Gay Print Culture

Gay Print Culture

A Transnational History of North America

JUAN CARLOS MEZO GONZÁLEZ

Duke University Press   *Durham and London*   2026

© 2026 DUKE UNIVERSITY PRESS. All rights reserved
Project Editor: Bird Williams
Designed by Dave Rainey
Typeset in Garamond Premier Pro and Anybody
by Westchester Publishing Services

Library of Congress Cataloging-in-Publication Data
Names: Mezo González, Juan Carlos, [date] author
Title: Gay print culture : a transnational history of North America / Juan Carlos Mezo González.
Description: Durham : Duke University Press, 2026. | Includes bibliographical references and index.
Identifiers: LCCN 2025021623 (print)
LCCN 2025021624 (ebook)
ISBN 9781478033042 (paperback)
ISBN 9781478029588 (hardcover)
ISBN 9781478061793 (ebook)
Subjects: LCSH: Gay liberation movement—North America—Periodicals. | Gay rights—North America—Periodicals. | Homosexuality and literature—North America. | Homosexuality and the arts—North America. | Politics and culture—North America—History.
Classification: LCC HQ76.8.N7 M48 2026 (print)
LCC HQ76.8.N7 (ebook)
DDC 302.23/208664097—dc23/eng/20250625
LC record available at https://lccn.loc.gov/2025021623
LC ebook record available at https://lccn.loc.gov/2025021624

Cover art: Photograph and flowers from a shoot for *Macho Tips*, no. 19, 1987. Photograph by Jim Moss. Text overlay from *The Body Politic*, no. 13, May/June 1974.

This book is dedicated to my parents María and Carlos,
to my sister Carla,
to my partner Paolo, and to Louis (†)

contents

Acknowledgments
ix

Introduction
1

| 1 |

Periodicals, Coming Out, and the Visualization of Gay Liberation
23

| 2 |

Sexual Imagery, Transnational Communities, and the Politics of Visualization in The Body Politic
67

| 3 |

Liberationist Politics, Colonial Optics, and the Desire for Latin America in Gay Sunshine

103

| 4 |

Gay Masculinity and the Commodification of the Mexican Body in Macho Tips

141

| 5 |

The Gay Editorial Market and the Transnational Production of Racialized Desires

185

Conclusion

221

Notes

227

Bibliography

253

Index

269

acknowledgments

This book on the transnational history of gay print culture is the product of a transnational network of support comprised of mentors, colleagues, friends, family members, and institutions based in Canada, Mexico, and the United States. I owe the completion of this book to this network, and I am pleased to take this opportunity to express my gratitude and appreciation for the help, guidance, time, and financial resources of countless people. *Gay Print Culture* began as a PhD dissertation at the University of Toronto about ten years ago. My doctoral supervisor, Elspeth Brown, received this project with enthusiasm and guided me at every stage, offering the brightest feedback and strongest encouragement. The same applies to the members of my dissertation committee, Kevin Coleman and Luis van Isschot. I am so honored for having worked alongside such professional, knowledgeable, inspiring, and kind scholars and I am so thankful for their invaluable contributions to my professional development over the years. Elspeth, Kevin, Luis, I really cannot thank you enough. Other wonderful scholars who read, commented on, and offered insightful feedback on this project before it took the form of a book manuscript were Anne Rubenstein and Víctor Macías-González. I extend my deepest gratitude to them for their guidance, suggestions, and willingness to always help. Anne, you have been a wonderful mentor and a source of much inspiration in my work.

Numerous people have also read portions of my work over the years in the form of essays, journal publications, and drafts of chapters. I wish to thank them for their feedback, which is certainly reflected in this book. In alphabetical order, these people include, but are not limited to, Brian Alavez Trujillo, L. K. Bertram, Libardo Gómez Estrada, Martín H. González Romero, Dan Guadagnolo, Tom Hooper, Valeria Mantilla Morales, Mari Ruti (†), Vannina Sztainbok, Uriel Vides Bautista, and Michael Weaver. Also included are the members of the Toronto-based Latin American Research Group (LARG) who read and commented on a portion of my work in one of our sessions. Especially important were the careful readings and insightful feedback of Dot Tuer, Tamara Walker, and of some of the scholars already mentioned above. I also had numerous opportunities to present and discuss my work at conferences and academic events, where amazing scholars and colleagues offered valuable feedback, guidance, and much encouragement. These include David Churchill, Ailén Cruz, Carina Guzmán, Daniel Laurin, Mireille Miller-Young, Virgilio Partida Peñalva, and Zeb Tortorici.

I am deeply grateful for the work of various editors and anonymous reviewers who have helped me strengthen my work over the years. Previous versions of chapters 2 and 4 from this book were published in *Left History* and *Hispanic American Historical Review*. I am indebted to the anonymous reviewers and editors of these journals, especially Sean Mannion, who read my work, offered insightful feedback, and improved the writing style. Of course, I am also grateful for the tremendous support of Duke University Press's editorial team. I particularly thank Alejandra Mejía, who believed in my project and supported me at every stage of the publication process. Likewise, I am grateful for the generous feedback of the anonymous reviewers who contributed their time and expertise to help me write a better book.

My research has benefited from the financial support and resources that numerous institutions provided me with over the years and without which this book would simply not exist. At the University of Toronto, I am deeply thankful to the Department of History, which welcomed me first as a graduate student and then as a postdoctoral fellow. This fellowship allowed me to spend a year preparing the first draft of a book manuscript while teaching gender, sexuality, and Latin American history to wonderful undergraduate students. I thank Alison Smith, Heidi Bohaker, Luis van Isschot, and Steve Penfold for this opportunity. I also thank the Department of History, the Department of Historical Studies, and the School of Graduate Studies for providing major awards that allowed me to conduct archival research across North America and present my work at various conferences. I am also deeply thankful to the Mark S. Bonham Centre for Sexual Diversity Studies, where I found a diverse, warm, and inspiring community. With the Centre's support, I presented my work at various conferences, and I particularly thank its current director, Dana Seitler, for always supporting my scholarship. My research also received funding from Mexico's National Council of Humanities, Sciences, and Technologies (CONAHCyT), the Mexican Ministry of Education (Secretaría de Educación Pública), and the Ontario Graduate Scholarship. The Phil Zwickler Memorial Research Grant, offered by the Division of Rare and Manuscript Collections at Cornell University, was also of great help to complete research for this project. I finalized revisions for this book as a Visiting

Scholar in Sexuality Studies at York University's Center for Feminist Research, and I thank Elaine Coburn and Nick J. Mulé for this opportunity. I also thank the American Men's Studies Association and the Research Society for American Periodicals for recognizing and supporting my scholarship. Moreover, although the research for this book began at the University of Toronto, my academic journey began in the Licenciatura en Historia at the Universidad Nacional Autónoma de México, where students receive world-class education for the symbolic amount of 20 cents per year. I owe so much of my training as a historian to the amazing faculty, mentors, and friends I met at the Facultad de Estudios Superiores Acatlán between 2009 and 2013. This book is indebted to those formative years of my life.

I extend my deepest appreciation to the people who agreed to be interviewed for this project and to those who have helped me gather primary sources and navigate archival collections. These people include the activists and former editors, photographers, contributors, and readers of the gay periodicals I examined throughout this book. I particularly appreciate the help of José Luis Bueno, Juan Jacobo Hernández, Tim McCaskell, Gonzalo Pozo Pietrasanta, and Juan Carlos Yustis. I thank everyone who assisted me in archives, special collections, and libraries across North America. I am especially grateful for the help of Alan Miller and Lucie Handley-Girard at The ArQuives: Canada's LGBTQ2+ Archives; of Bettina Gómez Oliver and the staff at the Centro Académico de la Memoria de Nuestra América (CAMeNA); and of Michael C. Oliveira and Loni Shibuyama at the ONE National Gay and Lesbian Archives. A special thanks goes to my dear friend David Fernández, head of Special Collections at the Thomas Fisher Rare Book Library. His teachings and guidance have been transformative and crucial in my work with print culture.

My deepest gratitude is with my family. I am forever grateful to my parents, Carlos Mezo Peña and María de la Paz González Márquez, for all their love, teachings, and support, and for always being by my side. Papás, gracias por todo su amor, sacrificios, enseñanzas, y por siempre estar a mi lado a pesar de la distancia. The same applies to my sister Carla Elena Mezo González, whose encouragement, feedback, and help were so important to complete this book. From the moment we met, my partner Paolo Frascà has also been a major source of support and inspiration. He read multiple versions of this book's chapters, and I am deeply grateful for his love, superb feedback, and encouragement. I would not have finished this book without his reminders to take it easy, *un pasito a la vez*, one step at a time. Finally, I wrote much of this book in the company of our little Chihuahua, Louis, sitting calmly on my lap or next to me. His presence, love, and charm, as well as our daily walks, gave me the peace of mind and energy boosts I needed to complete this project. He left this world in April 2025, but his pawprints are all over this book.

introduction

Print magazines have been one of the most important mediums for gay men to circulate information, make contacts, build community, and offer positive visual representations of homoerotic desire. This was particularly the case in the 1970s–1990s period, which followed the emergence of the modern gay liberation movement and predated the popularization of the internet. An unprecedented growth in gay publishing took place during this period and developed in close relationship with the gay liberation movements that surfaced around the globe. One of the magazines that emerged in this context was *Nuestro cuerpo* (Our Body), which the Mexico City–based group Frente Homosexual de Acción Revolucionaria (FHAR) launched in 1979. FHAR presented *Nuestro cuerpo* as a nonprofit publication that pursued three main goals: strengthening the revolutionary homosexual movement in the country, raising gay and lesbian awareness and pride, and linking the homosexual movement with other popular struggles.[1] As its title suggests, the magazine also aimed to offer a space to reflect on the body and its role in the movement. The body, as many gay and lesbian activists thought, was a vehicle to achieve one's liberation, both political and sexual. This thought, further discussed below, was also present in other gay liberation publications of the time, such as the San Francisco–based *Gay Sunshine* (1970–1982) and the Toronto-based *The Body Politic* (1971–1987), both of which inspired FHAR's editorial work. Like *Nuestro cuerpo*, these and similar publications discussed the relationship between body and liberation while featuring nudity and erotic imagery to offer positive and celebratory representations of homoerotic desire. The inaugural issue, for example, featured artwork by Guillermo Santamaría that represented nude men and celebrated male beauty (figure I.1). But unlike *Gay Sunshine* and *The Body Politic*, which published 46 and 135 issues, respectively, *Nuestro cuerpo* disappeared in 1980 after printing its

FIGURE 1.1. Published in Mexico City in 1979, the first cover of *Nuestro cuerpo* featured artwork by Guillermo Santamaría that celebrated the male body. Colectivo Sol Online Archive, Magazines Collection.

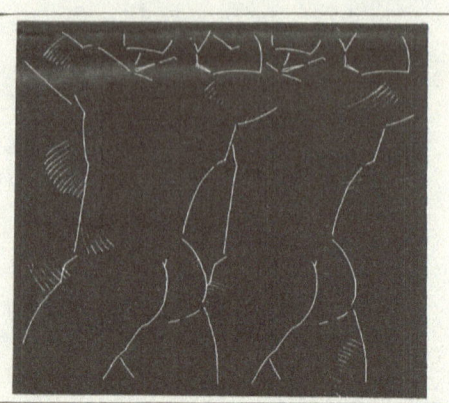

second and last issue. The other two gay liberation periodicals based in Mexico City at that time faced a similar fate: *Política sexual* (Sexual Politics), another initiative of FHAR, published its only issue in 1979, while the Grupo Lambda de Liberación Homosexual published only five issues of their magazine *Nuevo ambiente* (New Scene) between 1979 and 1983.[2] This brief though meaningful chapter in the history of gay publishing in Mexico opened the doors for another chapter in the mid-1980s, when the magazine *Macho Tips* changed the gay editorial landscape in the country.

The Mexican accountant Aurelio Refugio Hidalgo de la Torre launched *Macho Tips* in Mexico City in 1985, publishing twenty-three issues until 1989. In 1990, he relaunched his magazine as *Hermes* and published twenty-six issues through 1994 amid a growing market of gay erotic and consumer magazines. *Macho Tips* became popular and successful in Mexico because of its color centerfolds and covers that celebrated Mexican male beauty (figure I.2). It also became popular because of its rich editorial content, which included local and international gay news, articles about sexual health and AIDS, publications on gay culture and history, and a vibrant section of classifieds that provided readers with the opportunity to meet other queer people in Mexico and abroad. Shaped after US gay lifestyle and erotic magazines, *Macho Tips* was significantly different from the leftist gay liberation periodicals that published in the late 1970s and early 1980s in Mexico City. In contrast to those publications, *Macho Tips* did not employ a radical and revolutionary language, and it did not challenge the Mexican State. Nonetheless, selling an openly gay magazine with erotic imagery in the newsstands of 1980s Mexico was no small feat considering the conservative climate of the time. And in that context, the visually appealing content of *Macho Tips* fulfilled an important liberationist task: It visualized and celebrated homoerotic desires. In this particular way, *Macho Tips* was not so different from those publications that preceded it and whose content was more explicitly connected to the project of gay liberation. By engaging with this liberationist project, *Macho Tips* became part of a larger history of gay print culture in North America, a history that constitutes the focus of this book.

Gay Print Culture investigates the relationship between transnational gay liberation politics, periodicals, and images in Mexico, the United States, and Canada from the early 1970s through the mid-1990s. The book examines the production, content, circulation, and reception of leading gay periodicals published in these countries, including gay liberation newspapers, lifestyle, and erotic magazines. In bringing this diverse corpus of materials together, *Gay Print Culture* explains how, in many regards, these diverse publications actually performed quite similar work. The book demonstrates how these periodicals aimed to visualize the political goals of gay liberation, particularly those concerning the liberation and celebration of homoerotic desires. Visualizing these goals allowed activists, editors, publishers, and artists to foster the formation of gay communities and identities, while also advancing gay liberation movements at the local, national, and international levels. As readers will discover, the sexual and erotic imagery printed in these publications was at the heart of such efforts.

This book's focus on the relationship between gay liberation and the politics of visualization invites readers to reconsider the meaning of "gay liberation." This concept generally refers to the radical and leftist movements that emerged in the late 1960s and early 1970s in anglophone North American contexts, and in the 1970s more broadly in much of Latin America. As part of their movements, gay liberation activists across the two regions sought to transform sexual norms and fought against their oppression, linking their movements to other struggles against structures of oppression, which included colonialism, capitalism, imperialism, racism, and sexism. It was in this context that body, pleasure, and desire became intertwined with the politics of gay liberation. Inspired by the writings of Marxist philosophers, gay activists in this period began to advocate for the liberation of the body and, particularly, for a reconceptualization of eroticism and pleasure. It was also in this context that the visualization of those principles in gay periodicals became essential to advance gay liberation movements. *Gay Print Culture* follows the evolution of this project from the early 1970s through the 1990s, studying how activists, editors, publishers, artists, and readers imagined gay liberation, and how they worked to visualize those ideals.

This book argues that gay periodicals were at the center of the transnational history of gay liberation, both because they facilitated the circulation of information across borders and because they produced images that visualized the political goals of the movement, which included the liberation of desires and sexual representations. Before the popularization of the internet, gay periodicals were the most important resource to learn about and report on local and international news regarding struggles for gay rights around the world. They were also the most important resource to develop a strong visual and political language that encouraged people to embrace and celebrate their homoerotic desires, come out, join the movement, and appreciate the international nature of this struggle. As an editorial of the San Francisco–based *Gay Sunshine* declared in October 1970, "The oppression of Gay People, international in scope, arises from heterosexual chauvinism, religious dogmatism, police persecution, and other forms of discrimination and social intimidation."[3] These were issues that gay people faced around the globe, and gay periodicals were the most important medium to write about, contest, and visualize them. Their pages included

FIGURE 1.2. Published in Mexico City in 1989, the cover of *Macho Tips*' twenty-first issue featured a photograph by Juan Carlos Yustis. Almost all issues of *Macho Tips* featured artistic male nudes on their covers, and most of this erotic imagery was locally produced. Centro Académico de la Memoria de Nuestra América, Mexico City.

numerous depictions of gay oppression and resistance, as well as images that defied heterosexism by celebrating gay sexuality. The transnational movement of activists, publishers, and readers, combined with the circulation of gay literature and imaginaries, shaped the visual content of gay periodicals and made it legible across borders. For this reason, gay periodicals were instrumental in consolidating a politics of gay liberation and in visualizing those principles through their production and use of images. They published writings on gay liberation theory alongside erotic images that presented the body as an important vehicle to achieve gay liberation, as a site of pleasure and eroticism, and as a contested terrain in which liberation and oppression often clashed.

Gay Print Culture examines this transnational history by focusing on three thematic threads. The first of them is the transnational nature of gay periodicals. The activists, editors, writers, entrepreneurs, and artists involved in the production of gay periodicals worked to connect with one another across borders in order to circulate and exchange information and to expand their markets in an increasingly commercial landscape. As a result, periodicals not only influenced one another, but they also enabled the emergence of transnational gay networks and communities from the early 1970s through the 1990s. This book shows that the people producing gay periodicals were invested in internationalizing their publications, in terms of both content and circulation. For a number of these people, particularly for those who were also activists, connecting with other gay men and building local, national, and transnational communities was an important strategy to advance gay liberation. For example, the activists who published the first gay liberation periodicals in Mexico sought international connections with organizations like the Toronto-based *The Body Politic*, which by the late 1970s had reached a wide distribution and maintained a lively correspondence with gay communities around the globe. In July 1979, the Grupo Lambda wrote to *The Body Politic* to introduce their organization and their magazine *Nuevo ambiente*. The letter explained that Grupo Lambda was "comprised of Lesbians and Gay men dedicated to the struggle for a society free of sexism and oppression in all its forms." The letter also proposed an exchange of publications, as well as of information regarding the gay liberation movement in Mexico and Canada.[4] The members of *The Body Politic* editorial collective were also invested in this same struggle and were enthusiastic about the exchange. In their response, the Canadian gay activist Tim McCaskell emphasized the importance of having regular contact and circulating news relevant to the movement. This, he claimed, would help to strengthen the solidarity between their movements, and to exchange critical opinions on the politics of gay liberation.[5] As the following chapter explains, one factor that helped to connect gay communities across the

Americas was the leftist and internationalist mindset that many activists shared. Indeed, this mindset facilitated McCaskell's identification with and interest in Latin American gay struggles, as well as his notion of a transnational gay community. But the exchange between *Nuevo ambiente* and *The Body Politic* illustrates just one of the reasons why publishers and activists sought international connections. For entrepreneurs and some artists, for example, building such communities and cultivating gay markets was an effective way to make a profit from the circulation of periodicals and erotica, while also contributing to gay liberation in their own particular way. For instance, the creator of *Macho Tips*, Aurelio Hidalgo de la Torre, sought international connections and exchanges both to circulate his magazines abroad and to acquire content for them. Although his archive is virtually lost, some sources discussed in chapters 4 and 5 demonstrate that from the mid-1980s to the mid-1990s, Hidalgo de la Torre established communication and exchanges with activists, artists, and publishers in the United States and Europe, such as with the California-based editor John Rowberry. Periodicals were therefore documents, and in many instances also commodities, meant to circulate across borders and appeal to or serve transnational readerships.

The second thread is the relationship between gay liberation politics and visual culture. By focusing on a selection of Mexican, US, and Canadian publications, the book examines different ways in which the production and use of images in gay periodicals intersected with the project of gay liberation and how that intersection adapted to changing social, economic, and political landscapes over the years. The analysis pays particular attention to images that centered on the body, gay sexuality, and homoerotic desire, but it also discusses how the visual representation of gay oppression, resistance, and pride was a core component of gay periodicals. The book also explores how these images circulated across borders, influencing and shaping the visual content of gay periodicals, which developed a shared visual language. For example, chapter 1 examines this visual language by focusing on how gay liberation periodicals visualized ideas of gay oppression and resistance in the 1970s. A fascinating example of this language is the cover of *Gay Sunshine*'s fourteenth issue, published in 1972. The cover featured a collage by James Reed that evoked the severe oppression that gay and other marginalized groups faced, but that also communicated an important message of resistance and hope (figure I.3). At the bottom of this collage, a police officer faces a city and what appears to be a prison. Behind the prison's wall, two dogs and an armed man patrol the area, while a crowd of individuals—perhaps prisoners, judging by the numbers written on their hats—seem to protest with their fists raised. A skeleton holding a scythe on the right side of the collage and pointing to a nude gay couple in an embrace reminds the viewer about the life-threatening

FIGURE 1.3. Cover of *Gay Sunshine*'s fourteenth issue, published in San Francisco in 1972. The cover features a collage by US artist James Reed that uses symbols such as the butterfly, the eagle, the police, and the raised fist to offer a message of resistance, liberation, and hope. Pennsylvania State University Libraries, Digital Collections.

nature of oppression, which affected not only gay men but also other marginalized communities—as a legend above the couple states: "We are all fugitives." One of the most striking features of this collage is the presence of an eagle at the top of the page that chases two butterflies while a nude woman seems to emerge and fly away from the scene. Significantly, the butterflies' bodies are constituted by raised fists, a symbol that the Black Power movement popularized. As the following chapter explains, the butterfly was a recurrent symbol of liberation in gay cultural production, and similar allegories of repression and resistance, such as the one on this collage, appeared in other gay liberation journals in the 1970s, which made them legible across borders.

The third thread in this book is the existing tensions between the liberation of some and the oppression of others as it arises in gay print culture. The publishers of the periodicals studied viewed the relationship between images and liberation from different political, aesthetic, and ethical perspectives. Consequently, the erotic and sexualized imagery they produced acquired different meanings for readers, activists, and fellow publishers. For example, some of these individuals praised the publication of images of nudity, sadomasochism (S&M), and pornography, while others regarded these images as sexist and oppressive, as shown in chapter 2. In other cases, racial representation complicated liberationist projects. Most gay periodicals presented white men as objects of desire, particularly in the 1970s and early 1980s. In subsequent years, some publishers aimed to diversify their erotic imagery, either to address issues of representation, to expand notions of the erotic, or to make a profit. As part of this transition, some periodicals eroticized but also fetishized nonwhite individuals for the consumption of others, giving rise to a visual culture that reinforced colonial imaginaries of non-Western sexualities. At the same time, many of these images challenged dominant representations of homoerotic desire and offered alternatives on the market. For instance, *Macho Tips* began as a publication that emulated US gay lifestyle and erotic magazines such as *Blueboy*. As in those magazines, the erotic imagery in the first issues of *Macho Tips* featured mostly white men. Over time, though, the magazine began to feature models who resembled what most consumers would have identified as Mexican men based on dominant ideas of race in the country: mixed-race-appearing brown men. In fact, these types of models illustrated most covers of both *Macho Tips* and later *Hermes* and played a significant role in Hidalgo de la Torre's editorial success. These representations eroticized and celebrated an ideal of Mexican male beauty at a time when gay magazines continued to favor white desirability. Even the Mexican magazine *Del otro lado* (On the Other Side), which gay liberation activists like Juan Jacobo Hernández edited between 1992 and 1996, favored this dominant desire—Hernández had been a member of *Nuestro cuerpo*'s and *Política sexual*'s editorial collectives and had also worked as editor for *Macho Tips* in the 1980s. The commercialization of locally produced erotica in *Macho Tips* and *Hermes* served to offer positive and celebratory representations of homoerotic desire, which had been a core project of gay liberation politics for many years. Much of this imagery, though, built on exoticizing imaginaries that portrayed nonwhite models as primitive, hypersexual, and/or closer to nature. In some respects, these images could be questionable, but in appreciating racialized male beauty they also reconceptualized what could be considered erotic in a Mexican gay market. Therefore, one of the main goals of *Gay Print Culture* is to analyze the intersections between the production and consumption of erotic imagery and the transnational history of gay liberation. The book does not assume a liberatory nature in any of the materials studied. Instead, it examines how gender identity, class, and race shaped the production, content, reception, and circulation of gay periodicals, as well as how they shaped readers' understandings of liberation and oppression. Moreover, the book does not aim to set the boundaries of what constituted liberatory and oppressive visual representations. Instead, the focus is on the way activists, editors, publishers, artists, and readers negotiated the meanings of the images they produced, published, circulated, and consumed.

Periodicals and the Formation of Gay Communities

Gay Print Culture centers periodicals and their visual content in the transnational history of gay liberation for two major reasons. The first one is that the local, national, and international circulation of gay liberation imaginaries, as well as the formation of transnational gay networks and communities across the Americas, would not have been possible without the existence of gay periodicals. As historian and gay activist John D'Emilio asserts, prior to the technological revolution that the internet brought, "the community press was, really, the only resource other than word of mouth for letting people know that a new world, a new outlook, and a new community were in formation."[6] In the late 1960s and through the 1970s, gay liberation activists across the region turned to the printing press as a tool to advance their liberationist movements and to build local, national, and transnational communities. Many of the earliest gay liberation periodicals in the region had the specific purpose of documenting gay liberation movements and encouraging people to "come out." Coming out, connecting people across borders, and circulating information about these movements was crucial to advancing gay liberation, and the gay press was at the center of that process.

Alternative media has played a central role in social movements because of its capacity to build community and forge identities. In his transnational study of 1980s gay Polish magazines, Łukasz Szulc argues that "the chief function of alternative media created by social movements is to create and sustain the movement's identity. The focus is on the self: self-definition, self-representation and self-expression of a particular group, community, or movement."[7] The question of what makes a publication "alternative" is not easy to address, but the concept generally refers to publications with a small-scale production and limited distribution, and whose content is not typically found in mainstream printed media.[8] The gay periodicals studied in this book fall within this broad spectrum. As such, and echoing Szulc's observations, gay periodicals in the 1970s–1990s period played a crucial role in creating and validating a sense of common gay identity among the producers, contributors, and readers of these publications.[9] They also played a crucial role in the formation and consolidation of local, national, and international gay communities. Therefore, it is fundamental to study the histories of gay periodicals using a transnational lens and with a focus on the relationship between the history of gay political activism and the production, content, reception, and circulation of these publications.

Aside from facilitating the flow of information, periodicals also performed the important task of producing and circulating images that visualized the cultural and political imaginaries of the gay communities that created and consumed these publications. This is the second reason for which this book focuses on gay periodicals so attentively. Gay newspapers and magazines visualized images of gay pride and resistance, of homoerotic desire, and of same-sex sexuality that could not be found in mainstream media outlets. Much of this content reflected the desires, emotions, and concerns of the papers' readerships; since most of these periodicals relied on sales and advertising to survive, they constantly tried to be more visually appealing and sought to cater to consumers' demands. Therefore, gay periodicals offer valuable insight into the cultural history of gay liberation, community, and identity at the local, national, and international levels.

Indeed, through their vibrant editorial and commercial content, and through their wide circulation, gay periodicals connected gay men across borders and allowed them to imagine and form nationwide and international gay communities. Historians such as Marc Stein and David Johnson have examined the relationship between gay periodicals and community-building in the context of the United States. Commenting on the Philadelphia-based gay magazine *Drum* (1964–1969)—a publication that featured both news and erotic imagery—Stein writes that the magazine "confirms Benedict Anderson's argument that language has the 'capacity for generating imagined communities, building in effect particular solidarities.'" *Drum* magazine, Stein claims, illustrates how "print media have played a central role in the development of imagined communities."[10] Most gay periodicals with wide distribution in the twentieth century, including commercially oriented periodicals, had a similar outcome. Johnson asserts that, aside from the images and the merchandise, publishers of pre-1969 physique magazines provided their customers with "contact, both real and imagined." They also provided them with the opportunity to publish letters, participate in contests, and submit photographs, as well as with business directories and pen-pal clubs where customers could interact directly with one another and find information about photography studios, book services, and gay bars.[11] "Buying magazines, writing letters, and exchanging photographs were central features of this network," Johnson writes.[12] Szulc has identified a similar process in studying the histories of 1980s Polish gay magazines. These publications were crucial for developing a common sense of identity among readers and for establishing transnational communication between Poland and other European countries during the late Cold War period. Building on these scholars' work, *Gay Print Culture* demonstrates how gay liberation, lifestyle, and erotic magazines published in Mexico, Canada, and the United States between the 1970s and 1990s also allowed gay men to establish meaningful connections across borders and imagine transnational communities. Examining the role of images in the formation of those communities and networks is one of the main goals of this book.

In tracing the transnational formation of gay communities and identities through the production and circulation of gay periodicals and images, this book echoes Martin Meeker's assertion that gay and lesbian community-building is a process with local, regional, national, and global dimensions.[13] This occurs because, in gay and lesbian history, identity-formation and community-building are interconnected. Those who identify as homosexual, Meeker writes, "recount the process by which they came to that identity as one that involved feeling, longing, sensing, and thinking ... [;] the desire to contact others like themselves is a logical next step."[14] Such desire to connect helped to justify not only gay existence but also activism. Cross-border connections, Meeker contends, facilitated the exchange of information, advanced a self-awareness of gay identity and oppression, and led to the organization of collective action against that oppression.[15] Significantly, Meeker studied the role of homophile periodicals in this process, analyzing how they fostered the formation of nationwide communities in the United States in the mid-twentieth century.

As shown by existing scholarship, gay magazines in the twentieth century played a crucial role in the formation of gay identities and communities, and they were central to the transnational history of gay liberation. As the chapters of this book demonstrate, the international focus of gay periodicals published in North America from the early 1970s to the mid-1990s allowed activists, editors, publishers, artists, and readers to identify a common experience among gay communities in different contexts. This international focus also allowed these communities to develop a similar visual language that offered powerful representations of their experiences, desires, and liberationist projects. Furthermore, it allowed gay publishers and entrepreneurs to create markets for those representations, which further consolidated the existence of gay communities and identities.

A Visual and Transnational Approach

Gay Print Culture is the first major research project to examine gay periodicals and their visual content in a transnational context focused on Mexico, the United States, and Canada. To pursue this task, the book builds on and contributes to two bodies of scholarship: one that focuses on national and transnational histories of gay liberation across the American continent, and another that examines gay print culture with a focus on local, national, and, to a lesser extent, transnational contexts. The first body of literature includes the works of scholars who have focused on gay and lesbian liberation movements in the United States and Canada, such as Becki Ross, John D'Emilio, Miriam Smith, Gary Kinsman, Nan Alamilla Boyd, David Churchill, Marc Stein, Tom Warner, Kevin Mumford, Emily Hobson, and Tim McCaskell, among many others.[16] This literature also includes the works of scholars who have focused on gay and lesbian liberation movements in Latin America, such as James Green, Norma Mogrovejo, Rodrigo Laguarda, Jordi Díez, Lucinda Grinnell, Adriana Fuentes Ponce, Omar Guillermo Encarnación, Pablo Ben, Joaquín Insausti, Javier Fernández Galeano, Felipe Caro Romero, Patricio Simonetto, and Martín González Romero, among others.[17] Although I am indebted to the work of all these authors, much of this scholarship has been dominated by approaches that pay little attention to print and visual culture, treating them mostly as sources and rarely as objects of analysis.

In situating print culture and images at the center of transnational LGBTQ+ history, *Gay Print Culture* contributes to another body of scholarship. Specifically, it joins the efforts of several scholars who have made significant contributions to the study of gay and lesbian media and/or visual culture. This body of literature includes book-length projects by Rodger Streitmatter, Martin Meeker, David Johnson, and Łukasz Szulc.[18] It also includes various journal articles, book chapters, and recent doctoral dissertations by scholars such as Richard Meyer, Lucas Hilderbrand, Robert Dewhurst, Scott de Groot, Patricio Simonetto, Nick Hrynyk, Valerie Korinek, Kelly Phipps, and Bryan Pitts, among others.[19] The work of all these scholars contributes to our understanding of gay print culture and visuality in the second half of the twentieth century. But unlike most of them, my work transcends nationally bound frameworks, investigating instead the shared histories of gay periodicals across North America, while also considering other Latin American contexts.

Thus, although *Gay Print Culture* draws from and contributes to these two bodies of scholarship, it departs from them in important ways. The historiography on gay liberation in Canada and the United States has focused mostly on either local or national histories, or on anglophone North American contexts. While scholars of Latin America have been more attentive to the relationship between gay liberation in the region and in anglophone North America, their works also remain very much focused on national contexts, and in most cases, they adopt social and political approaches only. A similar situation has shaped Canadian histories of gay liberation, some of which trace relationships to US contexts, but not to Latin America. *Gay Print Culture* shows how these local and national histories were mutually constitutive. It also shows how gay communities helped to advance gay liberation across borders through the production and circulation of periodicals and images. During the period covered by this study, periodicals were the dominant form of gay print culture and the only effective resource to connect communities at various levels. Analyzing their content and histories from a transnational lens is therefore crucial for understanding the cultural history of gay liberation in the Americas. It is also crucial for understanding how gay activists, editors, publishers, artists, and also readers worked transnationally to shape and advance gay liberation politics.

This book employs an interdisciplinary methodology and a wide variety of sources to examine the production, content, circulation, and reception of gay periodicals. These sources are grouped into three categories: documentary, oral, and visual. The first category is comprised of newspapers and magazines, their administrative files, and letters sent to and by their editorial teams. These sources are housed in numerous archives across the Americas, including institutional and community-based archives, as well as digital repositories. Representative archives include the ONE National Gay and Lesbian Archives in Los Angeles, the GLBT Historical Society in San Francisco, the Centro Académico de la Memoria de Nuestra América in Mexico City, and The ArQuives: Canada's LGBTQ2+ Archives in Toronto. The second category is comprised of oral history interviews I conducted between 2016 and 2022 with individuals who produced, read, or contributed to gay periodicals, including activists, editors, writers, photographers, illustrators, and artists. I conducted these interviews in various locations, either in person or online, and in both English and Spanish. Interviewees include people from Mexico, Canada, the United States, and other nationalities. A copious visual archive constitutes the third group of sources. Each chapter of this book engages in close readings of the visual content of gay periodicals, particularly of their erotic imagery. The discussion considers the production and reception of these images, the ways in which publishers used them, and the messages they conveyed. This interdisciplinary methodology allows *Gay Print Culture* to have us reconsider our understanding of gay periodicals by situating them, and their visual cultures, at the center of a transnational history of gay community-formation and liberationist politics.

Since it would be impossible to study all the periodicals published in the Americas from the early 1970s to the mid-1990s, this book focuses on a selection of North American newspapers and magazines that had a wide distribution and an international scope, and that were leading voices of gay liberation in major cities. These periodicals varied from community-based gay liberation publications to commercially oriented gay lifestyle and erotic magazines. Thus, their gay politics and use of images differ significantly. The gay liberation and community-based periodicals examined in this book include magazines such as *Gay Sunshine* (San Francisco, 1970–1982), *The Body Politic* (Toronto, 1971–1987), *Gay Community News* (Boston, 1973–1999), *Política sexual* (Mexico City, 1979), *Nuestro cuerpo* (Mexico City, 1979–1980), and *Nuevo ambiente* (Mexico City, 1979–1983). Aside from being leading periodicals with an international scope and wide circulation, their publishers were part of transnational networks of gay liberation activists. Moreover, the content of these publications helped to advance gay liberation and community-building through the visual representation of gay sexuality and homoerotic desires, as well as of gay resistance and pride. This happened at a time when the access to such representations in the mainstream media was largely unthinkable. On the other hand, the gay lifestyle and erotic magazines analyzed in this book include *Macho Tips* (Mexico City, 1985–1989), its refurbished version *Hermes* (Mexico City, 1990–1994), and *Del otro lado* (Mexico City, 1992–1996). These magazines advanced gay liberation through a different approach: the production and circulation of erotic imagery alongside news and information on gay sexuality and culture. In addition to these sources, the book is also attentive to the histories, content, and international connections of other Latin American publications, such as the Argentinian *Somos* (Buenos Aires, 1973–1976).

Studying the histories of these magazines posed various methodological challenges, particularly in relation to the disparate levels of documentation they left behind. For instance, the archival records of *The Body Politic* (*TBP*) in The ArQuives are rich and abundant. The histories of *TBP* and the archives are actually linked; initially called the Canadian Gay Liberation Movement Archives, this community-based archive was founded in 1973 out of the *TBP* newspaper collection. From the beginning, the editorial collective of *TBP* kept almost every single document they produced and received over the years—a decision that has produced more than one hundred boxes of archival sources related to the history of this publication. Similarly, the *Gay Sunshine* records at the ONE National Gay and Lesbian Archives are comprised of eighty-one boxes and other related materials, while another, though much smaller portion of these records, is housed at the GLBT Historical Society in San Francisco. Since both magazines had a wide distribution and correspondence with individuals and organizations from across North America and beyond, it is easy to also locate the materials they produced in other collections. For instance, they are found at the Special Collections of various university libraries that house personal papers of gay activists and publishers (see the archives section of this book's bibliography). In contrast to these publications, the Mexican magazines studied in this book left very few archival records other than the magazines themselves. Although it is possible to also locate letters and other materials they produced in various US and Canadian archives and collections, as well as in government archives in Mexico, the documentation is limited and fragmented.

When archival silences and erasures produced crevices in my research, oral history helped to fill in those gaps. The memories of gay and lesbian individuals who interacted with gay periodicals as producers, contributors, or readers were a valuable source of information to reconstruct the histories of the gay press. They were also valuable sources to trace the international circulation of gay periodicals and the networks that gay activists, editors, publishers, artists, and readers established across borders. This was particularly important when researching Mexican magazines, as their subscription lists and most of their correspondence no longer exist. In each of the following chapters, I treat oral history interviews in almost the same way I treat other primary sources: drawing from them and contrasting peoples' recollections of the past with evidence from other primary sources. Engaging with deeper discussions on historical memory or the politics of remembering is beyond the scope of this book, but those interested in oral history as a methodology will hopefully appreciate the central role of such sources in this book.

Another methodological challenge faced throughout the research for this book was the whiteness of the archive. Despite their radical liberationist politics, many of the periodicals studied in this book were not particularly inclusive. For example, scholars and activists have long criticized *TBP* for presenting and promoting an implicitly white and cisgender gay male experience in its pages; the same could be said about *Gay Sunshine* and other similar publications. Claiming that these were leading voices of gay liberation in the anglophone-speaking world might be triggering for some readers whose experiences were absent or misrepresented in the pages of those magazines. The analysis in this book does not mean to reproduce what some consider a "whitening" of the queer archive, whereby queer people of color are disappeared from the record.[20] Despite my admiration and respect for these magazines, this book is not oblivious of their scope and role in the history of gay liberation—hence the attention to the tensions between liberation and oppression. Nonetheless, the undeniable work of these magazines to establish connections across borders made them central to the transnational history this book aims to reconstruct.

Finally, the rich visual content of gay periodicals also deserves some commentary. Each chapter of this book examines photographs, drawings, advertisements, and all kinds of illustrations. These media possess different characteristics that inform their use in gay periodicals and the engagement of readers with them. For instance, photography was the leading medium to visualize and provide powerful depictions of gay pride and resistance in gay periodicals, and the indexical nature of photography was central to accomplish those goals. In photography, indexicality refers to the ability of a photograph to capture an image of something that existed and happened at a particular time and in a particular place. To what extent a photograph represents reality has been the subject of much debate. However, what matters in this book is that, at its most basic level, photography allowed readers to appreciate and circulate *actual* moments of gay liberation. In his famous work on photography, *Camera Lucida*, Roland Barthes explains that the essence of photography is simple: "that has been." The photograph, he notes, "is an extended, loaded evidence—as if it caricatured not the figure of what it represents (quite the converse) but its very existence."[21] The object or scene that a photograph captures *existed* and was *there*. For this reason, as discussed in chapter 1, photographs of protests, of same-sex love, and of liberation in gay periodicals nourished activism across borders.

Drawings and other kinds of illustrations in gay periodicals were also powerful ways to visualize the political goals of gay liberation. As shown throughout the book, editors and readers alike took drawings, collages, comics, and other images very seriously. These images constituted another vehicle to circulate messages of gay resistance and liberation, as well as to celebrate gay sexuality and homoerotic desire. Although they were not as effective as photography in producing visual pleasure, they were no less stimulating. The fact that they triggered important debates, such as those analyzed in chapter 2, shows how these images produced and were charged with emotions and feelings. It also shows that these images had a strong cultural significance, especially considering the absence of similar representations in the mainstream press. Something similar occurred with advertising, which, aside from using appealing imagery to invite viewers to consume a product, played a crucial role in the formation of gay identities across borders. As the chapters in this book show, the imagery in gay advertising had deep roots in an international visual culture of gay consumerism.

Thus, the methodology of this book places a diverse corpus of sources—written, oral, and visual—in dialogue with one another. The analysis of these primary sources also involves drawing on a rich literature that includes social and cultural history, visual and media studies, queer theory, and scholarship on gender, sexuality, and race in Canadian, US, and Latin American contexts. This methodology allows *Gay Print Culture* to offer a novel approach to the history of gay print culture in the Americas.

Narrative Arc and Organization of the Book

Gay Print Culture follows the boom in gay publishing in Mexico, the United States, and Canada from the early 1970s to the mid-1990s, while also drawing connections to other cultural contexts in the Americas. In the 1970s, gay presses across all three countries began to publish liberation journals featuring political and visual content that bolstered the ideological foundations of the movement in each of its local contexts. Yet by the end of the 1980s and throughout the 1990s, many gay publishers had turned their attention away from overt political discourse and toward expanding into more lucrative markets, such as pornography. This change constitutes the narrative arc of this book. Through a close reading of gay periodicals, visual analysis of their content, archival research, and oral history interviews, the book explores how and why gay communities turned to the printing press over the period of study, and it follows the evolution of the markets they created. The book examines how in the 1970s and early 1980s, gay communities used the press to advance their liberation movements through the creation and circulation of periodicals with strong political and visual discourses. Then, the book examines how in the 1980s and 1990s, as sex acquired a more central role in the formation of gay community and identity, gay periodicals left behind their political content but continued to be invested in the liberation and visualization of homoerotic desires. Each of the five main chapters that constitute this book explores the intersections and tensions between gay politics, ideas of gay liberation, uses of the erotic, and changing visual representations that aimed to liberate and celebrate homoerotic desires. This arc begins in the early 1970s with the emergence of the first activist-oriented gay liberation periodicals in North America. It then moves to the 1980s to focus on commercially oriented gay lifestyle and erotic magazines. Toward the end of the book, the focus shifts to consumer and pornographic gay periodicals with little politics and big profits.

Chapter 1 focuses on the relationship between gay liberation movements, visuality, and the gay press from the late 1960s to the early 1980s. Specifically, the chapter examines how gay liberation activists used periodicals and images to advance their movements and build communities across borders. The chapter argues that gay liberation periodicals were central to the formation of communities because these publications developed an ideological and visual language legible at the local, national, and international levels. The development of this shared language was possible because the radical activists who published these periodicals were inspired by the same theories of gay liberation. These theories built on Marxism and traced connections between sexual and political liberation, while also linking them with the liberation of the body and erotic desires. To support this argument, the chapter focuses on various gay liberation periodicals, with particular attention to those published in Toronto and Mexico City. These periodicals presented the body as a vehicle for gay liberation, and used images that evoked pride, joy, and resistance to foster community-building.

Chapter 2 delves deeper into the role of the body and desire in the transnational history of gay liberation through a close analysis of the use and reception of erotic and sexualized imagery in gay liberation periodicals, with a particular focus on *The Body Politic*. The chapter examines the debates on nudity, sexism, and pornography that this imagery prompted among the editorial collective, contributors, and local and international readers of this publication from 1971 to 1987. The chapter argues that the contestation of this imagery was instrumental in the formation of gay liberation identities among the people who both produced and consumed periodicals like *The Body Politic*. To support this argument, the chapter compares these debates with similar disputes about erotic imagery in other gay liberation publications, such as the Boston-based *Gay Community News* (1973–1999). The chapter shows how the publication of sexualized and erotic imagery embodied the gay liberationist goals that brought gay liberation papers into existence. It also demonstrates how these images triggered debates because readers and editors ascribed different meanings to "pornography," "sexism," "gay liberation," and "community."

Chapter 3 focuses on two areas of analysis. The first one is the role of images in *Gay Sunshine* and the larger Gay Sunshine Press. The second one is the production of Latin American content for both the magazine and the press, as well as the formation of transnational networks of gay activists, writers, and visual artists who established contact across the Americas thanks to the production of such content. The chapter argues that *Gay Sunshine* and Gay Sunshine Press publications fostered gay liberation across the Americas through the visualization of homoerotic desires, the production of Latin American content, and the formation of transnational gay networks. Moreover, by analyzing the work of *Gay Sunshine*'s editor Winston Leyland and of his collaborators Erskine Lane and Edward A. Lacey, and by engaging with scholarship on queer theory, the chapter discusses the intricate relationship between gay mobility, consumerism, liberation, and oppression in the context of transnational gay history. The chapter offers a critique of the contradictions evident in the ways publishers and readers in the United States and Canada related to Latin America. Some in the Global North expressed solidarity with their Latin American counterparts, but also reinforced colonial imaginaries of non-Western sexuality through the reproduction and circulation of exoticizing discourses about Latin America.

The roles of images and homoerotic desire in transnational gay liberation are further examined in chapter 4 through an analysis of the Mexican gay magazine *Macho Tips*. Hidalgo de la Torre launched this magazine in 1985, inspired by a long tradition of US gay print culture. The magazine quickly became famous for its erotic representations of brown Mexican models and for its celebration of gay masculinity—it was so popular that by 1987 some pirate copies began to circulate in Mexico City. The chapter argues that the production and content of *Macho Tips* were integral to the transnational history of gay liberation movements that placed homoerotic desire and its visual representation at the center of community-building and identity formation. Building on scholarship of race, gender, popular culture, and sexuality in modern Mexico, the chapter also argues that the editorial and visual content of *Macho Tips* reproduced Mexican national discourses of race and gender to appeal to domestic and international consumers and to challenge stereotypes that marginalized gay men. Hidalgo de la Torre continued this project in the early 1990s, relaunching *Macho Tips* as *Hermes*. Through his editorial work in these magazines, he created a gay market for the brown Mexican body in Mexico and, as chapter 5 shows, this undertaking was part of a larger history of North American gay consumer culture.

Chapter 5 focuses on the growth of the gay publishing industry in Mexico, and it also examines how, since the late 1980s, some gay publishers, editors, visual artists, and pornographers in North America began to think of brown Mexican, Latin American, and Latino men as marketable. Some of those individuals were the Mexican editor Hidalgo de la Torre, the US editor and publisher John

Rowberry, and the US visual artists, editors, and pornographers Jim Moss and John Shown. The chapter argues that by creating a network and by producing and circulating gay magazines, erotic imagery, and pornography that capitalized on brown bodies, these men expanded notions of the erotic and helped to consolidate a gay market for these representations in Mexico and the United States. The chapter situates this process against the backdrop of the gay editorial market in Mexico and the United States while also examining its relationship with the larger history of gay liberation. At the same time, the chapter discusses how the editorial, artistic, and entrepreneurial work of these men fits into the larger history of the emergence and growth of the US Hispanic market. Moreover, the chapter also offers a critique of these men's work; while it expanded notions of the erotic and offered alternatives on the gay market, their work also drew on and reinforced colonial mindsets that profited from the production of exoticizing images for white and/or middle-class gay consumers.

A Note on Terminology

Throughout this book I use the terms *gay* and *homosexual* when necessary but prioritize the former in most cases. My choice is guided by the historical contexts I examine. From the late 1960s through the 1970s, gay men in anglophone North America began to increasingly replace the term *homosexual* with the term *gay* to refer to themselves and to their movement. Whereas the former was semantically charged with the harmful legacy of medical and criminal science, the latter is "tied to happiness, pride, community, and the declaration of legitimacy and difference."[22] In contrast, Latin American activists, particularly men, adopted the term *homosexual* in Spanish and Portuguese—despite its medical connotations existing also in their contexts—to refer to themselves and to their movement and to challenge more harmful terms that society had cast upon them. For instance, throughout the 1970s and early 1980s in Mexico, activists referred to their movement as the Movimiento de Liberación Homosexual and they founded organizations like the Frente de Liberación Homosexual (FLH) and the Frente Homosexual de Acción Revolucionaria (FHAR). However, in the specific context that I explore in this book, many middle-class Latin American activists, editors, artists, readers, and many other men who sexually, erotically, and affectively desired other men also began to use the English word "gay" to refer to themselves. In fact, the word was used frequently in the Latin American gay press since the 1970s. Numerous Latin American activists knew about, learned from, identified with, and linked their struggles to Canadian and US gay liberation movements, which explains their adoption of the term "gay" and justifies my using of it.

| 1 |

Periodicals, Coming Out, and the Visualization of Gay Liberation

A picture published in 1972 on the back cover of the Canadian gay liberation magazine *The Body Politic* (*TBP*) is evocative of the relationship between periodicals, images, and community-building in the history of gay liberation. The photograph portrays eleven young, white, and cheerful individuals building a human pyramid at the beach (figure 1.1). The ten men in the picture constitute the basis and body of the pyramid, while the only woman stands at the top. A combination of bathing suits, sunglasses, shirtless torsos, smiles, and sand suggested that the photograph was taken on a warm and happy summer day. Indeed, Jearld Frederick Moldenhauer took this photograph during the gay picnic held on Ward's Island, Toronto, in August 1972. Publishing this photograph in *TBP*,

FIGURE 1.1. Published in the fall of 1972, the back cover of *The Body Politic*'s sixth issue featured a cropped version of this photograph, which showed eleven people building a human pyramid with the only woman, Chris Fox, on top. The US gay liberation activist Jearld Frederick Moldenhauer took this photograph on August 20, 1972, at Toronto's first gay pride picnic on Ward's Island. Courtesy of Jearld Frederick Moldenhauer.

where it appeared within a bright yellow frame, served various purposes. One of them was to visualize and support one of the main goals of *TBP*: to build a gay and lesbian community. Community-building was a central project of gay liberation politics, and this project relied on encouraging people to come out. For that reason, gay periodicals produced and circulated images that offered powerful depictions of gay pride, resistance, and community, which, in turn, invited people to join the gay liberation movement. The photograph also evokes the relationship between the body, community-building, and liberation. The people in the picture are literally using their bodies to build something, and, as some of their facial expressions suggest, that was not an easy feat. For many gay and lesbian liberation activists, as this chapter discusses, the body constituted a vehicle to achieve their liberation. For that reason, representations of and discussions about the body featured prominently in both *TBP* as well as in other gay liberation periodicals. By publishing images such as this photograph, these periodicals aimed to visualize some of the ideological and political bases of the gay liberation movement. And in doing so, they developed a similar visual and political language that communicated powerful representations of gay resistance and liberation. These images visualized the existence of local, national, and international gay communities, while inviting readers to come out and join the movement. They also visualized same-sex love, homoerotic desires, and the leftist politics of gay liberation.

Gay liberation activists across the Americas shared a leftist political agenda and opposed structures of oppression. The Stonewall riots in New York City are generally considered the event that sparked the gay liberation movement, although different forms of gay and lesbian activism already existed, not only in the United States but also in other countries.[1] The riots took place in late June and early July 1969 in Greenwich Village, Manhattan, after the New York Police Department raided the gay bar Stonewall Inn on June 28. LGBTQ+ individuals took to the streets after the raid to protest police violence and repression. These events sparked the emergence of numerous organizations across the United States comprised of gay and lesbian radicals who, in Emily Hobson's words, "sought not just rights or inclusion but a fundamental transformation in the meanings of sexuality, a wholesale end to sexual limits and norms."[2] Gay and lesbian radicals in other latitudes, as explained below, also shared this view. In the US and Canadian contexts, gay and lesbian liberationists came of age during the 1960s civil rights, women's liberation, anti–Vietnam War, and student movements, as well as national liberation struggles. In Latin American countries such as Argentina, Brazil, and Mexico, gay and lesbian activists also came of age during a period of political upheaval that fueled the emergence of leftists and student movements, countercultural expressions, and sexual revolutions. Across the Americas, many of these gay and lesbian activists participated in socialist, Marxist, and Trotskyist organizations, and they linked their movements to larger struggles against structures of oppression, such as colonialism, capitalism, imperialism, racism, and sexism. They envisioned liberation for everyone based on the unity of all oppressed people and argued that only an end to capitalism would lead to equality.[3] This perspective did not mean that gay and lesbian liberation merged with other social movements. In fact, some queer activists complained about sexist and homophobic attitudes within other social movements, and, conversely, activists in those movements also complained about racism within the gay and lesbian movement.[4] However, despite the tensions and disagreements among them, all these movements shared a leftist political agenda and a struggle against oppression.

As part of their political projects, gay liberation activists around the globe turned to the printing press as a tool to advance their liberationist movement and to build local, national, and transnational communities. US and Canadian activists were the first in the Americas to launch gay liberation periodicals. Some representative titles include *Come Out!* (New York, 1969–1972), *Gay Sunshine* (Berkeley, 1970–1982), *Fag Rag* (Boston, 1971–1987), *The Body Politic* (Toronto, 1971–1987), and *Gay Community News* (Boston, 1973–1999). From the mid- to late 1970s, Latin American activists followed suit and published gay liberation periodicals as well, including Somos (Buenos Aires, 1973–1976), *El otro* (Medellín, 1977–1979), *Lampião da esquina* (Rio de Janeiro, 1978–1981), *Política sexual* (Mexico City, 1979), *Nuestro cuerpo* (Mexico City, 1979–1980), and *Nuevo ambiente* (Mexico City, 1979–1983). While some gay liberation periodicals were short-lived or published only a handful of issues, others managed to get a wide circulation abroad, especially in the anglophone-speaking world. Such was the case of *Gay Sunshine* and *The Body Politic*—two of the most influential periodicals of their time.

This chapter examines how gay liberation activists used periodicals and images to advance gay liberation, establish connections across borders, and build transnational communities from the late 1960s through the early 1980s. The chapter argues that gay periodicals enabled the emergence of a transnational gay liberation movement because they developed an ideological and visual language legible at the local, national, and international levels. The international focus of gay periodicals, the wide circulation of some of them, and the ability of some middle-class activists to travel abroad and communicate in different languages played crucial roles in this process. Also crucial was the fact that the activists who produced gay periodicals in the 1970s built on an international tradition of gay print culture with deep roots in North America. Another determinant factor was that gay liberation activists shared similar ideological foundations informed by Marxist theories that traced connections between sexual and political liberation. All these elements united gay activists across borders and provided them with a common political and visual language to frame their movements and editorial endeavors.

The chapter begins in the late 1960s and early 1970s with the emergence of gay liberation periodicals in North America. This first section presents *The Body Politic* as a case study because it was a sophisticated journal whose political and visual content exemplifies the main goals of liberationist publications in this formative period. As mentioned above, its powerful depictions of gay community served to encourage people to come out and join the movement. Such content, along with other gay magazines, inspired Mexican activists to launch their own gay liberation periodicals in 1979, as the chapter's second section explains. This section examines the history of gay liberation periodicals in Mexico City against the backdrop of North America's gay liberation movement, print culture, and visual culture. It discusses how the transnational circulation of gay periodicals encouraged Mexican activists to also use print culture and images to advance their movement.

The third section focuses on the role of the body in the transnational history of gay liberation. It discusses how the titles and content of gay periodicals during this period resonated with the theoretical bases of gay liberation, which were inspired by the works of Wilhelm Reich, Herbert Marcuse, Guy Hocquenghem, and Mario Mieli, among other Marxist thinkers. Through readings of their works and through the production of images, gay activists bridged sexual and political liberation while also celebrating their bodies and desires as vehicles for their liberation. The final section examines how transnational solidarity and the need to fight against a common oppressor—middle-class, male-dominated, capitalist, and heterosexist societies—helped to further unite gay activists across borders. It also examines how the production and circulation of images that visualized this fight were instrumental to fostering that union.

Gay Liberation Periodicals and Community-Building in North America

In November 1971, a group of gay and lesbian radical activists previously involved in the alternative newspaper *Guerilla* and Toronto Gay Action launched Canada's first gay liberation journal, *The Body Politic* (figure 1.2). During its fifteen years of publication, *TBP* was a leading voice of the gay liberation movement in anglophone North America and one of the most read queer newspapers in the English-speaking world. It provided gays and lesbians in Canada and other countries with a space for learning about, commenting on, and debating various issues, including civil rights, pornography, censorship, and intergenerational sex, among others. Its 135 issues featured articles, essays, local and international news, entertainment and community event listings, literature, and book reviews, as well as some erotic photographs, comics, and illustrations with sexual content. The paper printed about 1,500 copies of each issue (monthly or bimonthly), and it was distributed by mail or purchased at specific locations, such as Toronto's gay bookstore Glad Day.[5] Reproducing a common model of the late 1960s and early 1970s, *TBP* operated as a collective that "came together with a sense of relative equality, shared power, and mutual ownership."[6]

Throughout its fifteen years of history, *TBP* collective was comprised of gay and lesbian radicals, most of them white, who were embedded in a transnational network of gay liberation activism. For example, one of the founders of the paper was Jearld Frederick Moldenhauer, who was born in 1946 in Niagara Falls, New York. Moldenhauer graduated from Cornell University, where he and other male and female students founded the Cornell Student Homophile League, which later became the Cornell Gay Liberation Front.[7] In 1969, he moved to Toronto and helped found the University of Toronto Homophile Association, an organization that he left shortly after.[8] Following this episode, he moved on to help found other important organizations, including *TBP*. According to Peter Zorzi—another founder of the paper—Moldenhauer was heavily influenced by the example of *Gay Sunshine*, and he pushed for the creation of a similar periodical in Toronto.[9] Moldenhauer also helped found the radical and confrontational group Toronto Gay Action, the Canadian Gay Liberation Movement Archives (now The ArQuives), and Glad Day—the oldest surviving LGBTQ+ bookstore worldwide.[10] Other leading leftist and radical activists involved in the creation of *TBP* or who later joined the collective include the Canadian activists Gerald Hannon, Ed Jackson, Ken Popert, Tim McCaskell, and Chris Bearchell, and the US-born, Canadian immigrant activists Herb Spiers, Michael Lynch, and Rick Bébout.

TBP was born just a few months after the August 28, 1971, "We Demand" protest in Parliament Hill, Ottawa—the first public demonstration for gay rights in Canada. More than one hundred gay men, lesbians, and their supporters attended this protest to mark the second anniversary of the proclamation of Bill C-150, the federal government's 1969 omnibus legislation that changed the law to allow for homosexual acts between two consenting adults in private. While some scholars have referred to this bill as a "partial decriminalization" of homosexuality, historian Tom Hooper has recently argued that the bill should instead "be considered the recriminalization of homosexuality in Canada" because "these reforms enabled the expanded role of the criminal justice system in the everyday lives of queer people."[11] Indeed, from the time this bill was passed, queer people in Canada took a critical response to it, and those who joined the protest in Parliament Hill in 1971 proclaimed a ten-point platform for change, entitled "We Demand." The platform included demands against the higher age of consent for same-gender erotic practices, against police repression, and against gross indecency laws, among many other issues.[12]

The creation of *TBP* also occurred in the aftermath of the 1969 Stonewall riots in New York City, an event that constitutes a landmark in the history of the gay liberation movement around the world and that sparked the creation of dozens of gay liberation periodicals in North America.[13] Many of these publications had the specific purposes of documenting the gay liberation movement and encouraging people to "come out." This was precisely the case of *Come Out!*, a paper that the New York City chapter of the Gay Liberation Front (GLF) launched in November 1969. Richard Meyer explains that, consistent with the gay liberation movement's framing of coming out "as a public demand for visibility," the GLF aimed to make visible its social gatherings and political demonstrations; *Come Out!* allowed the GLF to position visibility as a central component of its broader mission.[14] The inaugural issue, which both gays and lesbians put together, invigorated people to "come out for freedom!" and to "come out now!" The editorial stated that the new publication "has COME OUT to fight for the freedom of the homosexual; to give voice to the rapidly growing militancy within our community; to provide a public forum for the discussion and clarification of methods and actions nexesary [*sic*] to end our oppression."[15]

In this early period, encouraging people to come out was a crucial part of the formation of gay community and therefore of gay liberation. The relationship between these two elements was particularly clear for the editorial collective of *TBP*. In the words of lesbian feminist and collective member Chris Bearchell, community-building was "the essence of the [gay liberation movement] agenda."[16] Consequently, *TBP* pursued a community-building project based both on the premise of coming out and on the importance of raising awareness about gay and lesbian oppression. Former *TBP* collective member Tim McCaskell recalls that the gay liberation movement "drew from the social solidarity promoted by socialism, Keynesianism, feminism, the civil rights movement, and anti-colonial struggles to produce the notion of 'community.'"[17] The building of this community was fueled by inviting people "to come out," to "Dare to be [themselves],"and to "deal with [their] own oppressive behaviour."[18] Another former collective member, Ed Jackson, recalls that the gay liberationists' theory in the early 1970s was that they "were creating a gay community"—they used the term *gay* in a broad sense. Gay liberationists, he notes, "conceptualized the community before there was a community and . . . created the community by that conception."[19]

One of the strategies that the *TBP* editorial collective employed to advance its liberationist and community-building project and to encourage readers to come out was to promote images that conveyed positive messages of resistance, pride, and joy. The photograph discussed at the beginning of this chapter illustrates this strategy, as do the covers of issues that featured photographs of gay protests from across Canada, including the inaugural issue (figure 1.2). While these photographs documented protests and struggles for gay rights, they also captured moments of joy, as evidenced by the presence of cheerful and smiling faces. Photography, as these and similar examples suggest, was used as a technology for community-building. Its indexicality—that is, the ability of a photograph to capture something that "has been" there, as Roland Barthes posited in *Camera*

FIGURE 1.2. The inaugural issue of *The Body Politic*, published in Toronto in the fall of 1971, featured a photograph that Jearld Frederick Moldenhauer took in August of that year in Toronto, as gay activists prepared for a trip to Ottawa to participate in the first gay rights demonstration in Canada. Canadian Museum for Human Rights, Digital Collections, Internet Archive.

Lucida—allowed gay periodicals to show readers seemingly natural, honest, and spontaneous depictions of gay resistance and community. This, in turn, was an effective way of encouraging readers to read these periodicals and join the movement. Depictions of same-sex love, intimacy, and desire also helped *TBP* to advance its liberationist and community-building work. One of these depictions appeared on the cover of the thirteenth issue. It was a drawing that represented a couple of nude young men resting peacefully, surrounded by nature, and looking at each other affectionately (figure 1.3). In another cover, a photograph captures a loving scene between two of *TBP* collective members—Gerald Hannon and his partner Robert Trow. In this picture, Hannon reclines his forehead and nose on Trow's smiling face while softly holding the neck of his sweater, thus offering a powerful image of same-sex love and intimacy (figure 1.4). Erotic imagery, as discussed in the following chapter, was also crucial to *TBP*'s liberationist and community-building work, particularly sex-positive representations. The absence of homoerotic and same-sex love images in the media turned gay liberation periodicals such as *TBP* into powerful referents of gay liberation. They also turned them into icons of resistance against homophobia and repression.

Despite a strong commitment to community-building, the editorial practices of *TBP* were not particularly inclusive. In fact, the community that most *TBP* collective members imagined and visualized in the magazine was implicitly white. Scholars and activists have long criticized *TBP* for representing only the voices and experiences of white and cisgender individuals, especially of men. This is particularly evident in the visual content of the magazine; aside from the fact that *TBP* featured mostly white men, its erotic and sexualized imagery also catered to the desires of their white male readership. Many scholars and activists have also exposed anti-Black racism in the paper's content and editorial practices.[20] Considering these issues in *TBP*'s history, the discussion presented in this chapter does not mean to overemphasize its influence on the life of every queer individual who came across the magazine. However, the discussion does acknowledge the powerful representations contained in *TBP*, as well as the undeniable significance they had in the transnational history of gay liberation.

Indeed, the images that *TBP* promoted were so influential that one of them, known as "Kiss in," circulated across borders. The photograph, which Gerald Hannon took in Toronto in 1976, captured a moment in which gay activists, including Tim McCaskell and Ed Jackson, passionately kissed at the corner of Yonge and Bloor Streets in Toronto to protest the arrest of two men who had kissed on the same spot (figure 1.5).[21] The six gay men in this picture kiss their partners with such fervor that they embrace each other with their arms around their necks and waists. Their pelvises are so close that a contemporary viewer

FIGURE 1.3. Cover of *The Body Politic*'s thirteenth issue, published in 1974. Canadian Museum for Human Rights, Digital Collections, Internet Archive.

FIGURE 1.4. Cover of *The Body Politic*'s seventeenth issue, published in 1975. Canadian Museum for Human Rights, Digital Collections, Internet Archive.

FIGURE 1.5. Canadian gay activist Gerald Hannon took this photograph on July 17, 1976. The photograph shows six gay activists, including Tim McCaskell and Ed Jackson, passionately kissing at the corner of Yonge and Bloor Streets in downtown Toronto.

can only imagine how unsettling or astonishing this scene may have been for those who witnessed it in the mid-1970s. The photograph was published in *TBP*'s twenty-sixth issue, in September 1976. Eleven years later, the Mexican gay magazine *Macho Tips* used this same picture in its fifteenth issue to illustrate a news item retrieved from the San Francisco–based *Sentinel*, published on May 22, 1987. The news reported on the successful appeal in court that granted a gay man in Philadelphia a compensation of $1,500 USD after he was erroneously arrested for having kissed another man in public—an alleged moral misconduct.[22] Although it is not clear where the *Macho Tips* staff found the photograph, their use of this image in 1987 shows the wide circulation of *TBP*'s visual content and its transnational influence. The circulation of this picture also suggests the power of photography as a medium able to capture *real* scenes of gay resistance and love. The indexicality of photography allowed viewers to see that these six gay men "had been there," confronting homophobia by ardently kissing in the middle of the street, right in front of drivers and passersby.

Such a strategic use of visual culture, and particularly of photography's indexicality, was not exclusive to *TBP*, but part of a more generalized practice in the history of gay liberation. Richard Meyer has discussed this use through an analysis of an iconic image of gay liberation that Peter Hujar created to invite people to "Join the sisters & brothers of the Gay Liberation Front." The now iconic photograph portrays over a dozen young white men and women cheerfully walking and running on the street in what seems to be a genuine and spontaneous depiction of liberation, joy, and pride. Meyer notes how this poster stands in stark contrast to previous images of gay resistance, which offer "a dramatically different approach to homosexual visibility." Those images include photographs of homophile protests with men and women marching peacefully while holding signs and wearing formal clothes. Despite this contrast, Meyer asserts, photography was instrumental in producing modern gay and lesbian visibility and it fueled both homophile and gay liberation movements.[23]

Images like those described above were vehicles to visualize local, national, and international gay liberation movements, and they also were powerful vehicles that brought young activists into those movements. One of them was the Boston-based gay liberation activist John Kyper, who helped found *Gay Community News* in the early 1970s. Kyper was inspired by the international press and by the visual culture of gay liberation. While reflecting on his friendship with the Berkeley gay liberation activist Pat Brown in the early 1980s, Kyper recalled that images propelled him into gay political activism: "I remember seeing a picture of Pat at a gay protest in the very first issue of the *Advocate* I ever had the courage to buy, in December, 1969. My envy for those 'gay guerillas' (as the *Advocate* called them), soon enough, inspired me into action."[24] This episode was just the beginning of a long life of activism. From the late 1960s through the 1980s, Kyper was involved in a number of leftist organizations and anti-war and gay liberation movements in Boston, the San Francisco Bay Area, and Mexico City. He helped found the Student Homophile League at Boston University and the Boston Gay Liberation Front, and he became a member of the Fag Rag collective, which published the radical tabloid *Fag Rag* between 1971 and 1987.[25]

The wide circulation of gay liberation periodicals and their innovative visual content had profound implications in the transnational history of gay liberation. It is important to note that these periodicals were not the first ones to create gay communities through their use of images. The physique magazines of the pre-1969 generation, which featured images of well-built nude men, not only created gay communities but also cultivated a gay market in the United States, as David Johnson has demonstrated.[26] However, the use of images in gay liberation periodicals was significantly different. Aside from visualizing homoerotic desires, these periodicals also visualized gay resistance, liberation, and pride. These images invited gays and lesbians to come out, celebrate, and join the gay liberation movement; and the powerful messages these images conveyed were legible among activists across borders. Indeed, when gay and lesbian activists in Mexico

City decided to launch their own periodicals, they were building on this international tradition of gay liberation print culture and visuality. *TBP* and other gay liberation periodicals such as *Gay Community News* and *Gay Sunshine* provided them with strong referents to embark on this crucial undertaking.

The Mexican Gay Liberation Press

Although the first gay liberation periodicals in Mexico were launched in 1979, gay and lesbian activism in the country began in the late 1960s and early 1970s, coinciding with wider movements for democratization. This was a time of political upheaval marked by the student movement and the Tlatelolco massacre of October 2, 1968—on this date, the military and police killed dozens of student protesters who were demanding justice and political changes in the country. Against this backdrop, gay and lesbian intellectuals and activists in Mexico City began organizing awareness groups that questioned the stigmatization and social oppression of homosexuals. Some of them, such as Nancy Cárdenas and Carlos Monsiváis, had links with gay and lesbian communities in England and the United States and were inspired by the liberation movements that were developing in those countries.[27] In 1971, these and other Mexican leaders formed the first homosexual group in the country, the Frente de Liberación Homosexual, which operated underground due to the prevailing climate of repression. The group disappeared in 1973 without having established a solid ideological platform, and it would not be until 1978 that a stronger and more public movement would take to the streets. Scholars consider July 26, 1978, as a watershed in the history of homosexual activism in the country. On this date, a group of gay and lesbian activists participated in a march commemorating the twenty-fifth anniversary of the beginning of the Cuban Revolution. Later in the same year, on October 2, a larger group joined the commemorative march of the Tlatelolco massacre. Although gays and lesbians had been involved in different social movements in Mexico, including the student movement, their participation in these marches strengthened and gave more visibility to their own movement. From 1978 to the mid-1980s, three organizations led the homosexual liberation movement in Mexico City: Frente Homosexual de Acción Revolucionaria (FHAR), Grupo Lambda de Liberación Homosexual, and Oikabeth. The FHAR and Grupo Lambda had both male and female members, while Oikabeth was a lesbian group.[28]

A 1977 political reform enabled the public appearance of the homosexual liberation movement in Mexico City in 1978. Spearheaded by President José López Portillo, this reform opened new spaces for political participation in the country. The reform sought to recover the regime's legitimacy by opening electoral procedures and allowing the formation of new political parties—the Partido Revolucionario Institucional (PRI) had ruled Mexico since 1929. The 1977 reform strengthened the left, which the PRI had severely castigated since Miguel Alemán's presidential term during the early Cold War. For example, the Mexican Communist Party had been proscribed from competition since the 1940s, but in 1982 it could participate legally in elections thanks to the passing of a new Law of Political Organizations and Electoral Procedures, known as the LOPPE. The PRI, however, maintained total control of the electoral bodies and held onto power until 2000. The reform also enabled the participation of new social actors in the public sphere, such as trade unions and the '68 Committee for the Defense of Democratic Liberties, which included victims of the 1968 massacre.[29]

The political reform was also significant because the 1970s were the most violent years of the so-called Dirty War that the Mexican government undertook against guerrillas, political dissidents, and social movements on the grounds that they posed a threat to national security. This Dirty War made difficult the political organization and mobilization of homosexual liberation groups, not only because of their sexual dissidence, but also because alternative and countercultural movements and lifestyles defied authority and traditional notions of masculinity, as well as sexual and religious norms. As Gladys McCormick points out, those participating in such movements represented a threat to the established order and were seen as dangerous and subversive, which turned them into potential subjects of repression.[30] Despite this Dirty War, after 1968 the PRI governments were able to simulate an approach with the leftist youth and applied selective repression. Already with the presidency of Luis Echeverría (1970–1976)—who played a significant role in planning the Tlatelolco massacre—there had been important political changes. When Echeverría took office, he tried to make peace with the left by announcing an "apertura democrática" (democratic opening). His aim was to co-opt student leaders by offering them public positions, but he continued to repress social movements during his government.[31] The Echeverría government's inability to quench political dissent, a deteriorated regime, and an economic crisis in 1976 led to the 1977 political reform and to a subsequent Amnesty Act that granted pardon to 1,539 political prisoners.[32] Neither Echeverría's democratic opening nor López Portillo's political reform ended state repression, but they did expand opportunities for free expression, particularly in the media.[33] With less repression and hostility toward new organizations and political forces, the gay liberation movement in Mexico was finally able to come out publicly.

It was in this context that queer activists published the first gay liberation periodicals in the country. In 1979, gay and lesbian activists involved in FHAR and the Grupo Lambda published three periodicals that, despite their efforts, would not survive for too long because they lacked sufficient funds. In May of that year, members of FHAR such as Juan Jacobo Hernández, Ignacio Álvarez, Fernando Esquivel, Teresa Incháustegui, and Braulio Peralta, among others, launched *Política sexual* (Sexual Politics) and *Nuestro cuerpo* (Our Body), which published only one and two issues, respectively (figures I.1 and 1.6). In June of the same year, Grupo Lambda launched *Nuevo ambiente* (New Scene), which published five issues over four years—the last one in the summer of 1983. Like other gay liberation magazines, these periodicals published local and international news concerning gay and lesbian liberation movements, literature, historical, political and theoretical essays, letters, some erotic imagery, and visual representations of same-sex love, among other content. All of them were printed in tabloid format, and their number of pages varied—*Política sexual* was twenty-nine pages long; the first and second issues of *Nuestro cuerpo* twelve and twenty pages, respectively; and *Nuevo ambiente* varied between seven and seventeen pages.[34]

These periodicals and the gay and lesbian liberation movement in Mexico City were part of a transnational history of gay and lesbian activism, as the personal experiences of leading gay and lesbian activists suggest. For instance, Ignacio Álvarez was an international activist whose leftist politics, middle-class background, and connections abroad played a significant role in Mexico's gay liberation movement. In a 1981 interview, Álvarez defined himself as "a mix of middle class: My father is Jewish bourgeoise, and my mother is proletarian."[35] He remembered coming to political consciousness in 1967 when he visited the United States and witnessed the hippie movement. According to his account, it was during that trip that he realized how the hippie movement opened the road for the women's movement, while the latter, in turn, opened the road for the gay movement. In 1968 he got involved with the Mexican student movement and spent two days in jail, after which his academic records disappeared from the university, as if he had never studied there. In response, he moved to San Francisco to work for a while and then to Europe. Living in Paris in 1971, Álvarez became familiar with the gay movement, particularly with the work of the *Front homosexuel d'action révolutionnaire*, a name that some Mexican activists would later appropriate. Years later, in 1974, he became one of the founders of a gay liberation group in Geneva and another one in Basel. Between Paris and Switzerland, Álvarez grew conscious of the relationship between feminism, the left, and gay liberation. He spent six years in Europe working with gay movements and then returned to Mexico. In 1978, he and other activists considered it the right time to create a political group of gay people, which was how FHAR was born.[36]

FIGURE 1.6. The second cover of the magazine *Nuestro cuerpo* repurposed an engraving by the famous Mexican artist José Guadalupe Posada (1852–1913). The original engraving depicts a man haunted by seven demons that represent the capital sins. On this cover, each demon represents a homophobic slur. This was the last issue of *Nuestro cuerpo*. Colectivo Sol Online Archive, Magazines Collection.

Juan Jacobo Hernández Chávez was another leftist whose international experiences and connections shaped his political and gay liberation consciousness and activism. He was born in León, Guanajuato, in 1942 and moved with his parents to Mexico City in 1948. His grandparents had migrated from Mexico to Nebraska during the Mexican Revolution, but his parents went back to Guanajuato a few years later. In Mexico, Hernández grew up speaking both Spanish and English and acquired proficiency in the latter when he was sent to live with his aunt in the United States for a short period of time. He was also fluent in French, as he studied French literature at the Universidad Nacional Autónoma de México. Because of these language skills, he worked as a teacher of literature, French, English, writing, and theater until 1992. In the early 1970s, he got involved in Mexico City's homosexual liberation movement, becoming a member of the Frente de Liberación Homosexual.[37] As this and subsequent chapters show, Hernández's ability to read and communicate in English and French allowed him to bridge the Mexican gay liberation movement with gay organizations in North America. It also allowed him to draw on international gay periodicals while working with the Mexican gay press.

The transnational circulation of gay liberation periodicals, the visual content of these publications, and the movement of activists across borders played a key role in the emergence of the Mexican gay liberation press. In a recent interview, Hernández recalled that FHAR was particularly inspired by the kinds of texts, themes, and images that *The Body Politic*, *Gay Community News* (*GCN*), and the French paper *Gai pied* promoted. Following the example of those periodicals, members of FHAR decided to publish *Política sexual* and *Nuestro cuerpo* to take control over the representation of gays and lesbians in the media and to have their "own voice."[38] Hernández also recalled how periodicals like *TBP* and *GCN* sought to establish contact with gay organizations in Mexico. People involved in the production of those papers often traveled to Mexico and brought materials, including periodicals, with them. Many of these activists and travelers—who came from places like San Francisco, New York, Los Angeles, Boston, and Toronto—began an international correspondence with the people they had met in Mexico. Gerald Hannon, for example, visited Mexico City in 1974, participated in the gay scene, and published an article in *TBP* about this visit (see chapter 3). Gay groups in Mexico would also subscribe to papers such as *TBP* and *GCN*, or they would bring them back to Mexico after traveling abroad. With over forty years of distance, Hernández remembers those exchanges with excitement: "There was quite an interesting effervescence in those years because there was indeed a shared interest, a crossroads of ideas, of people, of loving relationships, because the first phase of the movement had a lot of that explosion. It combined everything: the personal and the political."³⁹ It is important to note that already in the 1950s and 1960s gay periodicals from the United States had some circulation in Mexico City and enabled communication among gay men in both countries. For example, Víctor Macías-González notes that ONE *Magazine* (1953–1967) and other international homophile periodicals had some subscribers in Latin America and published numerous stories about the region. US homophile groups, the author explains, had connections with middle- and upper-class Mexicans, and they often visited each other.⁴⁰ In the case of *Nuevo ambiente*, a key figure who helped to connect the magazine with gay activists abroad was Danny Laird, a young US activist who moved to Mexico City in 1977. Soon after his arrival, Laird became involved in the Mexican homosexual liberation movement and joined Grupo Lambda. In a recent interview, he recalled that, from the late 1970s through the early 1980s, he performed various tasks in the group; significantly, he collaborated as editor of *Nuevo ambiente* and oversaw their international relations with organizations like TBP and the International Gay Association.⁴¹

In the abovementioned interview, Juan Jacobo Hernández underscored how images were crucial to FHAR's liberationist project. He recalls that during its early years FHAR explored and benefited from the production of images—drawings, photographs, and other kinds of pictures that they got printed and distributed among people. These "seeds," he noted, eventually became an initiative to launch *Política sexual*.⁴² Moreover, like TBP, FHAR's periodicals featured photographs that evoked resistance, pride, and joy. In one of these photographs, taken at the first gay pride march in Mexico City in 1979, a group of five protesters seem to repeat a chant with a mix of pride, joy, and also shyness—as suggested by their expressions, poses, and gestures (figure 1.7). For instance, the person on the far right of the picture, while seemingly happy, joins the chants timidly with their hands clasped in front of them. In contrast, the second protester from the left holds a banner and chants louder. Their unbuttoned shirt, gestures, and the movement of their body suggest a proud and defiant attitude that defends the message in their banner: "We are neither sick nor criminals!"

Thus, building on a transnational history of gay print culture, Mexican gay liberation activists used gay periodicals and images to advance their movement. The transnational nature of gay liberation periodicals around the globe helped them to do it, as well as the ability of some activists to travel abroad and communicate in different languages. The interactions between Canadian, US, and Mexican gay activists were mediated by people who were middle-class, educated, and fluent in English and Spanish, such as Hernández, Álvarez, and Laird. But equally important to establishing transnational connections were the theoretical grounds that united gay liberation activists across borders. As the following

FIGURE 1.7. The second issue of *Nuestro cuerpo* included photographs from the first gay pride march in Mexico City, which took place in June 1979. Colectivo Sol Online Archive, Magazines Collection.

section explains, shared ideas about gay liberation allowed activists to identify with each other and shaped the visual content of their periodicals.

The Liberation of the Body and Its Visual Representation

In addition to images of resistance, gay liberation periodicals in the 1970s and early 1980s published images that promoted the liberation and celebration of the body, as well as of homoerotic desires. Gay liberation activists across the Americas, and also in Europe, drew on the same theories that bridged Marxism and sexual liberation; as a result, the visual content of their periodicals promoted similar values that situated the body and homoerotic desire at the center of their liberationist and community-building projects. Some influential literature included Wilhelm Reich's *The Sexual Revolution: Toward a Self-Governing Character Structure* (1936), Herbert Marcuse's *Eros and Civilization* (1955), Guy Hocquenghem *Le désir homosexuel* (1972), and Mario Mieli's *Elementi di critica omosessuale* (1977). This Marxist literature enabled gay and lesbian activists to identify a relationship between the family, the capitalist order, and the oppression of women and homosexuals.

During the 1960s and 1970s, the revolutionary youth in the Americas and elsewhere read this literature and drew from it to advance a criticism of class and sexual oppression, as well as to oppose authoritarian and repressive regimes. For example, the works of Reich and Marcuse were a significant source of inspiration for university students in Mexico who sympathized with a revolutionary left and participated in the student movement. The works of both authors were part of the university curricula around those years, and in 1966 Marcuse himself participated in the winter courses organized by the Faculty of Social and Political Science at the Universidad Nacional Autónoma de México.[43] Toronto-based gay activists were also avid readers of these authors in the mid-1970s. The collective known as the Marxist Institute offered courses, sponsored debates, and facilitated the formation of study groups devoted to Reich, Marcuse, and other Marxist philosophers. Prominent gay activists like Tim McCaskell and Gary Kinsman attended and participated in such activities.[44] Since the works of both authors underlined the close connection between social and sexual revolution, they provided gay and lesbian activists with a powerful language to frame their political demands.

The similarity in the titles that gay activists chose to name their organizations and publications reflect their shared theoretical basis. For instance, Marxist theories and psychoanalysis had constituted the basis of the Mexican group Sex-Pol, whose name evoked the idea that sexuality was political; founded by the Mexican gay activist Antonio Cué in 1974, this group would later give rise to the Grupo Lambda de Liberación Homosexual. Similarly, Mexican gay activist Braulio Peralta has noted that the title of the magazine *Política sexual* alluded to Reich's theories that regarded sexual liberation as a vehicle for political liberation.[45] These theories had also constituted the basis of Argentina's Grupo de Política Sexual. As Patricio Simonetto observes, the activists who named this and similar organizations were inspired by the same theories of the liberation of desire and, particularly, by the principle that "the revolution should not only liberate the proletariat from the forced sale of their workforce, but also from the subjection of their desire and their sexed body."[46] Titles like *Política sexual* or Sex-Pol also evoke the strong influence that the feminist movement had on gay liberation. Kate Millett's *Sexual Politics*, published in 1970, was one of the most influential texts of the feminist movement and of the early stage of the gay liberation movement in the United States and beyond.[47] The strong influence of feminist theories in gay and lesbian liberation movements is reflected in the recollections of lesbian activists. For example, in a recent interview, the lesbian activist and former FHAR member Teresa Incháustegui elaborated further on the title *Política sexual*. She explained that the title responded to the militants' interest in reflecting on corporality and to the fact that "power was not only a rational, ethereal thing outside of us, but it was also found in corporeal territories, embodied." For this reason, they sought to understand the body as "a space of struggle and liberation."[48]

Indeed, the body was central to gay liberation movements across the Americas, as suggested by titles like *The Body Politic* and *Nuestro cuerpo*. Gay liberation activists in the region were inspired by Marxist theories that made connections between body, pleasure, and liberation—liberation from both sexual repression and the capitalist order. For example, in *Eros and Civilization*, Marcuse called for "a *transformation* of the libido: from sexuality constrained under genital supremacy to eroticization of the entire personality."[49] Gay activists in the 1970s recuperated this claim and argued for the liberation of the body. For instance, building on Marcuse and other Marxist theorists, Argentina's Frente de Liberación Homosexual published the manifesto *Sexo y revolución* in 1973. In this document, the Frente discussed how, in our society, the libido is reduced to the genitals to ensure that the rest of the body fulfills its role in capitalist production. In this "society of domination," the document stated, "genitalization removes from the body its capacity to produce pleasure, thus turning the body into an instrument of alienated production and reducing sexuality to reproduction. For this reason, our society condemns all sexual activities that are not the introduction of a penis into a vagina."[50] FHAR's magazine *Nuestro cuerpo* drew on the same principles and honored their invitation to liberate the body. In this instance, former FHAR activist Juan Jacobo Hernández explains that the title of the magazine honored the group's decision "to work with our bodies to lose fear and be able to go out publicly."[51] It also alluded to an effort of gay activists "to recuperate their sexuality." This effort was ideologically inspired by Italian philosopher and gay activist Mario Mieli, whom Hernández remembers as "a strong ideological referent who nurtured their movement." It was also inspired by the French philosopher and gay activist Guy Hocquenghem.[52]

The works of Mieli and Hocquenghem were strong referents of gay liberation theory across borders. Their major contributions, *Le désir homosexuel* and *Elementi di critica omosessuale*, were accessible to gay liberation activists in the Americas either in their original languages or in translated editions published in the late 1970s and early 1980s—Hocquenghem was first translated into English in 1978 and Mieli in 1980. Although these English translations came relatively late in the history of the movement, US radicals became familiar with the "antirationalist dimensions" of French theory—of which Hocquenghem was an exponent—through other means. One of them was the 1975 "Schizo-Culture" Conference, organized at Columbia University, which helped to bring post-1968 French scholarship to US audiences. The conference brought together French scholars such as Michel Foucault and thousands of US activists, including Black Power, feminist, and gay liberation activists.[53] In the Spanish-speaking world the reception and circulation of European gay liberation theories were somewhat different. The first translation of Hocquenghem's work was published in Buenos Aires in 1974 under the title *Homosexualidad y sociedad represiva*, while the first translation of Mieli's work was published in Barcelona in 1979 under the title *Elementos de crítica homosexual*. These works, as well as those by Michel Foucault, David Thorstad, and other writers, comprised the gay liberation theory that informed the Mexican movement.[54]

Mario Mieli was a leader of the Italian sexual liberation movement and a strong advocate for the liberation of the body, desires, and pleasures. In 1972, he co-founded the Italian Revolutionary Homosexual Liberation Front, "F.U.O.R.I.!" (*Fronte unitario omosessuale rivoluzionario italiano*), and its homonymous gay liberation periodical *Fuori!*," which had some circulation in the Americas. His *Elementi di critica omosessuale*, considered the most important work of critical theory on sexuality in the Italian context, posits that institutionalized heterosexuality is as a problem not only for homosexuals, but for people of all genders and sexual orientations.[55] Mieli drew on Marxism and psychoanalytical theory to criticize the repression of our bodies and desires. He believed that "the liberation of sexual desire—starting with the (re)discovery of anal pleasure in men—is one of the most important steps in the journey towards a harmonious future and a collectivist social order."[56] One of the arguments in *Elementi di critica omosessuale* that Juan Jacobo Hernández readily recalls is Mieli's claim that gay desire lives within us all. Mieli considered that most people rejected this desire because patriarchal, capitalist societies inscribe this rejection in their bodies and minds.[57]

Through readings of similar theories and through influences between periodicals, the visual content of gay liberation journals included similar representations that suggested the liberation, eroticization, and celebration of the body. For example, gay liberation periodicals regularly published photographs or drawings of male buttocks on their covers and back covers. Such representations resonated with the literature that gay liberation activists read in the 1970s and early 1980s. In addition to celebrating the body, these images invited readers to decenter eroticism from the genitals and to celebrate an important vehicle for homoerotic pleasure: the anus. Such was the case of the back cover of *Gay Sunshine*'s second issue, which featured a collage by Paul Mariah that put together numerous

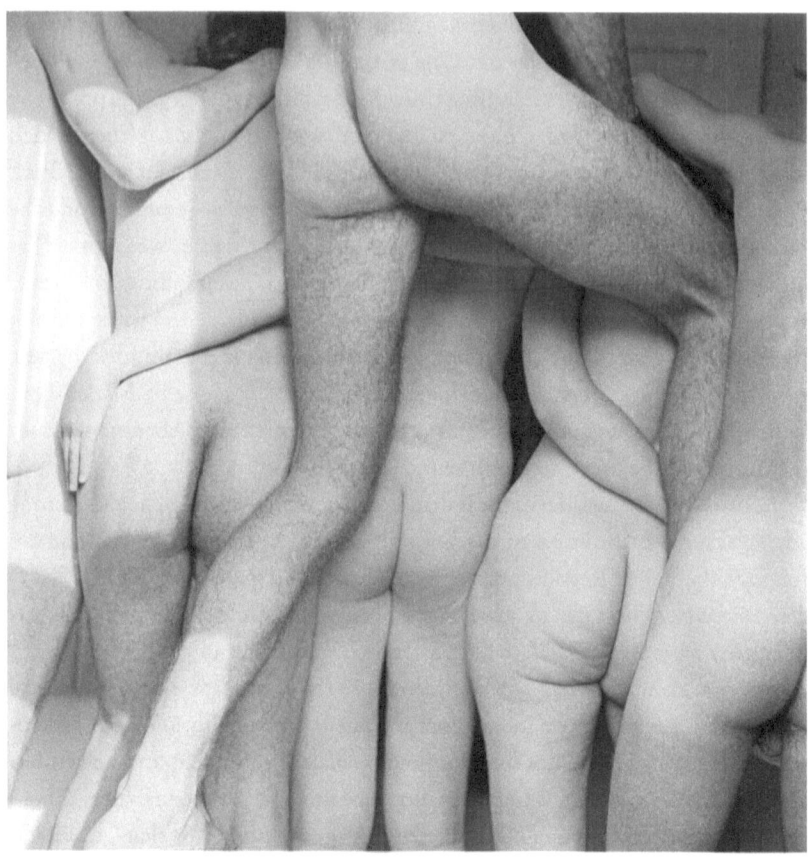

FIGURE 1.8. The back cover of *The Body Politic*'s fifth issue published a cropped version of this photograph that Jearld Frederick Moldenhauer took in 1972—the published image does not show the man on the far right. Courtesy of Jearld Frederick Moldenhauer.

clippings of male buttocks. The silhouette of a fist and forearm emerging from the bottom of the page metaphorically and literally penetrates the collage. Written within this silhouette, a poem tells the reader, "I want you to know how it feels to have a fist the size of a poem up yr ass."[58] Another example is the photograph featured on the back cover of *TBP*'s fifth issue, which portrayed the backs of some collective members while they playfully hugged each other and one of them, presumably Gerald Hannon, seems to jump on top of the others (figure 1.8). Moldenhauer took the picture at an orgy the collective had organized. Explaining the organization of this orgy over three decades later, a participant recalled, "There were a lot of silly ideas about breaking down inhibitions" and "naïve concepts of brotherhood" at that time.[59] A third example is the cover art by

Guillermo Santamaría on *Nuestro cuerpo*'s inaugural issue (figure I.1). Along with the title, his drawings of nude men announced to readers a clear relationship between sexual liberation, body, and desire. One drawing depicts men with athletic bodies and rounded glutes, while the other depicts men lying down with spread legs and showing their genitals, both images evoking an ideal of male beauty, musculature, and masculinity. The cover is akin to those images featured in *Gay Sunshine* and *TBP*, and despite the contrast between the medium—photographs versus drawings—and between the intention of these images' production—the provocative, the intimate, and the erotic—all of them convey explicit messages of liberation and celebration of the body. They were also powerful reminders of the potential of the body as a vehicle for gay community-building.

Along with the celebration of the body, images such as the one featured in *TBP* encapsulated other core values of gay liberation, specifically a belief in personal authenticity and acceptance. These principles were promoted in intimate spaces such as gay communes, which activists formed in a number of major cities across the United States and Canada in the early 1970s. Visual records of communal life and peoples' recollections of their experiences in queer communes reveal the importance of nudity and physical or intimate contact among members. Stephen Vider has discussed some of those records and experiences, observing that they suggest "the importance of authenticity and self-revelation," as well as the "emotional connection and the potential for erotic contact" in communal living.[60] Gay activist Nikos Diaman, whom Vider quotes, recalled that "openness was equated with freedom, the elimination of shame."[61] The depiction of nudity in gay liberation periodicals thus worked to advance the need to promote freedom, reject shame, liberate the body, and embrace authenticity and acceptance, as well as to celebrate the body. "Celebrate the Body" was actually the title of a publication by Gerald Hannon in *TBP*'s fifth issue that included another picture from the same orgy mentioned above. A legend at the bottom of the publication claimed: "In these photographs we present the body unashamedly as object, a joyous, potent object. Celebrate it." Commenting on the heterosexist portrayal of the body in the mainstream media, which mostly objectified the female body and lacked the inclusive or celebratory undertones of gay liberation aesthetics, Hannon declared: "It is our business to boldly offer alternatives. In this case the alternative is an exploration, a re-examination, a re-discovery of the body's potential." The alternate aesthetic, he went on, exhibited qualities that made the gay liberation movement "a varied and vibrant force in contemporary society— openness, honesty, joyfulness, a sense of play, a sense of brother/sisterhood, and embracing the young, the old, the male, the female, the beautiful and the not so beautiful."[62] In line with Hannon's observations, the *TBP* editorial collective celebrated the body, and most of its members supported the publication of sexual and erotic imagery in the paper. But as chapter 2 will explain, the reception of these images was far more complicated, particularly because of diverse understandings of liberation and oppression.

Various drawings and photographs depicting nude bodies in the periodicals of FHAR and Grupo Lambda also underscored the centrality of the body in gay liberation politics, sometimes by drawing from an international visual culture of gay liberation. For example, the cover of *Nuevo ambiente*'s second issue featured a drawing that conveyed a powerful message of gay and lesbian liberation through the representation of the body. The drawing depicts a man and a woman, both nude, emerging from a flower and stretching upward toward a symbol of same-sex love; their gestures and bodies suggest a hard, yet determined struggle to reach their liberation (figure 1.9). This drawing is similar to other images that appeared in the international gay press. For example, in 1971 *Gay Sunshine*'s eighth cover was illustrated with a drawing of a man and a woman, both nude, who seem to celebrate breaking the chains that kept them oppressed; still with chains hanging from their wrists, they both seem proud for having reached their liberation (figure 1.10). Years later, FHAR would use the same drawing in one of the pamphlets they published to promote their work (figure 1.11). Mexican gay activists had access to *Gay Sunshine* at least since 1972, when members of the Frente de Liberación Homosexual sent a letter to this magazine to present their objectives and get some international attention—*Gay Sunshine* published this letter in its eleventh issue and invited people to correspond with the Mexican group.[63] FHAR's use of this drawing in the late 1970s or early 1980s shows how gay liberation periodicals not only developed a similar visual language; they also borrowed from each other. It also shows how the transnational circulation of gay periodicals and images connected gay activists across borders.

Another example of how these periodicals represented the relationship between body and liberation is a photograph in *Nuestro cuerpo* situated in the middle of two news articles, one about the Mexican National Front for Women's Liberation and the other one about police repression. The photograph portrays a nude person laying on their side and tied with a cord. The shadows in the photograph prevent the viewer from identifying the person's gender, age, or facial features; all we see is a person in a semi-fetal position, touching the ground with their face while holding one leg closer to the stomach. Despite the artistic nature of this picture, the image evokes repression, a struggle for liberation, and even dehumanization; all we see is a body trapped and repressed—by society, by the police, or by their own inner selves.

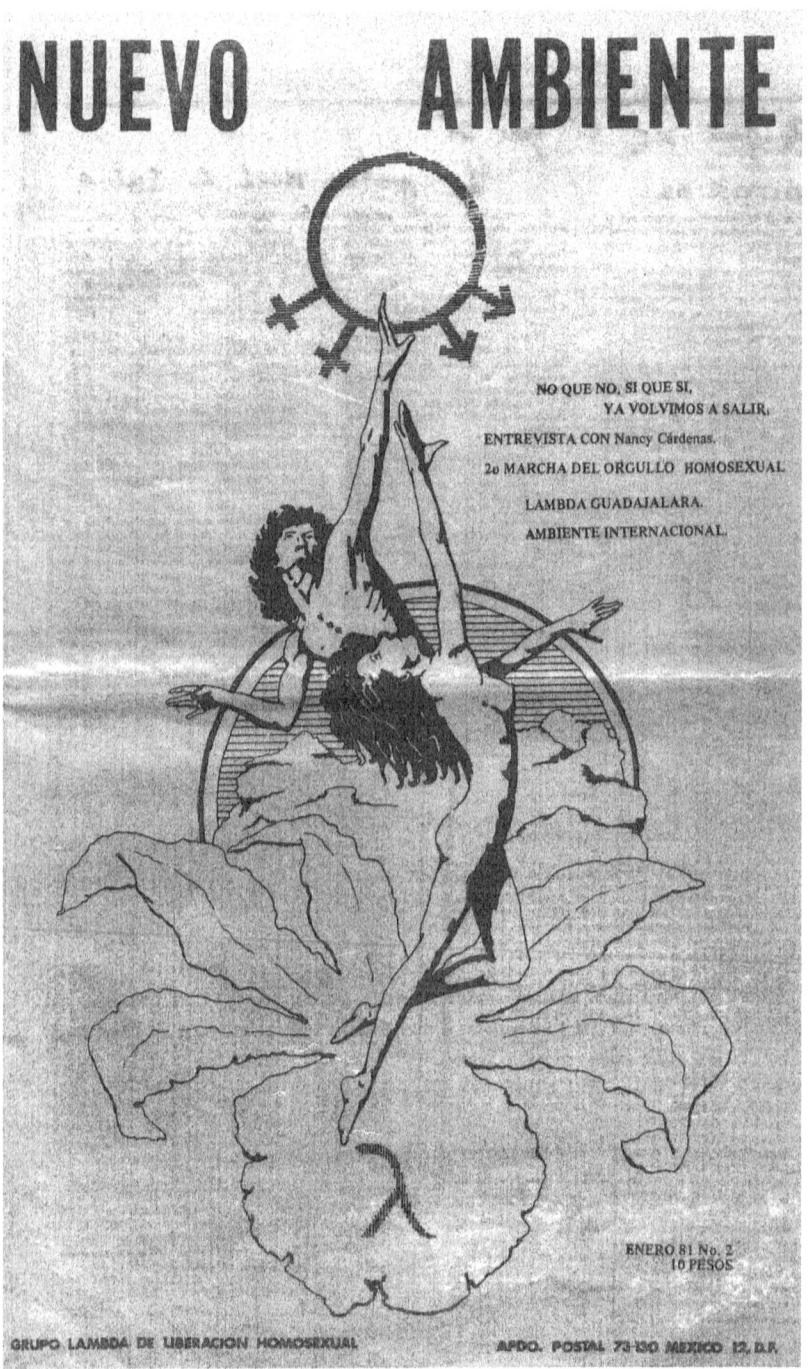

FIGURE 1.9. Cover of *Nuevo ambiente*'s second issue, published in Mexico City in January 1981. The ArQuives: Canada's LGBTQ2+ Archives, Toronto.

FIGURE 1.10. Cover of *Gay Sunshine*'s eighth issue, published in 1972. The ArQuives: Canada's LGBTQ2+ Archives, Toronto.

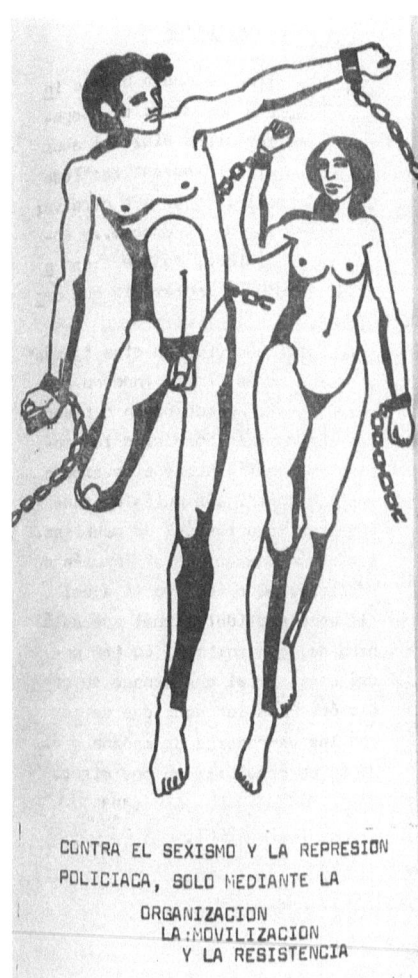

FIGURE 1.11. The Mexico City–based group Frente Homosexual de Acción Revolucionaria reproduced the same drawing from *Gay Sunshine* (figure 1.10) to promote their work. Cornell University Libraries Special Collections, Robert Roth Papers, Ithaca, New York.

It was precisely because of the repression of the body that, aside from the powerful influence of gay liberation theories and imagery, Gestalt therapy and bioenergetic exercises were crucial to the beginning of the Mexican gay liberation movement, as they helped gay activists to prepare their bodies to come out—both physically and politically. In a 2019 interview, Hernández argued, "The movement in Mexico would not have surfaced at the time it did without the powerful antecedent of Gestalt therapy and bioenergetic exercises," both of which prepared their bodies for political and physical action. He noted: "They prepared our bodies to break up armors of resistance, of fear, of shame ... and to be ourselves. The title [*Nuestro cuerpo*] alludes to that stage of building courage and deconstructing fear; a stage of fierce acceptance, which propelled us into the streets."[64] Antonio Cué, gay activist and Gestalt psychotherapist, led these sessions with his brother Leonardo—as mentioned above, Cué had founded the group Sex-Pol in 1974. The gay activist Braulio Peralta has recently written about how important it was for Cué to "break up the armor, first with awareness then with bioenergy, his methods of work."[65] This type of queer consciousness-raising was part of a larger tradition in which feminist consciousness-raising played a formative role as a technology of community-building and political mobilization.[66] In the words of a feminist activist, the purpose of consciousness-raising groups was to "trace the outlines of our pain" and to "delineate the scaffolding of a society that has arranged our crucifixion."[67]

Hernández's recollection of some of these sessions underscores the relationship between the body and the beginning of the Mexican gay liberation movement. In these sessions Cué would ask participants to question themselves about who they were, why they felt so ashamed of their homosexuality, why they would allow others to humiliate them, why they would shake when hearing homophobic slurs, why they would feel so enraged when seeing the police arresting and humiliating other gay men, and why they would not tell their mothers they were gay, among other questions. Then, Cué would ask them to begin corporeal exercises, "ridiculous, but terribly effective exercises," such as sitting for several minutes on a chair's edge with tiptoe feet and arms up, and he would ask them to remain in those positions until they started to shake. This would be followed by other movements and difficult positions that brought participants to the point of screaming and howling out of pain; but Cué would not let them stop. Instead, he would challenge them to resist with homophobic slurs—"¡Ni madres, pinches putos!" he would shout ("No way, fucking faggots!"). Finally, the sound of a drum would release the participants, some of them shaking and crying. Cué would then light incense and play music to help participants to calm down. At the end, participants would form a circle and share their experiences. Hernández observes that Cué generated such a powerful connection between participants "that he made us a group; we were not a group, he made us lose fear and recover the dignity of being. This was fundamental. Without this, the movement would have been delayed another two, three, four, five years or more to take to the streets, and it would not have done it the way it did."[68] While Hernández's opinion may be colored by a nostalgic or affective remembrance of the gay liberation movement, in the early 1980s Ignacio Álvarez also declared that working with Sex-Pol for about eighteen months organizing awareness and consciousness groups gave

FIGURE 1.12. Activists holding a banner at a gay pride march in Mexico City. The text reads: "A person is not free if they do not own their body." Colectivo Sol Online Archive, Archivo Histórico Gráfico de las Primeras Marchas.

him "the key to come out politically."[69] Interestingly, the visual language of gay liberation periodicals resembled the political language displayed during gay protests. For example, photographs of gay pride marches in 1980s Mexico City show individuals holding banners with messages such as: "A person is not free if they do not own their body"; "They [heterosexist people] ignore what the body can do"; and "Do you really think that only queers have anal sex?" (figure 1.12).

Gay activists elsewhere had been incorporating Gestalt and other therapeutic practices into their meetings since the early 1970s as a way to further advance their political and sexual liberation. For instance, gay liberation activists in Sydney incorporated Gestalt therapies into their sessions; they argued that such practices had a potentially transformative power because they enabled an exploration of the self.[70] In the British context, men's consciousness-raising groups also built on counseling, Gestalt therapy, and primal therapy to look for more positive emotions and to work through feelings and traumas.[71] Gay male collectives in the United States also drew on the model of consciousness-raising, and some groups brought in professional Gestalt therapists to lead group sessions.[72] Yoga was another practice that some gay activist valued because of its potentially liberating power. Writing for the Boston-based *Fag Rag* in 1972, an anonymous gay writer from California stated: "Gay liberation means to me the union of my mind and body so that I can transcend both of them." The author explained how his experiences performing physical activities such as weightlifting, dancing, and hatha yoga intersected with his political views and desire to deal with and transcend sex roles.[73]

In addition to their shared interest in liberating and celebrating their bodies, there were other equally important aspects that united gay activists across borders and that featured prominently in their publications, such as their opposition to police violence, authoritarianism, capitalism, and state repression. As the section below explains, because of these shared values, goals, and political views, gay liberation activists recognized the importance of circulating periodicals across borders. This allowed them to advance their movements, form transnational gay communities, and fight oppression.

Building Networks and Advancing Gay Liberation
Through Print Culture

Gay liberation activists across the Americas recognized the importance of periodicals and the power of images to advance liberation movements and to build transnational communities. A shared experience of sexism, homophobia, police violence, and their engagement with leftist politics played an important role in connecting gay liberation activists across borders and allowed them to identify a common ground for their movements. Equally important was their commitment to transnational solidarity. Gay activists produced and circulated periodicals and images that resonated with those experiences and principles. These materials were crucial to communicating messages of transnational gay resistance, mutual support, and liberation.

TBP offers an excellent opportunity to illustrate this point, in part because of the work of one of its most dedicated activists, Tim McCaskell, who helped to connect *TBP* with Latin America and other parts of the world. Through the 1970s and 1980s, McCaskell traveled to the region on several occasions to establish contact with gay communities there. He published three lengthy articles about gay oppression and resistance in Argentina, Colombia, and Nicaragua.[74] And he also kept a frequent correspondence with Latin American gay friends and colleagues to provide them with information, periodicals, and contacts, or to exchange other materials with them. McCaskell was born in 1952 in Beaverton, a small town in Ontario, and he attended Carleton University in the late 1960s. After the first year, he dropped out and joined a group of people from Western Europe and the United States traveling through North Africa, the Middle East, and India. Back in Toronto, he became involved in socialist, Marxist, and anti-racist groups, the anti-apartheid movement, and in the gay liberation movement.[75] He became a collective member of *TBP* in 1975, though it was not until 1977, upon his return from a one-year recreational trip to Africa and Asia, that he took a more active role. In 1977, *TBP* collective members wanted to expand the international news section of the paper, and they proposed that McCaskell take on the task. By that point, *TBP* had exchanged subscriptions set up with numerous gay magazines from around the globe, and many collective members had correspondence with gay groups and individuals abroad. His work as international news coordinator required McCaskell to read gay periodicals from all over the world to select news for publication. Most of the periodicals that *TBP* received came from the United States, but they also received materials from Europe, Australia, South Africa, the Caribbean, and Latin America, among other places.[76]

The 1970s and 1980s were a time of political turbulence across Latin America because of the Cold War and US interventionism, hence the importance of writing about the region in the gay liberation press. During those years, South and Central American nations were experiencing a wave of right-wing, US-backed military dictatorships, state violence, and authoritarianism. Some of the most representative outcomes of the Cold War in Latin America included the 1964 Brazilian coup that overthrew President João Goulart and established a military dictatorship that lasted until 1985; the 1973 Chilean coup that overthrew the socialist president Salvador Allende and established a military regime led by Augusto Pinochet until 1990; and the 1976 military coup in Argentina that overthrew the government of Isabel Perón and established a military dictatorship that lasted until 1983. In Central America, the situation was similar. Following the 1954 CIA-orchestrated coup, a civil war in Guatemala lasted from 1960 to 1996. During those years, several military dictatorships, such as that of Efraín Ríos Montt (1982–1983), strongly repressed, tortured, and killed political dissidents and committed genocidal violence against the country's Indigenous Maya majority. Similarly, the 1979 military coup in El Salvador led to a civil war that lasted until 1992; by the mid-1980s, conservative military figures held political power in alliance with the Christian Democrats, with the support of the United States, and with José Napoleón Duarte as president. Significantly, Nicaragua was undergoing a revolutionary process that had resulted in the 1979 overthrow of the forty-three-year-long Somoza dictatorship and the establishment of a Marxist-leftist government led by the Sandinista National Liberation Front.

One factor that helped to connect gay communities across the Americas was the leftist and internationalist mindset that many activists shared. As Emily Hobson has demonstrated, gay and lesbian leftists sought to bridge sexual politics with an internationalist left; for this reason, many of these activists participated in solidarity movements that fought against dictatorial regimes in Central and South America, as well as against US imperialism. Mexican, US, and Canadian activists participated in these movements. For example, in the United States, gay and lesbian solidarity gained force in 1979 through the group Gay People for the Nicaraguan Revolution, and it became a main concern of the gay and lesbian left in the 1980s.[77] Meanwhile, the three organizations that led the Mexican homosexual liberation movement—FHAR, Grupo Lambda, and Oikabeth—participated in the Comité Mexicano en Solidaridad con el Pueblo Salvadoreño and attended meetings and demonstrations to show their support to the Nicaraguan Revolution. One of these demonstrations was organized in June 1979 to protest the Somoza dictatorship in Nicaragua, and dozens of FHAR members participated.[78]

Some Canadian activists, such as Tim McCaskell, also participated in this transnational solidarity movement, and *TBP* became involved in it through his political consciousness and personal interest in Latin America. McCaskell believed that connecting with Latin American gay communities was constitutive of *TBP*'s international solidarity work with gay liberation movements around the world. In a 2016 interview, he recalled that "the idea was to look for the stirrings of this new gay liberation consciousness . . . and gay identity and how it was organizing itself and seeing what we could do to produce connections." According to his own recollections, the *TBP* collective believed that the US and Canadian gay liberation movements "had a head start" compared with movements in other parts of the world. Some collective members also considered that Canadian gay communities were not facing as much oppression as in other places. For these reasons, they wanted to connect with other movements, such as those in Latin America, to see how they could assist them and what they could learn from them.[79] Indeed, by the mid-1970s the Canadian gay movement was significantly stronger than the Latin American movements. In both regions, gay and lesbian activists were organizing through the 1970s, but the political and social climate in Latin American countries prevented their movements from advancing at the same pace as their Global North counterparts. For example, while Global North gay and lesbian activists also faced repression, gay Argentinians, as explained in chapter 3, were targets of state violence both before and especially after the 1976 coup.

A shared experience of sexism and homophobia and a leftist political stance facilitated McCaskell's identification with gay struggles in Latin America and his notion of a transnational gay community. For instance, following the 1976 coup, he wrote an article on Argentina's Frente de Liberación Homosexual (FLH) that discussed the state of gay activism in the country, police violence, and the emergence of the gay press in Buenos Aires, among other topics.[80] He also discussed the content of *Sexo y revolución*—the major theoretical document of the Argentinian FLH. McCaskell sympathized with the FLH's claim that they were waging a revolution that sought to change people's sexual and interpersonal relationships. Sexism and machismo, they maintained, "were ideological pillars of Argentinian capitalism which had to be overcome if the revolution was not to fall back."[81] McCaskell celebrated *Sexo y revolución* and related to homosexual liberationists in Argentina who were "constantly engaged in a difficult uphill struggle for acceptance from its allies on the left, and constantly under attack from its real enemies on the right"—something that McCaskell had experienced firsthand. From the late 1960s and through the 1970s, many gay and lesbian activists across the Americas were marginalized, discriminated against, and even expelled from leftist organizations. Because of this discrimination, McCaskell criticized the revolutionaries whose "pseudo-Marxist" justifications of homophobia claimed that gays were "the result of decadent capitalism," that gay liberation was "part of imperialist cultural penetration, or that any concern with sexual matters was petit bourgeois individualism."[82]

Examples of homophobia in leftist organizations during that period abound. Throughout the 1960s, the Trotskyist Socialist Workers Party (SWP) in the United States expelled gays from its membership because homosexuality was deemed a "bourgeois disease that does not exist under socialism."[83] However, according to gay left activist John Kyper, in the early 1970s the party suddenly rediscovered gay liberationists "as a promising source of recruits."[84] For the activist and scholar James N. Green, it was hard "to reconcile" his gay and leftist identities while living in Philadelphia in the early 1970s because most leftists organizations were anti-gay. Despite the openness of some groups, he always felt that gays were not treated as equals.[85] This homophobia, Green observes, was typical of the Cold War period, when most leftists thought that "gay men were unstable, that they had weak emotional relationships, that they couldn't be trusted, that they would be vulnerable to telling secrets, that they were flighty." There was also a widespread romanticization of revolutionary masculinity—embodied by Ernesto "Che" Guevara—that "idealized a cold, contained male who sacrificed for the cause."[86] Mexican gay activists such as Mario Rivas and the lesbian activists Nancy Cárdenas, Yan María Castro, and Trinidad Gutiérrez were also militants in leftist organizations but faced homophobia and hostility.[87]

McCaskell's article on Argentina reveals how an international circulation of gay periodicals and images played a significant role in moving information and making it legible across borders. To write this piece, McCaskell drew on the magazine *Somos* (We Are) to denounce the violent repression of homosexuals in Argentina. *Somos* was an initiative of the FLH in Buenos Aires and was the first gay periodical published in Latin America. It published eight issues from 1973 to 1976, and according to one of its founders, the gay leftist activist and writer Néstor Perlongher, it had a circulation of five hundred issues, was published clandestinely, and was distributed by hand.[88] Its eight issues printed articles on politics and gay life in Argentina, declarations of the FLH, drawings, stories, and literature, as well as news on local and international gay struggles. In fact, according to McCaskell, it was through *Somos* that the world first learned of the massacre of gay men in Santiago following the Chilean coup d'état in 1973.[89] As chapter 3 explains, McCaskell had access to *Somos* through the Canadian gay poet Edward A. Lacey, who lived in Latin America in the 1960s and 1970s.

The image that accompanied McCaskell's article on Argentina effectively conveyed a message of political and sexual repression and resistance that resonated with the international visual culture of gay liberation. The image featured a map of Argentina, and a series of riot police officers armed with helmets, shields, rifles, and batons. Numerous butterflies emerge from the map and spread across the image, flying around the policemen and reaching the title "We will conquer a space full of light" (figure 1.13). Through this representation, the image challenged the political and sexual oppression in Argentina and delivered a message of hope. This illustration is akin to *Somos*'s fifth cover, which featured a powerful allegory of oppression and resistance through the representation of an eagle chasing a butterfly (figure 1.14). On the eagle's body and wings, numerous drawings and clippings evoke Latin America's experience with homophobic violence over the centuries and the political climate in the region during the Cold War. For example, representations of guns, a soldier at the top of the eagle's right wing, a riot policeman on the eagle's core, and an emblem of the Central Intelligence Agency remind viewers about the dirty wars that right-wing leaders in Latin America undertook against leftist and political dissidents in the second half of the twentieth century with the support of the United States—these dirty wars also targeted homosexual activists because of their close relationship with the left. At the same time, a representation of what seems to be a Spanish conquistador at the top of the eagle's left wing reminds viewers about colonialism and, specifically, the violent repression of homosexuality in Latin America over the centuries. The inclusion of this conquistador could be read as an invocation of the massacres against Indigenous men accused of sodomy during the colonial period. It could also be read as a critique of how Western societies had criminalized homosexuality since the medieval period and imported those values to the Americas in the sixteenth

FIGURE 1.13. Tim McCaskell's article on gay oppression in Argentina, published in *The Body Politic*'s twenty-sixth issue in 1976. Canadian Museum for Human Rights, Digital Collections, Internet Archive.

FIGURE 1.14. Cover of the fifth issue of *Somos*, published in Buenos Aires in 1974. Cornell University Libraries Special Collections, Robert Roth Papers, Ithaca, New York.

and subsequent centuries. In fact, the third issue of *Somos* featured an illustration of homosexual men being burnt at the stake during the medieval or early modern period. Yet such powerful representations of violence against political and sexual dissidents in the collage are counterbalanced by the figure of a butterfly that the eagle tries but fails to catch. The butterfly, with hearts on its wings, served as a symbol of gay resistance, liberation, and hope—a message that is further supported by the symbol of a raised fist on the eagle's right wing (just below the soldier). A somewhat similar illustration accompanies an article in the same issue of *Somos* that discussed police repression: "Veinte años de Razzias" (Twenty Years of Raids). This drawing shows two police officers flanking five seemingly homosexual men with chains around their shoulders. Over their heads, there is a strip of flowers, perhaps stylized representations of butterflies.

Gay liberation periodicals often included images of butterflies, an important symbol in the visual culture of the movement. The butterfly worked as an allegory of liberation because it symbolized a process of transformation and coming out. For this reason, the names of many gay organizations and the visual content of their periodicals referred to it. For example, the Gay Liberation Front in New York had a cell named "The Red Butterfly," and other organizations, perhaps following this tradition, also adopted a similar name. One of them was Mexico's FHAR, comprised of the Black and Red Butterflies collectives. *Gay Sunshine* had been featuring butterflies since the early 1970s, such as in the collage discussed in this book's introduction. By using symbols such as the butterfly, the eagle, the police, and the raised fist, the collage offered a potent message of resistance, liberation, and hope (figure I.3). The butterfly was also present on *Nuestro cuerpo*'s covers and in the pages of *Nuevo ambiente*. The third issue of this magazine featured a butterfly taking flight after emerging from its chrysalis, represented in the image as a globe. Since this drawing was used to illustrate an article about the International Gay Association, the message was clear: gay liberation at a global scale (figure 1.15). The use of the butterfly as a symbol to evoke transformation and liberation was even more explicit in the title of the first gay magazine published in the Mexican state of Jalisco, *Crisálida* (1983–1988). Interestingly, butterflies are also powerful reminders of the transnational nature of gay liberation politics and movements. Like some of the gay activists whose experiences are examined throughout this book, butterflies travel long distances across borders.

Defiant representations of the police were also frequent in gay liberation periodicals, as well as in the underground press of the 1970s and 1980s in various geographical and cultural contexts. For instance, in *Come Out!* and *Nuevo ambiente*, police officers were presented as predatory, animal-like figures. In a *Come Out!* illustration an officer adopts the form of a pig strangling a gay and a

FIGURE 1.15. The third issue of *Nuevo ambiente*, published in Mexico City in 1981, used this image of a butterfly emerging from a globe to illustrate an article about the International Gay Association. Cornell University Libraries Special Collections, Robert Roth Papers, Ithaca, New York.

lesbian with each of its hands. In *Nuevo ambiente*, an ogre-looking police officer or military official is ready to devour a man with the help of what seems to be an undercover agent (figure 1.16). These drawings expressed contempt for the police and others in authority and offered powerful statements against repression and violence that resonated with the experiences of gays and lesbians in the Americas and elsewhere.

Because of their potent messages of gay resistance and because of the need to advance a transnational movement, many gay left activists in North America sought to introduce or circulate gay periodicals in Latin America or to exchange materials with gay activists in the region. Two of these activists were Tim McCaskell and the New York–based Steve Forgione. Forgione was a flight attendant, a militant in the Socialist Workers Party (SWP) in the 1970s, and a member of the New York–based Lesbian and Gay Rights Monitoring Group in the 1980s.

FIGURE 1.16. The fourth issue of *Nuevo ambiente*, published in Mexico City in 1983, included this drawing to illustrate an article about police harassment and gay oppression in Colombia. Cornell University Libraries Special Collections, Robert Roth Papers, Ithaca, New York.

Throughout the 1970s, he tried to connect with gay groups in Latin America. He worked for Pan Am Airlines, which allowed him to fly frequently to the region. Close friends of Forgione's remember that he was interested in Latin American struggles, particularly in Central America, and his job allowed him to bring supplies like computers for the guerrillas in Guatemala—he even had a male lover in Guatemala who was a *guerrillero*.[90]

Forgione and McCaskell were both interested in Central American solidarity and were conscious of the importance of print culture to fostering gay political activism. In August 1981, Forgione was writing an article on Nicaragua for *Gay Community News* and got in touch with McCaskell—who had written a similar piece in *TBP*—to exchange some thoughts. Forgione mentioned he went to Mexico City recently and was glad to learn that some Mexican gay activists had Nicaragua in their minds, too. He was planning to return to Nicaragua in September of that year, after a short stop in Mexico City. He intended to place some issues of Grupo Lambda's *Nuevo ambiente* in Managuan bookstores and to convince one of his contacts there to have an exchange with international organizations. Forgione asked McCaskell for contacts: "people, bookstores of interest, etc.—anything—this time I intend to see how far concretely we can do something."⁹¹ McCaskell considered that the best thing they could do was to find contacts, flood Nicaraguans with information and literature, and let them figure out the next steps for themselves. In his view, despite the revolutionary air in Nicaragua, revolutionaries still needed to grapple with the relationship between leftist politics, revolution, and sexual liberation.⁹²

Another network that illustrates how gay periodicals and leftist politics led to the formation of transnational gay communities and networks is the one that brought together Juan Jacobo Hernández, Ignacio Álvarez, and John Kyper. At the time they first got in touch in the late 1970s and early 1980s, Hernández and Álvarez were leaders of Mexico City's gay liberation movement, while Kyper, based in the San Francisco Bay Area at that time, worked with *Gay Community News* (*GCN*). In August 1979, Hernández was introduced to Kyper in Berkeley while the Mexican activist was on a trip to connect with gay groups in the United States and to get international support—he had also visited San Francisco in January of that year with the same goal in mind.⁹³ Like Forgione and McCaskell, Hernández and Álvarez recognized the importance of receiving international periodicals and literature to nurture gay political activism in Mexico, and they relied on the continuous influx of these materials into the country, as well as on other kinds of support. When Hernández visited San Francisco looking for assistance, Don Jacobs of San Francisco Gay Rap asked him how people could support the FHAR if they were not able to send money. "With books, with literature," he replied; "if they send us books, that's money to us. American books are very expensive in Mexico. Send us newspapers, letters, anything."⁹⁴ For the FHAR, getting international support and attention from the gay press was essential to advance Mexico's gay liberation movement and to fight oppression. They wanted to use the gay press to make their presence known to gays outside Mexico and to circulate news about the repression of homosexuals in the country. They believed that the circulation of this news would lead to a more careful treatment of gay people in all countries. "It is a matter of life and death for the movement to receive outside support," Hernández claimed, because if they were isolated and had no outside help, they would lose their battle.⁹⁵

Kyper used the gay press to offer the Mexican movement the support they needed and to make visible the oppression that gay Mexicans were facing. In the early 1980s, he published several articles on Mexico in *GCN*, including interviews with Álvarez and Hernández, and reports on gay marches, protests, police repression, politics, and other happenings in the country. Over the course of the 1980s, Kyper, Hernández, and Álvarez continued working together to maintain and to form new transnational ties and, in the case of the Mexican activists, to get support, materials, and contacts from the United States. Hernández and Álvarez often asked Kyper for financial help to use in AIDS-related programs, to support archival projects, to pay their subscriptions to different newspapers and journals, or to pay the rents of their offices.[96] Álvarez also kept Kyper informed on Mexican politics, gay activism, and police repression, and Kyper would often report on those issues in *GCN*.[97] They also coauthored several articles about the Mexican gay movement.[98] After Álvarez's death, Hernández continued asking Kyper for books, *GCN*, and other magazines and newspapers.[99]

Gay activists from the United States, Canada, and Mexico such as Kyper, Hernández, Álvarez, and McCaskell, among many others, had more than a sexual preference in common. Leftist politics informed by Marxism, the lack of significant language barriers, and a shared interest in the gay press connected these activists and allowed them to form networks, to identify with each other, and to envision a common liberationist goal. At the same time, the visual content of gay liberation periodicals fulfilled a crucial role—it visualized what united gay activists across borders and facilitated their communication and identification with one another.

ONE OF THE STRATEGIES that gay liberation activists deployed to advance their movement was publishing periodicals with a rich visual culture that evoked the core principles of gay liberation and that invited readers to come out and join the movement. By using photographs and drawings strategically in their periodicals, gay activists visualized their experiences with homophobia, sexism, and repression while offering powerful messages of resistance, liberation, and pride. The invitation to celebrate the body and homoerotic desire, which drew from Marxist literature, was particularly present in these periodicals and gave rise to a shared visual language that made them legible across borders. This visual language shows the existence of transnational gay liberation movements that pursued similar goals and built on ideas, theories, periodicals, and images that circulated across borders. The international circulation of US and Canadian gay liberation periodicals was particularly important in this respect. Magazines such as *The Body Politic*, *Gay Community News*, and *Gay Sunshine* were some of the earliest and most successful publications in the world—they had a wide distribution, they published regularly, and they offered a forum for gay activists to learn about and discuss gay liberation politics. Their powerful depictions of gay sexuality and liberation inspired the work of activists in other regions, such as in Mexico, where gay and lesbian collectives began to use the press and visual culture to advance their movement in the late 1970s. Like those publications in the Global North, gay periodicals from Latin America also circulated across borders, and activists in Canada and the United States recognized the importance of reading and circulating those materials.

The visual representation of the body and homoerotic desire was so important for the work of gay liberation journals that some editorial collectives exercised a careful control in their use of images. Despite this control, the publication of sexual and erotic imagery was sometimes the object of heated debates that both advanced and complicated community-building efforts. The following chapter takes a close look at these tensions through an in-depth analysis of the production and reception of sexual and erotic imagery in the gay liberationist press.

| 2 |

Sexual Imagery, Transnational Communities, and the Politics of Visualization in The Body Politic

Throughout its fifteen-year run, the visual content of the Toronto-based gay liberation magazine *The Body Politic* (*TBP*) triggered various debates among editors, contributors, and local and international readers. The publication of erotic and sexualized images was particularly controversial, especially when some people perceived those representations as "sexist," "objectifying," or "pornographic." Lesbian feminists often complained about sexism and the objectification of the body in *TBP*, while some gay readers were troubled by the reproduction of gender stereotypes in sexualized images. In the mid-1980s, for example, a number of readers expressed disapproval of a new type of content in the magazine, the "Hot Pics." These were erotic and, in many ways, provocative photographs that began to illustrate the classified pages in June 1985 (figure 2.1). Many readers questioned the publication of these images, interpreting them as vulgar, offensive, and even violent sexual representations. These complaints emerged in the context of the so-called sex wars, a period when anti-porn and sex-positive feminists across the United States and Canada intensely debated issues concerning sexual practices and representations, including pornography, s&m sex, and censorship. The publication of these photographs in *TBP* at exactly this time made the magazine's stance clear: It would continue to celebrate and offer visual representations of gay and lesbian sexuality and homoerotic desires. The liberation of sexual desires and their representation had been constitutive of *TBP*'s liberationist project since the magazine began publishing in 1971, the same way that it had been for other gay liberation journals in the United States, Mexico, and elsewhere. Yet neither the *TBP* editorial collective nor its readers were a monolithic voice that could speak for all gay and lesbian liberationists in Canada and abroad. Instead, the people who produced and read the magazine had diverse and often clashing understandings of what liberation meant.

TBP was one of the most successful gay liberation periodicals of its time, and it provided gays and lesbians in Canada and abroad with a space for learning about, commenting on, and debating several issues, including civil rights, pornography, censorship, and intergenerational sex. As discussed in the previous chapter, *TBP* came into existence as part of a wave of gay liberation publications in North America propelled by the gay liberation movement in the late 1960s and early 1970s. During those years, gay and lesbian activists published periodicals to report on gay liberation politics and activism, to document protests and public events, to connect gay groups and individuals, to encourage people to come out, and to build community. *TBP* published 135 issues from 1971 to 1987, and it reached up to three thousand subscribers per issue, around 30 percent of whom were international, mostly from the United States.[1] In addition, more than two thousand people contributed to the magazine, including eighty regular correspondents from Canada.[2] Because of its wide circulation and readership, when the magazine encouraged debates on a particular topic, such as on the relationship between images and gay liberation, such discussions often became transnational.

This chapter examines some of these transnational debates against the backdrop of gay liberation politics and second-wave feminism in North America. The chapter focuses on *TBP* as a case study to deepen the analysis of the role of images—particularly those that visualized homoerotic desire—in the transnational history of gay liberation. The chapter argues that these debates about the politics of visualization reflected the intrinsic relationship between the body,

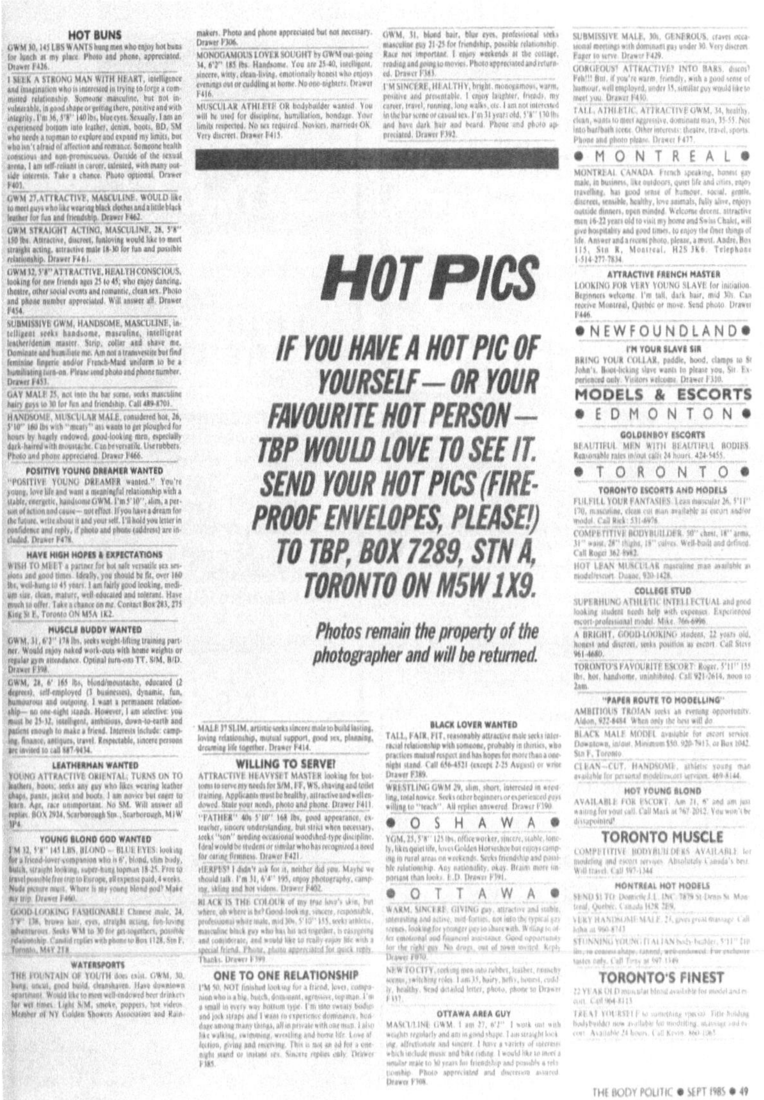

HOT PICS

IF YOU HAVE A HOT PIC OF YOURSELF — OR YOUR FAVOURITE HOT PERSON — TBP WOULD LOVE TO SEE IT. SEND YOUR HOT PICS (FIREPROOF ENVELOPES, PLEASE!) TO TBP, BOX 7289, STN A, TORONTO ON M5W 1X9.

Photos remain the property of the photographer and will be returned.

HOT BUNS

MONTREAL

NEWFOUNDLAND

MODELS & ESCORTS

EDMONTON

TORONTO

OSHAWA

OTTAWA

TORONTO MUSCLE

TORONTO'S FINEST

THE BODY POLITIC • SEPT 1985 • 49

FIGURE 2.1. In the 118th issue of *The Body Politic*, published in September 1985, the editorial collective invited readers to send their "Hot Pics" to be featured in the magazine. Canadian Museum for Human Rights, Digital Collections, Internet Archive.

sexual and erotic imagery, and the gay liberation movement. It also argues that the contestation of this imagery was instrumental in the formation of gay communities and identities at the local, national, and international levels. The publication of sexual and erotic imagery in *TBP* advanced some of the liberationist goals that brought this and other periodicals into existence—specifically, the visualization of gay sexuality and homoerotic desires. This content was so significant that the images and discourses promoted in *TBP* inspired some Latin American activists to launch some of the first gay liberation periodicals in the region, such as *Política sexual* and *Nuestro cuerpo* in Mexico City in the late 1970s. However, some images triggered debates because both readers and editors contested the meanings of "pornography," "sexism," "objectification," "liberation," and "community." They also triggered debates because feminist critiques emerging from Canada and the United States—but also present in other contexts—profoundly influenced the reception of the magazine.

Some of the debates over *TBP*'s sexual and erotic imagery evoke larger changes in the history of gay liberation in which images played a central role. One of these changes related to how gay communities began to see the visualization of homoerotic desires and sex as part of their liberation. This process has already been outlined in chapter 1 with a focus on Canadian, Mexican, and US gay liberation politics in the post-Stonewall period. At a more local level and later in this period, specifically toward the late 1970s and early 1980s, changes in Toronto's social and political landscape reconfigured how gay community was conceived. As explained below, sex became the main basis for politics among gay men—especially for those who were white—and a central factor in community formation. For some lesbians and gay men of color, though, this reconfiguration had a negative impact because it relegated issues such as sexism and racism to a secondary position. As former *TBP* collective member Tim McCaskell asserts, "elevating sexual desire to the centre of community formation potentially alienated those who found themselves excluded from those circuits, since it appeared to put sexual desire above criticism."[3] Thus, while the *TBP* collective advanced one of the most progressive and radical definitions of liberation, this definition was not widely accepted because it mostly favored the homoerotic desires of a white and middle-class gay community.

TBP could not encompass the experiences and voices of all gay and lesbian liberationists in North America. On one hand, the magazine's editorial collective, contributors, and readers were overwhelmingly white; on the other, its content centered mostly on male experiences, while the editorial collective was always male-dominated. Despite its failure to represent and include diverse voices of gay and lesbian liberation, the magazine honored its community-building project by encouraging its local and international readers to get involved in the magazine and share their views on its content—particularly on the visual content. On various occasions, the *TBP* collective gauged reader opinion on images, not only to become more familiar with their readership or to make changes to the magazine, but also to promote further debate and involvement on their part. Therefore, the magazine's use of images and their reception offer a unique opportunity to examine the role of images and homoerotic desire in the transnational history of gay liberation. This chapter further demonstrates that gay liberation communities and identities in the 1970s and 1980s were constituted through the production and circulation of periodicals and images that visualized homoerotic desires.

The chapter is divided in four sections, each devoted to analyzing local and transnational debates around sexualized and erotic imagery in *TBP* by drawing connections to similar debates in other gay liberation periodicals. The first section examines discussions about the politics of featuring nudity in a gay liberation journal, the kind of content that some lesbian feminists condemned for its alleged objectifying nature. The analysis situates such discussions within the larger history of second-wave feminism in North America while examining the relationship between the homoerotic imagery in gay periodicals and the formation of gay communities and identities. The second section discusses how the editorial collective and readers of *TBP* and other gay liberation periodicals took sexualized and erotic imagery very seriously. Most of them believed that this imagery was liberatory because it visualized and celebrated gay sexuality. However, others considered it was important to control the messages that these images conveyed in order to avoid reinforcing the oppression of some individuals. The third section focuses on the commercial representation of the body in advertising and how *TBP* and other periodicals navigated the tensions between this commercial use of the body and the principles of gay liberation. This section also examines the relationship between *TBP*'s visual content, a growing gay consumer culture, and the role of sex in the formation of gay communities and identities. The final section discusses how the visual content of *TBP* evolved in the 1980s and discusses the debates that some images perceived as pornographic triggered in the magazine. These debates are situated against the backdrop of the sex wars, which informed the nature of the discussions that readers and editors of *TBP* had over sexualized and erotic imagery in the 1980s. The sex wars also increased *TBP*'s efforts to visualize and defend the liberation and celebration of homoerotic desires.

The analysis of all these debates in the pages that follow avoids a condemnation of the alleged sexist or objectifying nature of *TBP*'s visual content. In this instance, the analysis builds on the theoretical framework that Jennifer Nash has outlined in her book *The Black Body in Ecstasy: Reading Race, Reading Pornography*. Although focused specifically on racialized pornography, Nash's framework is useful in this chapter because she reads racialized pornography not to find "evidence of the wounds it inflicts on black women's flesh," but for moments of racialized excitement and pleasures.[4] Drawing from film scholar Celine Parreñas Shimizu, Nash's work rejects "the long-standing presumption that images can be 'positive' or 'negative,' instead considering how minoritarian subjects are both constrained by and potentially liberated through representation."[5] In a similar way, this chapter pays more attention to how *TBP* readers and members of the editorial collective engaged with erotic and sexualized imagery in multiple ways. The aim is to show how most gay men appreciated the potentially liberating aspect of these kinds of images. As the analysis below demonstrates, most readers and editors of *TBP* experienced pleasure when seeing images that celebrated the body and visualized homoerotic desires and gay sexuality. They conceived of the production, publication, and circulation of these images as constitutive of a politics of gay liberation.

Debating Nudity, Sexism, and Objectification

In 1972, the publication of a nude portrait by *TBP*'s founding member Jearld Moldenhauer triggered the first debate over images among the editorial collective. The photograph, published on the back cover of *TBP*'s second issue, depicted a nude young man with his head to one side while sitting on a bed and resting his arms on each of his thighs, spread just enough to discreetly show his flaccid penis (figure 2.2). His name was Rolf, and Moldenhauer had photographed him in his dorm room at the University of Groningen the morning after meeting him during a trip to Europe.[6] With Rolf's calm look and relaxed posture, the picture evokes intimacy and tenderness, but it led some members of *TBP*'s editorial collective to accuse others of being sexist and of using the body to sell the magazine.[7] The main opponents to publishing the image were the only two women in the collective at that time, Jude and Aileen. The collective had initially decided against printing the photograph, but Moldenhauer insisted on publishing it, thus causing a division among the members. Peter Zorzi, one of *TBP*'s founding members, recalls that Moldenhauer had the intention of illustrating the paper with his portfolio of male photo studies, but some collective members—both men and women—opposed the idea. Jude and Aileen, who only used first names to oppose patriarchy, rejected the representation of nudity in *TBP* and claimed that Moldenhauer's photographs objectified the body.[8]

FIGURE 2.2. Photograph on the back cover of *The Body Politic*'s second issue, published in 1972. Courtesy of Jearld Frederick Moldenhauer.

Moldenhauer, who does not recall having a portfolio of male photo studies but only a few pictures, "pushed to use the photograph to counter the sex negative mentality of so many collective members."[9] Foreseeing the debate that this type of image might prompt, some male members also opposed publishing nudity. However, for most men in the collective, referring to the photograph as "sexist" was a "dogmatic assertion."[10] In a 1975 essay, collective member Ed Jackson recalled that most men could not understand such an interpretation, and the few who did support it could not clarify their reasons. "Everyone was a novice in [that] new way of perceiving things," he wrote.[11]

The critiques that Jude and Aileen put forth were informed by second-wave feminist politics, which emerged in major urban centers across North America in the mid-1960s, when women from various backgrounds began to develop feminist theories and to organize consciousness-raising groups to discuss their oppression. Their aim was to analyze the social relationship between the sexes in order to challenge patriarchy and sexism, to organize against violence against women, and to achieve women's freedom to decide over their bodies and personal lives. For women of color, advancing a theory of gender oppression attentive to racial oppression was also a priority. As part of their movement, second-wave feminists condemned the stereotypical and sexist representation of women in the mainstream fashion and beauty industries, as well as in pornography, because it reinforced and capitalized on women's subordination. Nonetheless, neither the early movement nor its adherents constituted a homogenous group, as women's experiences with sexism and oppression are shaped not only by their gender, but also sexual orientation, class, and race.[12]

The controversy around the photograph of the nude man caused a schism in *TBP* and made clear that, for some people, there was a tension between gay liberation and the feminist movement. This tension shaped the production and reception of the magazine, as well as how some members of the gay and lesbian community in Canada remember *TBP*. In fact, collective member Ken Popert recalls this controversy as one of the turning points in the magazine's history.[13] According to him, one of the most significant changes that the debate caused was that *TBP* "became more male-identified," because women "drifted away."[14] This assertion, however, needs some clarification. Although *TBP* was from the beginning a male-dominated journal, both gays and lesbians contributed to and read the paper. In fact, contrary to dominant narratives on the magazine's history, the participation of women in *TBP* was far from scarce. Kelly Phipps has recently demonstrated that the participation of lesbians in *TBP* was particularly consistent from the late 1970s onward, when five to ten women contributed to each issue and there was at least one female collective member, usually Chris

Bearchell.[15] Although male readers, contributors, and collective members of *TBP* indeed outnumbered women, Phipps argues that the latter were not *absent* from the magazine's history; instead, they have been *absented*.[16] Even in late 1984, at the peak of the sex wars, 20 percent of *TBP* subscribers were women—during the sex wars, many lesbian readers canceled their subscriptions to *TBP* for its alleged lack of support for women's issues.[17]

The work of sex-positive lesbians was actually instrumental in the history of *TBP*, as they helped to advance the goals of gay liberation politics. Such was the case of Chris Bearchell, who joined the *TBP* collective in 1978. Bearchell was the most influential lesbian contributor to *TBP* and dominated its lesbian content during the mid-1980s.[18] She was a leading activist in Toronto's gay liberation movement from the 1970s to the 1990s. She not only played a major role in *TBP*'s history, but also engaged in a number of gay and lesbian organizations such as the Gay Alliance Toward Equality, the Coalition for Gay Rights in Ontario, Lesbians Against the Right (LAR), and the Lesbian Organization of Toronto (LOOT).[19] In a 1996 interview, Bearchell recalled that LOOT was founded in the early 1980s to acknowledge that "there were women who worked exclusively within gay organizations, women who worked exclusively within feminist organizations, and women who worked in both, who were all lesbian and who had a common cause to make, and so it was in fact a deliberate attempt to bridge some of those differences."[20] For Bearchell, as Tim McCaskell recalls, bridging the gender divide among gays and lesbians was indeed a priority.[21] In Phipps's words, Bearchell was "a radical, revolutionary lesbian who was working with gay men, feminists, sex workers, and other marginalized groups to rebuild a collectivist and liberatory society."[22] In the late 1970s and throughout the 1980s, Bearchell strongly defended pornography and advocated against Canada's obscenity laws.[23] In fact, in 1984 she and a group of lesbians created the Super 8 porn film *Slumberparty*.[24] This film featured S&M scenes, a sexual practice that many lesbian feminists and some gay men considered outrageous, as discussed in the last section of this chapter.

Unlike Bearchell, though, most lesbian feminists in the 1970s and 1980s preferred to separate themselves from the organizations dominated by gay men, both in Canada and elsewhere. Examples of lesbians leaving male-dominated gay spaces because of alleged sexism abound, but one particularly relevant case is the break between lesbian and gay activists in the Mexico City–based Frente Homosexual de Acción Revolucionaria (FHAR). Disagreements over the relationship between gay liberation and the body played a central role in this break. The recollections of Teresa Incháustegui, lesbian activist and former FHAR collective member, shed light on this conflict. She recalls that the lesbians of FHAR sought to establish a deeper dialogue about the relationship between eroticism and genitality. However, this dialogue did not prosper because most group members were more interested in topics like cross-dressing, police violence, and "phallocentric eroticism." Indeed, the erotic imagery in FHAR publications—introduced in the previous chapter—was meant for a gay viewership, as most of these images were of nude males and erotic representations of the male body. For this reason, in the early 1980s the lesbians of FHAR decided to join other feminist and separatist groups, such as Oikabeth. In fact, the second and last issue of the magazine *Nuestro cuerpo* did not enlist any woman as collaborator. As discussed in the previous chapter, for many radical gay and lesbian activists the decentralization of eroticism from the genitals was constitutive of a liberationist agenda. In practice, though, depictions of male genitals in gay periodicals were the main vehicle to visualize and celebrate homoerotic desire and gay sexuality. This imagery left some lesbian feminists, such as Incháustegui, with the feeling of being "castrated" for not having a penis; and this concern, she recalls, was not sufficiently addressed in the FHAR.[25]

Discussions around erotic imagery in gay periodicals were thus central to the formation of gay communities and identities, as the cases above illustrate. Such discussions highlighted the various understandings of "liberation" that gay and lesbian individuals developed over the 1970s. They also provided opportunities for gay readers to interact with editors and shape the content of the gay liberation periodicals they consumed. For example, the debate on Moldenhauer's photograph was so significant that it led the collective to publish a poll in the paper's third issue where they asked readers for feedback on *TBP*'s general content and their opinion about advertising, about this photograph, and about images of that sort. The following issue reported that the response to the poll was overwhelming; though this report does not specify how many people responded to the poll, it is mentioned that 57.9 percent of the respondents were gay men, 10 percent were lesbians, 21.1 percent were bisexuals, 5.1 percent were straight, 2.6 percent did not know what they were, one respondent was a zoophilic, and another one was a mannequin.[26] According to the report, the controversy over the photograph of the nude young man "raised a lot of comment." The report noted that most readers seemed in favor of nude photographs, though the *TBP* collective feared that the young man in question had clouded readers' responses.[27] The magazine received comments such as: "Thought he was gorgeous!" and "Hunky and Delicious." Mr. B. Reynolds from Hollywood protested that "Those who object to tasteful and artistic nudes should join the Catholic Legion of Decency." Other commenters "found it much less than obscene"; for instance, a reader from London claimed, "The photography was just tacky. As a result its purpose was neither aesthetic nor masturbatory!"[28] What is clear in these responses is that most gay readers craved visual representations of the male body. The production, publication, and circulation of these images was a liberatory experience for them, and they wanted to buy a gay magazine that visualized their homoerotic desires.

Gay liberation periodicals were not alone in utilizing debates and conversations between editors and readers to advance community-building. These kinds of interactions are crucial in the formation of other magazine communities as well. Media scholar Brooke Erin Duffy asserts that "magazine communities are structured around imagined relations with editors," though "it is the participation of readers that keeps these communities intact" and fosters a "sense of kinship."[29] Through fostering this sense of kinship, gay periodicals like *TBP* were instrumental in building community and in cultivating political engagement among their readerships. The gay physique magazines that preceded the generation of gay liberation publications worked in a similar way. David Johnson has demonstrated how reading and purchasing these magazines put gay readers in contact with a national and international gay community, while making them participants in "a form of mail-order activism."[30] Consumers of physique magazines, Johnson argues, "came to understand themselves as part of a community of 'physique enthusiasts' enjoying and being excited by the same images, and being marginalized for that desire—even if it went unnamed."[31] Consumers of *TBP* and other gay liberation magazines also developed a sense of community by reading and looking at these periodicals; the visualization of homoerotic desires in gay magazines and the conversations around those representations played a crucial role in that process.

Following the debate on Moldenhauer's photograph, and after receiving feedback from their readers, the *TBP* collective began to feature more nudity. Images of buttocks, same-sex love, nude men, and even illustrations depicting sexual intercourse became more frequent. Some of these images, as collective member Gerald Hannon advocated for in 1972, aimed specifically to celebrate the body; other images appear to be more decorative and meant to simply appeal to readers.[32] The fact that few women were involved in *TBP* from the mid- to late 1970s might have eased debates over sexual representations in the magazine. Nevertheless, as the section below explores, opinions about the relationship between sexual imagery and gay liberation were not only determined by gender.

The Depiction of Sex as a Liberatory Force

In the May–June 1975 issue, *TBP* published a comic depicting oral sex between two men that earned the magazine a visit from the police department and triggered a transnational debate among the editorial collective and readers from across Canada and the United States (figure 2.3). "Harold Hedd," by Canadian artist Rand Holmes, showed two seemingly white, muscular men resting on a bed while reading passages from psychiatrist David Reuben's bestseller *Everything You Always Wanted to Know About Sex, but Were Afraid to Ask*—a book that the *TBP* collective regarded as homophobic and "the most vicious attack on gay people to date."[33] After laughing at the book, the couple kisses and performs mutual oral sex until they ejaculate in each other's mouths. For the collective, "this mocking illustration was a significant political statement."[34] They considered that the comic had a basic pro-gay, pro-sex message that should be repeated. Thus, they decided to run it, although conscious that the explicit representation of oral sex or the "unnecessarily large" size of the characters' penises would be problematic for some readers.[35] The "gratuitous" representation of "huge erections," as collective member Ed Jackson reflected a few months later, could be regarded as sexist because the penis "has come to symbolize the power and privilege which the male traditionally enjoys."[36] But for the police, the comic was more than sexist. The Toronto Morality Squad—a Toronto Police department—found it obscene and pornographic and ordered all issues containing the cartoon off Toronto's newsstands.[37] This outcome started the debate over the publication of the comic.

The diverse responses to the "Harold Hedd" comic illustrate how local and international readers of *TBP* took sexualized and erotic imagery very seriously; while some readers celebrated open depictions of gay sexuality, others thought it was important to control the messages such images conveyed. According to collective member Gerald Hannon, *TBP* received an unusual amount of mail commenting on the paper's decision to publish the comic. About half of the letters suggested that *TBP* "got what they deserved," for if they insisted "on publishing dirt," they would have to face the consequences.[38] The other half found the comic appealing and encouraged *TBP* to publish more images of that type. An anonymous writer thanked the collective for printing the cartoon. He especially appreciated the depictions of oral sex and ejaculation. He considered that gay people needed more of these images printed and available, because the mind of the public was "retreating from the new and gloriously open sexuality."[39] Greg Snyder, from Chicago, thought the cartoon was "witty, sexy, and still made a point."[40] Even a supposedly straight mother liked the comic and asked *TBP* to

FIGURE 2.3. "Harold Hedd" cartoon by Rand Holmes published in *The Body Politic*'s eighteenth issue in 1975. Canadian Museum for Human Rights, Digital Collections, Internet Archive.

"keep up the good work."[41] Conversely, critics of the comic complained that it was sexist and reflected stereotypes concerning gay life. Richard A. Maecker and his partner, owners of a gay bookstore in Jamestown, New York, disapproved of the collective's decision to print the cartoon, even if "the pictures were thrilling." Maecker's objection was that the comic had "a heterosexist base." He was troubled by the "outrageously large" penises and by the fact that the characters "were cast in masculine/feminine roles," following "the heterosexual myth of male-active, female-passive." He also complained that, in printing the cartoon, *TBP* supported the myth that "good sex need always be accompanied by a soothing drink or a relaxing cigarette." He considered that gay people needed to see same-sex relations "presented openly and positively," but gay publications needed "to enlighten the gay population, not just give it what it wants."[42] The Boston-based gay activist and *Gay Community News* (*GCN*) contributor John Kyper also criticized the comic and commented on the need to visualize diversity in erotic representations of same-sex sex. While he enjoyed the comic, Kyper agreed with Maecker's comments on the size of the penises and with his critique of smoking and drinking going hand-in-hand with sexual fulfillment. The latter, Kyper thought, mimicked another myth of our capitalist culture. In his opinion, though, the critique that one character was "butch" and the other "femme" was not as relevant as the fact that both men were white: "we need more good, un-exploitative and non-oppressive pornography. We need to see more Blacks, Orientals, Indians, interracial cocksucking, fat people, old people, people with small cocks, skinny people, etc." Gay life, he observed, is "more complex and varied than the currently fashionable images of well-hung white studs would have us believe."[43] At the core of all these responses from readers was an attempt to participate in the construction of a gay liberation politics, and in the creation of a visual culture that best defined what gay liberation, community, and identity meant for them.

TBP's response to the comic critics came from Ed Jackson in his article "Nudity and Sexism," published in the November–December 1975 issue. The use of images in *TBP* had been a point of debate throughout its then four-year run, and Jackson's article took "the first step towards a more open treatment of the subject."[44] Considering that readers had reacted in both positive and negative ways to the magazine's imagery, this article was more than a response to the comic critics; it was a justification of the paper's use of images in general. Jackson observed that the editorial collective had endlessly discussed the issues that revolved around the use of nudity, such as sexism, objectification, and "the commercial exploitation of the flesh so pervasive in a capitalist society."[45] He explained why the collective published certain images, such as Moldenhauer's photograph, the "Harold Hedd" comic, and an illustration depicting a winged man (or fairy) with a large, erect penis who held the legend "Be of good cheer." The latter was featured in the November–December 1974 issue because it made an important refutation of the anti-sexual ideology of the Christian church (figure 2.4). However, after its publication, it caused second thoughts among the collective and "rumblings from readers." Moreover, since the image was published on the issue's first page, as Jackson reflected, the magazine exhibited an unmistakable male orientation. The collective, he noted, never wanted to discourage lesbian readers, yet they effectively did so by using such images.[46]

The majority of the *TBP* collective regarded the publication of sexual imagery as a liberating practice that aimed to visualize and celebrate homoerotic desire, while fostering community-building. This standpoint is clear in Jackson's article. In his opinion, visualizing homoerotic desire served to confront homophobic attitudes toward gay sexuality. First, because images like the comic reminded viewers—particularly heterosexual viewers—that gay people are sexual beings. Second, because these images served to confront internalized homophobia. According to Jackson, since gay men have traditionally been seen as only sexual and promiscuous, many react negatively to representations that seem to support that stereotype. Fighting this kind of reaction was part of *TBP*'s liberationist agenda because, as mentioned in the previous chapter, in order to build community, gay liberationists had to deal with their own oppressive behavior. *TBP* tried to employ images in accordance with this liberationist ideology, and particularly with the pro-sex attitude that most of the collective members shared. These kinds of images were indeed liberating and had a positive impact among most readers, both local and international.

Interestingly, since images played a central role in gay liberation politics, the conversations and debates that the *TBP* collective had on the paper's visual content were also frequent in the editorial meetings of *GCN*. Launched in Boston in 1973, *GCN* published national and international news, letters, essays, book and film reviews, interviews, and entertainment, among other content, that made it one of the most influential and widely circulated periodicals of its time. *GCN* never had a circulation of more than five thousand, but it had male and female subscribers from all over the United States and twelve other countries. Former collective member Amy Hoffman notes that, while the paper was always short of money because their "politics frightened off most advertisers," it "had an influence way out of proportion to its circulation figures."[47] Part of *GCN*'s community-building efforts—like those of *TBP*—was fueled by engaging readers in conversations and debates over the paper's content. In Hoffman's words, "when an article was attacked from all sides, the staff knew they had done a good job."[48] Articles aside, the debates that *GCN* editors and readers had on images

FIGURE 2.4. Drawing published in *The Body Politic*'s sixteenth issue in 1974. Canadian Museum for Human Rights, Digital Collections, Internet Archive.

deemed sexist, pornographic, or exploitative intensified in the early 1980s and significantly impacted the paper's community-building project. Since *GCN* operated as a collective, all content—at least in theory—had to be reviewed and approved by everyone. In practice, though, some "problematic" images made it to the newsstands when people such as the art director were able to elude everyone's approval.[49] One 1981 *GCN* cover was particularly problematic, as it featured a drawing of a man whose genitalia were wrapped in barbed wire (figure 2.5). The "grotesque," "hyper-realistic drawing," as Hoffman recalls it, horrified everyone who saw the paper, except the art director and his cadre, who "implied that the objections came from people who were just too squeamish for gay liberation."[50] Most of the time, though, the collective members were able to make decisions together.

Making collective decisions about the visual content of *GCN*, and involving readers in the process, was central to the paper's community-building effort—an effort that was shaped by the tensions and intersections between gay liberation and feminist politics. In May 1981, a group of photographs by Michael Thompson depicting nude young white men on the beach gave the *GCN* collective an opportunity to gauge readers' and editors' opinions on the publication of sexualized images in the paper. The night that Thompson's photographs were ready to crop and size for the printer, several lesbians objected to reproducing photos of naked men, which could potentially upset the paper's female readership; the penis, they argued, represented the "source of patriarchal power." Other staff members, particularly gay men, disagreed and argued that it was appropriate to publish such pictures because their aim was to illustrate an article on nude beaches.[51] In the end, the clever solution of the *GCN* collective resembled the strategies that *TBP* employed to deal with contested images: They published them and asked for readers' opinions.[52] Hoffman's recollection of the incident is revealing: "We yanked the pictures from the resort supplement, distorting and confusing the design so that in the end hardly anyone actually made it all the way through Michael's article. Then—this is the genius part—we *published* the photos the following week, with commentaries pro and con by Michael, staff members, and layout volunteers. A final note invited readers to weigh in, not that they needed an engraved invitation."[53] *GCN* saw in pictures not only a contested space of liberationist politics but also an effective vehicle of community-building. The controversy over the beach photographs allowed the editorial collective to bring their readers into a conversation on sexism and objectification—both antagonistic to gay liberation—and into a debate on the role of sexualized imagery in gay print culture.

The reception of these photographs in *GCN* mirrors the reception of similar imagery in *TBP* in the late 1970s and early 1980s. Some *GCN* readers complained

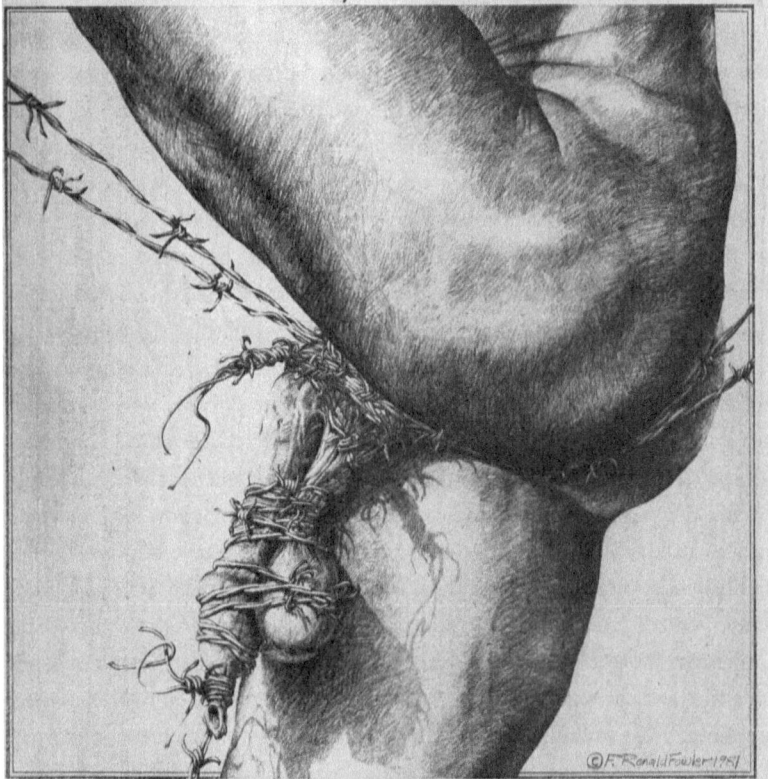

FIGURE 2.5. *Gay Community News* cover of October 17, 1981, featuring artwork by F. Ronald Fowler. Northeastern University Library, Archives and Special Collections, Bromfield Street Educational Foundation records (M64), Digital Collections.

that Thomson's photographs were ableist, ageist, racist, and sexist because they only represented white, athletic young men. Other readers believed that the publication of these images in GCN contributed to perpetuating "the destructive values of advertising and the mainstream media," which made people feel inadequate about their bodies and sexuality. Yet other readers found pleasure in the images and praised their aesthetic and technical qualities.[54] These contrasting responses show that the people who contributed to and read gay liberation periodicals had different opinions on what could be liberating. They also show that sexualized images both enhanced and undermined the community-building projects in which these papers embarked on.

The publication of erotic and sexualized imagery was central to the work of gay liberation periodicals, but some gay and lesbian activists rejected this content when it was meant to advertise or sell something. For some of them, the "commercial" use of the body was sexist and objectifying, and thus antagonistic to gay liberation. In fact, the possibility of using the body merely to attract the attention of newsstand readers always troubled the *TBP* collective. As Ed Jackson noted in 1975, collective members—only men at that time—knew that nude photos were what many male readers wanted; therefore, most members resolved that if appealing images moved people to buy the paper and read its articles, their publication was worthwhile.[55] Advertisers, too, knew that to catch readers' attention they needed to use appealing imagery. The commercial use of the body, particularly in advertising, thus became a particularly contentious topic in the history of *TBP* and other gay liberation journals. As the following section demonstrates, over the 1970s and 1980s gay periodicals offered a space to debate the liberatory and oppressive nature of advertising in a growing gay consumer culture. Such debates continued to be at the center of gay liberation and community-building at the local, national, and international levels.

Advertising and the Commercialization of Gay Culture

From the early 1970s, the *TBP* collective paid special attention to advertising and encouraged readers to participate in the magazine's decision-making over its ads policy. This effort offers another opportunity to evaluate the role of images in the transnational history of gay liberation, specifically those that aimed to visualize and capitalize on homoerotic desires. Although the *TBP* collective had initially refused to accept ads, they also realized that advertising could provide resources for publishing on a more frequent schedule, so they printed a poll in the third issue to ask readers what they favored.[56] Since 88.5 percent of respondents approved advertising in *TBP*, the paper's fourth issue began to include ads.[57]

However, the collective established an ads policy using the same criteria they applied to other submissions: As with any other article or letter, the collective discussed and voted on ads; any submission required a two-thirds' majority vote for acceptance. The collective was cautious to not accept ads from businesses that promoted sexism, or whose ads were exploitative in appearance, and until the late 1970s, their policy was to not allow any nudity in advertising.[58] Following another public questionnaire in 1981, the collective learned that more than a third of respondents wanted to see more advertising.[59] However, 52 percent of the male respondents said they would be willing to pay more for *TBP* if it had less advertising. Most respondents stated they would reject particular kinds of ads: materials that were false or misleading, racist, sexist, or anti-woman. A few readers were willing to turn away anything overtly sexual, such as sex toys, pornography, nudity, and S&M paraphernalia.[60]

TBP's stance on advertising was similar to that of other contemporary gay liberation journals such as *GCN* and *Gay Sunshine*. In the late 1970s, the *GCN* ads policy forbade ads that "exploited the human body to sell things"—even though there was no consensus on what constituted exploitation.[61] Some collective members did not mind the publication of erotic imagery, or even pornography—which they defined as "material created for the specific, utilitarian purpose of sexual arousal"—but they complied with the policy to not undermine *GCN*'s principles.[62] In fact, former collective member Amy Hoffman considers that this policy helped the paper to retain their female readership and staff; people involved in *GCN*, she notes, "were pro-sex but anti-exploitation."[63] The *Gay Sunshine* collective in San Francisco also avoided advertising in their paper, at least over the course of its first year, but in 1972 they had no other choice than to start featuring ads in order to continue publication. Since they probably knew that some of their readers—who were mostly male—would disapprove of the inclusion of ads, they published an editorial in early 1973 explaining their decision.[64]

The critical view on advertising from a feminist perspective began with the second wave of feminism in North America, along with denunciations of the role of mainstream fashion and beauty industries in perpetuating women's oppression. By the mid-1960s, women began organizing in the United States to actively campaign against the advertising industry. They objected to the typical depiction of women in domestic roles, their objectification and sexualization, and the imposition of unrealistic standards for female beauty. Organizations like Women Against Violence Against Women (WAVAW) and Women Against Violence in Pornography and Media (WAVPM) argued that media played an important role in women's oppression and discrimination, and in perpetuating ideas of women's inferiority. Such denunciations of the relationship between women's oppression and the advertising, fashion, and beauty industries soon spread to other major urban centers in North America, including Toronto.[65] For example, in November 1975, ten lesbians joined at the staging of the Miss Canada Pageant in that city to protest the degrading and sexist nature of the contest. During their protest, they handed out leaflets announcing: "Happy International Women's Year and Smash Sexism."[66]

All these critiques and debates on the complicated relationship between images, advertising, and oppression informed gay liberation periodicals' decision-making. Some *TBP* collective members regarded advertising in the magazine as a "necessary evil," either because gay liberation was critical of the commercialization of gay culture or simply because ads tended to be controversial.[67] In the March 1978 issue, the collective acknowledged that the use of sexual imagery in ads was the topic of their "longest-running serialized debate."[68] Some members thought it was wrong to use sex to encourage readers to buy something; others thought it was only wrong if the item or service being sold had nothing to do with sex.[69] Such debates sparked from the fact that the commodification of gay culture conflicted with some of the foundational principles of the gay liberation movement. Through the 1970s, many groups made up of lesbian feminists, sexual liberationists, and gay and lesbian leftists followed a radical agenda and linked their liberation movements to struggles against structures of oppression, such as capitalism. As Allen Young claimed in *Out of the Closets*, a foundational anthology of gay liberation literature, "there can be no freedom for gays in a society which enslaves others through male supremacy, racism and economic exploitation (capitalism)."[70]

Although gay liberation was ultimately unsuccessful in overturning capitalism and even contributed to the growth of a gay commercial culture, this contribution could also be considered an integral part of a gay liberation agenda.[71] For instance, through the 1970s *TBP* and Toronto-based gay business owners clashed over conflicting perspectives on gay movement politics—*TBP* was especially critical of gay commercial spaces that could potentially work as forms of containment and segregation. However, in the late 1970s and early 1980s, in the context of a series of bathhouse raids, the *TBP* collective began to realize that the basis of gay community increasingly depended on the commercialization of gay culture.[72] As Catherine Nash has demonstrated, the raid of the Barracks Bathhouse in 1978 brought together the otherwise antagonistic groups of gay activists and gay businessowners. By June 1981, some collective members of *TBP* began to emphasize the virtues of gay and lesbian commercial spaces and the need to protect them.[73]

Moreover, despite *TBP*'s initial radical stance against gay commercial culture, the magazine was a product meant to be bought and sold. Since sales alone could not finance *TBP* unless it was high-priced, it reluctantly depended on advertising. By the early 1980s, about 30 percent of *TBP*'s income came from commercial display ads and classifieds, which occupied 25 percent of the space in every issue.[74] In December 1979, collective member Michael Lynch observed that the more they increased advertising in *TBP*, unless they handled it carefully, the more two things happened: "we tie ourselves to advertisers, and we suggest that gay liberation is a matter of gay consumerism (To be gay you must buy gay)."[75] For other collective members like Chris Bearchell, advertising was not so bad. In 1979 she claimed that there was "no need to be squeamish about dirty money," since increasing the proportion of advertising in the magazine would be one of the easiest ways to increase their revenue.[76] The problem for Lynch was that the paper was increasingly moving toward a business structure, thereby importing other financial, competitive motives that were "not very liberationist." The magazine, he asserted, "was not a commercial object," since collectivism, volunteerism, and commitment were part of *TBP*'s central ethos.[77]

In the context of late 1970s discussions over advertising, a new debate in *TBP* took place. In 1978 the *TBP* collective and readers discussed whether the paper should run an ad for The Club baths in Ottawa, which seemed to promote a stereotypical gay life and foster increasingly normative representations of gay masculinity.[78] The ad depicted a drawing of a young, muscular white man wearing an open coverall that exposed his body from chest to pelvis. His gaze, almost visible genitalia, and his touching of his left nipple sexualized the image; while his garment, muscles, and hairy chest eroticized an ideal of gay masculinity (figure 2.6). The ad was published just a few months after the collective had overturned the policy of not allowing any nudity in advertising. However, some collective members regarded the image as too stereotypical and thought that it reinforced the idea that gay men were only interested in sex. Some members also noted that images of that sort were sexist and offended female readers. Those who challenged the critiques claimed that the image was realistic and celebrated a gay male sexuality. No one was completely comfortable with the illustration, but neither were any of them ready to accept all arguments against it.[79] As with any other ad containing images of male sexuality, the collective discussed its publication and rejected it by a tie vote, though they published it on the editorial page so readers could participate in the debate.

Readers framed their analysis of this ad either in line with or in opposition to feminist critiques of advertising, and in sharing their opinions in *TBP*, they played an active role in defining what gay liberation meant. Greg Bourgeois, from Toronto, was concerned with the reproduction of stereotypes in images that emphasized the sexual character of gay people. Magazines like *TBP*, he claimed,

This Issue

Sex and money, or what can you find wrong with this picture?

This column, as people may recall, exists to open up to readers some of the discussions the collective went through in putting together this issue. Too often in the past, a contentious point which may have preoccupied or educated or divided us showed up in the pages of the paper only as mute evidence of the final decision — a particular article or letter or ad, for instance. Or maybe nothing showed up at all.

That could have been the fate of what you see below. It was submitted by the Club Baths in Ottawa to run as a quarter-page ad in the next ten issues of *The Body Politic* beginning this month. It was discussed by the collective, as is any advertising copy which contains images of male sexuality. It was rejected. By a tie vote. The Club has allowed us to reproduce the ad here so that you might see what had us so divided.

Not that this is a new issue. The use of sexual imagery in advertising is the topic of what must be the collective's longest-running serialized debate. The last round was in September, when it was decided that the then-existing policy of not allowing any nudity in advertising copy was too simplistic. At that point an ad for Dudes (which appears in this issue on page 27) was accepted by a margin of one vote. The arguments since have gone around and around:

"It's wrong to use sex as a come-on to try to sell something."

"Sure, if what you're selling is washing machines or floor wax, but what if what you're selling is sex, or at least the opportunity for it? After all, that's what the baths are for."

"Well, maybe, but the image is so stereotypical."

"But some people really do look like that and other people do find it attractive."

"But we don't all look like that. And besides, things like that offend a lot of women. If

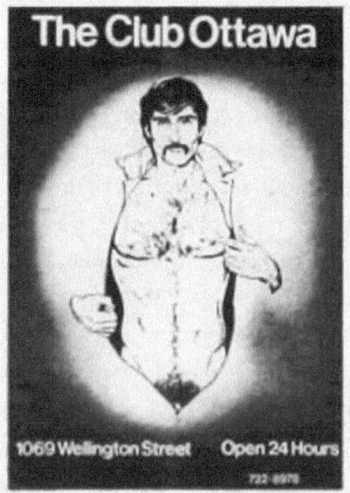

FIGURE 2.6. Editorial page from *The Body Politic*'s forty-first issue, published in March 1978. Canadian Museum for Human Rights, Digital Collections, Internet Archive.

were the only resource for most gays to contact peers, but images like that in The Club ad implied that "you've got to make it as a sexy object." He asked the editors to preserve *TBP* as a meeting place where his "validity" was not dependent on his "desirability."[80] His critique resonates with Ed Jackson's 1975 article, which noted that certain images were problematic for some individuals who would "measure themselves against impossible ideals, find themselves wanting, and in so doing have their social and sexual interactions gravely impaired."[81] Most men, however, were not troubled by images of that sort, and criticized the use of feminist discourses to interpret gay imagery. In fact, some male readers of *TBP* condemned the supposedly female opposition to The Club ad and urged the magazine to run it even if it reinforced stereotypes of gay life. John Duggan, on behalf of the Gays of Ottawa Political Action Committee (GO), urged *TBP* to publish the ad because The Club was one of the few places where gay men in Ottawa could go to meet other gay men. While baths are not liberating, he noted, "they do provide a safe and relatively supportive place for gay men."[82] GO did not find the ad sexist, for they felt it was necessary to explore and celebrate gay male sexuality, and believed that lesbians and gay men must allow one another the space and freedom to express their sexuality.[83] Paul Goldring, from Montreal, thought that the ad's debate had been "clouded by feminists assuming that what applies to the exploitation of women applies equally to men's sexuality."[84] Douglas A. Campbell, from Syracuse, asked why ads containing male nudity were censored while other depictions of female nudity were allowed in *TBP*.[85] His opinion is interesting if one considers how depictions of nudity in *TBP*, as well as erotic or sexualized imagery, were perceived differently depending on the space they occupied in the magazine. For instance, when these kinds of images illustrated articles or book reviews, they did not incite complaints.

Since many gay readers regarded *TBP*'s stance on nudity and sex as "prudish," a number of local and international readers pressured the collective to overcome this attitude.[86] This can be attested in a debate that took place in 1980, when another ad created some controversy. While putting the November 1980 issue together, regular lesbian contributor and former collective member Mariana Valverde was bothered by a Montgomery Leathers ad, which she found offensive and tacky because it depicted a hypermasculine man wearing a harness. The image, she later argued, "could be described as at best unrealistic and at worst pornographic."[87] The collective did not think depictions of the penis were offensive, but they recognized that some commercial uses of them could be, so they published the ad and once again asked readers for their opinion.[88] Only one out of the six men who commented on the ad thought *TBP* should not have run it. Warren A. Putas, from Washington, DC, did not find the ad offensive, but he did have some reservations about it; he thought that publishing the ad in *TBP* served to establish a precedent for other similar ads to contain sexual imagery.[89] The other five readers—based in Quebec, Toronto, Minnesota, San Francisco, and Los Angeles—urged *TBP* to publish more of these ads. One of them argued that advertisers had the right to use sexy images to sell something sexy; another one argued that people should not be ashamed of something as beautiful as the penis; and the San Francisco reader believed that censoring images of this sort was simply counter-revolutionary.[90]

It is important to note that some of the sexualized images that *TBP* published, especially those in ads, were part of a transnational circulation of erotica that played a significant role in the formation of a gay masculine aesthetics in the 1970s and 1980s. According to Nick Hrynyk, much of *TBP*'s erotic imagery came from stock image banks that supplied gay publications around the world based on US and European advertising practices. For this reason, Hrynyk notes, stock images perpetuated cultural values that associated gay male style with Western beauty, aesthetic musculature, and whiteness.[91] Chapters 4 and 5 will return to these publishing practices to discuss how Mexican gay magazines in the 1980s and 1990s used stock images combined with locally produced erotica to visualize a Mexican model of gay masculinity.

Throughout the 1970s, people who opposed *TBP*'s sex-positive liberationist stance, or who were disappointed with the lack of support for women's concerns, had left the paper, which noticeably influenced *TBP*'s visual content. For example, Mariana Valverde, exhausted with the paper's scarce interest in women's issues, decided to leave *TBP* in May 1979. In her resignation letter, she lamented not finding much support for feminist views in *TBP*. In fact, because of her work in a male-dominated publication, she found herself "alienated from both the gay and the women's community."[92] Without significant resistance to the publication of sexualized imagery since the early 1980s, the *TBP* collective stopped being so concerned about issues like nudity, sexism, or objectification, and started printing more ads like those for The Club and Montgomery Leathers. A number of ads for nightclubs, baths, or sex shops depicted nudity, sexual intercourse, and hypermasculine men wearing tight clothes in a San Francisco clone style.

Despite disagreements over erotic and sexualized imagery, *TBP* had always advocated for the liberation and visualization of homoerotic desires, and this stance became more pressing in the late 1970s and early 1980s. During that time the magazine underwent significant structural and ideological changes that responded to the social and economic landscape in which it published. On one hand, the Toronto gay community increasingly faced state repression, as reflected in the bathhouse raids, in *TBP*'s fight with the state for their right to publish, and in the ongoing censorship of material at Toronto's gay bookstore Glad Day. On the other, neoliberalism was pushing the collective to redefine the paper's content, adapting it to a gay market that capitalized on sex. Neoliberalism, which began to inform Canadian politics in the 1980s, significantly increased *TBP*'s financial difficulties. According to Tim McCaskell, through the 1970s *TBP* had a couple of paid staff who cycled off and on unemployment insurance, which helped support the non-paid staff. In the 1980s, though, neoliberal politics cut back social programs and such benefits were harder to get. Thus, the *TBP* collective became concerned with selling more issues. Since they were a small business, they had to accept more ads and sell more papers to survive. This meant, in McCaskell's words, "shrink[ing] the politics a little bit so [*TBP*] would be interesting for a broader number of people"; they needed "to be sexier rather than political."[93] Furthermore, in the 1980s sex acquired a greater importance for gay men and the liberation movement. According to McCaskell, in the early days of the gay liberation movement the unity of gay people had to do with the common oppression they faced. After the 1981 bathhouse raids, however, the notion developed that gay community arose "because of the sexual networks that gay men would develop." Since sex held the gay community together, McCaskell notes, *TBP* had to address the topic of sexuality and show sexuality. They also had to discuss pornography, both because of the contemporary government repression of porn and because of the increasing distribution of sexually explicit material.[94]

One of the collective's strategies to make the paper "sexier" was to include more varied visual content. Aside from "sexy" ads, the paper also featured erotic photographs as a tool for attracting readers and increasing their revenue. A series of photographs known as "Hot Pics" were included beginning in 1985 and helped to fulfil these purposes. The final section of this chapter examines these images and their relationship with *TBP*'s community-building project, situating their reception within the broader historical context of North American gay liberation politics and feminist debates of the mid-1980s.

Pornography, S&M, and the Threat of Censorship

A photograph of a suture needle piercing a female nipple in *TBP*'s April 1986 issue triggered the last major debate over sexualized imagery in the paper's history. The erotic, yet somewhat disquieting photograph was a close-up of a female breast with no other context beyond the act of piercing and the author's name above it: Ryan Hotchkiss (figure 2.7).[95] This lack of context led some readers to describe the image as "pornographic" on the grounds that it was obscene,

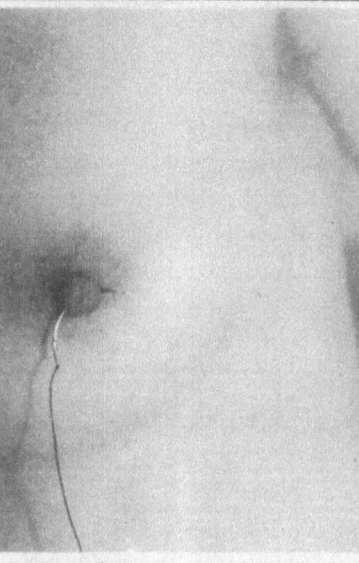

FIGURE 2.7. "Hot Pic" by Ryan Hotchkiss published in *The Body Politic*'s 125th issue in 1986. Canadian Museum for Human Rights, Digital Collections, Internet Archive.

promoted S&M, and denoted contempt for the body. This response was part of a larger conflict about diverse and incompatible understandings of pornography in North America, a conflict that was constitutive of the sex wars and that began in the late 1970s with the emergence of an anti-pornography movement. In the United States, three influential feminist reform groups emerged during this period and led the movement against pornography through the following decade: WAVAW, WAVPM, and Women Against Pornography (WAP).[96] In Canada, groups like Toronto's WAVAW also organized demonstrations against pornography in the late 1970s and pressured the federal government to expand the definition of obscene material to address depictions of violence against women that were not necessarily sexual.[97] Anti-pornography feminists argued that pornography violated women's dignity, reflected hostility toward them, undermined their right to liberty and equality, and inculcated misogynist attitudes in men because it portrayed women as mere objects for their sexual gratification.[98] In the late 1970s and early 1980s, radical feminists such as Andrea Dworkin and Catharine MacKinnon in the United States, and Susan G. Cole in Canada, defined pornography as "the presentation of sexual subordination for sexual pleasure," and claimed that porn set "certain standards for what women are for and what they should look like."[99] Pornography, in the words of Dany Lacombe, came to be perceived as "the source of sexism," while "its eradication, through the enactment of anti-pornography legislation, became the promise of equality and freedom."[100]

Although critiques that linked pornography with sexism and oppression originally arose within feminist organizing, some men were also concerned about it, but for different reasons. For example, as early as in 1971 a group of Toronto-based gay activists—Jearld Moldenhauer among them—complained to CBC for airing a TV program in which the gay lifestyle was inaccurately portrayed. They protested that the program led the viewer "to associate gay life with pornography, anonymous sexuality, sexual addiction and sadomasochism," thus giving the impression that everything in the gay world was centered on sex. The writers did not condemn pornography per se, but they found the representation of pornography shops "especially insidious." Their "extremely sordid aesthetic," they thought, would make a significant visual impact on viewers.[101] Pornography was not a major concern in gay liberation politics, which promoted the visualization of gay sexuality. However, this complaint shows that controlling the uses and meanings of these kinds of images was also important for some men, especially to avoid perpetuating harmful stereotypes of gay life. As David Churchill asserts, gay and lesbian liberationists fought against "negative, disfigured, and unfair" representations of same-sex sexuality; key for them "was the rejection of external definitions and characterizations of their own identity, sexual practices, and behaviours."[102] It was precisely for this reason that readers and editors of *TBP* and other gay liberation journals exercised a careful control of these publications' visual content.

At the same time that the anti-pornography movement was on the rise, numerous feminists, lesbians, artists, and gay men in Canada and the United States challenged the attacks on pornography and opposed censorship. The latter, they argued, did nothing to attack the roots of women's oppression and could be detrimental for sexual minorities, including lesbian feminists.[103] For instance, when WAVPM held its first public protest against pornography in the United States in 1977, writer Pat (now Patrick) Califia and feminist academic Gayle Rubin denounced the organization as conservative and puritanical. This encouraged them to found Samois, a San Francisco–based lesbian-feminist S&M rights group that operated from 1978 to 1983.[104] Other academics joined the debate and discussed pornography and censorship in events such as the 1982 Feminist Conference at Barnard College, "Towards a Politics of Sexuality." The event, which became a landmark in the history of the sex wars, sought to promote a movement that could speak "as powerfully in favor of sexual pleasure as it [did] against sexual danger."[105] In Canada, lesbian and gay liberationists expressed concerns about how anti-pornography legislation could potentially impact gay and lesbian communities, as they anticipated that same-sex sexuality would be the prime target. Lesbian feminists such as Mariana Valverde in 1979 and Chris Bearchell in 1983 warned that pornography laws could be used against gays and lesbians. Bearchell was particularly concerned about "minority tastes, violent or not," because they would be the first to be hit by the law; "the hotter lesbian pornography becomes the more vulnerable it will be to the whims of the guardians of public morality," she claimed.[106] These warnings proved to be true in 1992, when the US lesbian-feminist porn magazine *Bad Attitude* came into trial in Canada and was found obscene.[107] *TBP* collective members Merv Walker and Gerald Hannon, as well as some readers, also thought that government regulations could lead to the closing down of magazines because of their sexual content. For Hannon, the trial *TBP* faced after publishing the controversial "Men Loving Boys Loving Men" article was an example of how obscenity laws would be used against gay magazines.[108]

From the late 1970s through the mid-1980s, the *TBP* collective, readers, and contributors participated in various conversations about pornography. In 1978, when anti-pornography campaigns became more prominent, the magazine received letters that discussed the relationship between pornography, censorship, feminism, and gay liberation. Due to the importance of the topic, the editorial collective published a selection of these letters in the August 1978 issue, hoping to receive further responses.[109] Some collective members and readers critiqued the censorship movement for posing a threat to the gay and lesbian community.

In contrast, other male readers supported pornography legislation, claiming that men also suffered the impact of the sex industry and criticizing *TBP* for publishing content that divided feminist women from feminist men.[110]

In the context of the sex wars, *TBP* implemented changes in its format and visual content, including the addition of more erotic images as well as advertising, which by 1985 occupied 30–40 percent of the magazine. One of those new additions were the "Hot Pics." A memo from the collective stated that these "sexy" photos would occupy one quarter of the page, "should be by as many different photographers as we can get our hands on, should be hot, imaginative, and of high quality photographically. A chance to help suggest what the erotic might look like, in the middle of the sex ads."[111] As of June 1985, each issue of *TBP* included two Hot Pics with their respective credits, and in September 1985, the magazine published an ad inviting readers to send their own Hot Pics—in a way, this was an invitation for readers to be involved in a more intimate way in the paper (figure 2.1). Some of the first Hot Pics featured in *TBP* included photographs by Canadian visual artist David Blair (also known as Terry David Silvercloud). These were studio photographs of nude men wearing gas masks and holding swords, as shown in figure 2.8. Other pictures depicted male and female nudes, as well as scenes of queer love and intimacy by photographers like Robyn Budd, Konnie Reich, and Doug Grenville, among others. At first, these images had no other purpose than to illustrate the classifieds section to appeal to readers. But as of May 1986, the pictures incorporated some of the photographers' contact information should readers wanted to purchase their artwork, thus turning the images into ads as well.

While the first twenty Hot Pics did not produce a significant response, Hotchkiss's photograph triggered a heated debate. Some readers critiqued this photograph on the grounds that it contravened *TBP*'s liberationist undertaking. For instance, Robert D. Butchart, from Meaford, Ontario, associated the image with s&m sex and complained that "the monstrous close-up . . . celebrate[d] the deliberate infliction of pain on others or on oneself, . . . a cause incompatible with *TBP*'s noble mission."[112] The pro-sex, anti-censorship feminist Gillian Rodgerson, who at the time helped in the selection of Hot Pics as a member of the *TBP* collective, responded to the letter. She understood Butchart did not find Hotchkiss's photograph sexually exciting, since the collective did not expect "every 'hot pic' to turn every reader on."[113] However, she discarded Butchart's interpretation of the image by highlighting the risks of defending "normative" behaviors within the gay community. Her selection of photographs, she claimed, was "guided by an exploration of the perverse, not a definition of a norm."[114] Butchart's response to Hotchkiss's photograph shows what Jennifer Nash refers

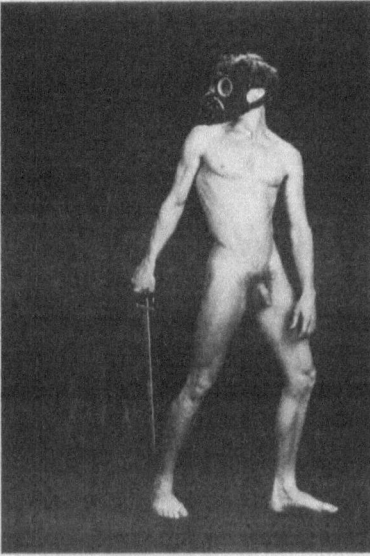

FIGURE 2.8. "Hot Pic" by David Blair (also known as Terry David Silvercloud) published in *The Body Politic*'s 116th issue in 1985. Canadian Museum for Human Rights, Digital Collections, Internet Archive.

to as a "protectionist" reading of sexual representations, while Rodgerson's interpretation "centered on complex and sometimes unnerving pleasures."[115]

S&M sex had divided gay and lesbian liberationists since the early 1970s because of the power dynamics it involved, and by the late 1970s it became entangled in debates over pornography and censorship. For instance, between 1972 and 1973, *Gay Sunshine* provided their local and international male readers with a space to comment on and debate this practice, with most of them, including the Canadian activist Ian Young, defending it.[116] For many gay men, S&M sex was potentially radical and liberatory. Guy Hocquenghem—the French theorist highly regarded by gay radicals in Mexico and elsewhere—conceived of fisting and S&M as powerful, radical sexual practices that counterbalanced homosexuality's domestication and gay reformists' assimilationist calls.[117] Conversely, critics of this practice argued that S&M reproduced the power dynamics of a patriarchal sexual ideology. While feminists such as Samois members had maintained that S&M implied a consensual exchange of power, others denounced its participants for not challenging the social construct through which such a practice had emerged.[118] Though a minority voice among gay liberationists, some men like the US writer John Rechy also condemned S&M gay sex on the same grounds; in 1977 he wrote that this was "the straight world's most despicable legacy."[119] Local and international readers of *TBP* also used the magazine as a forum to debate S&M in the late 1970s and early 1980s. For example, Mariana Valverde's 1979 and 1980 articles on S&M—where she reflected on the tensions between her own sexual desires and political views—sparked numerous responses.[120] Lesbian readers such as Peg McCuaig from Toronto, Amy Groves from Ohio, Judith Zutz from British Columbia, and the San Francisco–based Samois member Terry Kolb expressed their disagreement with Valverde's stance.[121]

The fact that in the 1980s some feminist women and a few gay men across North America considered S&M an outrageous sexual practice helps to explain why some readers reacted so negatively to Hotchkiss's photograph of a pierced nipple. People like Gillian Rodgerson defended their own understanding of liberation, which included expanding notions of the erotic and pleasure. For some readers, though, featuring Hotchkiss's photograph in *TBP* was an offensive way to explore alternative sexual practices. Considering that in the 1980s antipornography groups sought to redefine pornography as any representation that outraged the female body or promoted violence against women, these reactions are not surprising. What is interesting to note is that most of the people who complained about Hotchkiss's photograph were men. While this is understandable given that most of *TBP* readers were men, it is notable that many of them had adopted an anti-pornography stance.[122] As mentioned previously, some men were particularly concerned about the reproduction of sexualized images that stereotyped gay life. For instance, in the April 1986 issue B. Benson complained that the Hot Pics and other nude sketches and pictures in *TBP* made it seem as if sex was all gay people thought about.[123] His critique, as shown throughout this chapter, had been a long-lasting concern among some gay men.

Moreover, the decision to publish erotic images in the middle of the classifieds section invariably shaped their reception among readers, as the relationship between nudity and advertising had always been a matter of debate in gay liberation politics. K. McCarthy from Toronto complained that if the magazine wanted to attract readers by including "artistic" photographs, it should have placed those "raunchy" images in another section, for readers would assume that every ad solicited only non-intimate, casual sex. Pornography, he concluded, "should not be forced on anyone."[124] David G. Thomas, from Gloucester, Ontario, asked *TBP* what their purpose was in publishing those "bizarre" photographs? While he had tolerated previous Hot Pics, Hotchkiss's photograph prompted him to write because it bespoke "mutilation and contempt for the body."[125] Despite some disapproval, the purpose of the Hot Pics was indeed to provide a sexy illustration for a sex-oriented section, and to be as visible as possible. To borrow from Robert Dewhurst's analysis of *Gay Sunshine*'s sexual imagery, the Hot Pics turned the browsing of classifieds into a "visual reading experience," thereby "expanding the range of pleasures" such pages could offer.[126]

One of the most striking letters criticizing *TBP* came from "The Sheaf Collective," a group from the University of Saskatchewan who decided to cancel their subscription to the paper because of its visual content. Some content in *TBP* contravened the Sheaf's policy against accepting pornographic publications, such as those featuring ads using close-up photos of male torsos, ads depicting crotches strapped into leather and metal devices, or the full-colored ads "Hot American Tapes for Cold Canadian Nights."[127] The Sheaf felt that such images placed unnecessary emphasis on the violent power dynamics of sexuality, and perpetuated stereotypes of a gay lifestyle. They also complained about the August 1985 Hot Pics, which loosely evoked S&M.[128] Although the Sheaf did not explicitly refer to Hotchkiss's photograph, it is likely that the picture and the debate around it had encouraged them to express how offended they felt about *TBP*'s new visual content. The *TBP* collective's response came from Gerald Hannon, who saw the Sheaf's critique as a radical feminist stance. He criticized authoritarian ways of interpreting pictures because they allowed an image the possibility of making only one statement.[129]

The mid-1980s controversy over *TBP*'s sexualized and erotic imagery was the last episode in a long history of contested images, and it overlapped with serious discussions about racism in the magazine's editorial practices. In 1985 the *TBP* collective debated the publication of a classified personal ad by a white gay man seeking "a young well-built BM [Black Man] for houseboy." The collective published the memos of their discussions to bring readers into the debate, and, shortly after, they decided to run the ad. Hannon was one of those in favor of publishing it, as this would be in line with the paper's sexual politics—politics that had always advocated for the liberation of homoerotic desires, however contested they may have been.[130] But contrary to this understanding of gay liberation that favored white, middle-class men, a number of gay and lesbian readers of *TBP* in Canada and abroad condemned the explicit racist nature of the ad and the decision to run it. Commenting on the debate that this decision triggered, David Churchill has noted that it "was a continuation of a larger political dispute around political ethics, consent, and power that had created conflict between the predominately male members of the newspaper's collective and lesbian feminists."[131] The ad also reflected the racialized politics of sexual liberation, whereby the sexual desires of a white man were being placed at the forefront of gay liberation, despite the racism implicit in those desires. The debates over the Hot Pics and other sexualized images in *TBP* were part of these major disputes about the racial and gender politics of gay liberation. Specifically, they questioned how far the liberation of homoerotic desire could go without undermining other social and political struggles, such as feminist or anti-racist movements.

The debate over the Hot Pics and other images in *TBP* also illustrates how gay periodicals and their visual content facilitated (and triggered) discussions over the meanings, promises, and limits of gay liberation. Throughout the fifteen years of the paper's publication, *TBP* readers and members of the editorial collective developed multiple understandings of desire, liberation, and oppression. In the process, it became clear that gay liberationists did not constitute a monolithic group that shared political views, desires, and goals. It also became clear that, for the vast majority of gay men across North America, the defense of erotic and sexualized imagery was constitutive of a gay liberation project.

WITH TRANSNATIONAL GAY LIBERATION and feminist theory as its backdrop, conflicts and clashing understandings of oppression and liberation profoundly shaped the reception of *TBP*'s visual content at the local, national, and international levels, the same way they shaped the reception of similar content in other gay liberation periodicals, such as *GCN*. Through the 1970s, when feminist groups across North America were campaigning against the media's objectification of women, concerns about sexism and the objectification of the body shaped discussions over sexual and erotic imagery in *TBP*. Through the 1980s, concerns about pornography and S&M were current, reflecting contemporary debates among feminist groups in Canada and the United States. A lingering concern about the stereotyping of gay life through the visual spanned both decades. While most collective members opposed sexism, objectification, or mainstream stereotypes of gay life, there was hardly a consensus on the meaning of these concepts, nor was there a homogeneous collective whose ideas every member shared. For instance, while some collective members and readers disapproved of commercial use of sexual imagery, others thought it was necessary, either to celebrate the body and gay sexuality or to make the magazine more appealing.

The relationship between images, gay liberation, and community-building in anglophone North America evolved over time because of social and cultural changes. Members of the gay and lesbian community perceived this relationship in a variety of ways, depending on their gender, race, personal politics, or life experiences. Because of these factors, the responses of the *TBP* editorial collective to criticism varied during the paper's fifteen-year run. Whereas in the 1970s *TBP* seemed more eager to solicit feedback on the paper's visual content, Gerald Hannon's and Gillian Rodgerson's responses to readers in the mid-1980s reveal a less conciliatory attitude toward the reception of images in *TBP*. This does not mean that Hannon and Rodgerson were less sensitive to readers' concerns, but it does suggest that by the mid-1980s the collective was tired of and less interested in dealing with sex-negative, moralistic, or anti-porn critiques that conflicted with *TBP*'s liberationist stance. Those critiques also conflicted with the *TBP*'s fight against censorship, the magazine's adaptation to a neoliberal economy, and its dependence on advertising. Moreover, those critiques hardly fit into the contemporary social and political landscape wherein sex had acquired a new importance among the gay community in North American major urban centers. All these debates demonstrate how the sexual and erotic imagery in *TBP* and other gay periodicals both advanced and complicated the development of gay liberation identities, as well as the community-building projects of these publications.

This and subsequent chapters show how gay liberation politics and community—local, national, and transnational—were constituted through print culture and images from the 1970s through the 1990s. The chapters that follow discuss how US and Mexican gay periodicals such as *Gay Sunshine*, *Macho Tips*, and *Hermes* handled the relationship between sexual and erotic imagery and gay liberation politics. Similar to *TBP* and *GCN*, the content of these periodicals and the transnational networks they created helped to advance gay liberation across borders while placing the body and homoerotic desire at the center of their projects.

| 3 |

Liberationist Politics, Colonial Optics, and the Desire for Latin America in Gay Sunshine

In 1981, the San Francisco–based editor Winston Leyland published an English translation of the Mexican novel *El vampiro de la colonia Roma* (1979), a foundational piece of Mexico's gay literature by Luis Zapata. Translated as *Adonis García: A Picaresque Novel*, its cover featured a black-and-white photograph of a racialized young man standing outside a wooden construction and leaning against its door (figure 3.1). The man, who may be in his early twenties, wears a leather jacket, with nothing underneath, and a pair of white jeans. He gazes directly at the camera with a stern, yet seductive look. His left hand rests on his hip, while his right arm leans against the wall and his hand is thrust forward in a fist. His jeans, which are below his navel, are so tight that they wrin-

FIGURE 3.1. Photograph by David Greene featured on the cover of *Adonis García: A Picaresque Novel*. Published by Gay Sunshine Press in 1981, this is the English translation of Luis Zapata's *El vampiro de la colonia Roma* (1979). ONE National Gay and Lesbian Archives, *Gay Sunshine* Papers, Los Angeles.

kle and accentuate his genitalia. Written on the wall, the phrase "Esta noche," which means tonight, and an arrow pointing toward the man suggest the idea of a potential sexual encounter. Indeed, everything in the image leads to a sexual reading, and by presenting Adonis as an Indigenous-looking macho man, the picture also evokes a Global North fantasy of racialized hypersexuality and sexual availability. This reading is not surprising considering the protagonist's profession: prostitution. What is surprising, though, is that Adonis was not Indigenous. Winston Leyland knew his market well, and with this book cover he appealed to North American gay consumers' desires for an exotic, racialized, and sexually permissive Latin America.

As the editor of the San Francisco–based *Gay Sunshine* journal and the creator of Gay Sunshine Press, Leyland was particularly interested in producing Latin American content that was appealing to his readers. Through the 1970s and early 1980s he traveled across the region to collect material on its gay life, history, and cultural production. His travels and the work of two of his collaborators and friends, Edward A. Lacey and Erskine Lane, resulted in two special Latin American issues of *Gay Sunshine*, the publication of two anthologies of Latin American gay literature, the translation of *El vampiro de la colonia Roma*, and the publication of Lane's autobiographical narration *Game Texts: A Guatemala Journal*. In collecting, translating, and publishing Latin American gay content for an anglophone, North American audience, Leyland and his collaborators connected the gay worlds of the Americas; not only did they situate Latin American gay histories and cultural production within the larger history of gay print culture in the Americas, but they also helped to connect gay activists, artists, and communities across borders. However, while producing this content and illustrating it with an exoticizing visual content, Leyland and his collaborators also reproduced and capitalized on neocolonial imaginaries of non-Western sexualities.

In using visual culture strategically to appeal to readers, visualize their desires, and increase sales, Leyland was building on a long tradition of gay liberation print culture, a tradition that *Gay Sunshine* helped build since it launched its first issue in the summer of 1970. Over its twelve years of publication, images occupied a central place in *Gay Sunshine* because of the intrinsic relationship between gay liberation politics, periodicals, and the visualization of homoerotic desires. In fact, contrary to contemporary gay liberation periodicals like *The Body Politic*, *Gay Sunshine* never questioned this relationship. From the beginning, the paper aimed to visualize and celebrate gay sexuality and, when Leyland became the sole editor in 1973, he began using images strategically to also ensure the economic success of both the paper and Gay Sunshine Press publications.

This was particularly clear in the imagery that accompanied Latin American content, imagery that was used to create a marketable depiction of the region and its people.

Scholarship on *Gay Sunshine* and Gay Sunshine Press has either celebrated their internationalist scope as a manifestation of transnational solidarity or condemned it as the outcome of a colonial mindset. The works of Daniel Balderston, José Quiroga, and Robert Dewhurst reflect this contrast. Balderston and Quiroga have described the work of Leyland, Lane, and Lacey in Latin America as "neo-colonial," "imperial," and even "sinister" because of these men's sexual exploitation of "boys" in the region.[1] They argue that the Latin American anthologies that these white, middle-class gay men put together were part of a "marketing operation" and were "imperial constructions."[2] Conversely, Dewhurst sees *Gay Sunshine*'s "research in gay lifestyles and literatures past, present, and international" as part of a "radical editorial vision" and "a politics of radical solidarity."[3] The analysis in this chapter is indebted to the interpretive frameworks that these three authors have advanced; however, these frameworks do not fully account for the tensions and intersections between the "radical" and the "objectionable," the "liberatory" and the "oppressive," in the works of Leyland, Lane, and Lacey. As well, they do not account for the ways in which the production of Latin American content for the journal and press during the Cold War fueled gay activism across borders while also reinforcing neocolonial imaginaries of non-Western sexualities.

Building on this scholarship, this chapter deepens the analysis of the complex relationship between gay liberation politics, print culture, and the visualization of homoerotic desires in North America by taking *Gay Sunshine*, its visual culture, and Leyland's production of Latin American content as case studies. Focusing on these areas of analysis, the chapter further demonstrates the role of images and periodicals in the transnational history of gay liberation and the way in which these materials fostered the formation of gay communities, identities, and networks of gay liberation activists. In discussing the work of Leyland, Lane, and Lacey, and the Latin American content they produced for anglophone North American gay consumers, this chapter also examines the tensions between gay liberation politics, transnational community-building, and the use of erotic and sexualized imagery in gay periodicals. The chapter argues that *Gay Sunshine* and Gay Sunshine Press publications fostered gay liberation across the Americas through the visualization of homoerotic desires, the production of Latin American content, and the formation of transnational gay networks. Neither Leyland nor Lane nor Lacey were gay liberation activists, but their work was embedded in and helped to create transnational networks that contributed to gay liberation movements across the Americas. Their editorial work and travels allowed them to circulate information and connect gay communities across the region. They also allowed them to contribute to the liberation, celebration, and visualization of homoerotic desires. This contribution, however, was mainly beneficial for Global North gay communities. In fact, their interactions with Latin Americans were complex and unequal because of racial, class, and age imbalances. Although they fueled gay activism across borders through print culture, these men put self-indulgence and/or profit at the forefront of their editorial work and of their efforts to connect with Latin America. As seen in the previous chapters, the liberation and visualization of homoerotic desires were constitutive forces of gay liberation politics. For some gay men, these included desires that fetishized racial, age, and class differences and hierarchies. Gay Sunshine Press publications, for instance, produced and visualized desires for racialized and youthful Latin Americans, as well as desires for a backward, tradition-bound, and sexually permissive Latin America. As this and subsequent chapters demonstrate, the existence of these desires shaped many of the interactions among gay communities in North America in the period studied in this book. For instance, they shaped how Leyland, Lacey, and Lane imagined and visualized Latin America in their editorial and literary work.

This chapter begins with an exploration of *Gay Sunshine*'s history, from its emergence in the aftermath of the San Francisco Bay Area's gay liberation movement until its demise in 1982. This first section also discusses the relationship between the paper's visual content and its community-building work, emphasizing how gay liberation's principle of visualizing same-sex desire informed the paper's use of erotic and sexual imagery. The second section focuses on the production of *Gay Sunshine*'s Latin American special issues and of the anthologies of Latin American gay literature. The section discusses how their production was indebted to the existence of transnational gay networks across the Americas, and how this production also nurtured those networks. The third and fourth sections examine how Leyland's market-oriented approach shaped his portrayal of Latin America to appeal to a largely white, middle-class, and cosmopolitan gay consumer base. Both sections examine how the Latin American issues and anthologies of the journal and press featured erotic and sexualized imagery to produce pleasure and celebrate homoerotic desires. They also examine how this imagery drew on colonial and racist discourses that regarded Latin America as an exotic and backward sexual paradise. Such a portrayal, the chapter shows, catered to racialized desires that have been at the core of the formation of modern gay identities for over a hundred years.

Visualizing Desire and Building Community

Against the backdrop of the San Francisco Bay Area's gay liberation movement, a group of activists affiliated with Berkeley's Gay Liberation Front published the first issue of *Gay Sunshine* in 1970. The gay liberation movement in the Bay Area emerged in the late 1960s and early 1970s in close relationship with the left and anti-war movement and directly linked to the region's long tradition of homophile activism and counterculture.[4] Because of the confluence of these factors, as Nan Alamilla Boyd points out, in the late 1960s and early 1970s San Francisco "became the headquarters of a spirited and nationally focused gay liberation movement."[5] Following the Stonewall riots in 1969 and the formation of the first Gay Liberation Front (GLF) in New York City, similar organizations were formed in major urban centers across the United States. Two of them were the San Francisco GLF—founded in 1969 out of the Committee for Homosexual Freedom—and the Berkeley GLF—founded in 1970. In the fall of that year, a collective affiliated with the Berkeley GLF launched *Gay Sunshine*; some collective members included the gay activists Nicholas Benton, Gary Alinder, and Konstantin Berlandt.[6]

Prior to the creation of *Gay Sunshine*, gay and lesbian communities in California already had a strong print culture tradition. The three periodicals that pioneered the gay and lesbian press in the United States—*One*, *Mattachine Review*, and *Ladder*—were all founded in California in the 1950s. In 1953, the gay and lesbian rights organization One, Inc., founded *One* in Los Angeles. In 1955, the homophile organization Mattachine Society created *Mattachine Review* in San Francisco. And in 1957, the lesbian organization Daughters of Bilitis created *Ladder* in this same city. These periodicals were sold in newsstands and helped to connect homophile organizations as well as gay and lesbian readers across the country. As Martin Meeker has demonstrated, the communication networks that these publications helped to create were central to the homophile movement and to subsequent forms of gay and lesbian political and social organizing at the local and national levels.[7]

Gay Sunshine started as a visually stylish liberation tabloid that reported on local, national, and some international news concerning gay liberation and politics. From 1970 to 1973, the paper operated as a collective comprised of several gay liberation activists who put together news articles, literature, and art in about twenty tabloid-sized-pages (~15.74 × 9.84 inches). The inaugural issue included news on the gay liberation movement, gay student organizing, women's liberation, and the Cuban Revolution, as well as poetry, photographs, collages, and drawings that visualized same-sex love and homoerotic desire (figure 3.2). This

FIGURE 3.2. Inaugural issue of *Gay Sunshine*, published in 1970.

editorial trend continued throughout the entire history of the paper, though Winston Leyland implemented important changes after he took the lead in 1971. Under his leadership, the paper kept its tabloid format, but the number of pages increased from about twenty or thirty to up to fifty over the years. The paper also began to include classifieds and more ads, and the artistic content increased—both the visual and the literary.

Leyland was a former Catholic priest with expertise in literature, philosophy, and publishing. He was born in Lancashire, England, in 1940 and moved to Providence, Rhode Island, with his family in 1952. He studied for eight years at the seminary of the Society of St. Columban in Milton, Massachusetts; earned a BA in philosophy in 1963; and completed four years of graduate work in theology with a minor in literature. He was ordained a Roman Catholic priest by Cardinal Cushing in 1966, but he resigned two years later because of the Church's silence on the Vietnam War and other social issues and to pursue creative literary interests.[8] Since early 1969, he worked as a proofreader for the *Los Angeles Times* while living in Hollywood and earning an MA in history from the University of California, Los Angeles, in 1970. Though he was offered a permanent position on that paper, he decided to move to northern California; once in Berkeley, he became involved with *Gay Sunshine*.[9] The paper was a product of the 1960s counterculture, which had also shaped Leyland's philosophical approach to gay sexuality, politics, and literature.[10]

With Leyland's intervention, the content and operational structure of *Gay Sunshine* changed rapidly, as he began to take over editorial duties progressively and the artistic content of the paper began to surpass the political one. According to his own account, he resurrected the paper in the spring of 1971 after the collapse of the Berkeley GLF in early 1971 and subsequent dissolution of the original *Gay Sunshine* collective.[11] That spring, a second collective took the lead with Leyland as the main coordinator—other members included Paul Mariah, Morgan Pinney, and Tony DeRosa.[12] During this second stage of *Gay Sunshine*, spanning issues 6 to 15 (1971–1972), Leyland did most of the work required to keep the paper alive, including coordinating typesetting and printing, and securing funds. During this period Leyland also took the initiative to solicit and print more gay literary material in the magazine. The third stage of the paper began in 1973 when the people who had been involved in previous issues moved on and Leyland alone coordinated and put out the paper—at least until Bill Rick took over typesetting in the mid-1970s.[13] This third stage spanned issues 16 through 47 (1973–1982). During this period, Leyland renamed the magazine *Gay Sunshine: A Journal of Gay Liberation* and continued to publish the paper in tabloid format. He increased the number of pages and actively sought "innovative and pioneering material for publication," including historical and literary essays, "Third World gay literature," and gay fiction and poetry. It was also around this time that Leyland began a series of in-depth interviews with gay writers and artists, such as Christopher Isherwood, John Rechy, Jean Genet, William Burroughs, and Allen Ginsberg.[14] In his hands, as Robert Dewhurst comments, *Gay Sunshine* transitioned from a local, activist publication into "a formidable international newspaper of the arts."[15] As part of this same project, in 1975 Leyland created Gay Sunshine Press to publish in book format "literary writings of high quality which in some way have a bearing on gay consciousness."[16]

Although by the fall of 1971 *Gay Sunshine* already presented itself as an international publication with distribution in most of the major cities in the United States and in countries like Italy, England, and Australia, under Leyland's leadership this distribution further expanded.[17] Leyland employed various strategies to distribute *Gay Sunshine* in the United States and abroad. One of them was to seek out exchanges with other gay periodicals. For example, in 1974 Leyland and *The Body Politic* collective member Jearld Moldenhauer got in touch to set up an exchange. At that time, the Toronto-based magazine had 550 regular subscribers, while *Gay Sunshine* had 970; of these, 625 were regular paid subscribers and the rest were prison, exchange, or complementary subscribers. Leyland hoped that Moldenhauer could sell some copies of *Gay Sunshine* in his Toronto gay bookstore Glad Day.[18] Another strategy was to publish materials in collaboration with other gay organizations. For example, in 1974 *Gay Sunshine* published a joint issue with the Boston-based radical periodical *Fag Rag*; the issue was printed in San Francisco and published in June of that year. Another strategy of Leyland was to circulate issues of *Gay Sunshine* among his international friends, including those based in Latin America, such as the Mexican writer Luis Zapata, the Mexican visual artist Ricardo Regazzoni, and the Argentinian writer Alberto Nigro.[19]

The events described above resonate with the narrative arc of this book. First, the creation of *Gay Sunshine* in 1971 by a gay liberation collective was part of a larger trend in North America. As discussed in the previous chapters, following 1969 gay activists began using the press to advance gay liberation movements, encourage people to come out, build communities, and facilitate the circulation of information across borders. The 1973 demise of the original collective and Leyland's resurrection of the paper was also another common trend in the history of the gay press. Most gay liberation journals had short lives; they published only a handful of issues and disappeared shortly after their creation—this was the case of the Mexican gay periodicals *Política sexual*, *Nuestro cuerpo*, and *Nuevo ambiente* examined in chapter 1, and of many other gay magazines. Some gay periodicals managed to survive, but in order to do it, they had to become more visually appealing. This meant reducing the political content and giving more space to advertising, erotic imagery, and entertainment. This is what happened with *Gay Sunshine* under Leyland's leadership, which allowed the magazine to regain force and survive until 1982. Other gay liberation journals like *The Body Politic* also incorporated these changes, particularly toward the mid- to late 1970s, as discussed in the previous chapter. In the mid-1970s, *Gay Sunshine* was experiencing a financial crisis due to increases in typesetting, printing, and postal costs. Though Leyland claimed to have no intention of commercializing his journal, the reality is that *Gay Sunshine*, much like other gay liberation periodicals at that time, did become a commodity.[20] Moreover, with the creation of Gay Sunshine Press in 1975, he was able to participate in a growing gay consumer culture with the commercialization of both gay magazines and gay literature books while continuing to engage with the larger project of gay liberation in the United States and abroad.

From the beginning, *Gay Sunshine* aimed to be a vehicle to create a sense of community and advance the gay liberation movement in the San Francisco Bay Area and beyond. In the inaugural issue, collective member Nicholas Benton explained the rationale for creating this publication: "a gay newspaper would be a powerful tool in the homosexual fight for equal rights, as it would be a catalyst that could call forth the political potential of a subculture such as the one in San Francisco that constitutes more than 10 percent of the total population."[21] Benton's claims were further supported in Charles P. Thorp's "A Gay Liberation Manifesto," published in the third issue of *Gay Sunshine*. In this text, Thorp expressed the importance of developing a gay community through education; having "an all-Gay magazine" was part of this effort, as it was one of the techniques available for gay men to "liberate our minds and help bring about Identity-Community."[22] Initially, the editorial collective pursued this community-building work by informing and commenting on issues concerning gay rights and the movement, but over time, as discussed above, the visual and literary arts acquired a more prominent role. In Dewhurst's words, "the newspaper's archival politics and aesthetics cooperated to create a vital and coherent sense of community in the present."[23] This can be attested in the way former readers of *Gay Sunshine* remember the paper. One of them was the poet Steve Abbott, whom Dewhurst quoted in his analysis of *Gay Sunshine*. Abbott claimed that, without this magazine, "there would not have evolved the strong sense of Gay culture and community I feel proud to be a part of today."[24] Moreover, *Gay Sunshine* always invited readers to make their voices heard by contributing articles, poems, letters, or artwork. As the *Gay Sunshine* collective wrote in 1970, these contributions were integral to community-building: They encouraged readers to "add your energy to the community by letting the community in on your creativity."[25]

In line with a politics of gay liberation, *Gay Sunshine* used visual culture to nurture this sense of community. The publication of sexual and erotic imagery that celebrated same-sex love and promoted the liberation and visualization of homoerotic desires was particularly important to accomplish this goal. For instance, a drawing of a nude male fairy on the cover of the inaugural issue announced to readers that sexual desire and the liberation of the body were integral to both gay liberation and *Gay Sunshine* (figure 3.2). The fairy flies with gracious movements under the sunshine and above flowers while looking at his erect penis. Although "fairy" is a derogatory term often used for gay effeminate men, depictions of fairies appearing joyful and proud were quite common in the visual culture of gay liberation journals, as demonstrated by the drawing in *TBP* shown in figure 2.4 (the reception of which was discussed in chapter 2). In subsequent issues, *Gay Sunshine* continued publishing numerous drawings and photographs that conveyed a positive and celebratory view of gay sexuality. One example of such liberationist imagery is a drawing published in the second issue that depicts two men kissing as their erect penises intertwine (figure 3.3). Over the years, the magazine published very similar representations of gay sexuality, as well as more explicit representations of oral and anal sex. The homoerotic art of Joe Brainard, for example, featured prominently in *Gay Sunshine*, particularly his drawings of gay sex. Equally important was the imagery that conveyed messages of gay liberation and resistance, such as the collage published on the cover of the fourteenth issue (figure I.3). As discussed in this book's introduction, the collage used the symbol of the raised fist, as well as the metaphor of the eagle chasing butterflies, to offer powerful representations of the gay liberation struggle. Moreover, depictions of lesbian love, though less frequent, were also present in *Gay Sunshine*, particularly in its first issues.

Though some activists across the United States and Canada debated the use of erotic and sexualized imagery in their publications, the editors of *Gay Sunshine* never questioned the intrinsic relationship between these kinds of images and gay liberation. As Nick Benton argued, "Such publications that play into the hands of this mentality—that perpetuate the stupid haggling over whether or not ... a naked body is fit material for the expense of printer's ink—are not newspapers in the sense of actualizing the right to free press."[26] What was needed, Benton continued, was a newspaper that could "harken to a greater cause—the cause of human liberation of which homosexual liberation is just one aspect."[27] This view did not mean that members of the *Gay Sunshine* collective were not critical of certain images and of the way they had been produced. For instance,

DISMISSED

by Cherie Matisse

Three of us were on our way to a party. Apparently, we did a no-no driving and the S.F. pigs stopped us. Driver's license, registration of the car were presented to the pigs (1814, 1911 badge numbers). As flashlights zoomed about the interior of the car, our political literature and banners were suspiciously looked upon. "Where are you going?" asked the pig. To a G.L.F. party answered Sandy. "Open the door!" demanded the pig with his hand on his gun. POW! The pig threw Sandy against the car and frisked him. The other pig told me to get out, "Are you arresting me?" I asked. "If you keep HARASSING ME, I'll have to" he retorted and pulled me out of the car. I repeated, "Are you arresting me, and if so, for what?" and he threw me in the pig-car. Davi and Sandy were placed in with me as the pigs searched the car and found a lid of grass in the trunk of our borrowed car. Another case of illegal search and seizure, people!

While being booked, Davi and I were attacked with such witty statements as "Are you a girl or a boy? Hey, butch, hey dyke. What do you lesbos really do? I've never talked to a lesbian before." etc. We were all booked with possession, a felony. Convenient for the pigs. Can't have those "lunatic activists" spreading their propaganda among the people, you know, I'm gay. so automatically I'm a criminal. As I yelled POWER TO THE PEOPLE to Sandy when I was being fingerprinted on five 5x7 cards and mug shots were taken of my profile and full-face, I couldn't help thinking of Arlo Guthrie's song, Alice's Restaurant. Now, I'm distinguished by having my fingerprints and pictures in Sacramento, San Francisco, Washington, D.C. and God knows where else.

The first night Davi and I were put in a cell together. We decided the blankets were fucked, so we got it on (you haven't lived until you've made love in prison) and I came all over the fucker. Miss Closet-Dyke Matron, the following morning, saw us sleeping together and said, "We can't have this in our prison! We'll have to put you two in separate cells." Which they did.

When I say that hole is a pigsty, I mean it literally. In three days, no one was given towels or soap (which reaffirms that we're all dirty commie criminals,). The "food" was so bad people vomited. It's impossible to get any deep sleep, so mental and physical fatigue sets in. The second day, after ensuing harassment from the pigs, I was really getting fed up with this shit. One pig said, "You know, you're really sick." I retorted, "You're the one who's sick" and yelled, "You fascist pig!"

The third night the case was dismissed. The pigs knew they didn't have a case. The whole thing was simply another instance of further harassment of gays. The harassment, the murders, the social ridicule, the job discrimination, etc. must stop. We must unite and take affirmative action. The time is now, ALL POWER TO THE PEOPLE!

Willie Brown

California Assemblyman Willie Brown—minority whip and a probable S.F. mayoral candidate—agreed last week to boycott ABC TV and radio. He will also try to persuade other assemblymen not to grant interviews or news to ABC until it drops its discriminatory policy against Gay people. Brown's action was in response to a request from Leo Laurence fired last year by KGO for being an outspoken homosexual. The Black Panthers and other groups will be asked to join the boycott. Brown previously boycotted ABC when KGO editorialized for a round up of prostitutes in the Tenderloin.

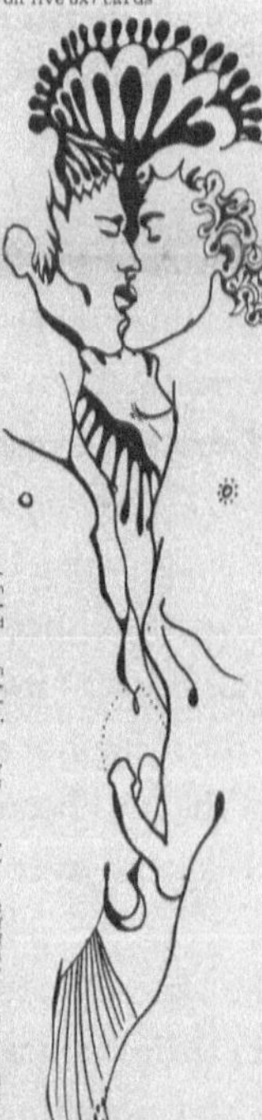

EDI-TORIAL

It has been the frustrating experience for radical homosexuals and others, and Gay Liberationists in particular that in broaching our demands to all political groups from Establishment homosexuals to Radical heteros, we have been denied inclusion in their programs.

This has not been the case with the Peace and Freedom Party. In February 1970 both San Francisco and Los Angeles Gay Liberation were approached and invited to send delegates to the state Convention in Long Beach. Both areas did so.

The result was the first Gay Liberation Plank ever in any U.S. political party's Platform and is reprinted here below:

******GAY LIBERATION********

(Statement of information: "GAY" refers to types of non-heterosexual expression including the female and male homosexual, bisexual, transexual, transvestite, etc.)

The Peace and Freedom Party recognizes and affirms that the goals and aims of Gay Liberation are an essential part of the general struggle against oppression. The oppression of Gay People, international in scope, arises from heterosexual chauvinism, religious dogmatism, police persecution, and other forms of discrimination and social intimidation.

We recognize and affirm:

I. The primary right of self-determination to. members of the Gay community in the free expression of their true sexual natures;

II. The necessity to work to abolish all laws and institutional practices of U.S. governments—federal, state and local—that in any way discriminate against any persons because of actions expressive of their sexual natures;

III. That no person shall be denied any of the rights asserted by the Declaration of Independence, the U.S. Constitution and the Bill of Rights because of her or his sexual nature or preferences;

IV. That all forms of economic and social exploitation of the Gay community be abolished.

V. That all "sex education" programs should accord the same validity to homosexual and other forms of expression as to heterosexual forms;

VI. That all persons incarcerated in prisons and in mental institutions on charges of non-victim sexual crimes should be released at once and restored to full participation in society.

VII. That as a part of the sanctity of the person, each individual has the right to determine the uses of her or his own body as in sex-change operations and others.

****

The rest of the platform incorporates a wide range of far reaching social reforms into a libertarian socialist composite which even ultra-liberal and working class Gays and others should be able to relate to and identify with.

Peace and Freedom offers all those Gay voters who would ordinarily go to the polls only to vote for Willie Brown an out-of-the-closet alternative to the War and Racist politics of the Democratic Party.

Therefore far the foregoing we can only conclude that it is our responsibility in speaking out in the interests of the Gay community to urge you, if you vote, to vote Gay, vote Peace and Freedom, vote for Willie Brown as the only San Francisco Democratic candidate who has spoken for the gay community in the state assembly. The Peace and Freedom Party is the only political party to speak courageously for our rights without being pressured to do so.

There are two rallies being planned in the Gay Bay Area at which the Gay community will have the opportunity to meet the Peace and Freedom candidates and find out how they will implement the Gay and other proposals in the Peace and Freedom Platform. The people will be informed about the times of the rallies by movement radio stations and leafletting.

POWER TO THE PEOPLE! GAY POWER TO GAY PEOPLE!

FIGURE 3.3. Page from the second issue of *Gay Sunshine*, published in 1970. Pennsylvania State University Libraries, Digital Collections.

in an editorial published in the tenth issue, the collective criticized ads in the San Francisco–based gay magazine *Vector* that featured well-muscled young models. These ads had been sponsored by some of San Francisco's and Los Angeles's largest modeling agencies. The collective referred to these images as oppressive, not because of the naked bodies in them, but because these models were being exploited: "Never having been exposed to the ideas of gay liberation which would help them to liberate their minds and bodies, these models bond themselves to model agencies and are caught in a vicious cycle," the collective wrote. *Vector*, they claimed, was "promoting this vicious exploitation by printing ads from such modeling agencies."[28] By the time they wrote this editorial, the *Gay Sunshine* collective had begun accepting paid porn ads for the paper to survive. Though the collective thought that these ads "were far from ideal," they also considered that pornography was "relatively innocuous in exploitative content" compared with the modeling agencies: "We hope that our liberated articles will offset any bad vibes from an occasional alienating ad," they wrote.[29]

The erotic and sexualized imagery in *Gay Sunshine* had a positive impact among many readers who equated the publication of this imagery with sexual liberation. Reflecting on the stimulating nature of *Gay Sunshine*'s imagery, in 1980 the US poet Kenneth Royal Murdoch recalled the first time he saw an issue of the paper as an adult in 1975: "I remember the feeling of shock when I pulled it out of my postoffice box and saw on the cover the American Statue of Liberty adorned with an enormous phallus. With what excitement and incredulity I perused the contents. I am an old man now but each issue brings me a renewed sense of liberation."[30] Images such as this homoerotic rending of the Statue of Liberty (figure 3.4) could have been shocking for some gay men unaccustomed to this kind of imagery in the press, but the experience of seeing such provocative and stimulating representations was indeed liberatory. Murdoch's visual experience is evocative of the one that the Boston-based activist John Kyper had a few years prior; as discussed in chapter 1, the photographs documenting the gay liberation movement in *The Advocate* impressed Kyper and propelled him into the gay movement. The impact of *Gay Sunshine*'s erotic and political imagery is also reminiscent of how *The Body Politic*'s visual content fueled its community-building project.

Although the community of *Gay Sunshine* readers was largely based in the United States, Leyland was particularly interested in internationalizing the paper's scope. This interest led to the publication of several articles and special issues on what he referred to as the "Third World," including Latin America. It also led to numerous attempts to connect with gay groups and artists abroad. These kinds of efforts were also integral to the work of other gay liberation

FIGURE 3.4. Cover of *Gay Sunshine*'s twenty-fourth issue, published in 1975. Pennsylvania State University Libraries, Digital Collections.

periodicals in anglophone North America and responded to gay activists' desire to establish meaningful connections with the Global South. They also responded to their understanding of gay liberation as a movement intimately related to the struggle against systems of oppression, such as colonialism and imperialism. As the following section demonstrates, publishing on Latin America and connecting with gay communities there allowed Leyland, his collaborators, and several Latin Americans to advance gay liberation across borders and to foster the formation of transnational gay communities and networks.

Bridging the Gay Cultures of the Americas

Leyland placed Latin America at the center of his international community-building project, and to do so he relied on the collaboration of a number of people either living in or traveling through Latin America. These (mostly white) gay men contributed to *Gay Sunshine* and Gay Sunshine Press with news articles, essays, and artwork related to Latin America or with translations from Spanish and Portuguese into English. Contributors included activists, writers, scholars, and academics, among many others. Some of these people were one-time contributors, while others were long-time collaborators and close friends of Leyland's, such as the US translator Erskine Lane and the Canadian poet and translator Edward Lacey. Their work for the journal and press helped to build an image of Latin America that appealed to North American gay readers while facilitating the exchange of information across borders and the formation of transnational networks of gay activists at a crucial time in Latin American history: the Cold War.

Connecting with and publishing on Latin America was not an unprecedented practice in the US gay press, since this practice was beneficial for Global North gay communities and their editorial endeavors. For example, tracing the existence of homosexual practices, communities, and movements around the world was necessary for homophile and gay liberation activists to argue for the normalization of same-sex desire. As David Churchill writes, "The existence of non-Western homosexual others afforded homophiles in Europe and North America a scientific authority for the claim that homosexuality was not merely the product of the West, of civilization, but something that existed across the globe among all peoples."[31] Homophile periodicals continuously sought and published material that supported this claim. At the same time, representations of Latin American sexual cultures in homophile periodicals often underscored the differences between these cultures and those in the United States, as Shlomo Gleibman has shown.[32] Thus, publishing on Latin America fulfilled an important role in gay activism. But many of these publications also catered to a readership simply eager to learn about non-Western sexualities, particularly those considered to be more "primitive."³³

Another factor encouraging the Global North gay press to write about Latin America in the 1970s and 1980s was the political climate in the region and the repercussions of this climate on the lives of gay men. As discussed in chapter 1, the Cold War triggered a wave of right-wing, US-backed military dictatorships, state violence, and authoritarianism across the region. Because of the close relationship between sexual liberation movements and the left, gay liberation activists in Latin America were deemed sexual and political dissidents and became a target of state violence. For example, the Argentinian coup d'état in 1976 gave rise to a "Process of National Re-Organization" characterized by a dirty war against political dissidents and "social deviants" that resulted in as many as thirty thousand killings.³⁴ Since gay liberationists in Argentina and elsewhere had adopted a Marxist, working-class, and anti-capitalist politics, the Argentinian Frente de Liberación Homosexual self-dissolved shortly after the coup and its leadership fled to Spain, Brazil, and other countries.³⁵ The editorial work of gay activists and the existence of an international gay press were crucial to visualize these and other forms of violence against gay communities. The article on Argentina that Tim McCaskell published in *TBP* in 1976 illustrates such efforts to publicize this violence (see chapter 1).

It was against this backdrop that Winston Leyland published the first Latin American issue of *Gay Sunshine* in the 1975–1976 winter edition (figure 3.5). The issue featured contributions by activists, anthropologists, and travelers, among others. For instance, the US anthropologists Clark Taylor and Joseph Carrier, the Mexican-American awareness-group organizer Bob Figueroa, and the US gay activist Nikos Diaman contributed with articles on "gay life" in Mexico.³⁶ The issue also included excerpts from Erskine Lane's Guatemala journal, an article on "Indian homosexuality" by Maurice Kenny, and documents on Argentina's gay liberation movement. These documents included a letter that Argentina's Frente de Liberación Homosexual sent to gay liberation activists in Australia and a document from the Argentinian right-wing paper *El caudillo* that stated the need to get rid of homosexuals.³⁷ According to his own recollection of the events, gay activist Nikos Diaman collected the material for this issue and then delivered it to Leyland after a twelve-week trip across Mexico in 1975.³⁸ Looking back at his trip in a 2019 interview, Diaman recalled how, once in Mexico, he thought about researching gay life in the country, especially in Mexico City, as an "amateur anthropologist."³⁹ He collected material on this subject, and after returning to the United States, he thought about publishing it in either *Fag Rag* or *Gay Sunshine*; he then decided it would make more sense to publish it in San Francisco, as it

FIGURE 3.5. In 1975–1976, *Gay Sunshine* published its first Latin American issue. Its cover featured an engraving by Mexican artist José Clemente Orozco. Pennsylvania State University Libraries, Digital Collections.

had been part of Mexico. Leyland was interested in the material but declined Diaman's offer to edit a Mexican issue with his friend Rodrigo Reyes—in part because the material on Mexico was not sufficient for an entire publication. Diaman's article "Reflections on the Pyramid: A Mexico City Diary" was the introduction he had envisioned for a Mexican issue, but Leyland published it as just another contribution.[40] It is also important to note that, prior to this special issue, *Gay Sunshine* had been publishing material from or about Latin America at least since 1972, including content on Mexico, Brazil, Cuba, and Argentina in the eleventh, thirteenth, and fifteenth issues.

Launched in the winter of 1979, the second Latin American issue of *Gay Sunshine* focused on Brazil, and various activists working with the Brazilian gay periodical *Lampião da esquina* (Lamppost on the Corner) contributed articles and literary material (figure 3.6). Participants included Aguinaldo Silva, Darcy Penteado, João Silvério Trevisan, and Gaspariano Damata, as well as other writers and poets. The issue included a supplement with pictures that Leyland had taken during the Carnival of Rio de Janeiro; one of them was featured on the cover. A review of this special issue in *Lampião da esquina* commented that the supplement clearly showed the "typically relaxed nature" of Brazilians *("a chamada 'descontração' do brasileiro")* through the representation of carnival blocks such as the *Cacique de Ramos*. In this block, the reviewers noted, male participants exchange caresses or affection, which is always justified because, "at the end of the day, it is a carnival."[41] This special issue was a prelude to the first anthology of Latin American literature, which included works by some of the same writers and was also published in 1979.

The production of these special issues of *Gay Sunshine*, and of the anthologies of Latin American gay literature, would not have been possible without the transnational circulation of gay periodicals, contacts, and information. When Diaman arrived in Mexico from San Francisco in 1975, he already had the contact information of some gay men from Mexico City who introduced him to the local scene. According to his "Reflections on the Pyramid," upon arriving in Mexico City he looked over the names and phone numbers of gay men he was given by friends before leaving San Francisco.[42] Thanks to these contacts, he met people such as Ricardo Regazzoni, who was creating homoerotic art at that time, and the Argentinian writer Manuel Puig, who was staying at Regazzoni's house in Coyoacán. On his third evening there, Diaman met with Bob Figueroa and Clark Taylor, who wrote articles for the first Latin American issue of *Gay Sunshine*.[43] He also attended one of the Sunday meetings of the gay study group that the performer Javier Yépez organized. Diaman could have found the contact information of both Figueroa and Yépez in the 1973 or 1974 editions of

FIGURE 3.6. In 1979, *Gay Sunshine* published its second Latin American issue. Its cover featured a photograph from the Carnival in Rio de Janeiro. Pennsylvania State University Libraries, Digital Collections.

the *International List of Gay Organizations and Publications*, compiled by the US lawyer Robert Roth and published in New York City by the Gay Activist Alliance. Figueroa and Yépez were the only Mexican entries in those two editions, and they had been on the list since the early 1970s.[44] It is also possible that Diaman had learned about Figueroa in *The Body Politic*. The Canadian activist Gerald Hannon had met Figueroa in Mexico City in 1974, and upon returning to Toronto, he published an article on Mexican gay life in *The Body Politic* that included Figueroa's contact information (figure 3.7).[45]

Leyland was also able to connect with gay communities in Latin America thanks to his connections with various gay groups and his own travels. He visited the region regularly, especially during the summers. In 1974, 1975, and 1976 he traveled to Mexico and Guatemala; in 1977 to Mexico, Guatemala, and Brazil; and in 1978 to Guatemala, Colombia, and Ecuador. Subsequent travels included a trip to Brazil and Chile in December 1982 and January 1983, to Mexico in December 1984, and to Peru in December 1991.[46] Some of these travels were motivated by Leyland's desire to meet with his partner Manuel in Guatemala—this trip required Leyland to stay for a few days in Mexico. They were also motivated by Leyland's interest in connecting with gay communities abroad and by other personal incentives, including tourism. In his travels to Mexico City, he met with some of the same people that Diaman had encountered during his trip, including Regazzoni and Taylor.[47] Leyland and Diaman may have had access to the same information prior to their travels—including access to Roth's *International List*—or they may have exchanged information at some point. Thanks to his connections, Leyland was able to penetrate Mexico City's gay scene, connect with gay writers, and collect materials for his first anthology of Latin American gay literature.

Two crucial collaborators helping Leyland to bridge *Gay Sunshine* and Gay Sunshine Press with Latin America were the Guatemala-based US writer and translator Erskine Lane and the Canadian writer Edward Allan Lacey. Lane was born in Gadsden, Alabama, in 1940. He earned a BA in French with a minor in Spanish from Jacksonville State University in 1962 and received an MA in romance languages and literatures from the University of Alabama in 1968. He taught Spanish and Spanish-American literature at Eastern Michigan University from 1969 to 1971 and traveled through Mexico and Central America for several months. He then returned to the United States in the fall of 1972 to work as a temporary instructor in French and Spanish at Concord College, in West Virginia. He returned to Guatemala in August 1973, became a permanent resident, and co-owned the 4 AHAU gallery, which sold Indigenous-related art. He became associated with *Gay Sunshine* in 1974 and 1975 through the publication

FIGURE 3.7. Article on homosexual oppression in Mexico, published in *The Body Politic*'s thirteenth issue in 1974. Canadian Museum for Human Rights, Digital Collections, Internet Archive.

of various translations, original poems, and prose diary excerpts. In 1976, he became a contributing editor of the journal and an officer at the Gay Sunshine Press.[48] In 1978, the press published his autobiographical account *Game Texts: A Guatemala Journal*.

Edward Lacey was born in Lindsay, Ontario, in 1937.[49] He graduated from the University of Toronto in 1959 and earned a master's degree in linguistics from the University of Texas, Austin in 1961. While living in the United States, he often crossed the border into Mexico to enjoy greater levels of tolerance for drinking, drugs, and homosexual encounters. Eventually, he decided to stay there for a longer period and established himself in Torreón, where he taught English for three years until he accepted an appointment at the University of Alberta in 1963.[50] Lacey considered his years in Mexico to be the "formative period" of his life. This was, in his own words, his "first direct contact with a third-world society," and he "integrated quickly into, and came to love, Mexican (and hence all Latin-American) culture." He also "learned the language and customs, was thrilled by the personal and emotional freedom Mexicans enjoy, and [was] indelibly marked by this experience."[51] In 1965, he joined the Department of Spanish at the University of the West Indies, in Trinidad. He remained there for a couple of years and then moved to Brazil, where he taught English again. After his parents died, he inherited an estate that allowed him to continue his travels, and in 1978 he embarked on a journey that took him to Europe, North Africa, India, Indonesia, and Thailand.[52] While living in England, he worked as an English teacher for the former president of Brazil Juscelino Kubitschek during the latter's exile following the Brazilian military coup of 1964.[53]

Leyland published the two anthologies of Latin American gay literature with the help of Lane and Lacey as translators. In the mid-1970s, Leyland planned the first anthology and, to collect materials for the volume, he traveled through Latin America to contact gay intellectuals, writers, and activists. Published in 1979, *Now the Volcano: An Anthology of Latin American Gay Literature* collected works of major figures of Latin America's gay literature, such as the Mexican writers Salvador Novo and Xavier Villaurrutia; the Brazilian authors Adolfo Caminha, Darcy Penteado, and João Silvério Trevisan; and the Colombian writer Porfirio Barba-Jacob. The translators for this volume were Erskine Lane, Franklin D. Blanton, and Simon Karlinsky. Edward Lacey translated the material for the second anthology, *My Deep Dark Pain Is Love: A Collection of Latin American Gay Fiction*, published in 1983. This volume featured work by famous writers, such as the Argentinians Néstor Perlongher and Manuel Puig, the Mexican Luis Zapata, and the Cuban Reinaldo Arenas, among many others. According to Fernández Galeano, the Argentinian philosophy student Carlos

Oller provided Leyland with some of the material for this anthology—Oller met Leyland in San Francisco in 1982 and connected him with Perlongher, who gathered the material.⁵⁴ With the publication of these literary anthologies, as Daniel Balderston and José Quiroga assert, Leyland played an important role in the dissemination of Latin American gay writing, although his role was that of a promoter, not a founder. He took most of the Brazilian material in *Now the Volcano* from the first Latin American anthology of homoerotic writing, *Histórias do amor maldito*, which Gasparino Damata had edited in 1969.⁵⁵

A celebration of gay sexuality and homoerotic desire, as well as a market-oriented strategy, shaped the portrayal of Latin America in *Gay Sunshine* and Gay Sunshine Press publications, which in turn became part of a larger tradition of gay liberation print culture. First, as Balderston and Quiroga have pointed out, the anthologies focused mainly on those excerpts and texts that specifically dealt with homosexuality and sexual content.⁵⁶ The authors are right in suggesting that this decision left aside more subtle representations of homoerotic desire in Latin American literature, but it is also important to consider that this focus engaged with a politics of gay liberation that situated sex at the center of gay community-building and identity, even if Leyland's main purpose was commercial. The choosing of *Now the Volcano* as a title demonstrates how a market-oriented strategy shaped the production of this anthology. According to Leyland, someone suggested this title as a metaphor that described the book: "the dormant volcano underground being the suppressed gay masses of Latin America, and the suddenly arisen volcano a metaphor for the sudden appearance of this book expressing tabooed ideas and feelings."⁵⁷ Erskine Lane had a different appreciation. He recommended a one-word title directly relevant to the contents of the book, such as "Entendido: An Anthology of Latin American Gay Writing," because *entendido* was a Portuguese and Spanish word that gay men in South America used to refer to themselves.⁵⁸ He considered that *Now the Volcano* was rather confusing because the material in the book was not "a volcanic eruption" but "a timid oozing of magma through a lithospheric fissure."⁵⁹ Yet the "abstract" title "Entendido" did not convince Leyland, because Gay Sunshine Press distributors, Bookpeople, maintained that the title "Now the Volcano" would have a significant effect on sales.⁶⁰ This, after all, was one of Leyland's main concerns, as Gay Sunshine Press financed the publication of its books in one of three ways: through grants from the National Endowment for the Arts, through regular Gay Sunshine Press income from sales of other books, and through gift funding.⁶¹ Therefore, Leyland and his distributors may have praised Balderston's and Quiroga's critique that the title of the anthology "was fully suggestive ... of gushing erotic releases."⁶² And unlike "entendido," the term "volcano" in the title was legible to US readers. It evoked stereotypes in US popular culture of the "fiery," "explosive," and "passionate" Latin lover. It also resonated with the use of "volcano" as a metonym for Latin America in Western culture.[63]

The publication of these anthologies and the special Latin American issues of *Gay Sunshine* may have been commercial projects, but the histories behind their production are intimately connected to the larger history of gay liberation, not only in the United States but in the Americas in general. This is particularly clear when tracing how Winston Leyland, Erskine Lane, and Edward Lacey began to collaborate. The existence of transnational gay networks connected these men, which they, in turn, helped to expand. Canadian gay activist and poet Ian Young, who in the 1970s and 1980s contributed to *The Body Politic* (*TBP*) and *Gay Sunshine*, connected Leyland and Lacey in 1975.[64] A year later, Leyland connected Lacey and Lane, giving the former Lane's address in Guatemala City.[65] Leyland also connected Lacey with Argentinian gay liberation activists, including Héctor Anabitarte, who had previously contacted Leyland in early 1976 to send him some material on gay liberation in Argentina. At that time, *Gay Sunshine* was one of the most renowned and widely distributed gay periodicals in the world, and Anabitarte was hoping to establish a meaningful connection with San Francisco and Leyland. Knowing that Lacey was in South America in the mid-1970s, Leyland wrote to him to inquire whether he had met with the Buenos Aires gay liberation group and to provide him with Anabitarte's information in case Lacey wanted to establish contact.[66] Once in contact with gay activists in Buenos Aires, Lacey connected them with *TBP* in Toronto and provided the newspaper with material on Argentina's gay liberation movement, on the Frente de Liberación Homosexual, and on the gay periodical *Somos*. Lacey sent this material to Young, who in turn forwarded it to *TBP* collective member Ed Jackson.[67] Tim McCaskell drew on this material to write the article on gay liberation and oppression in Argentina discussed in chapter 1.[68]

Although Edward Lacey had no interest in politics or activism, he played a crucial role in connecting *TBP*'s Spanish-speaking staff with Argentinian gay activists seeking refuge in Canada after the 1976 coup.[69] Two of these activists were Carlos Molina and Pablo Stajnsznajder, who fled their country shortly after the coup.[70] In June 1976, after receiving the newspaper's mailing address from Lacey, the then-twenty-year-old Stajnsznajder wrote to *TBP* saying that he, his sister Mónica, and his bisexual brother-in-law Carlos Molina were planning to move to Montreal. According to his letter, both Stajnsznajder and Molina were members of the Frente de Liberación Homosexual and were interested in learning about and connecting with Montreal's gay life and organizing. They specifically asked for information on the gay movement in that city, for contacts, and for information on immigration laws to explore the possibility of entering Canada and staying, either legally or not.[71] While their first letter was addressed to Jackson, he forwarded it to Gerald Hannon because the latter spoke Spanish and was somewhat familiar with immigration laws.[72] Hannon provided Stajnsznajder with information on the process of applying for residency, with suggestions to successfully enter the country, and with information on gay organizing in Montreal. Once in Montreal, Molina wrote to *TBP* on November 15, 1976, to exchange opinions and materials on gay liberation, and to get more contacts. He also asked for some issues of *TBP* so he could send them to gay activists in Buenos Aires before they fled the country.[73] The fact that he asked for these issues on several occasions (in October, November, and December 1976) suggests that Molina, much like other gay activists at that time, recognized the importance of circulating the gay press across national borders in order to advance gay liberation.

Another contribution to transnational gay liberation was Leyland's visit to Brazil in 1977, which allowed him not only to collect materials for this anthology but also to nurture the gay liberation movement in that country. In fact, James N. Green regards Leyland's visit as a catalyst for the emergence of this movement. When Leyland visited São Paulo and Rio de Janeiro, a new political climate that followed the most repressive years of the Brazilian dictatorship was favoring the emergence of a gay and lesbian movement. During his visit, Brazilian magazines and journals interviewed Leyland on his projected anthology and on the gay liberation movement. Green argues that Leyland's presence and his meetings with intellectuals in those cities inspired a dozen writers, journalists, and scholars to organize and found the country's first gay periodical, *Lampião da esquina*.[74] Although a 1979 article in this magazine referred to this alleged inspiration as a "legend," it is possible that Leyland had indeed played a role in the emergence of this magazine.[75] But despite this role, he did not travel to Brazil with the explicit aim of advancing gay liberation, much less of planting the seeds of a gay journal. As he himself wrote in a letter, his main objective "was to gather literary material for the anthology of Latin American literature."[76] In fact, despite the important outcome of his visit, he was not even planning to visit the country that year.[77] Nonetheless, his travel did have an important outcome: it contributed to gay liberation and the growth of gay print culture in the Americas.

The contributions of Leyland, Lane, and Lacey to gay liberation movements show the centrality of gay periodicals in this transnational history, but their role in this history was far more complicated. These men were able to connect gay activists across the Americas and to publish on Latin America because of their privileged positions. They, and many others like them, benefited from the mobility that their race and class afforded them. Living in, traveling to, and writing about Latin America allowed them to connect gay communities and to fuel gay activism through print culture. But as the section below explains, they used their mobility as white, middle-class gay men to materialize desires that eroticized and celebrated racial, class, and age imbalances. Much of the work they created built on and visualized those desires, which made it legible and appealing to US and other Global North gay consumers.

The Desire for Brown Bodies

In an "Open Letter" published in the spring 1976 issue of *Gay Sunshine*, Leyland emphasized the need to see gay liberation as a struggle connected to other movements against oppression. He maintained that gays should support other groups striving for political and social changes, such as the American Indian Movement and the Chicano Movement. He also maintained that gay liberationists should support demonstrations against fascist regimes abroad, such as those in Chile and Iran, and should condemn imperialism. Aware of structures of oppression along the lines of race and class, he also claimed that "Gay liberation will have achieved little if it merely means that it's all right for a select group of white, middle-class people to 'have sex' in a different way."[78] Leyland thus argued for an end to exploitation. However, his work and collaborations with Lane and Lacey complicated this liberationist discourse. Their interactions with Latin Americans were shaped by racial, class, and age imbalances, while their production of Latin American content profited from the eroticization of those imbalances.

The work and life experiences of Leyland and his collaborators evoke critiques on cosmopolitanism in queer scholarship. In 2002, a special issue of *GLQ: A Journal of Lesbian and Gay Studies* on queer tourism helped to lay out the relationship between mobility, queernesss, and globalization. In her contribution, Jasbir Puar posited that "cosmopolitan queerness" is partially indebted to its mobility, while Dereka Rushbrook explained that "To be cosmopolitan is to display openness and curiosity about other cultures, to seek out the different." In many cases, Rushbrook noted, such openness and curiosity may imply claiming the right to consume other races and cultures.[79] The term "cosmopolitanism" has had a mostly positive connotation in sociopolitical philosophy because it "is based on a liberal conception of human beings as a single community in which all have equal entitlement to dignity and to fundamental freedoms."[80] However, scholars such as Hiram Pérez have later used the term "gay cosmopolitan" to advance an interpretative framework that traces a relationship between cosmopolitan gay modernity, colonialism, and US empire from the late nineteenth century through its contemporary manifestations. In Pérez's work, "gay cosmopolitan" designates "a subject position originating with (but not limited to) a white, urban, leisure-class gay male whose desire is cast materially onto the globe at the close of the nineteenth century."[81] This form of gay modernity, he contends, has played a significant role in colonial and neocolonial expansion. He argues that the "desires comprising the cosmopolitan gay male subject... reinscribe oppressive racial hierarchies while enjoining gay men of color to both authenticate and celebrate those desires and the sexual cultures they organize."[82]

If cosmopolitanism means "belonging to all parts of the world," as Peter Nyers explains, and it also entails consuming other races and cultures, then it becomes clear how some gay cosmopolitans could benefit from social, racial, and other imbalances while feeling entitled to consume "the other."[83] Peter Nyers explains that cosmopolitanism is "universalistic in its aspirations. It is well known for disregarding the particularistic logic of nationalism, with its imagined spatial communities and territorialized identities."[84] The problem with this universalistic aspiration, as Nyers himself clarifies, is that it does not benefit everyone equally, to the extent that some may ask whether "today's cosmopolitans [are] none other than the subjects of Empire."[85] Indeed, white, middle-class gay cosmopolitans such as those who contributed to or read *Gay Sunshine* participated in circuits of queer cosmopolitanism premised on mobility and consumerism. Many of these circuits, as explained below, had a negative impact on Global South queer subjects.

Thinking about the work of Leyland, Lacey, and Lane through the lens of cosmopolitanism allows to reflect on what they and their readers desired about Latin America, and on how those desires manifested in the gay print culture of anglophone North America. It also allows us to reflect on the role of those desires in the transnational history of gay liberation and to examine the complicated racial, age, and class imbalances that shaped these men's interactions with Latin Americans. Leyland, Lane, Lacey, and many others like them used their gay cosmopolitan mobility to satisfy their erotic desires in places like Latin America; their cosmopolitanism, in turn, allowed their readers to experience their gay mobility. In Pérez's view, mobility is constitutive of gay identity and cosmopolitanism; being gay, he asserts, "requires some kind of travel, actual or imagined."[86] As we shall see below, the visualization of "Third World" sexualities and cultures in *Gay Sunshine* and Gay Sunshine Press publications gave readers an opportunity to exercise their mobility and cosmopolitan desires through *imagined* travels.

One example that illustrates the gay cosmopolitan desires of Leyland, his collaborators, and readers is the visual content in the anthologies of Latin American literature published by Gay Sunshine Press, particularly the representation of adolescents and young men. *Now the Volcano* included six black-and-white erotic images by Latin American artists that depict nude men and oral-sex scenes. A painting by Brazilian artist Darcy Penteado of a nude young man against an abstract backdrop introduces the reader to the anthology. The use of this image suggests to the reader that sexuality and eroticism will be main features of this literary anthology. This and another painting by the same artist eroticize men with fit, almost hairless bodies and flaccid, albeit bulky genitals, while conveying a message of innocent male sexuality. In contrast to these images, there is other artwork in *Now the Volcano* that offers more explicit representations of same-sex sexuality. This artwork catered not only to readers' cravings for sexual representations but also to erotic imaginaries that oversexualized Latin America or that conceived it as a region of sexually available men. For example, the anthology included two images that evoked oral sex scenes, one performed by a young individual and the other by an older man in leather. In each representation, the emphasis appears to be on the seemingly submissive role of the oral-sex giver, who appears kneeling or squatting. The young man even has the elbow of his sexual partner resting on top of him, as if to suggest an act of domination. Moreover, the idea of Latin America as a region of sexually available men, and the invocation of power dynamics in sex, is further suggested by Luis Caballero's painting of a headless, nude man with lifted arms and a cord around his armpits. These messages may not be the ones that the artists originally intended. But placing these images in an anthology of Latin American gay literature produced by and for North American or Global North gay men invariably provides these images with new meanings. The anthology and its visual content were part of a gay cosmopolitan imaginary that eroticized racial, class, and age imbalances.

The cover and the two illustrations by Argentinian artist Jorge Gumier Maier in *My Deep Dark Pain Is Love* also show how both anthologies catered to North American gay men's desires for an exotic Latin America with sexually available (and racialized) young men. The cover features an image of an erect penis from which a white line emanates and frames the title of the book. The only illustrations in the volume are two drawings that depict nude males with hairless bodies and uncircumcised penises—such features arguably racialize their bodies for a white North American viewership. One of these illustrations is a drawing of a somewhat muscular adolescent or young man kneeling on a bed; his uncircumcised, semi-erect penis and the feet in front of him suggest that he is about to initiate a sexual interaction with another person, most likely taking an active role. The other drawing shows what seems to be an adolescent leaning toward one side and crossing one leg in front of the other. He wears socks and a cord around his waist that accentuates his hips, and he holds a small bouquet of flowers in his right hand. The boy is slim, his penis is small, and his body hair is scant. The drawing is reminiscent of the famous pictures that the German photographer Wilhelm von Gloeden took in Mediterranean Europe in the late nineteenth and early twentieth century. His photographs of young men, adolescents, and boys in places like Sicily popularized the region "as a kind of homosexual utopia."[87]

From the late nineteenth century until the mid-twentieth century, the desire for youthful bodies was a central feature of homosexual identity in Europe and North America, with famous homosexual artists from those regions enthusiastically participating in the production and visualization of this desire. Some of these artists were the writers Walt Whitman, Oscar Wilde, Marcel Proust, Jean Cocteau, and André Guide; the painter Henry Scott Tuke; the pictorialist photographers Wilhelm von Gloeden, Vincenzo Galdi, Thomas Eakins, Wilhelm Plüschow, and Fred Holland Day; and the writer and activist Adolf Brand, who published in Berlin the first homosexual magazine in history, *Der Eigene* (1896–1932).[88] The visualization of this desire was particularly evident in this magazine, with photographs and drawings of boy-adolescents increasingly being featured in every issue, especially after 1919. These erotic and sexualized images presented the desire for youthful bodies as a marker of homosexual identity. It was around this time that European photographic studios were most prolific in the production of orientalist erotic imagery of youth. As Kadji Amin notes, these studios produced "ethnopornographic" images with exoticized Arab themes for European consumers with "pederastic fantasies."[89] Over the twentieth century, numerous gay periodicals in Europe and the Americas reproduced these images, including the Mexican gay liberation periodicals examined in chapter 1. In publishing this type of imagery, these periodicals were presenting their readership with a visual culture of homoerotic desire easily recognized and with deep roots in gay culture.

The work of Leyland and his collaborators must be situated within this larger context of gay cosmopolitanism. The anthologies of Latin American literature and the special Latin American issues of *Gay Sunshine* offered readers the experience of traveling to exotic destinations: By reading and enjoying the visual content of these documents, consumers came close to Latin America and its people and exercised their cosmopolitan mobility, which allowed them to possess other cultures and races. In turn, by catering to gay cosmopolitan desires, Leyland ensured the economic success of his books and magazines. Creating appealing products that could be successful in the gay market was indeed a priority for Leyland, and when those products were about Latin America, capitalizing on racial differences was central to that success.

One visual record that demonstrates Leyland's ability to capitalize on ideas of race to sell Latin American content is the cover of *Adonis García*, the English translation by Edward Lacey of *El vampiro de la colonia Roma*. The book takes the format of a monologue in which a male hustler, Adonis García, narrates his daily life and sexual adventures with men in Mexico City. Adonis is the son of a Mexican mother and a Spanish father; therefore, the covers of Mexican editions have featured either pictures of white men or images that seem inattentive to race. Many of these Mexican covers have also featured colorful depictions of urban landscapes that reflect the modern appearance of Mexico City in the 1970s and 1980s (figure 3.8). In contrast to these covers, the Gay Sunshine Press cover featured a black-and-white photograph of an Indigenous-looking young man (figure 3.1). Since the man on this cover does not match the description of Adonis, it arguably aimed to appeal to a specific North American readership that desired youthful brown bodies and that could only think (or would want to think) of Mexicans as racial others. Aware of the rationale behind the selection of this cover, the author Luis Zapata told Leyland in 1981: "I think the photo is very good, very suggestive. Although the boy of the photo is not exactly the idea I have of the main character of *El vampiro*, I think it can work, and I suppose your choice is based on the public that might read the book (which I suppose you know very well)."[90] Indeed, Leyland knew his market, as the book, which was distributed by Bookpeople, sold relatively well: 4,900 paperback copies were printed along with 200 regular hardcover and twenty-six specially signed hardcovers.[91] According to Leyland, by October 1981, about 700 copies were sold. It was "not a huge amount," he told Zapata, but reminded him "that there are well over 100 gay books currently in print and in circulation."[92] In the course of the next few months, the book continued to sell, though somewhat slower than Leyland had expected—which he continued to attribute to the competition from the large number of gay-oriented books in the United States.[93] By April 1983, sales had slowed considerably, but the book was still selling; the critical response had been "mostly favorable"; and Leyland continued to send Zapata royalty checks through the 1980s.[94]

The imagery of racialized young men in *Gay Sunshine* and Gay Sunshine Press publications with Latin American content situated the body and homoeroticism at the center of gay liberation politics and cultural production. The gay cosmopolitan desire for the primitive, the exotic, and the brown body that Pérez identifies in US cultural production and considers "fundamental to gay modernity" was at the center of the Latin American anthologies and *Gay Sunshine* issues that Leyland produced.[95] These works, and specially their visual content, could be deemed objectionable by some, but they offer insight into readers' desires and consumer patterns. Moreover, the production, content, and circulation of these works helped to advance gay liberation while fostering the formation

FIGURE 3.8. *El vampiro de la colonia Roma*, by Luis Zapata, published in Mexico City in 1979.

of gay communities and identities across borders. But as the final section of this chapter further demonstrates, the outcomes of these works were mainly beneficial for white and North American gay subjects.

Gay Identity and the Sexuality of the "Other"

The gay liberation politics that Leyland advanced through his editorial work on Latin America centered the desires of anglophone North American consumers, and more generally of Global North gay consumers. These desires, and the visual culture they produced, should be contextualized within colonial and neocolonial travel logics and understandings of non-Western sexualities. They should also be analyzed in relation to the formation of a modern gay identity. The Latin American content that Leyland produced and marketed not only exoticized the people of this region but also presented them as the "backward other" whose sexuality stood in stark contrast with that of the modern Western gay reader. In this instance, rather than emphasizing the shared experiences of gay men across the Americas to foster community-building, these publications accentuated their differences and reinscribed racial hierarchies. For that reason, the final section of this chapter examines how the liberatory politics of these publications complicated the larger project of transnational gay liberation and community-building.

Scholars have discussed how, since the nineteenth century, Western gay travelers have advanced a colonial binary framework to depict the sexuality and ethnicity of postcolonial subjects. As Gordon Waitt and Kevin Markwell observe, this framework "imagines the people of the United States and Europe as mobile and the nations as 'First World' modern, the site of progressive social organizations." Conversely, non-Western individuals "are imagined as fixed in place, devoid of time," and "presumed to be 'Third World,' traditional, premodern, and 'primitive,' particularly in regard to sexuality." Such conceptions, the authors note, draw on nineteenth-century conceptions of nature, race, history, and civilization according to which regions outside the West were "unrespectable" places where "anything was imaginable, including same-sex desire, nudity, prostitution, and polygamy."[96] This mindset also informed the association of Latin America with economic underdevelopment, "lack of civilization," and "cultural simplicity." All these conditions were attributed to the political instability and racial mixing in the region.[97]

Such ideas of Latin America, and more generally of the "Third World," have persisted over the years and can be identified in contemporary narratives of non-Western sexualities. For instance, analyzing early 2000s versions of the gay travel guide *Spartacus*, Waitt and Markwell found that "Non-Western territories are coded as tradition bound, poor, undemocratic, 'backward,' and potentially life-threatening to gay people," while the sexual practices in those places are "portrayed as belonging to the past."[98] Such narratives around Latin American sexualities can also be identified in contemporary discourses around heterosexual sex tourism in the region. For example, in her ethnographic work on sex tourism in the Dominican Republic, Denise Brennan has identified how Global North male buyers eroticize gendered and racial differences as part of their paid-sex experiences with local women, often regarding them as more sexual, compliant, and traditional. Some men would even say that Dominican women have "fiery blood," while others associate darker skin tones with more "sexual proficiency." Interestingly, some of these women capitalize on those imagined differences, performing the stereotype of the "hot" Latina.[99] Thus, the encounters between sex tourists and sex workers, as Megan Rivers-Moore argues, "are produced through a variety of intersecting sites of power."[100] Writing specifically about Costa Rica's sex tourism enclave Gringo Gulch, Rivers-Moore explains that "sex tourists are more than just racist neoimperialists." Instead, both buyers and sellers "are involved in complicated processes of class mobility that must be situated within the neoliberal marketization of leisure, consumption, and sex."[101] Some sex tourists, the author explains, "have taken up a specifically transnational response to their experiences of disempowerment (whether imagined or real), and crossing borders allows them to claim a level of social mobility that would be unavailable to them at home."[102] This argument may help explain the experiences of Global North gay men traveling to Latin America looking for sex, as well as the experiences of those who read magazines like *Gay Sunshine*. Both traveling and consuming these periodicals provided Global North gay men with the opportunity to challenge experiences of disempowerment at home by imagining, constructing, and reproducing racial and class hierarchies in relation to Latin America.

Indeed, neocolonial racial and sexual fantasies and stereotypes informed much of the Latin American content in Global North gay magazines like *Gay Sunshine*. These publications often sexualized the region and portrayed it as backward, exotic, and atemporal. For example, their news articles on gay life in Latin America were often illustrated with images that evoked the Indigenous or precolonial history of the region, even when such themes were not the focus of the texts. This was the case in Gerald Hannon's abovementioned article on gay life in Mexico City, published in *The Body Politic* in 1974. This article was illustrated with images of Mayan hieroglyphic writing (figure 3.7). The Maya writing system, though, had fallen into disuse since the early colonial period; it was never used in Central Mexico; and it had no relation to the content of the article.

Another portrayal of a backward and/or atemporal Mexico is found in Diaman's article "Reflections on the Pyramid: A Mexico City Diary," published in the first Latin American issue of *Gay Sunshine*. The title borrowed from Mexican writer Octavio Paz's essay "The Other Mexico: Critique of the Pyramid." However, considering the lack of a meaningful discussion on Mexican culture or history, Diaman's use of this metaphor seems bizarre. Despite the reference to precolonial architecture, Diaman's "Reflections on the Pyramid" centered mostly on his search for sex while exploring Mexico City—according to the text, he could not even visit the Teotihuacan pyramids because the archaeological site had closed before he could get there: He had spent the afternoon having sex in the baths. Moreover, the publication was only illustrated with an abstract phallic painting by Ricardo Regazzoni (figure 3.9). Although this kind of art was in line with the visual culture of gay liberation because of its celebration of homoeroticism, it did not contribute to Diaman's "reflections" on gay life in Mexico City. Instead, it implied that the only thing the city had to offer was sex. If somehow Diaman's portrayal of Mexico as backward, lost in time, and exclusively sexual was missed, his closing paragraph reinforced the message. He wrote: "I am finally headed home on a train.... My mind drifts somewhere between consciousness and sleep. I feel like a swimmer slowly rising from the dark bottom of the sea toward the cold clear light above. And for a moment I catch a glimpse of a Mesoamerican pantheon of godesses [sic] and gods standing silently at the edge of my reality knowing I will soon be safe across the border."[103]

The fascination with and commodification of Indigenous Latin America responded both to these authors' desire to trace non-Western genealogies of homoerotic desire and to an effort to idealize a primitive past of sexual permissiveness. Shlomo Gleibman has found that many authors in homophile periodicals wrote about the "homosexual customs" of Indigenous Latin Americans. Some of them romanticized the region's precolonial past, "where there was greater openness to homosexuality and gender transgression."[104] Therefore, Indigenous-related content and imagery may have been well received among most of Leyland's readers, especially because this content and imagery were already part of the visual content of other gay periodicals such as physique and travel magazines, including *Grecian Guild Pictorial* and *Ciao!*[105] One of these readers was Thomas Wright, who wrote to Leyland to congratulate him for the publication of Lane's *Game Text* and for his overall editorial work. He thought that the "pre-colonial" cover of this book was "vivid and exceptionally attractive." "I should imagine that Gay Sunshine Press is beginning to get a tremendous reputation among sensitive aware persons. No one seriously interested in modern literature can afford to dismiss it," he wrote.[106]

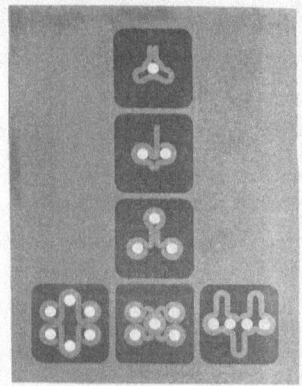

FIGURE 3.9. Page from the first Latin American issue of *Gay Sunshine* featuring artwork by Mexican visual artist Ricardo Regazzoni. Pennsylvania State University Libraries, Digital Collections.

Finally, the fact that Diaman's narration centers on his search for sex in Mexico City tells us more about him and his intended audience than about gay life in the city. Like him, many other white cosmopolitan gay men who visited Mexico or other Latin American countries in the 1970s did it with the purpose of conducting sex tourism. If we are to believe Diaman's account, he began searching for sex as soon as he set foot in the city, which shows what the main purpose of his visit was.[107] Even the more "scientific" or research-oriented travels of white, US gay men to countries like Mexico were often shaped by sexual drives. The work of two anthropologists who contributed to the first Latin American issue of *Gay Sunshine* illustrates this point. Clark Taylor conducted extensive research in bathhouses in Mexico City in the 1970s as a participant observer in order to document cruising and sexual practices of Mexicans and to experience firsthand how such practices occurred. His research methods, though, and those of his fellow colleague Joe Carrier have been seriously questioned by anthropologist Pedro Bustos-Aguilar.[108] The latter reproaches the researchers' under-theorized methodologies and their decision to engage in sexual practices with their informants without critically assessing their privileged positions and the power dynamics at play.[109] In the case of Diaman's portrayal of Mexico in this special issue of *Gay Sunshine*, it surely resonated with what readers expected from a "Third World" country. Latin America was constructed as an exotic, dangerous, and backward region: At least one reader thanked Leyland for this "terrific Latin issue"; he "especially liked the diaries, confirming all one's worst fears about Mexico et al."[110]

Similar to the first Latin American issue of *Gay Sunshine*, writings by Erskine Lane and Edward Lacey also constructed an image of Latin America as an exotic and backward region with sexually available boys and men. As Balderston and Quiroga have discussed, in Lane's *Game Texts* "there are endless encounters with boys [and] observations on native habits and customs.... There are no dates to guide the reader on a temporal journey.... Lane seeks to account for a timeless present—his aim is to give the sensation of space, not of time."[111] In regard to Lacey's poems on Latin America, the authors notice a sense of "nostalgia produced by a temporal and spacial dislocation" supported with an "overabundance of palm trees, Indian ruins," and naked young bodies.[112] Moreover, Lacey's correspondence with people like Leyland, Lane, and Ian Yong contains multiple references to his sexual interactions with boys and working-class men in Latin America. In those unsettling references, whose analysis is beyond the scope of this book, Lacey worships unequal relationships and power disparities with Latin American boys and young men.[113]

Latin America thus provided gay cosmopolitan men with an exotic place to explore, have sex, and research homosexual practices. It also provided them with rich and exciting material to write about in the anglophone North American gay press. For them and their readership, learning about Latin American sexual cultures advanced their sense of liberation. By covering this content alongside vibrant depictions of homoerotic desire, the gay press showed that homosexuality was universal and promoted a sense of gay pride. This sense of liberation, though, developed in close relationship with neocolonial constructions of non-Western, "primitive," and/or "backward" homosexual cultures and practices. The editorial and creative work of Leyland, Lacey, and Lane built on and contributed to these constructions, which they eroticized for their own pleasure and recognition.

WINSTON LEYLAND REVOLUTIONIZED THE gay publishing industry in the United States with his contributions to *Gay Sunshine* and the subsequent creation of Gay Sunshine Press, the oldest publishing house of gay material in the country.[114] His interest in the cultural history of homoerotic desire, specifically in literature and the visual arts, cultivated a strong sense of community among his readers. However, as this chapter has discussed, the gay world that Leyland's editorial work imagined and created was shaped by racial and class hierarchies. This was a world for Global North and, to some extent, privileged Latin American gay readers where working-class and racialized men were objects of desire but not necessarily members of the same community. Leyland, Lacey, and Lane imagined a transnational gay community along the lines of race and class, and these factors determined whom they connected and identified with. The knowledge they spread about Latin America and the reception of this knowledge among readers had a similar effect. While *Gay Sunshine* and Gay Sunshine Press connected the gay worlds of the Americas by selling an image of "gay" Latin America to an anglophone North American audience, many Global North readers desired the region and its inhabitants precisely because of the "otherness" of their sexuality and their presumed inferiority. Thus, *Gay Sunshine*, Gay Sunshine Press, and specifically the editorial work of Leyland, Lacey, and Lane played a crucial role in the transnational history of gay liberation. Aside from connecting communities across borders, they advanced the goals of liberating, celebrating, and visualizing homoerotic desires through their work—though some of these desires were not liberatory for everyone.

To a significant extent, the desire for brown, youthful, and working-class individuals was at the center of transnational gay history from the 1970s onward. As the following chapters will demonstrate, similar desires informed much of the sexual imagery in Mexican and US gay magazines published in the 1980s and early 1990s. Each of these magazines addressed these desires in significantly different ways in order to appeal to both domestic and international gay consumers.

| 4 |

Gay Masculinity and the Commodification of the Mexican Body in *Macho Tips*

In a 2019 interview, a former reader of gay erotic magazines based in Mexico City described with excitement the pleasure it gave him to purchase, leaf through, and collect these periodicals. "Owning the magazines was like owning those men featured in their pages ... instead of something I needed to read, the magazines became something I needed to possess," he recalled. One of the magazines that this reader was particularly fond of was *Macho Tips*, which was published in Mexico City from 1985 to 1989. Its creator was the public accountant Aurelio Refugio Hidalgo de la Torre, who envisioned a gay magazine that could serve a Mexican gay readership by publishing relevant information for them, as well as erotic imagery. Its first cover, which featured a seemingly white young man wearing jeans and a tank top, presented *Macho Tips* as a magazine with information about services, classifieds, and reportage for the people of "mucho ambiente," a coded way to refer to homosexual men (figure 4.1). With a vibrant editorial content and an appealing visual culture that celebrated masculinity and the male body, the magazine quickly became popular. Its twenty-three issues included local and international gay news, and content on politics, sexual health, gay history and culture, entertainment, lesbian content, and classifieds. *Macho Tips* also provided readers with the opportunity to make contacts, to build community, to control their representation in the media, and to enjoy erotica, especially pictures of brown Mexican-looking models, which began to increasingly illustrate the magazine in 1986. This editorial trend continued after Hidalgo de la Torre renamed his magazine *Hermes* in 1990 and until this periodical ended publication in 1994 after producing twenty-six issues.

The mid-1980s was a difficult but significant time to publish a gay magazine with this kind of content because of the prevailing climate of neoconservative politics and economic crisis in Mexico. At the time, the "moral renovation campaign" of Miguel de la Madrid's presidential period (1982–1988), neoliberal reforms, internal divisions within gay and lesbian activism, and the AIDS crisis had severely weakened the homosexual liberation movement. By 1984, this weakening had led to the demise of the three groups that directed the movement in Mexico City: the Frente Homosexual de Acción Revolucionaria (FHAR), Grupo Lambda de Liberación Homosexual, and Oikabeth. *Macho Tips* filled an important editorial gap in the city because the periodicals that FHAR and Grupo Lambda had launched in 1979 had already disappeared by 1983: *Política sexual*, *Nuestro cuerpo*, and *Nuevo ambiente*. However, filling this gap came at a greater risk, considering both the content of *Macho Tips* and the context in which it published. For these reasons, Hidalgo de la Torre's editorial initiative was a radical and remarkable achievement. This initiative would not have been possible without his knowledge of Mexican politics and bureaucracy, his familiarity with the international gay press, and his blatant support of the authoritarian ruling party, the Partido Revolucionario Institucional (PRI). His political affinities were tangible in the seemingly conservative content of *Macho Tips*; unlike previous gay liberation periodicals that criticized the government and envisioned revolutionary changes in the sociopolitical realm, Hidalgo de la Torre's magazines promoted an assimilationist approach that aimed to present gay men as masculine, respectable, and productive individuals. Even the magazine's erotic imagery resonated with the PRI's enactment of revolutionary nationalism during its long hegemonic rule (1929–2000). This enactment—performed in historical commemorations and official discourses—became particularly useful to counteract the growing crisis of

FIGURE 4.1. Inaugural issue of *Macho Tips*, published in Mexico City in 1985. The cover featured artwork by Mexican artist Rubén Gómez-Tagle. Courtesy of Ernesto Reséndiz Oikión.

legitimacy of the regime, increased by the 1982 economic crisis.[1] Revolutionary nationalism highlighted, among other themes, the pre-Hispanic and mestizo (racially mixed) heritage of Mexico. The fact that Hidalgo de la Torre's magazines celebrated the brown and hypermasculine Mexican-looking body may not have been a direct engagement with revolutionary nationalism, but that context certainly influenced much of the Mexican cultural production of the time.

By analyzing the production and content of *Macho Tips*, this chapter develops two arguments that engage with scholarship on both transnational gay liberation and race, gender, and sexuality in Mexico. The first argument is that the production and content of *Macho Tips* were integral to the transnational history of gay liberation movements that placed homoerotic desire and its visual representation at the center of community-building and identity formation. In this respect, *Macho Tips* joined a long tradition in the history of gay print culture and consumer culture, a tradition that has been presented in previous chapters through an analysis of gay liberation periodicals such as *The Body Politic*, *Gay Sunshine*, and the Mexican magazines mentioned above. This tradition, however, has a longer history that predates the 1970s. For instance, David Johnson's scholarship has shown the relationship between physique magazines, consumerism, and the emergence of the gay rights movement in the United States from the 1940s to the late 1960s. Although they were not advertised as gay publications, most physique magazines catered to a gay consumer base and were crucial to the formation of gay communities and identities. Selling images of athletic and well-built men to a male readership not only celebrated the masculine body but also cultivated a homoerotic desire for it.[2] Like those physique and gay liberation magazines that centered the body and the visualization of homoerotic desires—magazines that actually inspired Hidalgo de la Torre's work—*Macho Tips* contributed to gay liberation and community-building by means of this type of content.

The second argument in this chapter is that *Macho Tips* appropriated, eroticized, and commodified Mexican national values of race and gender to make a profit, to appeal to domestic and international gay consumers, and to challenge the marginalization of gay men in Mexico. Evoking Mexico's master narrative of racial identity, *mestizaje* (race mixture), the erotic images that *Macho Tips* published in most covers and centerfolds after 1986 celebrated an idea of racialized Mexican masculine beauty. These images resonated with the cult of masculinity in Mexican society, which was very present in the popular culture of the postrevolutionary period beginning in the 1920s and 1930s.[3] However, while *Macho Tips* drew on national discourses of race and gender, the magazine also reconceptualized their meaning. *Macho Tips* detached macho aesthetics from heterosexuality and successfully blurred the line between straight and gay Mexican masculinities. Through this strategy, *Macho Tips* "nationalized" homosexuality and appealed to the desires of the gay middle classes who sought to consume the Mexican masculine body.

The discourse of *mestizaje* has served as a cohesive force of national identity in many Latin American countries, while popular culture has been instrumental in negotiating national discourses of race and gender. As Nancy P. Appelbaum, Anne S. Macpherson, and Karin Alejandra Rosemblatt contend, "race has been central to gendered and sexualized constructions of nationhood" in the region, and both elite and nonelite people have either contested or engaged with national ideologies of *mestizaje* to pursue specific goals. Subordinated peoples, they claim, "have participated in the transnational, national, regional, and local production of race and nation" by using "racial discourse to their own ends."[4] Other scholars have shown how popular culture can be used "to challenge or uphold local gender ideologies," and how "people sometimes make claims based on gender status to get what they need from political, cultural, or religious institutions."[5] Such individuals, as Víctor Macías-González and Anne Rubenstein point out, "deploy the set of words, images, stories, and ideas about gender that are already available to them to form their arguments," which in turn "reinforces existing hierarchies."[6] Moreover, social movements in Latin America such as women's liberation, human rights, and gay movements have "reconfigured the state's democratic discourse on rights, citizenship, and the 'nation'" and have "reimagined nations."[7] Like those groups, *Macho Tips* also drew on racial and gendered national discourses to reimagine the Mexican nation and the belonging of gay men therein.

In commercializing an idea of racialized Mexican male beauty, *Macho Tips* exemplifies a turning point in the history of gay print culture, one that moves from gay liberation politics to consumerism without necessarily breaking entirely with the former. While the narrative arc of this book began in the early 1970s with the emergence of the first activist-oriented gay liberation periodicals in North America, the focus of this and the next chapter is on commercially oriented gay lifestyle and erotic magazines with few politics and significant profits. Winston Leyland's *Gay Sunshine* had already stood in stark contrast with contemporary, but more radical publications such as *The Body Politic* or *Gay Community News*; unlike them, the San Francisco journal became more concerned with the arts and literature than with politics. In a somewhat similar way, *Macho Tips* did not follow the same editorial practices of *Política sexual, Nuestro cuerpo*, or *Nuevo ambiente*, but it was certainly an outcome of the Mexican gay liberation movement. Its format had no resemblance to those previous publications studied in chapter 1, but much of its content continued to play a crucial role in the Mexican gay movement: Its news coverage, AIDS-related content, classifieds, and erotic imagery were all relevant for building gay community and fostering political organization. People like Leyland and Hidalgo de la Torre were not only editors, but also entrepreneurs. For them, publishing gay periodicals represented both a business and an opportunity to advance gay liberation through an editorial and entrepreneurial activism. Their work was akin to that of US publishers of physique magazines, which Johnson deems undeniably activist.

The pages that follow examine the production, content, circulation, and reception of *Macho Tips* against the backdrop of social, cultural, and political changes that shaped the history of gay print culture in Mexico and other countries in North America. The first section discusses the creation of the magazine after the heyday of Mexico's gay liberation movement by drawing connections to the histories of other gay magazines whose focus was mostly commercial rather than political. This section also examines the role of *Macho Tips* in the formation of local, national, and international gay communities in the 1980s and how Hidalgo de la Torre's work became part of a larger history of North American gay publishing. This topic is further examined in the second section, which examines how Hidalgo de la Torre's editorial work constituted a form of activism. On one hand, his magazines played a crucial role in mobilizing information about AIDS and sexual health among the gay public in Mexico; on the other, his fight against censorship ensured that not only information about AIDS would circulate across Mexico, but also erotic imagery produced by and for gay men. As this section demonstrates, the international gay press provided Hidalgo de la Torre with both inspiration and tools to defend his magazines from censorship attempts. The last two sections of the chapter examine the discursive and visual representation of masculinity and race in *Macho Tips*. The third section examines how *Macho Tips* built on the cult of masculinity in both the Mexican and larger North American gay cultures. Engaging with this cult allowed the magazine to confront stereotypes of homosexuality, develop and promote a particular form of gay identity, and advance gay liberation. The fourth section analyzes how much of the erotic imagery in *Macho Tips* reproduced, deliberately or not, the Mexican ideology of *mestizaje*. The analysis explains how, in commercializing images of the Mexican body and homoerotic desire to advance gay liberation, *Macho Tips* participated in a larger trend in the history of gay print culture.

A Pioneering Gay Magazine in Mexico

Building on the legacy of a vibrant local gay liberation movement, Aurelio Refugio Hidalgo de la Torre created the first long-running gay magazine in Mexico City and helped to launch the Mexican gay publishing industry. As discussed in chapter 1, Mexico City's gay press emerged in 1979 alongside the homosexual liberation movement. Gay and lesbian activists involved in FHAR and Grupo Lambda published three periodicals that, despite their efforts, did not survive for long due to their lack of resources and support from the homosexual community. *Política sexual*, *Nuestro cuerpo*, and *Nuevo ambiente* were all launched in 1979 but published only one, two, and five issues, respectively. Though short-lived, these periodicals, and the gay liberation movement in Mexico, set in motion changes that would allow for the emergence of *Macho Tips*. As Hidalgo de la Torre acknowledged in 1986, the opening of spaces for the expression, development, and awareness of gay issues in Mexico—especially those related to culture—was the result of the homosexual liberation movement.[8]

Little is known about Hidalgo de la Torre's personal and professional life. He was born in Guadalajara City on September 30, 1947. He studied public accounting at the Universidad de Guadalajara and obtained his degree in the early 1980s (Licenciatura como Contador Público y Auditor). He married in this city in 1971 and had a son. About a decade later, he moved to Mexico City, perhaps to live as a gay man, and became affiliated with the PRI. Some of his former collaborators assert that Hidalgo de la Torre worked with political leaders affiliated with this party, and that this work allowed him to amass some wealth and pursue his dream of launching a gay magazine. They also assert that both his wife and son were aware of Hidalgo de la Torre's sexual orientation and editorial work.[9]

Although Hidalgo de la Torre had close links with the PRI, publishing a magazine like *Macho Tips* in 1985 constituted a major challenge because of the prevailing neoconservative climate in Mexico. Through the 1980s, President Miguel de la Madrid's "moral renovation campaign" and neoliberal reforms were profoundly affecting the gay liberation movement in Mexico. Shortly after taking office in 1982, de la Madrid amended the civil and penal codes, criminalizing "moral damage" and the publication of anti-government materials. As Lucinda Grinnell asserts, implicit in de la Madrid's amendment and public discourses was the idea that gays and lesbians were delinquents.[10] The government's neoliberal reforms were also acting against gays and lesbians; these reforms brought campaigns that promoted the nuclear family—composed of a working father, a housewife mother, and children—as the norm, which further marginalized these groups.[11] This conservative climate led to rising repression and unemployment rates among queer people. For example, on March 9, 1984, Mexico City witnessed the biggest raid up until then; the aim was to clean up the streets of delinquency, female sex workers, and homosexuals.[12] With neoliberal reforms also came a renewed authoritarianism. As Lorenzo Meyer explains, to impose the reforms and control inevitable reactions against them, the PRI had to rely on their traditional authoritarian practices; thus, the new "economic liberalism" was made possible by "political anti-liberalism."[13]

Along with this neoconservative climate, divisions within gay and lesbian activism and the AIDS crisis were profoundly affecting the gay liberation movement in Mexico. As Jordi Díez has explained, disagreements over the aims and strategies of gay and lesbian activism were weakening their movement and collective identity. One of the most significant disagreements concerned opposing views on how to achieve social change. While some activists advocated for radical revolutionary transformations, others promoted a reformist approach that relied on the existing system to pursue sociopolitical changes.[14] Meanwhile, AIDS arrived in Mexico at the end of 1983, triggering a social panic and a discourse that blamed the "promiscuous" lives of homosexuals for the onset and spread of the virus. Conservative groups such as the Catholic Church saw the epidemic as divine punishment. The emergence of this discourse and the panic it created, Díez writes, destabilized the Mexican gay and lesbian movement and erased it from the public sphere.[15]

In such a fraught context, *Macho Tips* intermittently published twenty-three issues between 1985 and 1989, and then twenty-six issues from 1990 to 1994 under the name *Hermes*. The size of *Macho Tips* was about 9.05 × 6.69 inches and was comprised of thirty to sixty pages, of which only the covers and a central supplement with male nudes were printed in color. While the first eleven issues of *Hermes* had a similar format, the following fifteen were printed in color, had a larger size, and included more pages with classifieds and sexual imagery (figure 4.2). In addition to content relevant for gay men, *Macho Tips* also included a three-page-long section titled "Amazonas" that was edited by female writer Cherie J. Vaughan and featured articles she wrote for a lesbian readership. Though the Amazonas section often appeared at the back of the magazine, the *Macho Tips* editors claimed that they wanted the section to grow and encouraged female readers to give feedback on the section and male readers to inform lesbian friends about it.[16]

Little is known about why Hidalgo de la Torre chose the title *Macho Tips*, which suggested that the magazine offered recommendations and helpful information for Mexican gay machos. This title may have appealed to middle-class gay readers who incorporated foreign words—such as tip—to denote sophistication, modernity, or cosmopolitan taste. It is also not clear why Hidalgo de la Torre had to rename his magazine, and why he then chose the title *Hermes*. According to a former collaborator of *Macho Tips*, the photographer José Luis Bueno, Hidalgo de la Torre renamed his magazine in 1990 because some public officials considered that the title *Macho Tips* was inappropriate; this assertion,

FIGURE 4.2. The Centro Académico de la Memoria de Nuestra América, in Mexico City, houses an almost complete collection of *Macho Tips* and all issues of *Hermes*.

however, cannot be verified by any written documentation.[17] Regardless of the reason, it is important to consider that, since the 1960s, gay organizations, periodicals, and commercial ventures in Europe and America had adopted names and imagery that evoked the ancient world, specifically the classical Greek trope.[18] Hidalgo de la Torre may have drawn upon the same tradition to rename his publication, even if, compared with *Macho Tips*, the new title was less significant for a Mexican readership.

Throughout the years, *Macho Tips* brought together a diverse group of activists, journalists, writers, intellectuals, artists, and other professionals that included both Mexicans and foreign nationals. Among Hidalgo de la Torre's main collaborators were the gay left activist and former FHAR member Juan Jacobo Hernández, the editor Gonzalo Pozo Pietrasanta, the photographer José Luis Bueno, and the staff members Tita Bárcenas and Rocío Sosa. Other contributors included Cheríe J. Vaughan, the visual artist Enrique Villena, the Spanish photographer Tony Brehton, and the US photographer, editor, and visual artist Jim Moss, whose work will be discussed in the following chapter. Another important collaborator was Rubén Gómez-Tagle, who was also a member of the famous Mexico City–based arts collective Taller Documentación Visual. His artwork illustrated the first five covers of the magazine, as well as the pages of many other issues, and his comic *Inches* appeared from the second to the eleventh issue. Unlike most gay liberation journals in the 1970s and 1980s, such as those examined in previous chapters, *Macho Tips* operated not as a collective but as a business. Hidalgo de la Torre, with the help of the editors, made most decisions regarding magazine content.

Macho Tips was an effective, innovative, and valuable vehicle to connect gays and lesbians in the country and to build community at the local, national, and international levels. Part of its impact and success was because it was the first gay magazine sold in Mexico's newsstands. This was no minor accomplishment, for it increased the visibility of the Mexican gay population, encouraged a sense of pride among some gay readers, and produced a gay public. For J.R., a reader from Mexico City, being able to acquire the magazine in any kiosk was extremely fulfilling, not only because it was a "special and accurate" magazine for gay people but also because it was a very important step toward recognition.[19] Yet informants recall that *Macho Tips* and *Hermes* were sold inside a plastic bag and were often concealed or located in a restricted section of the newsstands, which put consumers in the uncomfortable position of having to ask for them specifically.[20] Despite this discomfort, the presence of *Macho Tips* and *Hermes* in newsstands helped readers to imagine a local and national community of gay men. In 1987, the reader Rubén P.L. from Guanajuato congratulated the editors for editing the magazine so skillfully. *Macho Tips*, he noted, was extremely important to gay men living in states like Guanajuato where there was no institution or place of "ambiente." For Rubén and his small group of friends, the magazine was the only means of communication with Mexico's gay scene.[21] Although *Macho Tips* could hardly speak for the experiences of all gay Mexicans—or of those men who experienced same-sex desire—the lack of venues in the media for LGBTQ+ people turned the magazine into the leading gay periodical in the country. Moreover, like other contemporary gay periodicals around the world, *Macho Tips* provided gay Mexicans with a vehicle to connect with gay people abroad through the magazine's classifieds and advertising. For instance, Oscar Laguna Maqueda, an assiduous reader of the magazine, recalls having looked for friends regularly in the classified sections of *Macho Tips*. He especially remembers becoming friends with a young man from Poland who published an ad in the magazine. They exchanged letters frequently for a few years until they were able to meet in person in Poland. While Laguna Maqueda was eager to make gay friends in his adolescence, he was also afraid of being identified as homosexual by someone he knew. *Macho Tips* allowed him to get in touch with men in the farthest possible places of the world.[22]

Macho Tips was enthusiastically received in the cities where it circulated, and some sources claim that by 1987 it had a monthly circulation of around thirty thousand issues.[23] However, neither *Macho Tips* nor *Hermes* really published monthly; they published in a more intermittent way. According to the editor Gonzalo Pozo Pietrasanta, Hidalgo de la Torre's strategy was to sell out an issue before publishing a new one.[24] Every time the editorial team had a new magazine ready to publish, they would print it and take it to the Unión de Voceadores for distribution, which oversaw the distribution of all periodicals in the city.[25] After a few days, the *voceadores* would return the issues that had not been sold in the city's newsstands. *Macho Tips* staff would then send those issues to other Mexican states, such as Guanajuato, Puebla, Jalisco, and Tamaulipas, among others.[26] With few exceptions such as Guadalajara, where the gay paper *Crisálida* was published from 1983 to 1988, most cities in the country lacked a local gay newspaper.[27] For that reason, many readers across the country appreciated the existence of *Macho Tips*.

Although the internal office records of *Macho Tips* are virtually lost, its classifieds and letters sections reveal that people in various countries had access to the magazine, particularly in the United States, Latin America, and Europe. Informants do not recall whether *Macho Tips* actually sold abroad, but the covers of issues 14–20 included legends such as "USA, Canadá, Centro y Sudamérica $3.5 US dólares." Since *Macho Tips* targeted middle-class readers, presenting it as an international magazine could have been simply a sales strategy. But some issues did circulate abroad thanks to international subscriptions, exchanges of periodicals, and foreigners who purchased the magazine in Mexico and took it back to their home countries. One of those exchanges happened between *Macho Tips* and the French gay periodical *Gai pied* (1979–1991). Aside from exchanging letters and magazines, one of the *Gai pied* editors, Frank Arnal, even met with the *Macho Tips* editorial team in Mexico City in July 1986.[28] Another exchange occurred between Hidalgo de la Torre and the US editor John Rowberry in the early 1990s; their interactions and exchanges are examined in the following chapter.

Hidalgo de la Torre modeled *Macho Tips* after US erotic and pornographic magazines that he had collected over the years. Some of his close collaborators and friends, such as Juan Jacobo Hernández, Pozo Pietrasanta, and Milton Robles, recall Hidalgo de la Torre's enormous archive of international gay periodicals, which the editorial staff often perused for content to publish in *Macho Tips*. A portion of this archive, today in Robles's home, is comprised of numerous issues of 1970s and 1980s gay lifestyle and pornographic magazines.[29] These include *Manpower!*, *Manacle*, *Heat*, *Blueboy*, *Hot Chaps*, *Beef Chunks*, *Beach Punk*, and *Playgirl's Sexy Men*. Some covers of *Manpower!* and *Blueboy*—which began publishing in 1969 and 1974, respectively—were particularly similar to those of *Macho Tips* and *Hermes*. For instance, a 1980 cover of *Blueboy* and a 1986 cover of *Macho Tips* look fairly alike. The *Blueboy* cover features two white models, one with a naked torso who looks directly at the camera, and another one wearing sunglasses, a black leather jacket, and a leather hat with metallic ornaments (figure 4.3). The model on *Macho Tips* also shows a naked torso and wears a leather hat with metallic ornaments, as well as other accessories made of the same materials. Like *Blueboy*'s, the *Macho Tips* cover image also plays with light and shadows to partially conceal the face of its model (figure 4.4). Yet, regardless of the similitudes between *Macho Tips* and some US porn magazines, Hidalgo de la Torre was careful to not present his magazine as "pornographic" and apologized to people who bought it hoping to find pornography.[30]

Hidalgo de la Torre's claim necessitates revisiting how pornography is not only a contested term but also a form of sexual representation with profound implications in the history of gay and lesbian liberation. Chapter 2 examined how Canadian and US gay and lesbian liberationists in the 1970s and 1980s had diverse and often clashing understandings of what pornography was. As well, they had different appreciations of the relationship between pornography and sexual liberation. For instance, most gay men celebrated the representation of sexually explicit content in the Toronto-based *The Body Politic*, but a few of them were also

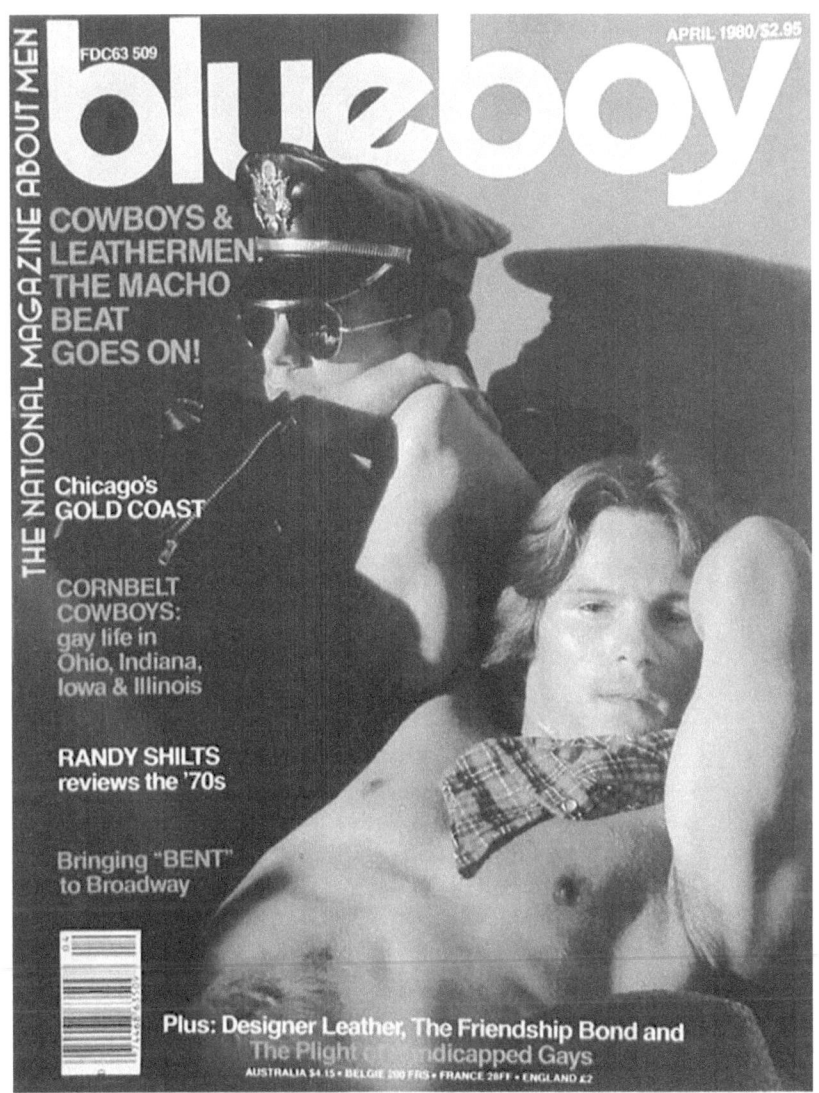

FIGURE 4.3. Cover of *Blueboy*, published in April 1980.

FIGURE 4.4. Cover of *Macho Tips*' ninth issue, published in 1986. Centro Académico de la Memoria de Nuestra América, Mexico City.

concerned about perpetuating stereotypes of gay life—particularly promiscuity. For lesbian women, the situation was far more complex, especially through the 1980s in the context of the sex wars. While sex-positive lesbians also celebrated the production of erotic and pornographic representations by and for women, other lesbian feminists advocated for stronger censorship laws—concerns about sexism, objectification of the female body, and violence against women were some of the issues that informed their perception of pornographic representations. Hidalgo de la Torre's standpoint seems more pragmatic, though. Distancing his magazines from the "pornographic" label helped him to elude censorship. Nudity featured prominently in his magazines, but *Macho Tips* never displayed erections, intercourse, or any kind of sexually explicit content. Though he surely enjoyed pornography, he would not risk the existence of his magazine.

Aside from fashioning *Macho Tips* after several US erotic and pornographic magazines, the editorial team also borrowed artwork from US and European artists to illustrate it. Some of these images are reminiscent of transnational gay liberation imagery, and the way in which *Macho Tips* used them is also reminiscent of how other gay periodicals had employed similar images before. Such was the case of the "safe-sex" illustration that was featured in several back covers of the magazine—specifically in issues 17, 18, and 19 (figure 4.5). This illustration, by US artist Michael Sabanosh, shows the back of a man who wears a blue T-shirt and tight jeans that draw attention to both his buttocks and the condom in his back pocket. The featuring of this image in *Macho Tips* is evocative of a common practice in other gay magazines that had featured male buttocks in their back covers, including *Gay Sunshine*, *The Body Politic*, and *Nuestro cuerpo* (see chapter 1). Like those magazines, *Macho Tips* published this art to celebrate the male body, gay sexuality, and homoerotic desire. In the particular context of the AIDS epidemic, this sex-positive image also served to promote safe sex.

Despite the success of *Macho Tips*, several activists had conflicting feelings about the magazine's visual content. In gay activist and scholar Xabier Lizarraga Cruchaga's view, *Macho Tips* was seriously questioned by most gay and lesbian liberation activists in Mexico because it did not adopt a *"posición sexopolítica."* Yet its content was celebrated and justified by the vast majority of the gay population not involved in the gay liberation movement.[31] Lizarraga was glad that magazines such as *Macho Tips* were able to publish and sell in newsstands, but he disliked that the "hook" to attract readers was erotic pictures of nude men instead of a more serious discourse.[32] Other activists such as Alejandro Brito were simply not interested in magazines like *Macho Tips*. Though he now regards it as a significant historical document, Brito did not read the magazine in the 1980s because it did not seem serious enough.[33] Moreover, some people remember

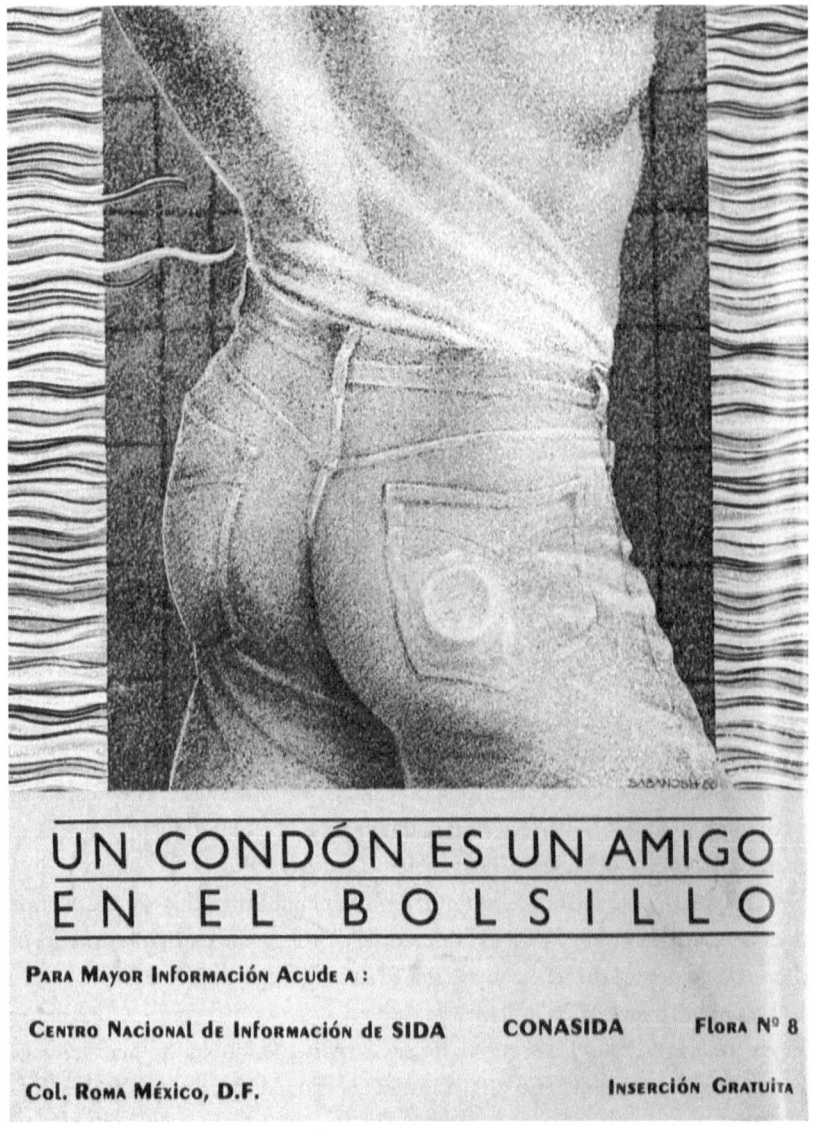

FIGURE 4.5. Some back covers of *Macho Tips* featured this illustration by US artist Michael Sabanosh. The legend reads: "A condom is a friend in the pocket."

Macho Tips as a commercial project only vaguely committed to gay liberation politics. Gay activist Braulio Peralta has observed that, following the failure of the first Mexican gay periodicals, entrepreneurs tried to make a profit by publishing magazines that featured nude men, because such magazines would compete with the international papers that circulated in the country. Peralta noted that periodicals like *Macho Tips* and the 1990s *Hermes*, *Apolo*, and *Del otro lado* were pioneers in the search for a gay market, and this, he believed, undermined their editorial quality.[34] From an international point of view, *Macho Tips* was not alone doing this kind of work. Chapters 2 and 3 have already examined how even gay liberation periodicals like *The Body Politic* and *Gay Sunshine* used erotic and sexualized imagery strategically to attract readers in the 1970s and 1980s. *Gay Sunshine* editor and entrepreneur Winston Leyland actually went a step further and founded Gay Sunshine Press publications in 1975 in order to commercialize both a gay magazine and gay literature books. Moreover, in 1984 *The Body Politic* began publishing the smaller and more commercial *Xtra!* magazine, which relied on advertising to operate. Though it was distributed for free in Toronto every second week, it allowed *The Body Politic* to raise money by appealing to a gay readership interested in consumption rather than politics.

In contrast to those who disapproved of the magazine's visual content, some people who participated in the production of *Macho Tips* grew disenchanted with Hidalgo de la Torre's apparent assimilationist stance.[35] Juan Jacobo Hernández contributed to *Macho Tips* since the periodical's second issue in 1985 and became associate editor in 1986. From 1986 to 1987 he played a central role in putting the magazine together, but eventually he resigned. In a phone conversation with US journalist Patrick Oster in the late 1980s, gay activist Mario Rivas (then Hernández's partner) observed that "Juan Jacobo hadn't liked what the magazine represented. It was careful, conservative, and safe. Its photographs of men were not very provocative. They were certainly less pornographic than those in the heterosexual skin magazines. Juan Jacobo thought Mexican gays needed more."[36] As discussed in chapter 1, through the 1970s and 1980s Hernández was deeply influenced by the most radical stance of gay liberation. In 1992, he and other activists launched the magazine *Del otro lado*, which built on the legacy of Hidalgo de la Torre's work but competed with *Hermes*, as the following chapter explains.

Macho Tips emerged out of the gay liberation movement and soon became widely circulated in Mexico City and in other major cities. Its success was at least partially attributable to its publication of erotic imagery, though the magazine also published articles covering a wide range of issues and offered readers ways of connecting with other gay men. For some gay activists in the Mexico City scene, the magazine was also a reflection of the publisher's commercial ambitions, and more conservative politics. The somewhat conservative and assimilationist stance of the magazine, as the sections below show, was particularly evident in its representation of gay masculinity and respectability. However, despite this conservative content, publishing a magazine like *Macho Tips* in 1980s Mexico was no small feat. Through his editorial work and defense of his right to publish, Hidalgo de la Torre joined a long tradition in the history of transnational gay liberation politics. This tradition, which is further explained below, brought together print culture, the visualization of homoeotic desire, and activism.

Hidalgo de la Torre, the Mexican State, and the
International Gay Press

Hidalgo de la Torre's work constituted a form of activism that capitalized on the publication of gay magazines with erotic imagery while facilitating the circulation of information relevant for gay communities in Mexico and resisting censorship. In this instance, his work was similar to that of other North American gay publishers in the second half of the twentieth century, including those who published the physique magazines that inspired his work. As David Johnson observes, the publication of physique magazines began in the postwar years when photographers and magazine publishers created a commercial network around the physical culture movement. These individuals capitalized on a male desire for physique photography and created a genre of magazines that served and united gay men throughout the United States.[37] Similar to these publishers, Hidalgo de la Torre also capitalized on the visualization of a desire for the athletic, masculine, and, in this case, racialized Mexican body. Moreover, like the publishers of physique magazines, Hidalgo de la Torre also politized that desire and created a community of gay readers who shared a similar interest in gay erotic imagery. His determination to market this desire and defend it from government censorship was a form of activism that helped to advance gay liberation in Mexico. For that reason, Hidalgo de la Torre's magazines became part of a larger history of gay print culture and liberation politics in North America; in fact, international gay periodicals, as the discussion below demonstrates, provided Hidalgo de la Torre not only with inspiration but also with tools to defend his magazine from censorship attempts.

Hidalgo de la Torre's training as an accountant, his involvement in politics, and his relationship with local government officials gave him the necessary skills to navigate Mexican bureaucracy and laws and to effectively elude censorship. Every periodical in Mexico must be registered and approved by the Comisión Calificadora de Publicaciones y Revistas Ilustradas, a government body that evaluates the content of printed publications to either ban or grant them the permission to publish.[38] To be able to circulate in the country, magazines need a "Certificado de licitud de contenido" (Legal Content Certificate), which *Macho Tips* never fully obtained.[39] In fact, in December 1987, *Macho Tips* was among a list of publications that had been suspended for infringing the law. According to an article in the newspaper *El porvenir*, this and forty-six other suspended magazines included content that contravened "Mexican social values, education, and culture."[40] The Comisión Calificadora destroyed their records of *Macho Tips* some years ago, which makes impossible to know what their assessment of the magazine was. However, considering that the magazine continued publishing in 1988, it is safe to assume that Hidalgo de la Torre reached an agreement with the Comisión and was able to elude censorship, at least until he had to rebrand the magazine as *Hermes*. The Comisión did grant *Hermes* a Certificado de licitud de contenido after assessing the first three issues of *Hermes*, which were very similar to *Macho Tips*. Interestingly, this Certificado simply mentions that the magazine included information on culture, health, and entertainment for "a special sector" of the population, without mentioning anything about its visual content.

While the sexual and erotic imagery in both *Macho Tips* and *Hermes* may have troubled the Comisión Calificadora, and indeed upset some conservative groups, this content did not prevent these magazines from circulating in the country. For instance, in 1990 the right-wing organization Alianza para la Moral (Alliance for the Moral) tried to get *Hermes* out of circulation. Members of the Alianza wrote to the Comisión Calificadora expressing their disapproval of this magazine and noting that it "was no other than the publication Macho Tips, with its same vices." They were particularly troubled by the male nudes in *Hermes*, by the ads of gay organizations that offered to "orient our children and youth," and especially by the classifieds section. They complained that this periodical was now "international, and homosexuals, bisexuals, and lesbians advertise themselves and offer their favors." The magazine, they claimed, should only circulate among the gay community instead of being sold and exhibited in newsstands.[41]

To undermine conservative critiques, Hidalgo de la Torre ingeniously and rightly reminded the Comisión Calificadora of the essential role that his magazines played in the fight against AIDS, a role that justified the use of sexual imagery to attract readers. Indeed, *Macho Tips* was from the beginning committed to informing readers on matters of sexual education and AIDS. As the journalist Federico Campbell observed in 1987, the magazine acquired special importance in the country as the most effective source of information on the epidemic.[42] Several doctors, psychologists, and psychotherapists collaborated with *Macho Tips*, including the physicians Juan Luis Álvarez Gayou, Juan Salazar Green, and Víctor Hugo Villalobos Leaño (Hidalgo de la Torre's partner), as well as the psychologists Enrique Ortiz and Mario Luis Heredia Filio. Doctors affiliated with governmental institutions also collaborated with *Macho Tips*, such as José Antonio Izazola Licea, Samuel Ponce de León, and Camilo César Guzmán Delgado. A number of articles in *Macho Tips* informed readers about the causes, transmission, symptoms, prevention, and detection of AIDS and offered useful information for practicing safe sex. Izazola Licea, coordinator of the Research and Early Detection of AIDS Program at the Secretaría de Salud (Ministry of Health), remembers being approached directly by Hidalgo de la Torre to report on AIDS for the magazine. He not only agreed but also received authorization to write on behalf of the Secretaría de Salud.[43] Hidalgo de la Torre also partnered with government officials and organizations such as the Consejo Nacional para Prevención y Control del SIDA (National Council for the Prevention and Control of AIDS, CONASIDA). Some issues of *Macho Tips* and *Hermes* also included a free condom. In fact, reminding us of the role of butterflies in the history of gay visual culture, some back covers of these issues featured a collage by US artist John Shown that depicted three colorful butterflies hovering above a condom-shaped butterfly net. A legend invited the viewer to "catch happy moments instead of risks" and to wear a condom. A smaller text box also reminded readers that the condom offered in these magazines was courtesy of the Secretaría de Salud as part of their efforts to fight AIDS and promote family planning (figure 4.6).

In the early 1990s, facing censorship attempts, Hidalgo de la Torre wrote to the Comisión Calificadora reminding them that *Hermes* was a strictly adult magazine whose main purpose was to assist in the fight against AIDS and "all the addictions that damage human health."[44] To accomplish this goal, he also requested the Comisión's consent to continue including a free condom in every issue of his magazine. This, he said, would strengthen his joint effort with CONASIDA.[45] Hidalgo de la Torre also forwarded to the Comisión materials that could attest to the positive impact of his editorial work.[46] Through these strategies, he successfully defended his right to publish and convincingly argued that erotic content was paramount in the fight against AIDS. Similar to *The Body Politic*'s justification for the use of erotic imagery in a gay liberation journal (as chapter 2 has explained), Hidalgo de la Torre argued that the visually appealing content in his magazines helped him to gain reader's acceptance and interest more easily.[47] Since the magazine published on such vital issues as the AIDS pandemic, getting as many readers as possible was a primary concern.

Hidalgo de la Torre approached the anti-AIDS campaign from a respectable, moralistic, and even nationalistic stance, which he sought to communicate to his readers and possibly to government officials as well. His September 1986 editorial

FIGURE 4.6. Some back covers of *Macho Tips* and *Hermes* featured this safe-sex collage by US artist John Shown. The legend invited readers to wear a condom and "catch happy moments" instead of AIDS. The text also informed readers that the condom included in the magazine was courtesy of the Ministry of Health.

noted that that month, in which Mexico commemorates its independence, was a good time to reflect on what he regarded as the current climate of freedom that gay Mexicans enjoyed. This freedom, he noted, had positive and negative outcomes: While it allowed the existence of *Macho Tips*, it also facilitated the propagation of AIDS. For Hidalgo de la Torre it was important that readers reflected on the boundaries of their freedom: "To live in liberty is to live in responsibility and love toward oneself and others. Selfishness, unconsciousness, and blindness are incompatible with libertarian ideals and with the Mexico we all wish for."[48] Against the backdrop of Miguel de la Madrid's moral renovation campaign and its impact on the lives of LGBTQ+ individuals, Hidalgo de la Torre's reference to a supposed climate of freedom seems deceptive, especially considering his political affinities. Nonetheless, this claim could have been one of his strategies to avoid censorship or a more severe punishment, as the president's amendment of the criminal and penal codes criminalized the publication of anti-government materials.

Regardless of how sincere Hidalgo de la Torre's claims were, his assimilationist and respectable stance permeated *Macho Tips*' overall editorial policy, which helps to explain why some people were suspicious about the links between the magazine and the government. Canadian scholar Ian Lumsden, who conducted fieldwork in Mexico City in the 1980s, wrote that the "glossy Americanized" periodical was for a while "the most visible public presence of the homosexual community in Mexico City" and "served to publicize and, in a sense, legitimize the existence of gays and lesbians."[49] However, he claimed, the magazine "was a commercial and possibly PRI-connected political venture, whose information was erratic, and which in no sense could be said to be a vehicle for communication between and on behalf of gays and lesbians. Its graphic images and editorial content in no way reflected the sexuality of most homosexuals in Mexico."[50] Hidalgo de la Torre was indeed affiliated with the PRI and had worked with politicians, but *Macho Tips* had no clear links with the PRI.[51] He never hid his political inclinations, though. Instead, he used his editorials to communicate his political sympathies and to influence readers' opinions. For instance, in the context of the 1994 presidential elections, an editorial in *Hermes* noted his intention to vote for the PRI candidate Ernesto Zedillo. His vote, he claimed, would be for those candidates with whom the gay community could fight shoulder to shoulder in the pursuit of political goals beneficial to the community and the country.[52] While a lack of documentation makes it impossible to draw any further conclusions, some informants do recall Hidalgo de la Torre's close relationship with politicians and local authorities. They even observe that to publish a magazine like *Macho Tips*, a person needed money and the support of certain government officials.⁵³ Yet the fact that Hidalgo de la Torre had to legitimize his work at the Comisión Calificadora, and was forced to rebrand his magazine, suggests that if this support existed, it had some limits.

Interestingly, the existence of an international gay press helped Hidalgo de la Torre to defend his right to publish a gay magazine with erotic imagery. In order to obtain a license to publish *Hermes*, he astutely claimed that the parameters of his printing press Febo Editores were based on the content of Mexican magazines with female nudes and of foreign periodicals with male nudes—the former had a license to publish and sell in the country. To support this argument, he forwarded to the Comisión Calificadora international gay magazines such as *Gai pied*, *Skin Flicks*, *Blueboy*, *Heat*, *All-Man*, and *Cumming Up*; the sexual imagery in all these magazines was much more explicit than in *Hermes*.⁵⁴ The female nudes in Mexican magazines, Hidalgo de la Torre argued, were much more "aggressive" than those in *Hermes* and in foreign gay magazines: "this is why it has been so hard for us to take these examples as parameters, because we are pioneers in representing male nudes in Mexico . . . our aim is the artistic nude and, to get there, we are in a constant search. . . . We need patience as we learn how to navigate this process," he claimed.⁵⁵ Hidalgo de la Torre's nationalistic rhetoric and his discussion of how his magazine compared with international gay periodicals resonated with the larger neoliberal context in which it was published. Anne Rubenstein's scholarship on comic books helps to elucidate this aspect. Rubenstein discusses how, from the 1940s through the 1970s, the Mexican publishing industry competed with the US industry. Like other local businesspeople, she explains, "Mexican publishers used nationalist rhetoric to encourage the government to protect local markets from foreign encroachment." This rhetoric aimed "to build national consensus around a kind of state capitalism" and became useful to warn against the "invasion" of US magazines, which, according to some publishers, threatened Mexican jobs.⁵⁶ The neoliberal politics of the 1980s and 1990s increased these tensions. As discussed in the following chapter, *Hermes* competed not only with new Mexican gay magazines but also with international gay periodicals with more explicit sexual imagery and, in some cases, a lower cost.

Hidalgo de la Torre's strategies to elude censorship prove the undeniable importance of his magazines in the 1980s and early 1990s in Mexico. At a time when most major cities in the country lacked a gay periodical, *Macho Tips* and later *Hermes* were crucial to circulating information about sexual health and AIDS among the LGBTQ+ population, particularly among gay readers. His battle against censorship also demonstrates how the creation of *Macho Tips* and *Hermes* should be situated within a larger, transnational history of gay publishing. Hidalgo de la Torre modeled *Macho Tips* after US gay magazines and used them to legitimize his own editorial work. This work was facilitated by a transnational circulation of gay periodicals, which was already in place by the time he launched his magazine. The success of *Macho Tips* and later *Hermes* was also indebted, at least in part, to Hidalgo de la Torre's ability to deal with government officials and to engage with a nationalist discourse. This engagement was particularly present in the visual and discursive construction of gay masculinity in *Macho Tips*, as the following section explains.

Visualizing Gay Masculinity

One of the ways *Macho Tips* fostered gay community-building was through the promotion and celebration of gay masculinity in its editorials, articles, and visual content, which included erotic photographs and advertising. This content also promoted the formation of a gay identity that embraced a macho aesthetic with deep roots in both gay and Mexican cultures. A significant amount of content in the magazine endeavored to highlight homosexuals' manliness by portraying them as masculine, virile, strong, and muscular men, thereby challenging their common depiction in the media as effeminate. Masculinity was both celebrated and exploited in the magazine for its consumption by a gay readership that had learned to idealize, desire, and emulate a gay macho aesthetic that originated in the 1970s internationally. As Martin Levine noted, from the explosion of gay liberation in the 1970s "gay men confronted, challenged and transformed existing stereotypes about male homosexuality, and the ways in which gender—masculinity—became one of the chief currencies of that transformation."[57] As part of this process, "gay men enacted a hypermasculine sexuality as a way to challenge their stigmatization as failed men, as 'sissies'"; bars, bathhouses, sex shops, and other businesses "catered to and supported this hypermasculine sexual code."[58] Men who adhered to such a style—which first emerged in San Francisco's Castro Street and Folsom Street districts as well as in other North American gay ghettos—came to be known as "clones." The clone style, in Whitney Davis's words, "was an intricately codified discipline of gay male comportment, encompassing the finest aesthetic details of facial and body hair, jeans, belts, and tees, boots and sunglasses, jackets and caps."[59]

Many of the North American gay magazines that published in the 1970s and 1980s participated in the construction, idealization, and commercialization of gay masculinity. Some magazines like *The Body Politic* did it hesitantly, while other papers such as the US periodical *Drummer* (1975–1999) profited from the consumption of gay macho culture. In relation to *The Body Politic*, Nicholas Hrynyk has discussed how the journal "mediated assumptions around what it meant to be masculine in the gay community by challenging, promoting, and visualizing macho style as an aesthetic throughout the 1970s and into the 1980s."[60] The macho aesthetic of the clone style was imported to Mexico City in the early 1980s and informed much of the visual content of *Macho Tips*. A 1986 article demonstrates that people who produced or contributed to the magazine were aware of this cultural context. The article noted that such a masculine style belonged to a generation of middle-aged gay men who had participated in the gay liberation movement or gay scene in the 1970s, following the Stonewall riots. This generation, the author continued, was characterized by their jeans, mustaches, hairstyle, and other features that were part of the macho image they promoted.[61]

While *Macho Tips* built on an international eroticization of the gay macho, the celebration of masculinity in Mexican culture has more profound implications. Scholars have discussed how, in the aftermath of the Mexican Revolution, effeminacy and homosexuality became incompatible with the new national culture the elites were trying to form, and how averting the contamination of Mexican machismo by homosexuality was central to that project.[62] Within this postrevolutionary mindset, male homosexuality—perceived as effeminate—contrasted with the exaggerated masculinity of revolutionary leaders such as Emiliano Zapata and Pancho Villa, who had "tacitly accepted the Porfirian conflation of nation, state, family honor, and male power."[63] The visual culture built around these leaders and their peasant and indigenous followers suggested that "their exaggerated manliness made up for their lesser class and ethnic status, marking them as true citizens of the nation they were hoping to remake."[64] Thus, for much of the twentieth century, mestizo, heterosexual, and hypermasculine men like Zapata epitomized an ideal of Mexican masculinity.

While definitions of Mexican machismo and macho abound, both terms broadly refer to a set of practices and ideologies that celebrate masculinity and virility. As Sergio de la Mora explains, machismo is "an ideology of heterosexual male supremacy that in Mexico gets wedded to the institutionalized postrevolutionary State apparatus."[65] Similarly, Macías-González and Rubenstein explain that macho "connotes men who expect the superior place in a vigorously defended gender hierarchy and the societies informed by such a hierarchy."[66] Recent scholarship, as Gustavo Subero observes, "shows that Latin American masculinity has evolved, and in many cases has also departed, from the stereotypical image of the macho that has been reinforced by popular culture."[67] However, while machismo and masculinity are not synonymous, the former invariably implies an enactment of the latter. Popular culture and particularly the film industry in the post-revolutionary years celebrated this vision of masculinity, while intellectuals established a correlation between machismo and Mexican culture.[68]

By the early 1970s, Macías-González and Rubenstein assert, "Mexicans appeared to agree on what typical male behavior was and seemed to know, too, what constituted exemplary male character."[69]

By enacting masculinity, *Macho Tips* "nationalized" homosexuality and engaged with a project of gay liberation—a project in which gay periodicals had played a central role since the 1970s. The appropriation of a macho aesthetic in the magazine went beyond the construction of a hypermasculine sexual code to attract Mexico's middle-class gay population. Considering that machismo and masculinity have been crucial components of Mexican culture, the appropriation of such values in the magazine constituted an effort by gay Mexicans to be participants in the construction and reproduction of a national ideology that helped them reclaim their status as Mexicans. The magazine reinforced previous efforts—such as those of FHAR discussed in chapter 1—to speak about homosexuality free of stigmas and to reclaim the public representation of homosexuals. In this regard, Sofía Argüello Pazmiño has demonstrated that the battle over the representation of homosexuality between homosexuals and the mainstream media was crucial for the development of Mexico's homosexual liberation movement. The stigmatization and misrepresentation of homosexuality in the media caused outrage among militants, bolstering the homosexual liberation movement and the participation of homosexuals in the public sphere.[70] Following in these footsteps, *Macho Tips* provided gay Mexicans with a space in the media to control their individual and collective representation. As Hidalgo de la Torre claimed in the magazine's twentieth issue, his editorial policy always focused on two main aspects: discrediting society's scandalous and negative image of homosexuals and raising consciousness about AIDS while working to avoid prejudices and misconceptions.[71] One of the ways to discredit scandalous and negative images of homosexuals was through the visual content of the magazine. By portraying gays as any other (masculine) Mexican man, the magazine sought to influence not only how heterosexuals—who might not read the magazine—saw homosexuality but also how gays might have seen, represented, and understood themselves. The magazine's visual content, editorials, articles, and classifieds encouraged certain representations and behaviors.

The publishing of photographs and advertisements played a significant role in *Macho Tips*' enactment of gay masculinity as well as in visualizing a homoerotic desire for it. Ads for bathhouses and bars in *Macho Tips* often included images of hunky, muscular men whose urban, industrial, and working-class attire epitomized a model of gay masculinity. This visual culture resonates with Levine's assertion that, since the 1970s, "gay men embraced other marginalized, but far more masculine definitions of masculinity. They expressed their new sense of self

FIGURE 4.7. Ad for the gay bar El Taller, published in some issues of *Macho Tips*.

by wearing the attire of the working class."[72] The imagery in ads for and articles about Luis González de Alba's gay bars El Taller (The Workshop) and La Cantina del Vaquero (The Cowboy's Pub) included representations of such men that idealized and eroticized working-class masculinity. One of the ads for El Taller showed a drawing of a shirtless, athletic man fixing a car; the bearded yet young mechanic wore overalls and black boots and carried a wrench in his back pocket. His image was framed by a tire topped with the silhouette of a naked body, which further eroticized the scene. In another ad, a middle-aged, attractive man was photographed wearing overalls and helmet to promote El Taller, his legs flanked by images of gears and wheels while he stands in front of the bar (figure 4.7).

An article in the magazine described El Taller as a men-only bar in a basement that promised the adventure of entering a labyrinth of screws, nuts, chains, and gears. El Taller, the article noted, sought to provide "to ALL MEN WHO LIKE MEN an ample and comfortable space."[73] The use of capital letters to highlight a portion of the phrase, along with the photographs accompanying the article, clearly conveyed what being a man meant as well as how he should look. The photographic record of El Taller and La Cantina del Vaquero in the magazine shows the bars' gay clientele and bartenders performing masculinity by sporting mustaches and wearing jeans, tank tops, overalls, and boots.[74] Some patrons of El Taller were also portrayed playing with the bar's decor, which emulated a mechanical workshop by including gears, chains, crane hooks, and presses. Among other gay businesses that used imagery of masculine men to advertise in *Macho Tips* was Spartacu's, a nightclub in the outskirts of Mexico City. Published regularly in the magazine, an ad for this nightclub depicted a muscular, seminude man whose attire evoked that of Roman gladiators or centurions. His posture, gaze, and stern expression signaled masculinity and virility, which illustrates Hrynyk's observation that, aside from a working-class aesthetic, macho style also evoked a Greco-Roman style of male musculature and whiteness that further confronted stereotypes of gay male effeminacy.[75]

In publishing these ads and photographs alongside other images that celebrated gay masculinity, *Macho Tips* contributed to the visualization of homoerotic desires and thus to a politics of gay liberation that had informed the history of gay print culture in North America since the 1970s. Its pages contained numerous drawings, photographs, and art that celebrated masculinity and macho aesthetics by featuring bodybuilders and muscular men in uniforms, leather, sporty attire, briefs, and jockstraps. For example, artwork by Tom of Finland and Harry Bush depicting hypermasculine men was featured in the magazine occasionally, such as in the eighth issue. *Macho Tips* also consistently reprinted images of masculine men (most of whom were white) that the editors had taken from US, Canadian, or European gay magazines. These images were used to illustrate articles, the classifieds, or entire pages of the magazine. Like other editors and entrepreneurs such as Winston Leyland, Hidalgo de la Torre knew his market well, and with these images he effectively catered to a homoerotic desire for masculine gay men at a time when no other magazine in Mexico would do so.

In some cases, *Macho Tips*' enactment of masculinity, and the way people responded to it, reflected a "politics of respectability" concerned with the assimilation of gay people into the dominant heteronormative values of Mexican society.[76] In a 1985 article, Víctor Villalobos Cuevas evoked a past when men were more preoccupied with appearing manly and respectful.[77] He recalled those men who visited El Eco, a discreet bar with an extremely manly gay clientele who dressed formally and sought nothing but conversation.[78] Since bars were places where, in his opinion, homosexuals could have fun, socialize, feel part of a community, and find sexual partners or love, it was important for the clients to be attractive to others—in other words, to be masculine. Nowadays, he complained, "it seems like pansies or transvestites were the most attractive."[79] A year later, Julián Pizá's article "Libertinaje vs. Gay" complained that homosexuals often confused liberty with debauchery. Homosexuals, he claimed, had to follow some scripts and norms that regulate life within society and had to practice their sexuality in private. For him, it was necessary to debunk clichés associated with homosexuality and to show that a gay man was a productive individual. Pizá's homonormative view led him to claim that the best way that gays could gain social acceptance was to be productive while avoiding effeminate, scandalous behaviors. Should someone display these behaviors, he suggested that they resort to legal, psychological, or medical guidance to overcome them.[80] The letters section of *Macho Tips* offers insight into how readers perceived the representation of gay masculinity and respectability in the magazine. A reader from Mexico City encouraged the editors to continue the laudable work of publishing the magazine so that all homosexuals "could be worthy exponents of the gay population" as well as be able to dignify their world by "debunking taboos with their proper conduct and behavior."[81] Another reader also highlighted *Macho Tips*' importance among Mexico's gay population; the magazine, he thought, helped to fight the "exhibitionism" and "ridicule" of homosexuals.[82] Both letters recall one of the major conflicts among gay activists throughout the 1980s in relation to the assimilationist stance of some groups. In 1984, for instance, the gay organization Colectivo Sol complained that some groups in the homosexual liberation movement were left powerless because they sold themselves to their desire for tolerance and social acceptance and started trying to convince others of being "de categoría" (of good rank) by, for instance, getting a stable and well-paying job.[83]

Although *Macho Tips* occasionally published articles about famous cross-dressers and drag performers, the magazine constructed and promoted a gay identity grounded in masculinity and that aligned with the current conservative climate in Mexico City.[84] In fact, the visual representation of and attention to cross-dressing in the magazine was quite marginal compared with the magazine's emphasis on masculinity. Even when gay bars such as Spartacu's or L'Baron advertised drag shows, their imagery alluded only to masculinity.[85] This occurred because, as Renaud René Boivin observes, an emphasis on virility was at the base of gay middle-class community formation in the 1970s and 1980s; this emphasis counteracted the effeminate image imposed by the heterosexual perspective, not only in Mexico but elsewhere. As a result of this process, some members of gay middle-class communities marginalized individuals who did not adopt the new conceptualization of gay masculinity. For example, in the 1980s, some of Mexico City's gay establishments began to replace drag shows with spectacles of muscled, virile men; other businesses, such as El Taller and La Cantina del Vaquero, even forbade entrance to women, trans people, and effeminate men and imposed a dress code.[86] Looking manly, though, was also a strategy to avoid police brutality. This was especially important in 1980s Mexico City, as police repression, extortion, and raids on gay and lesbian bars and communities had increased during Miguel de la Madrid's moral renovation campaign.[87]

Macho Tips thus appropriated, eroticized, and commodified Mexican national values of gender to make a profit, challenge the marginalization of gay men, and promote an image of gay respectability. But enacting masculinity was also at the core of the development of a middle-class gay identity at the local, national, and international levels; as the leading gay magazine in Mexico, *Macho Tips* played a central role in advancing and promoting this identity. This was particularly clear in the erotic imagery of the magazine, informed by national ideas of both gender and race. Through this imagery, the magazine participated in the construction and reproduction of Mexico's powerful discourse of race mixture in an unprecedented fashion in order to cater to both domestic and international consumers who craved the Mexican masculine body. Such imagery is the focus of this chapter's final section.

Mestizo Aesthetics and the Desire for Brown Mexican Bodies

Macho Tips is particularly remembered for its erotic visual content and especially for its color supplements and centerfolds with photographs of nude, and masculine, Mexican-looking men. In producing and commercializing these images, the magazine catered to and fostered a desire for these representations, and in doing so, it contributed to one of the central goals of gay liberation: the celebration and visualization of homoerotic desires. The previous three chapters have examined different ways in which gay periodicals in North America accomplished this goal. They have also examined how the body and its visual representation were central to the project of celebrating and visualizing homoerotic desires. The final section of this chapter continues to analyze both aspects with a focus on the erotic imagery of *Macho Tips*, imagery that was charged with Mexican national values of race and gender.

The erotic imagery in *Macho Tips* evolved over the years, emulating first the visual content of international gay periodicals and later developing its own identity. Various professional photographers collaborated with *Macho Tips* in the production of this imagery, including José Luis Bueno, Juan Carlos Yustis, Tony Brehton, and Jim Moss, among many others. In its first issues, *Macho Tips* presented white men as objects of desire, but by late 1986 the magazine began turning its attention from light-skinned, blue-eyed models to men with a mestizo appearance. The May 1986 issue published an ad informing readers that, if they were good looking and had a nice body, they could be the next *Macho Tips* model (figure 4.8). In December of the same year, the magazine informed its readers that it was looking for Mexican adults "of all types" to be featured in the following issues, although the editors pointed out their preference for masculine-looking men.[88] A few months later, the magazine explained that it sought to "enrich" its visual content by portraying the masculine body from "different perspectives": classic and contemporary, national and international, aesthetic and erotic.[89] Although white men continued to be featured in the magazine, Mexican-looking models quickly outnumbered the former. Over time, *Macho Tips* and later *Hermes* were easily identified by their covers with seminude brown men—full nudity was only featured in the color supplements—and many former readers remember both periodicals precisely because of their photographs of such men.[90]

The fetishization and commodification of the Mexican body in *Macho Tips* implied both a strategy to attract readers and a participation in the construction and reproduction of Mexico's national discourse of *mestizaje*, or race mixture. As Mónica Moreno explains, *mestizaje* is a term that encompasses both the processes of race mixture that started in Mexico with the sixteenth-century Spanish invasion and the "discourses of inclusion and belonging to the nation."[91] In the words of Florencia Mallon, this narrative emerged as an official discourse of nation formation "that denies colonial forms of racial/ethnic hierarchy and oppression by creating an intermediate subject and interpellating him/her as 'the citizen.'"[92] As a narrative of national belonging, *mestizaje* has been a recurrent trope in different forms of cultural and ideological production in Mexico. The invocation of *mestizaje* in Latin America, as Marilyn Miller observes, "is always framed by local histories and contemporary sociopolitical conditions, contexts, and conditions which, in turn, re-dress it according to specific national and transnational concerns."[93] In the case of *Macho Tips*, this invocation entailed a desire to link gay cultural production to a nationalist discourse while making a profit.

FIGURE 4.8. With this ad, the sixth issue of *Macho Tips* (1986) began informing readers that, if they were good looking and had a nice body, they could be the next model in the magazine.

Although Hidalgo de la Torre may not have intended to explicitly engage with a discourse of *mestizaje*, the erotic photographs in his magazines invariably negotiated and (homo)sexualized this powerful narrative of racial identity, as well as its gender and class connotations. In this regard, it is important to consider the relationship between machismo, race, and class. As Matthew Gutmann has pointed out, the portrayal of machismo in Mexico "has been uniquely linked to the poor, unsophisticated, uncosmopolitan, and un–North American"—or, one could argue, to the Mexican mestizo.[94] The photographer José Luis Bueno attributes the predominant depiction of brown Mexican-looking men in *Macho Tips* to Hidalgo de la Torre's particular preferences.[95] Other informants, such as Antonio González de Cosío and Pozo Pietrasanta, note that those were the models who agreed to be photographed in the magazine; since some of them already worked as strippers at gay establishments, they had nothing to lose by posing for a gay magazine.[96] Intentional or not, Hidalgo de la Torre's preference for brown models shows why scholars have referred to *mestizaje* as "a master narrative of national identity for much of Latin America."[97] The conscious or unconscious equation of Mexican with mestizo has been present in much of the country's cultural production throughout the twentieth century. The mestizo masculine models in *Macho Tips* embodied this master narrative of racial identity. Through the evocation and commodification of *mestizaje*, *Macho Tips* participated in nation-building and appealed to the desires of gay middle classes both in Mexico and abroad who craved the consumption of the Mexican masculine body.

Three series of photographs, published in the fourteenth, nineteenth, and twenty-first issues of *Macho Tips*, provide compelling examples of how the magazine advanced *mestizaje* as an aesthetic to represent the national body and offer appealing depictions of Mexican masculine men. Miguel, a young brown Mexican photographed by Tony Brehton, was featured on the fourteenth issue's cover wearing only a thong, a band on his forehead, and an armband decorated with what appears to be animal teeth. His rudimentary though suggestive attire, as well as his holding of wood sticks behind his back, evoked Mexico's precolonial, even primitive, past (figure 4.9). In another photograph in the color supplement, Miguel posed in front of a wall covered with *paliacates*, a traditional handkerchief commonly used in Mexican folk dances or simply as an accessory. The colorful wall was also reminiscent of Mexico's popular culture. The cover and color supplement of *Macho Tips*' nineteenth issue featured Sergio Andrade, a twenty-year-old student from Mexico City who was photographed by Jim Moss.[98] In some photographs, Andrade was portrayed wearing jeans, a tank top, and a straw hat, surrounded by agave plants (figure 4.10). All these features were clear signifiers of a *mexicanidad mestiza*, or a mixed-race Mexicanness. In

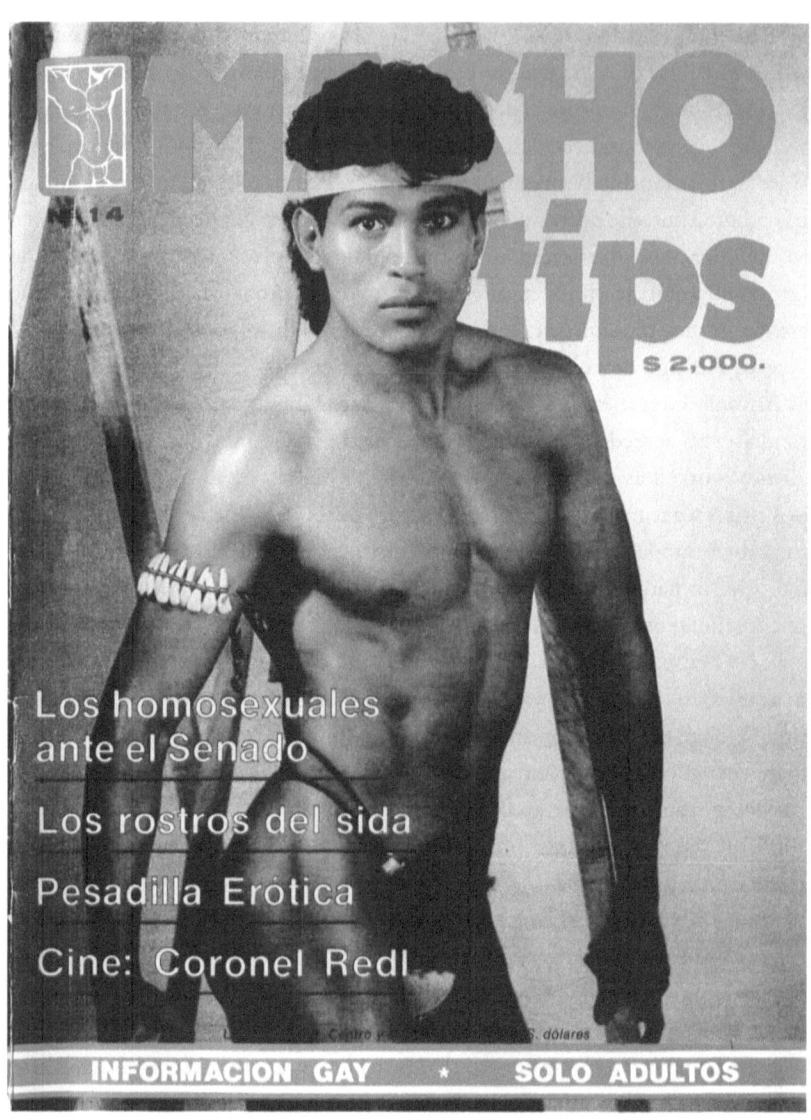

FIGURE 4.9. Published in 1987, the fourteenth issue of *Macho Tips* featured a model named Miguel Vázquez, photographed by Tony Brehton. Centro Académico de la Memoria de Nuestra América, Mexico City.

FIGURE 4.10. Published in 1987, the nineteenth issue of *Macho Tips* featured a model named Sergio Andrade, photographed by Jim Moss. Centro Académico de la Memoria de Nuestra América, Mexico City.

modelo **Adrián**
fotos de David Flores

FIGURE 4.11. The twenty-first issue of *Macho Tips*, published in 1989, featured photographs by David Flores. He photographed a model named Adrián in what appears to be a tropical setting. Centro Académico de la Memoria de Nuestra América, Mexico City.

other photographs, Andrade posed naked in settings with mud walls, old bejuco furniture, and cement floors. The conjunction of these elements was a sign of a poor, old-fashioned Mexico, which was also a component in other pictures. For example, in the ninth issue's color supplement, Brehton photographed Alejandro—another Mexican-looking model—in an old, dirty, and deteriorated bathroom.[99] The invocation of Mexico's indigenous heritage was clearer in a series of six photographs by David Flores printed in the magazine's twenty-first issue. In these black-and-white pictures, the young model Adrián posed naked in what seems to be a tropical setting, with tropical trees in the background. In three of those pictures, Adrián was portrayed sitting on top of an anthropomorphic stone sculpture (figure 4.11). The carving and the greenish landscape that surrounded Adrián evoked the Olmecs, an indigenous group that inhabited Mexico's tropical east coast and is well known for its monumental sculptures.[100]

The way that *Macho Tips* exoticized Mexico's indigenous past and popular culture while celebrating masculinity to appeal to gay middle-class consumers both in Mexico and abroad mirrors what for other North American periodicals was a sales strategy. Lucas Hilderbrand has examined how race and ethnicity intersected with sexuality in gay travel magazines' projections of gay male desire. US magazines like *Ciao!*, he argues, tended to construct images of "exotically primitive destination[s] with pliable, masculine young dudes for gays with 'liberated' identities."[101] In some cases, Hilderbrand notes, the models' "stylings attempted to suggest some kind of 'timeless' exoticism, even when the featured model was white."[102] In *Macho Tips*, the portrayal of an "exotically primitive," "timeless," and poor Mexico clearly sought to fulfill certain sexual desires and fantasies. This portrayal is reminiscent of the visual content that Winston Leyland included in *Gay Sunshine* and Gay Sunshine Press publications with Latin American content, the focus of the previous chapter. Similar to those images, the erotic imagery in *Macho Tips* portrayed, at least to some extent, what Hiram Pérez calls "the primitive brown body of cosmopolitan desire."[103] What is interesting about these images is that, despite their exoticizing attributes, most of them also disrupt the traditional canon of white gay primitivism; in marketing brown Mexican machos to gay consumers, Hidalgo de la Torre's editorial practices depart in significant ways from the work of other editors, like Winston Leyland. The men in *Macho Tips* are not the effeminate and/or passive receiver of the white gay male traveler. Their masculinity and agency are powerfully signaled in their frank stares at the camera, which do not read as a passive and pliable visual rhetoric.

Some of the formal features that accompanied the erotic content in *Macho Tips* and *Hermes* were also similar to those in other international, pioneering periodicals with erotic imagery. For instance, one interesting component of the color supplements and centerfolds in *Macho Tips* and *Hermes* was the addition of a short bio of the featured models, which may have served two purposes. The first one was to ease the reception of erotic and sexualized imagery among both a gay and straight viewership. Several models were introduced as students or young professionals, thus implying that they were respectable individuals. This is similar to what Johnson identified in physique magazines such as Bob Mizer's *Physique Pictorial*—founded in 1951, this was the first large-circulation magazine targeting gay men in the United States.[104] Johnson notes, "To counter the perception of both gay men and bodybuilders as degenerates, Mizer's biographical notes gave his models middle-class respectability, highlighting not only their physical attributes but also their alleged intellectual and professional ambitions."[105] This was also the strategy of *Playboy*'s founder and editor-in-chief Hugh Hefner. As Elspeth Brown observes, Hefner accompanied *Playboy*'s centerfold "with some sort of narratives about the girl's hobbies in an effort to deobjectify them."[106] The second purpose of these biographical notes in *Macho Tips* and *Hermes* was to present a fictional identity for the models to sell a fantasy of masculinity. The content of the photographs and the biographical notes indicates

FIGURE 4.12. A model named Alan was featured on the cover and centerfold of *Macho Tips*' sixteenth issue in 1987. He was photographed by José Luis Bueno.

that some of these models were bodybuilders, athletes, and strippers. For example, José Luis Bueno photographed Alan wearing his football uniform for the magazine's sixteenth issue. His bio stated: "Taurus, 21 years old. We owe his body to the practicing of football, diving, bodybuilding, aerobics, and to a generous Mother Nature" (figure 4.12).[107] One of the alleged secret desires of Mauro, a brown stripper from Veracruz photographed by Héctor Briceño in the twentieth issue, was "to be an actor, and to see, through a keyhole, two women making love."[108] In his pictures, Mauro posed as a mechanic, rubbing cotton fiber on his body, sitting on wheels, and surrounded by tires. That *Macho Tips* sold fantasies is further demonstrated by the fact that in 1991, two years after being featured in *Macho Tips*, Sergio Andrade posed for *Hermes* in cowboy attire, though this time he was introduced as "Valentin."[109]

The formal features of *Macho Tips*' erotic imagery, the composition of the photographs, and the engagement of the models with the camera were paramount to the successful representation of Mexican masculinity and to effectively cater to a desire for brown bodies. Scholars such as Elspeth Brown have demonstrated how "the production of desire" has been central to fashion photography as well as to commercial culture and queer history.[110] In her words, "The fashion industry, in particular, is in the business of producing such an eroticized affect, since desire is the prelude to buying."[111] She also observes that "the affective necessarily requires the work of the body in producing physiologically charged emotions."[112] Although *Macho Tips* was not a fashion magazine, the "affective labor" of its models and the emotions it triggered among readers were vital to the success of the magazine, as they acted as a hook for readers and led to sales. The covers and centerfolds in *Macho Tips* and *Hermes* offer numerous examples of how this occurred. For instance, one issue of *Macho Tips* with particularly charged emotions was the seventeenth. Its cover image features a photograph of the famous Mexican stripper Roger taken by the US photographer Jim Moss. In this photograph, Roger looks directly at the camera and strikes a seductive pose waist-deep in a pool, touching his head with both hands while water cascades down his body (figure 4.13). Roger was well-known among the gay community because of his show at the gay bar Spartacu's. People especially remember the part of the show in which Roger shook his penis inside their drinks. Because of the public's familiarity with Roger, this cover image must have attracted several readers who wanted to look at his pictures, and possibly the rest of the magazine. His fame undoubtedly shaped how readers perceived these images, because "the sociability of models off-camera," as Brown argues, is crucial to the success of their representations.[113] Interestingly, in this issue, Roger was featured with no other signifiers of Mexican masculinity beside his brown body. And the color supplement reveals what the cover image conceals; he appears fully naked in the centerfold. Also interesting is the fact that someone began to sell unauthorized copies of some *Macho Tips* issues in 1987, including this one. A note in the nineteenth issue warned readers about these pirated copies and asked readers to not buy them—some of these pirate issues can be found in the LGBTQ Serials collection at The ArQuives, in Toronto.

While *Macho Tips* arguably fetishized brown, Mexican male beauty, it is important to note that Hidalgo de la Torre did not simply "exploit" models. Informants recall how Hidalgo de la Torre, members of the *Macho Tips* staff, and some models often developed friendships and affective bonds, and willingly engaged in sexual interactions. Although the relationship between many of them was surely not equal—especially not with Hidalgo de la Torre, a businessman and employer—some level of comradeship must have been present. One visual record that attests to this comradeship is a black-and-white photograph from the mid-1980s portraying a number of men involved in *Macho Tips*, including staff, models, Hidalgo de la Torre, and some of his friends (figure 4.14). The group

FIGURE 4.13. The cover and centerfold of *Macho Tips*' seventeenth issue (1987) featured Roger, a famous Mexican stripper, photographed by Jim Moss. Centro Académico de la Memoria de Nuestra América, Mexico City.

FIGURE 4.14. Photograph featuring some members of *Macho Tips*' editorial team and models. Top row, from left to right: the photographer José Luis Bueno, the model and stripper Roger, the medical doctor Víctor Hugo Villalobos Leaño (Hidalgo de la Torre's partner), a model identified as Alan, and Hidalgo de la Torre. In the bottom row, the art collector Milton Robles is second from left. Courtesy of José Luis Bueno.

of men in the picture smile for the camera while sitting close to each other. On the top right of the picture, Hidalgo de la Torre poses with his arm on Alan's shoulder—the model featured on the sixteenth issue wearing football attire. On the opposite side, the photographer José Luis Bueno holds his camera looking serious and professional while Roger, sitting next to him, stares at the camera with his usual seductive look. Overall, the picture suggests a somewhat horizontal relationship, friendship, and some level of affection and respect among these men.

Finally, it is also important to note that the sexual imagery in *Macho Tips* and *Hermes* provided an alternative to the dominant erotic representations of white men for gay consumers in most contemporary gay periodicals. These periodicals, which included those that inspired Hidalgo de la Torre's work, associated musculature, manliness, and beauty with whiteness. Although the formal features and editorial content of *Macho Tips* and *Hermes* emulated those publications, the mestizo body acquired a chief role in Hidalgo de la Torre's magazines. In fact, the eroticization of the Mexican body in both magazines resonates with Gustavo Subero's analysis of the representation of mestizo men in the Mexican-produced pornography of Mecos Films. Subero argues that this pornography offers an alternative to dominant representations of Latinx homosexuality that already circulate in the gay imaginary; in this pornography, "the mestizo gay man is presented as a valid sexual choice who is not regarded as an inferior Other."[114] However, unlike Mecos Films, *Macho Tips* and later *Hermes* did not offer a satire or a parodic criticism of machismo. Both magazines actually engaged with and reproduced traditional representations of masculinity as portrayed in Mexican popular culture. They embraced and idealized macho and mestizo aesthetics but claimed them for the gay community by (homo)sexualizing and subverting their values.

Though *Macho Tips* never stopped featuring fairer, white-looking models, ten out of eighteen color supplements with male nudes featured mestizo-looking men. In *Hermes*, the numbers were also balanced because each issue included more than one supplement—there was a model for anyone's preference. However, almost all of the twenty-six covers of the magazine featured Mexican-looking models. Hidalgo de la Torre's editorial work thus expanded the options available for gay consumers in Mexico, offering them an option to purchase erotic magazines that evoked a racial and gendered discourse of Mexican male beauty. In visualizing a desire for such representations, Hidalgo de la Torre successfully created a market for them and expanded a visual erotic archive in gay print culture that celebrated homoerotic desires.

MACHO TIPS OFFERS A UNIQUE opportunity to examine how gay periodicals, images, and the visualization of homoerotic desires advanced gay liberation in Mexico, and beyond, in the 1980s. The somewhat conservative construction of masculinity and the eroticization of the "national body" in *Macho Tips* served a variety of purposes. One was to challenge stereotypes that marginalized gay men in Mexico, especially those that regarded them as effeminate. Presenting gay Mexicans as macho resonated with the cult of masculinity in Mexican popular culture and therefore helped to legitimize homosexuality in Mexico. This nationalistic rhetoric speaks for the larger sociopolitical context in which the magazine published. This context was shaped by President Miguel de la Madrid's moral renovation campaign, neoliberal reforms, the AIDS crisis, and conflicts among gay and lesbian liberation activists.

Considering this context, another purpose of engaging with national discourses of gender and race may have been to avoid censorship. Even though *Macho Tips* was a gay magazine with erotic imagery, its content did not threaten the Mexican state in significant ways. Establishing a connection between homosexuality, macho culture, and *mestizaje* was surely subversive, and promoting a gay lifestyle undermined the government's dream of moral renovation. Yet the somewhat "normative" representation of gender and race in *Macho Tips* resonated with and supported the revolutionary nationalism that shaped the long period of PRI's hegemonic rule from 1929 through the late twentieth century. In this instance, *Macho Tips* stood in stark contrast to foreign gay periodicals with circulation in the country and which celebrated Western male beauty. Unlike those foreign periodicals, *Macho Tips* and later *Hermes* provided gay Mexicans with a local magazine that presented Mexican men as objects of desire. Moreover, both magazines played an important role in the battle against the AIDS epidemic. Hidalgo de la Torre partnered with government officials and approached the anti-AIDS campaign from a nationalist and respectable stance. All these aspects, along with Hidalgo de la Torre's own links with the PRI, ensured the survival of his magazines.

Another purpose of *Macho Tips*' engagement with national discourses of gender and race was to advance gay liberation while also making a profit. Hidalgo de la Torre's editorial work built on a long tradition in gay print culture that placed sexual and erotic imagery at the center of gay community-building, identity formation, and sexual liberation. The visual content of his magazines advanced core projects of gay liberation, namely, the celebration and visualization homoerotic desires. The discursive and visual representation of masculinity and race in *Macho Tips* successfully appealed to the desires of domestic and international gay middle-class consumers who craved the brown, working-class, and hypermasculine Mexican-looking body. Through *Macho Tips* and *Hermes*, Hidalgo de la Torre created a gay market for these kinds of representations in Mexico, and as shown in the following chapter, his work was part of a larger history of North American gay consumer culture.

| 5 |

The Gay Editorial Market and the Transnational Production of Racialized Desires

When the US editor, artist, and pornographer Jim Moss moved to Mexico City in the 1980s, he began to produce erotica that featured brown Mexican-looking men and to work with the *Macho Tips* director Aurelio Refugio Hidalgo de la Torre. Aside from contributing to *Macho Tips* with photographs, Moss also connected Hidalgo de la Torre with other artists and editors based in the United States, including the visual artist John Shown and the editor John Rowberry. By the time Hidalgo de la Torre had renamed his magazine *Hermes* in 1990, his transnational network was expanding, and this allowed him to redesign his magazine and acquire new material for publication. In turn, this network also allowed US artists and editors to acquire material for their own publications and to expand their audiences. Like Moss and Hidalgo de la Torre, these gay artists and editors were particularly interested in producing or buying erotic and pornographic material that depicted brown Mexican and Latino models. Although whiteness dominated the visual content of gay periodicals in the 1970s and 1980s, in the late 1980s and through the 1990s some gay editors and artists in Mexico and the United States began to think of the Mexican and Latino body as marketable. Hidalgo de la Torre, Moss, and Rowberry were at the forefront of this change. Through their editorial and artistic work, these white, middle-class gay men created a network to produce and circulate gay magazines, erotic imagery, and pornography that centered on Mexican and Latino men and that catered to Mexican and US middle-class gay consumers. Although their US audience was implicitly white, their work also catered to Hispanic gay men, because this change in gay periodicals' erotic representations coincided with the growth of the US Hispanic market. This growth, outlined below, began in the 1960s but acquired greater force in the 1970s and especially in the 1980s.[1]

Considering this larger historical context, this chapter develops two interconnected arguments. The first argument is that Hidalgo de la Torre created a gay market for the brown Mexican body in Mexico through his editorial work in *Macho Tips* and *Hermes*. His motivations, this chapter contends, were both political and commercial. On one hand, his editorial work challenged dominant representations of homoerotic desire since the late 1980s through the eroticization of brown and masculine Mexican models. In doing so, he expanded notions of the erotic and advanced the liberation of homoerotic desire. On the other hand, because of his pioneering work in the previous decade, the 1990s saw the emergence of several gay lifestyle and erotic magazines in Mexico City, such as *Del otro lado* (On the Other Side), a magazine that also conceived of the visualization of homoerotic desire as constitutive of gay liberation. Since *Hermes* had to compete with these periodicals and with the international magazines that circulated in the country, Hidalgo de la Torre sought ways to differentiate his magazines from other gay periodicals. The eroticization of masculine brown models thus became the distinctive feature of his publications, while magazines like *Del otro lado* favored erotic imagery with white men—at least on its covers.

The second argument of this chapter is that the network that Hidalgo de la Torre, Jim Moss, John Rowberry, and John Shown formed in the late 1980s and early 1990s helped to consolidate a market for pornographic representations of Latino men for gay consumers in the United States. Their work, this chapter contends, fits into the larger history of the emergence and growth of the US Hispanic market. In a white-dominated gay consumer culture, these editors and artists identified a largely untapped market and began to produce erotic imagery and pornography depicting Mexican and Latino men for both white and Hispanic gay consumers. Neither this network nor any of its members alone could be credited with creating these markets. However, their communication and, especially, the network they created did have an important outcome: the consolidation of markets for pornographic representations of these type of men for gay consumers in North America.

This chapter discusses how the representation of racialized desires in gay periodicals published in the 1980s and 1990s intersected with the project of gay liberation in North America. Men like Hidalgo de la Torre, Moss, Rowberry, and Shown worked to reconceptualize what was considered erotic and desirable in gay cultural production. But as the analysis below demonstrates, some of their practices also perpetuated the exploitation of people because of their race and class. Drawing on different bodies of scholarship, the chapter tackles those tensions between liberation and oppression and examines the complex implications of sexual desire in the transnational history of gay liberation. The aim of this chapter is not to deploy an analytical framework that would merely describe the production and visualization of a desire for brown bodies in pornography as good or bad, as oppressive or liberating, as racist or simply sexy.[2] Instead, this chapter explains how the production and visualization of this desire fostered the formation of transnational networks of editors and artists invested in editorial projects that expanded notions of the erotic. While the chapter will critically assess the work and aims of these men, it will also explore how the emergence of a market for their work fits within, and complicates, the transnational history of gay liberation.

The chapter begins with a discussion of how *Hermes* continued the same editorial practices that had shaped *Macho Tips*, specifically regarding visual content. Then, the chapter discusses the expansion of Mexico's gay publishing industry, discussing how the erotic imagery of *Hermes* compared to the visual content of other gay magazines that circulated in the country in the 1990s. One of those magazines was *Del otro lado*, which the Mexico City–based group Colectivo Sol launched in 1992. The second half of the chapter discusses three key figures in the history of gay print culture and the network they created with Hidalgo de la Torre: Jim Moss, John Rowberry, and John Shown. By analyzing their work and their relationship with Hidalgo de la Torre in the late 1980s and early 1990s, the chapter traces the connection between this network, the growth of the US Hispanic market, and the increasing production of gay erotica and pornography depicting Latino brown men in North America during those years.

Hermes in (Trans)National Perspective

After Hidalgo de la Torre renamed *Macho Tips* in 1990, the content and format of the new magazine remained virtually the same. Under the new name of *Hermes* and with a circulation of forty thousand issues, the new magazine published twenty-six issues over four years.³ Like *Macho Tips*, *Hermes* continued to inform readers about important topics, such as the state of the AIDS epidemic, and it helped them to connect at local, national, and international levels through the classifieds section. The magazine also continued to be highly popular and successful among the Mexican gay public because of its sexual imagery that eroticized Mexican-looking masculine models. Although archival sources suggest that the Comisión Calificadora de Publicaciones y Revistas Ilustradas revoked *Macho Tips*' license because of complaints from conservative groups about the visual content and classifieds of *Macho Tips*, these features remained unchanged in the new magazine.⁴ Since most readers purchased these magazines for their erotic imagery and classifieds, it is understandable that Hidalgo de la Torre would not give in to any pressure to remove or change those sections.

In fact, *Hermes* contained more erotic material than its former version *Macho Tips*, and the representation of Mexican-looking models remained the most characteristic feature of the magazine, as its covers demonstrate. *Hermes* had more color supplements with male nudes and the models were quite diverse, as the color supplements in each issue featured both Mexican-looking and white models. However, the majority of the twenty-six covers of *Hermes* featured Mexican-looking models. The cover images on the seventh and tenth issues illustrate how *Hermes* followed *Macho Tips*' editorial practice of eroticizing brown, Mexican-looking, and masculine models to appeal to consumers. On both covers, a brown muscled model poses seminude against a setting that evokes a tropical landscape. On the seventh issue, the model wears nothing but a thong and poses against a background with sunset colors and a palm tree (figure 5.1); on the cover of the tenth issue, the model holds a hammock around his body and poses against a jungle backdrop with tropical vegetation, a toucan, and a macaw (figure 5.2). Both covers situate the Mexican body close to nature, following a representational strategy also present in other gay magazines' depictions of nonwhite models, particularly Blacks.⁵

These kinds of covers had been crucial to the success of Hidalgo de la Torre's magazines, not only because they appealed to readers' desires but also because these covers provided his magazines with an identity. On the one hand, readers were able to identify these magazines as periodicals that offered visual pleasure and relevant information for gay consumers. On the other hand, readers who

FIGURE 5.1. Cover of *Hermes*'s seventh issue, published in 1992. The model, named Armando, was photographed by Víctor Hugo Villa. The latter, according to some informants, was Víctor Hugo Villalobos Leaño. Centro Académico de la Memoria de Nuestra América, Mexico City.

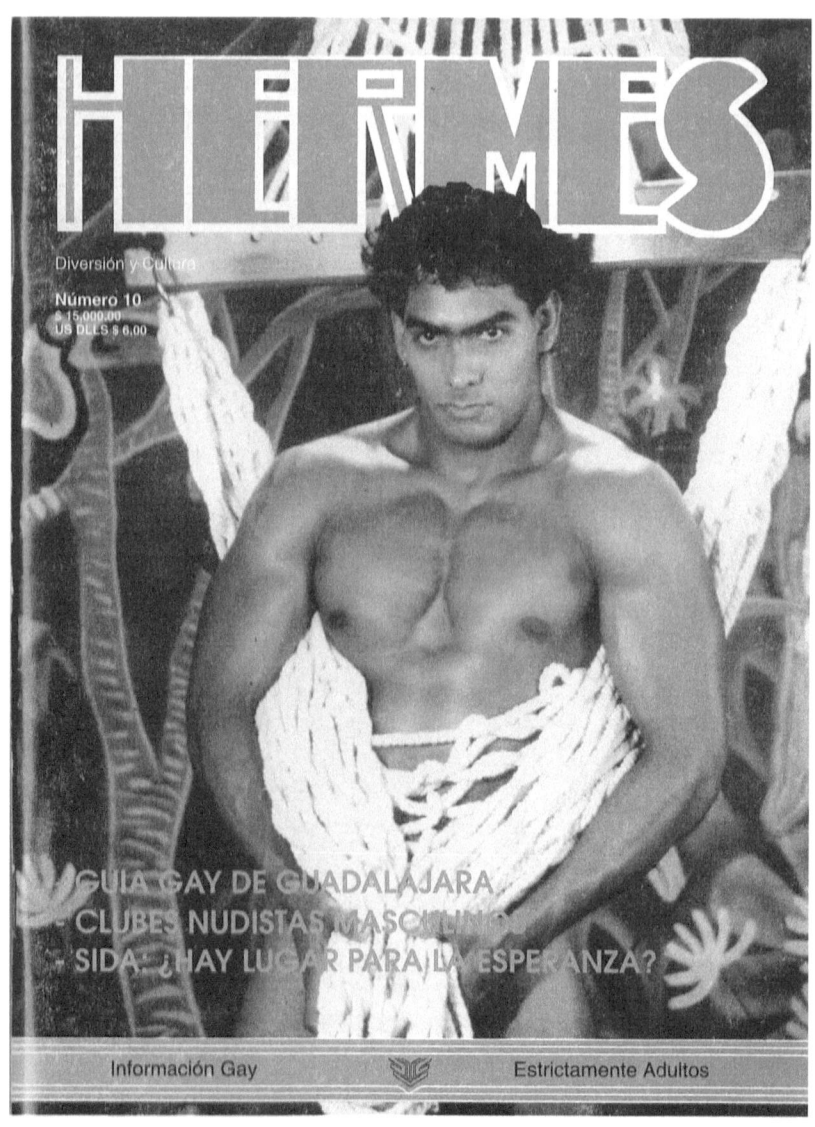

FIGURE 5.2. Cover of *Hermes*'s tenth issue, published in 1992. The model, named Sammy, was photographed by Víctor Hugo Villa (Víctor Hugo Villalobos Leaño). Centro Académico de la Memoria de Nuestra América, Mexico City.

enjoyed erotica depicting Mexican men could be certain that *Hermes* would cater to their desires. As discussed in the previous chapter, potential consumers were unable to leaf through magazines like *Macho Tips* and *Hermes* because they were sold inside plastic bags, hence the importance of appealing and suggestive covers. Media studies scholars explain that "The magazine cover is a metatext that seeks 'to persuade people that the media text they are thinking of consuming will be worth the investment of time, energy, and money.'"[6] The cover, as Mehita Iqani argues, "is the most crucial part of the entire magazine," because it presents "an image that the magazine wishes to promote about itself—an identity that will cause it to be recognized, differentiated from its competitors, purchased, read, or at least leafed through precisely so as to lead readers into the consumerist ideology that permeates the magazine as a whole."[7] This explains why even if *Hermes*'s erotic imagery included both brown and white models, nearly all its covers only featured the former.

Although the celebration of Western male beauty was not the selling point of *Hermes*, it played a central role in the magazine and featured prominently in numerous centerfolds and ads. This type of content built on a longer tradition of physique magazines that idealized whiteness, musculature, and youth, while also evoking ancient Greek culture. This tradition began in the 1950s and gave rise to physique magazines such as *Adonis, Grecian Guild Pictorial, Young Adonis*, and *Demi-Gods*. Like those magazines, *Hermes* adopted a title that evoked ancient Greece and idealized the same values. As discussed in the previous chapter, US gay magazines and visual cultures heavily influenced Hidalgo de la Torre's editorial work. Indeed, he and his staff often turned to international periodicals looking for illustrations and erotic material. Since these periodicals mostly featured white men, those were the images that *Hermes* repurposed. For example, inspiration, borrowing, and/or the existence of international image banks help explain why a 1990 ad of a Mexico City gay social club was so similar to other North American ads in their portrayal of male beauty and desirability (figure 5.3). This Mexican ad depicts a young, seemingly white, muscular man with a moustache opening his garment and exposing his chest and abs. The ad is almost identical to The Club Ottawa baths ad, which was published in *The Body Politic* in 1978 and triggered a debate among the editorial collective and readers, as discussed in chapter 2 (figure 2.6). Images like the one in The Club ad were usually acquired in image banks, and a significant portion of the imagery in *TBP* came from those repositories.[8]

Hidalgo de la Torre's magazines thus negotiated notions of male beauty and homoerotic desire; while his magazines celebrated Mexican beauty, they also participated in the construction of a longer, better established, and much more

FIGURE 5.3. Ad for a Mexico City gay club published in *Hermes* in 1990.

popular visual culture that idealized Western male beauty. Notwithstanding this celebration of "all types" of male beauty in *Hermes*, Hidalgo de la Torre had several good reasons to continue his previous editorial practice of specifically marketing pictures of Mexican-looking models. One of them was his own desire for these types of men and his goal of expanding notions of the erotic—topics discussed in chapter 4. Another good reason was the fact that Mexico City's gay publishing industry began to grow in the early 1990s. While in 1990 *Hermes* was still the only Mexican gay magazine with erotic imagery and nationwide circulation, this began to change in 1992 when the appearance of new gay magazines with diverse content pushed *Hermes* to find ways to differentiate itself from other periodicals and to rework its design and format. In that context, which is further discussed below, the eroticization of brown, Mexican-looking models remained the distinctive feature of *Hermes*.

The Politics of Race in Gay Commercial Magazines

The gay market for erotic and pornographic representations of Mexican and Latino brown men emerged in Mexico and the United States in the late 1980s and early 1990s. As discussed in the previous chapter, the attention given to the Mexican masculine body in a Mexican gay magazine had important implications considering the gendered and racialized constructions of national identity in this country. In the 1990s, this attention also acquired an increasingly commercial nature, as *Hermes* began to compete with other Mexican gay magazines. In this context, the representation of working-class, brown, and hypermasculine Mexican models, also known as "chacales," was a central feature of *Hermes*. A similar process was developing in the United States during the 1980s and 1990s with the growth of the Hispanic market. The pornographic depiction of Latino men and a genre known as "thug porn" became increasingly profitable. The gay markets for these representations emerged at the same time and in connection to one another. Hidalgo de la Torre created this market in Mexico through his editorial work in *Macho Tips* and *Hermes*, while in the United States several white and Latino editors tapped this market through their production of erotica and pornography.

As a result of Hidalgo de la Torre's pioneering work in the previous decade, the 1990s saw the emergence of several gay magazines in Mexico City, which coincided with an increase in the circulation of international gay periodicals in the country. Two of these Mexican magazines were *41 soñar fantasmas* (41 Dreaming of Ghosts) and *Del otro lado*. The former published four issues and was the journalist project of the Centro de Información y Documentación de las

Homosexualidades en México "Ignacio Álvarez," an archival project under the leadership of the gay liberation activist Juan Jacobo Hernández. The pilot issue was launched in June 1992 and the last issue was published in January 1993. *Del otro lado* was an initiative of Colectivo Sol, a group that Hernández cofounded in 1981 to fight for gay and transgender rights. This magazine was more successful than *41 soñar fantasmas*, as it published nineteen issues (one of them a double issue) between January 1992 and January 1996 (figure 5.4). Both magazines included information on the gay rights movement in Mexico and the world, material on sexual health and culture, and erotic imagery that was more explicit than in *Hermes*. One clear example of this contrast was the featuring of erections, an element that Hidalgo de la Torre had always avoided. Moreover, *41 soñar fantasmas* and *Del otro lado* had a size of about 10.62 × 8.26 inches and included several color pages. These were formal features that *Hermes* quickly adopted, most likely to better compete with Hernández's magazines.[9] As the previous chapter explained, Hernández worked with Hidalgo de la Torre in *Macho Tips* for several months, but he resigned in 1987 because the magazine was too conservative for him, a committed gay liberation activist. Hernández also thought that *Macho Tips*' photographs of nude men were not very provocative.

Hermes also had to compete with international magazines that began to circulate in Mexico in the early 1990s, specifically gay magazines published in the United States. According to Mexican geographers Álvaro Sánchez Crispín and Álvaro López López, beginning in 1992 several US gay magazines became available at newsstands in Mexico City, including *All Man* and the Spanish version of *Honcho*, both of which had a lower cost than *Hermes*. While in 1994 the latter sold for $8 USD, *All Man* sold for $7 USD. However, the authors also point out that these prices changed dramatically after the financial crisis of late 1994, which caused the devaluation of the Mexican peso. To name one example, after this financial crisis the Mexican gay magazine *Boys and Toys* was cheaper than $3 USD, while US magazines sold for more than $7.[10]

A major difference between *Hermes* and its Mexican and US competitors like *Del otro lado*, *All Man*, and *Honcho* was the attention given to Mexican-looking models who fell into a category that through the 1990s became popularized in Mexican gay culture: the "chacales." As an article in *Del otro lado* explained, a "chacal" could be defined as "a man with clearly masculine features; a man who does not need to exaggerate or perform his manliness, like the leather folk do, because in most cases the masculine attitude of Mexico City's chacales is natural."[11] In order to provide a visual image of what a *chacal* looked like, *Del otro lado* illustrated the article with the photograph in figure 5.5 and explained that most *chacales* were middle-aged, working-class, and uneducated; they tended to

FIGURE 5.4. Covers of *Del otro lado*, published in Mexico City from 1992 to 1994. Colectivo Sol Online Archive, Magazines Collection.

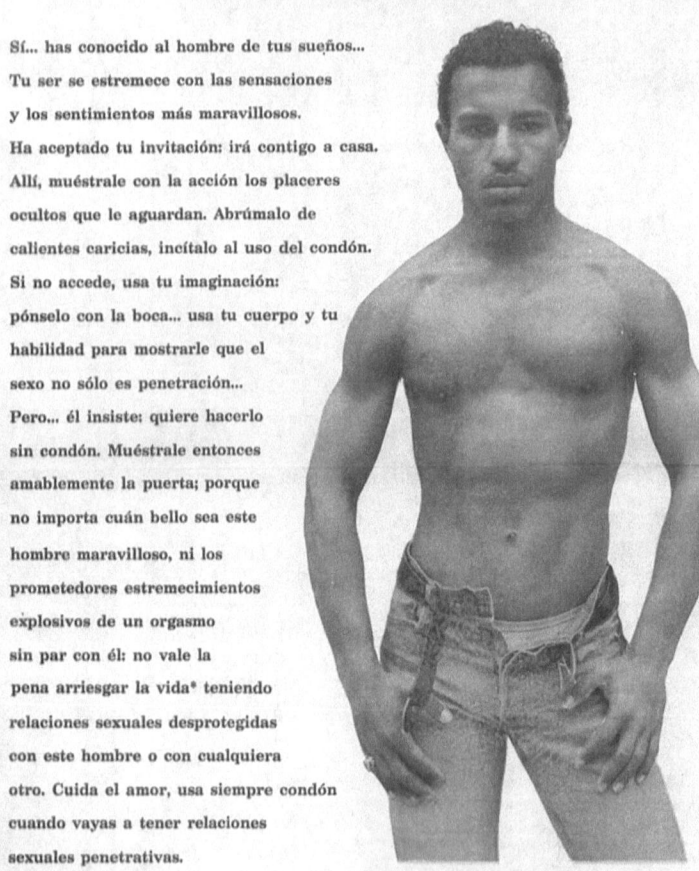

El hombre de tus sueños

Sí... has conocido al hombre de tus sueños...
Tu ser se estremece con las sensaciones
y los sentimientos más maravillosos.
Ha aceptado tu invitación: irá contigo a casa.
Allí, muéstrale con la acción los placeres
ocultos que le aguardan. Abrúmalo de
calientes caricias, incítalo al uso del condón.
Si no accede, usa tu imaginación:
pónselo con la boca... usa tu cuerpo y tu
habilidad para mostrarle que el
sexo no sólo es penetración...
Pero... él insiste: quiere hacerlo
sin condón. Muéstrale entonces
amablemente la puerta; porque
no importa cuán bello sea este
hombre maravilloso, ni los
prometedores estremecimientos
explosivos de un orgasmo
sin par con él: no vale la
pena arriesgar la vida* teniendo
relaciones sexuales desprotegidas
con este hombre o con cualquiera
otro. Cuida el amor, usa siempre condón
cuando vayas a tener relaciones
sexuales penetrativas.

* El virus de la inmunodeficiencia humana (vih), causante del mortal sida, se transmite a través de relaciones sexuales desprotegidas mediante el semen, la sangre o los fluidos corporales de una persona infectada. Hasta la fecha no existe cura para el sida.

PRACTICA EL SEXO MAS SEGURO

 Centro de Información y Documentación de las Homosexualidades en México (CIDHOM) "Ignacio Álvarez", del Colectivo Sol, A.C.
Apartado Postal 13-424, México, D.F. 03500

FIGURE 5.5. This photograph, published in the pilot issue of *41 soñar fantasmas* in 1992, was the same photograph published in the first issue of *Del otro lado* to illustrate what a "chacal" looked like. Colectivo Sol Online Archive, Magazines Collection.

wear jeans and T-shirts or tank tops of dark tones; and they liked to show off their bodies. In their sexual practices, they preferred an active role in sexual intercourse, but most of them did not "assimilate" the concept of "homosexual," at least not when they first became exposed to same-sex relations.[12] But aside from gender expression, in Mexican gay slang *chacal* is a racializing category. In this instance, *Del otro lado* explained that most *chacales* are mestizo looking—they are brown, hairless, and with scant moustaches, and only a few of them are light-skinned and hirsute. The Mexican intellectual Carlos Monsiváis famously defined a *chacal* as a "young proletarian with indigenous (or newly mestizo) features" who "embodies working-class eroticism" and whose "superb shape is the product not of aesthetic concerns but of manual labor."[13] Like the man in figure 5.5, many of the mestizo-looking masculine men featured in *Macho Tips* and *Hermes* illustrate this visual description of *chacales*.

The sexual imagery in magazines like *Hermes*, *Del otro lado*, and *41 soñar fantasmas* helped to advance gay liberation's goal of visualizing and celebrating gay sexuality and homoerotic desires, but these magazines approached this work from different angles. For example, in contrast to *Hermes*, only one out of four covers of *41 soñar fantasmas* and three out of nineteen covers of *Del otro lado* featured visibly brown models. According to an editorial in *Del otro lado*'s third issue, the magazine did want to feature brown models, but some readers objected to this content. They sent letters expressing their disapproval of some of the magazine's visual content, referring pejoratively to the color of skin of some models, as well as to their "tacky" appearance and alleged "vulgarity."[14] It was because of this response from readers that the headline on *Del otro lado*'s third issue asked: "Are Mexican Homosexuals Racist?" (figure 5.6). The editorial note further explained: "We are being asked—openly and covertly—that we comply with the 'hunky' stereotype that the gay commercial project promotes, and that we include more illustrations with masculine, handsome, and muscular men." The editors also received requests "to be bolder," and in order to respond to these requests, they began to feature erections with the aim of "reclaiming this unique source of masculine pleasure." The editors observed that the visual content in *Del otro lado* helped to "acknowledge homosexual sexuality and to accept it as valid and positive."[15] The magazine's visual content undoubtedly contributed to this liberationist project—a project in which Juan Jacobo Hernández had always been invested—but in doing so the magazine centered whiteness and Western male beauty. In fact, beginning with its fourth issue, *Del otro lado* only featured white models on its covers—the only exception being the sixteenth issue. Even though the editors criticized the desire for the "foreign body" instead of the domestic one (the editors referred to the latter as "that which is our own" and "that

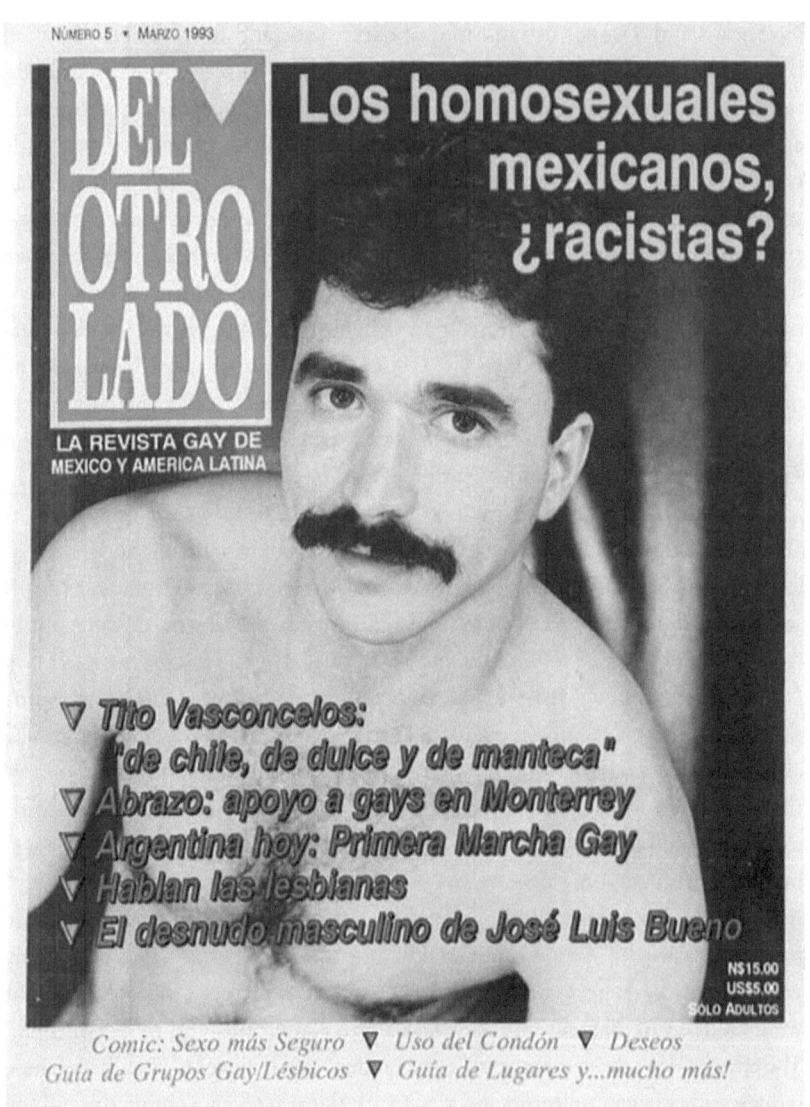

FIGURE 5.6. Fifth issue of *Del otro lado*, published in March 1993. The cover featured a photograph by José Luis Bueno and asked readers: Are Mexican homosexuals racist? Colectivo Sol Online Archive, Magazines Collection.

which identifies us and is what we are"), they chose to comply with readers' demands.[16] Moreover, it is likely that the images in their covers were acquired from foreign image banks or borrowed from foreign periodicals. As a result, these images are in stark contrast with *Hermes*'s locally produced erotica. *Del otro lado* was heir to the most important tradition of gay liberation politics in Mexico, one that Hernández and other leftist activists had led since the 1970s and that gave rise to periodicals like *Política sexual* and *Nuestro cuerpo* in 1979 (see chapter 1). However, even though *Del otro lado* offered more explicit representations of gay sexuality than *Hermes*, its celebration of male beauty did not challenge dominant representations of homoerotic desire, specifically regarding racial representation. In contrast, gay liberation politics did not constitute a central feature of *Macho Tips* or *Hermes*, but their erotic imagery did challenge dominant representations of male beauty by decentering whiteness; and in doing so, they also expanded notions of the erotic.

Two elements mediated Hidalgo de la Torre's decision to feature brown models in his magazines. One was the political and visual economy of the context in which he produced them; the other was the market. Chapter 4 has already discussed the first element, that is, Mexico's powerful discourse of racial identity and national belonging as well as the rise of the gay macho in North America. Regarding the market, it is important to note that gay periodicals have traditionally preferred to feature white models over racialized men. Through the fetishization of the brown Mexican body—a practice that in the late 1980s and early 1990s was even less common in gay magazines than it is now—Hidalgo de la Torre catered to racialized and liberated fantasies that other magazines were not satisfying. While the erotic imagery in *Del otro lado* fulfilled a similar purpose, it catered to a more mainstream, normalized, and less exoticizing desire for Western male beauty—a type of desire that has been at the center of a homoerotic visual culture for centuries.[17]

The preference for white models in North American gay magazines evokes complex issues regarding the relationship between gay politics, consumerism, and racialized desires that scholars have identified in other geographical and cultural scenarios. For instance, Bryan Pitts has recently analyzed "how desires and fantasies about blackness ... structured erotic and political representations of African descended men in *G Magazine*," a Brazilian gay periodical that published from 1997 to 2008.[18] Pitts discusses how the magazine's cover models were overwhelmingly white, even though Afro-Brazilians comprise at least half of the population. Afro-Brazilian men, he points out, "did appear on occasion, but when they did, the magazine's gaze was profoundly ethnopornographic, as it nearly invariably represented eroticized black and brown models as *malandros*, primitive natives, athletes, samba artists, or manual laborers, their racial and class 'otherness' granting them their value in a capitalist marketplace of same-sex desire."[19] As discussed throughout this book, similar portrayals and tensions between the political, liberationist, and racist can be identified in numerous North American gay magazines, including Mexican ones.

Del otro lado's struggle to cater to their readership, while at the same time advancing gay liberation, also underscores the centrality of racial representation in the formation of modern gay identities and communities. The readers who complained about the representation of brown men in this magazine were probably looking for alternatives to *Hermes*, whose erotic imagery did not satisfy their desires or did not represent them as members of the gay community. The abovementioned editorial of *Del otro lado* stated, "Racism and classicism among homosexuals, as well as homophobia, only hinder the relations within the community, polarize it, and divide gays, while clouding efforts to share strength and talent in the benefit of everyone."[20] The editors claimed to be "looking for the promotion of a positive image, in concordance with the reality of Mexican homosexuals, one that recovers the self-esteem of many dejected gays.... That does not mean to resign from the admiration and publication of images of beautiful men, but to diversify the concept." The editors knew that in their effort to diversify the notion of male beauty, centering the Mexican body and visualizing various gender expressions, they could potentially drive some readers away. Although the editors claimed to be willing to take that risk, the visual record of this magazine undermines their claim.[21] Furthermore, the fact that the editors used white models as a hook to attract readers evokes a common trend in the history of gay liberation periodicals: To attract readers and keep their magazines afloat, editors had to provide readers with the content they demanded, even if this content contravened the editors' political views.

The ways in which *Hermes* and *Del otro lado* tried to differentiate themselves in the market and to cater to different audiences reflect similar dynamics in the international sphere. In the mid-1970s and through the 1980s, the market for gay erotic magazines in the United States was thriving. Some of the most popular gay magazines of those years were *Blueboy* (1974–2007), *Drummer* (1975–1999), *Mandate* (1975–2009), *Playguy* (1976–2009), *Honcho* (1978–2006), and *Inches* (1985–2009). Many of these magazines catered to specific audiences and deployed various strategies to compete in the market over the course of the following decades. For instance, *Drummer* targeted the leather and S&M subcultures, while *Inches* gave birth to two specialized magazines, *Black Inches* (1993–2009) and *Latin Inches* (1997–2009), both dedicated to pornographic material depicting racialized men. Another specialized gay magazine was *Uncut: The Magazine of the Natural Man* (1987–1993), whose photographs, illustrations, stories, and articles celebrated, fetishized, and focused on the foreskin.

While commercial pornography depicting nonwhite models in the United States was still uncommon in the 1970s, by the mid- to late 1980s pornography featuring Black and Latino performers emerged as a specialized niche market.[22] One of the first gay entrepreneurs to turn his attention to Latino models was Brian Brennan, a former art director at *Blueboy* who founded the studio Latino Fan Club in 1985.[23] Jeffrey Escoffier notes that Brennan "was disappointed by the lack of Latinos in mainstream gay porn," which were his "favorite kind of men."[24] Brennan, together with pornographers working with Latinos through the 1990s, helped to define a genre known as "thug porn," a genre "that caters to and represents young black and Latino men."[25] Enrique Cruz was one of those pornographers who helped define and develop this genre. Cruz grew up in Spanish Harlem and the Bronx and in the 1990s began to follow Brennan's path; but unlike Brennan, Cruz was Latino. This meant that for him the interest in what came to be known as thug porn was a personal and political matter and not only a response to a taste for a particular other "kind of men." In Donald Suggs's words, by 1999 Cruz had "already assembled a small empire dedicated to the lofty proposition that black and Latino gay men should have a porn industry created in their own image."[26] In the late 1990s, white gay men made up over 75 percent of the gay adult market. Cruz identified the potential of marketing to Latino consumers, and in 1997 he launched his first pornographic film with Latino actors, *Learning Latin*. He then created the studio La Mancha Productions and became Latino Fan Club's main competitor.[27]

The desires of people like Cruz to tap a Latino market were part of a larger history of US commercial culture, specifically the formation of a Hispanic market and its growth in cities with large and diverse Hispanic populations, such as New York, Los Angeles, and San Antonio. This market began to emerge in the mid-twentieth century in relation to the migration of Cubans and Puerto Ricans to New York City in the 1950s. It also emerged in relation to the purchasing of TV stations in San Antonio and Los Angeles by Mexican television entrepreneur Emilio Azcárraga in the early 1960s, and to the involvement of other Latin American entrepreneurs in US Spanish networks throughout the second half of the twentieth century.[28] According to Arlene Dávila, the growth of the US Hispanic market coincided with or was triggered by important events that caused Hispanics to be recognized in mainstream society throughout the 1980s. These events included the civil rights struggles of the 1960s and 1970s and changes in the census categorization of Hispanics in the 1980s; the census revealed a rise in the number of Hispanics and encouraged people to identify themselves as such.

This larger social and political context became a selling point for advertising agencies.[29] Moreover, while these changes took place, the purchasing power of US Hispanics increased from $104 billion USD in 1982 to $221 billion USD in 1993.[30]

It was within this larger context that the market for Hispanic-oriented gay pornography began to emerge in the 1980s, but this context does not fully explain exactly how gay editors, artists, and pornographers began to market brown Latino men to gay middle-class consumers. Scholar José Quiroga has commented on the difficulty of identifying the social and cultural changes that led to the increasing eroticization of brown bodies in 1980s gay culture, or the exact moment when those changes took place. For instance, he has referred to the difficulty of determining exactly when personal ads in gay male publications began to ask explicitly for gay Hispanic or Latino men. He observes that "something happened at some point in the late 1980s—something that had to do with the niche market for Latino men that produced *Latin Inches* or that whole uncircumcised penis fetish—this in turn produced the manuals for regaining your absent foreskin and it led straight (no pun intended) out of, or into, one of the periodic 'Latin booms.'"[31] This chapter argues that the creation of a network comprised of the editors Hidalgo de la Torre, Jim Moss, John Rowberry, and John Shown was an important factor that contributed to the "Latin boom" in gay commercial culture across North America. Their editorial and artistic work, as the following section explains, shaped the trajectory of the gay press and porn industries in the region from the late 1980s and through the 1990s.

Mexican and Latino Men for North American Consumers

Macho Tips and *Hermes* were transnational magazines deeply embedded in an international tradition of gay print culture. International periodicals and collaborators had an influence on the production and content of these magazines and on their reception among domestic and international readers. Some international photographers and visual artists who moved to Mexico in the 1980s, particularly from the United States, contributed to these magazines with artwork, and they helped to give them an international reach. These artists had connections with other artists, editors, and entrepreneurs in the United States and were able to connect them with *Macho Tips* and *Hermes*. A central figure in this history was Jim Moss, also known as James Moss or Jimmy Moss. Through his work in the 1980s, Moss contributed to an emerging trend in gay print culture and pornography consisting of the representation of racialized men for a US male consumer base. Moss also facilitated the formation of a transnational network of men looking for profit and the opportunity to expand their audiences through the portrayal of Mexican and Latino brown men.

Jim Moss was a versatile and international artist. He was an actor, photographer, writer, editor, filmmaker, and pornographer whose photographs of male nudes, leather, and S&M appeared in numerous gay magazines worldwide. He was born in 1940 in Los Angeles to a poor family that had migrated from Arkansas during the Great Depression. During his childhood and early adolescence, he worked as an actor in Hollywood and participated in about thirty films by Fox and Warner, as well as in TV shows under the name of Jimmy Moss—for instance, he played Joan Crawford's son in *The Damned Don't Cry* (1950) and Burt Lancaster's son in *Jim Thorpe All American* (1951). At fifteen, he decided to quit the film industry and moved to New York City, where he enrolled at Columbia University and graduated with a degree in creative writing in 1965. According to an interview in *Gai pied*, Moss decided to leave Hollywood because there were hysterical reactions about homosexual actors in the 1950s and he was reluctant to hide his sexual orientation.[32] The money Moss had made as an actor allowed him to live comfortably in New York City and to pay for his education. At Columbia, he met the photographer Edward Wallowitch, who encouraged him to take his first professional pictures and introduced him to Andy Warhol, under whose guidance Moss undertook a two-year apprenticeship. At that time, Warhol was at the center of a queer subculture that was a focal point of New York City's cultural scene.[33] Warhol introduced Moss into that cultural scene, and in exchange, Moss introduced Warhol to some of his Hollywood acquaintances.[34] It was also around this time that Moss became interested in filmmaking—he wrote and directed his first film *Dragula* in 1974. However, by 1986 he had stopped distributing some of his films under his name out of fear of prosecution. At that time, the regulation of pornography in the United States had become stronger with the publication of the Meese Commission report, ordered by President Ronald Reagan. Reagan's attack on pornography led to a culture of "self-policing," and pornographers began to avoid "extreme" fetishes, such as bondage and even interracial sex, to avoid the attention of federal investigators.[35] After living in New York City for two decades, Moss decided to return to California. In 1986, at the age of forty-five, he was based in San Francisco; *Gai pied* described him as a public personage but also a lonely artist.[36]

Moss dabbled in print culture while living in New York City, though it was not until he moved to California in the late 1970s that his career as editor formally took off and allowed him to leave a footprint in the history of gay print culture. He first got involved with straight magazines in New York City, working as writer and editor. This work would later encourage him to launch his first gay magazine in the late 1960s, called *Where It's At*. After moving to California, he got involved with the S&M gay magazine *Drummer*, published by the San Francisco–based Desmodus Inc. Although Moss had a career on his own, his work for *Drummer* gave him more visibility among gay publics at the national and international levels. The magazine, in turn, benefited from Moss's experience in the visual arts. According to some, he introduced pictures of Black and older men, and he claimed to have invented the term "daddies."[37] Moss quit *Drummer* in the early 1980s because of disagreements with its founder, John Embry, and launched his own gay magazine, called *Folsom*, in 1981 (figure 5.7). This hardcore S&M periodical had more explicit sexual imagery than *Drummer* and even featured coprophilia to gauge people's responses to it. According to *Gai pied*'s interview, Moss did not limit himself to leather culture or S&M; instead, he explored what was "passionate and sexual" in the broadest sense of the terms.[38] However, while Moss's straight friends praised *Folsom*, some gays accused him of offering a "degrading" image of homosexuality. This response evokes the negative reaction that some sexualized or controversial images in gay liberation periodicals—such as those depicting S&M sex—produced among gay readers in the 1970s and 1980s (see chapter 2). *Folsom* only published four issues because, as Moss noted, with only that number he had already told everything he cared about.[39] By the early 1990s, his wide-ranging repertoire of photographs and articles had been published in numerous gay magazines across the globe. Some of these magazines were the US-based *Inches*, *Uncut*, *All Man*, *Hombres*, and *Latin Men*; the Paris-based *Gay lettres* and *Gai pied*; the Hong Kong–based *O.G.*; and the Mexico City–based *Macho Tips* and *Hermes*.[40]

Much of Moss's career took place in Mexico, where he began to portray brown models for Mexican and US gay consumers in order to expand his audience. He arrived in the country in 1986 and began to work with *Macho Tips* shortly after meeting Hidalgo de la Torre. Some of his most representative work for *Macho Tips* includes photographs of the Mexican models Roger and Sergio Andrade, featured in the seventeenth and nineteenth issues, both published in 1987 (figures 4.10 and 4.13). *Macho Tips* also published some of Moss's photographs of white men, most likely taken in the United States. His work depicting Mexican models circulated across the border and was featured in US gay periodicals.[41] One of these periodicals was *Uncut*. For instance, the cover image of the third issue, published in 1989, featured one of Moss's photographs of Sergio Andrade—though, in *Uncut*, he was introduced as Marc Anthony (figure 5.8). On this cover, Andrade looks flirtatiously at the camera holding the chin straps of his hat and wearing only a pair of partly unbuttoned jeans. The picture probably

FIGURE 5.7. Cover of *Folsom* magazine, edited by Jim Moss and published in San Francisco in 1981. GLBT Historical Society, San Francisco.

FIGURE 5.8. Photograph by Jim Moss featured on the cover of *Uncut* magazine in January 1989. *Macho Tips* had featured the same model in 1987.

belonged to the same series that was featured in the nineteenth issue of *Macho Tips* (see chapter 4). The erotic imagery that Moss produced in Mexico for Mexican and US gay consumers contrasts with the images he published in French periodicals and with most of the pictures he published in US magazines prior to his Mexican stay. For instance, his photographs in *Gai pied* and *Folsom* only depicted white, middle-aged, masculine men wearing leather, uniforms, and S&M paraphernalia (masks, chains, harnesses), as seen in figure 5.7.[42] It is possible that he discovered the brown body as an object of desire or as a source of profit in the late 1980s, upon moving to Mexico, or that it was easier to have access to and portray these types of men south of the border. Whatever the case, the opportunity to portray brown models and expand his audience did encourage him to settle in Mexico. He confirmed this motive in an interview with the former *Macho Tips* editor Gonzalo Pozo Pietrasanta. Moss explained: "My editors told me that if I wanted to come to Mexico or to go anywhere in the world, they would buy my pictures. I am here to photograph the Mexicans, the gay life in Mexico, the sensual and the erotic of this country. . . . [A]ll the pictures I have taken of Mexico have been sent to and published in the United States. This is the first opportunity for my work to be published and seen by Mexicans."[43]

Moss played an important role in connecting Hidalgo de la Torre with US artists and editors, and he helped to give *Macho Tips* an international reputation. Since he liked the magazine, he forwarded it to his editors in the United States and claimed that "they are all very impressed and they never believed that something like this was happening in Mexico. Its destiny is to grow and to be more complete."[44] One of these editors was John Rowberry, who in the 1990s also helped to connect Hidalgo de la Torre with other US editors. Moss and Rowberry had met around the time they both worked with *Drummer* magazine. In the late 1980s, Moss introduced Rowberry to Hidalgo de la Torre and soon after they began an exchange. The interaction between both editors was fueled by their shared interest in erotic imagery and specifically by their desire to acquire new material for their magazines.

John Rowberry (1948–1993) was a California-based editor and publisher who worked with and produced numerous gay lifestyle and porn magazines from the 1970s to the early 1990s. His career in print culture took off when he began working for *Drummer* in the late 1970s and especially when he became editor of that magazine, beginning with the fortieth issue in January 1981, a role that he performed until 1985.[45] Through the 1980s and early 1990s, he became the editor of several magazines published by George W. Mavety's Mavety Media Group, a company that had "the most far-reaching 'male' roster of titles in the world": *Mandate, Torso, Honcho, Playguy, Inches, Uncut, Male Insider, Heat, Stallion,*

All-Man, Friction, and *Honcho Overload,* among others.[46] Rowberry became interested in featuring racialized models in some of his magazines in the late 1980s, possibly because of the influence of Jim Moss's and Hidalgo de la Torre's work. It was thanks to this network that Rowberry acquired new visual material depicting Latin American models for his magazines. This new content was well received by some Latino buyers; one of them was the Los Angeles–based photographer Eduardo A., who wrote to Rowberry in 1990 to offer him photographs of Latino models and to express his appreciation of *Uncut*'s July 1990 cover and centerfold, which featured a model named Armando.[47]

Hidalgo de la Torre had always been interested in internationalizing his magazine, and with the help of his assistant, Rocío Sosa, as well as of Jim Moss and John Rowberry, he was able to advance this project. In 1993, Hidalgo de la Torre was actively trying to expand *Hermes*'s international outreach, and he wanted to purchase material from Rowberry, to whom he paid a visit at his office in Carlsbad, California.[48] Since Hidalgo de la Torre did not speak English well, Sosa's mediation was crucial in these negotiations.[49] Prior to Hidalgo de la Torre's visit, Rowberry wrote a letter to Sosa thanking her for the copies of *Hermes* and encouraging Hidalgo de la Torre to come to his office in Carlsbad: "I represent over 20 gay photographers who have photos to sell. In addition, I have a large personal library of photos that he will want to see, and which are available for purchase. He should plan to spend at least one day, maybe two days, looking through my inventory of photographic material," he wrote.[50] By 1993, Rowberry and his collaborators were the agents for a large number of photographers as well as a general source for stock male nude photographs; they had "photographic material of all types: young and fresh models (over 18 years of age); masculine models, muscular models, models in leather, etc."[51] Rowberry thus facilitated Hidalgo de la Torre's access to his stock image bank, and according to another 1993 letter, he connected him with every photographer and photo studio he knew of.[52] He also provided Hidalgo de la Torre with the contact information of the pornography producers Falcon Studios, Catalina Video, Colt Studios, Matt Sterling, Mavety Media Group, and Kristen Bjorn.[53] However, there is no documentary evidence of whether or not Hidalgo de la Torre actually met with any of these studios and photographers during this or any other trip. In fact, the outcomes of the exchange between Hidalgo de la Torre, Moss, and Rowberry did not fully materialize in *Hermes*. Moss died in 1991, and in 1994, exactly a year after the meeting and letter exchanges between Rowberry and Hidalgo de la Torre, *Hermes* ceased publication. In 1993, Hidalgo de la Torre became ill, and he began to face financial burdens that would ultimately lead him to sell his magazine. Rowberry, on the other hand, would face a similar fate, with his health rapidly deteriorating by the end of 1993, when he died. Nonetheless, their communication and, especially, the network they created did have an important outcome: the strengthening of a market for pornographic representations of Mexican and Latino men for gay consumers in North America. In fact, Moss played an important role in expanding that network.

Moss encouraged at least another US visual artist, John Shown, to move to Mexico to take advantage of the same things that he was benefiting from: a growing Mexican gay market and a US emerging market of racially diverse pornography. Shown was a visual artist, writer, lighting and scenic designer, photographer, and filmmaker who, like Moss, had also developed his skills in New York City. Born in San Antonio, Texas, in 1937, Shown studied art at Trinity University, in San Antonio, and at Brigham Young University in Provo, Utah, before moving to New York City, where he lived for eleven years. There, he studied at Lester Polokov Scenic Studio and worked for department stores making appliques and for theater productions designing scenery. His life and professional experiences in New York City around those years were particularly significant considering that, as Elspeth Brown notes, the city was the locus of the fashion industry during those decades.[54] Shown's artwork centered primarily on collages and tapestry. Many of his collages were published in various gay magazines and exhibited in numerous galleries in the United States, England, and Mexico, and so were his films.[55] Archival records in San Antonio and Los Angeles suggest that the communication between Moss and Shown began or became more active in late 1986. In December of that year, Moss, on behalf of Desmodus Inc., wrote to Shown praising him for his San Antonio–based art magazine *Forum* and for his artwork—Shown created *Forum* in 1984 to promote the arts in Texas; shortly after, *Forum* and Desmodus began an ad exchange. Moss also visited Shown in San Antonio and did three photo sessions of him for *Drummer*, *Gai pied*, and another French magazine. Moss would also introduce Shown to John Rowberry and Hidalgo de la Torre a few months later.[56]

Although Shown's motives to move to Mexico are unclear, his friendship with Moss, the possibility of expanding his audience, and the opportunity to find new material for his art played important roles in his decision. In 1986, Moss gave Shown the first incentive to move; he told Shown that Hidalgo de la Torre wanted to publish some of his collages in *Macho Tips*. Though the Mexican editor could not offer a payment, Moss pointed out that Hidalgo de la Torre would be a great host should Shown ever visit Mexico City.[57] One of Shown's lovers, Ray Murdock, was also working in Mexico at that time, and it is possible that Shown wanted to join him.[58] But even more powerful were the economic and professional motives that Moss mentioned in his letters. In one of them, he emphasized that Mexico City had 18 million people and the importance of having a large audience.[59] Another equally appealing benefit of moving to Mexico was the easy and cheap access to racialized men and to "exotic" settings: "You wouldn't believe some of the men I photographed or the incredible locations that were made available to me," Moss flaunted.[60] Finally, as white men from the United States, Moss and Shown could enjoy and benefit from certain privileges in Mexico. One of them was living a more-than-affordable life thanks to a devaluating Mexican peso, which Moss pointed out in a letter. Another benefit was the possibility of becoming acquainted with wealthy, upper-class Mexicans, which Moss had already done.[61]

Shown remained in Mexico for about four years, and during this time he continued to work in visual arts and magazines. Prior to his moving to Mexico, Shown had interacted widely with print culture and he worked with or contributed to numerous periodicals as editor, article writer, illustrator, and even as a model. For instance, he was featured in *Numbers, Manifest, LUST, Stroke, Drummer*, and in a book published by the Gay Sunshine Press.[62] He edited and contributed to a number of US periodicals, including the aforementioned *Forum* magazine, *Texas Monthly, San Antonio Magazine, San Antonio Express, Light Newspapers*, and *Gecu Magazine*. He also tried to publish two books with Gay Sunshine Press—an autobiography and a book with his collage art—but Winston Leyland rejected both.[63] On September 1, 1987, Shown resigned from his position as director of Artists Forum of Texas and from his editorship at *Forum* magazine because he planned to alternate his work and businesses between Los Angeles and San Antonio.[64] But soon after, he moved to Mexico. There, he worked as an art critic for the Mexican English-language newspaper *The News* and he launched a magazine, *Nuevo en todas las artes* (New in All the Arts), which targeted upper-class Mexicans.[65] He lived intermittently in Mexico City, Cuernavaca, and Acapulco from 1991 to 1993, and he remained in the country until 1994, when he returned to Texas.[66] In the late 1980s, Hidalgo de la Torre featured Shown's work in *Macho Tips*, specifically the collage shown in figure 4.6 to promote safe sex. In 1988, the magazine's twentieth issue also published an interview with him and featured his artwork (figure 5.9).

Both Moss and Shown became interested in producing erotic and pornographic material featuring Mexican men, since they identified a potential market for it. In December 1989, Moss intended to begin a "hardcore" video tentatively titled "Tropical Fantasies," which he planned to shoot in Houston, South Padre Island (Texas), Cuernavaca, and Guadalajara with a simple plot: "two American tourists from Houston who get fucked all over Mexico."[67] Around the same time, Shown envisioned a similar project. In a 1990 letter to John Rowberry, he men-

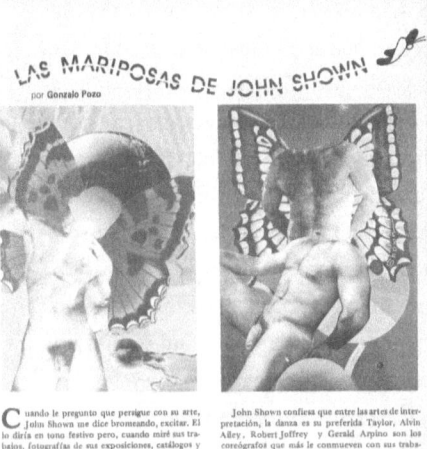

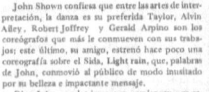

FIGURE 5.9. In 1988, Gonzalo Pozo Pietrasanta published this article in *Macho Tips*' twentieth issue, which focused on John Shown's artwork.

tioned he was planning to do a video in Mexico with himself and his thirty-six-year-old lover, Ray, as stars. They were "planning a gringos-go-to-Mexico and fuck with Mexican men video"; they thought that it would be a "one-of-its-kind" video.[68] Moss's and Shown's projects speak to some of the erotic fantasies of men like them and of their potential audiences; their intentions also suggest the lack of similar material in the porn industry and the potential benefits of creating a market for it. But unlike Shown, Moss did become quite prolific in producing pornography and erotica in Mexico that portrayed Mexican or Latin American actors. His porn videos shot in Mexico in the late 1980s and early 1990s, with a Mexican or Latin American cast, included titles such as *Viva Macho 1* and *2*, *Guys from Veracruz 1* and *2*, *Bronze Beach Boys*, *Mexican Beach Boys*, *5 Guys in a Hammock*, and the art tape *Men of Mexico*. Other films by Moss with nonwhite actors included *California Gold* and *Boy Sauce*, shot in San Francisco with an Asian cast.[69]

Moss made *Viva Macho 2* in collaboration with another US migrant based in Mexico, Ken Edwards, who owned a pottery store with his partner Jackie Saylor and who became interested in the gay porn industry through the influence of

Moss and Rowberry.[70] Edwards and Saylor had moved to Mexico at some point in the second half of the twentieth century and had settled in the state of Jalisco, where they established a pottery shop in the village of Tonalá. After Moss introduced Edwards and Saylor to Hidalgo de la Torre, they became good friends, and the latter visited the couple regularly in the early 1990s, particularly because his family also lived in Jalisco.[71] It was around this time that Ken Edwards became interested in making gay porn videos that exploited stereotypes of Latin American sexuality, perhaps to satisfy his own erotic fantasies or to participate in a growing industry. He thus tried to partner with Moss and Rowberry in order to produce at least one "professional quality hard core gay movie" and to have the "opportunity to learn something of this complex business at first hand from professionals." While he "would be happy to do a conventional movie using Latin actors and a Mexican setting," he was more interested in doing "a more Mexican movie using Mexican social and sexual attitudes and practices."[72] It is possible that *Viva Macho 2* was that video. According to Pozo Pietrasanta, for one of his videos Moss hired as actors some of the local young men who worked at a pottery business near Guadalajara, which could have been Edwards and Saylor's business.[73]

The fact that Moss's videos featured actual Latin American models in Latin American settings helped his work to stand out in the market while keeping the production cheap. For instance, Moss shot *Bronze Beach Boys* on Mexican beaches over a period of one year with "real-life Mexican beach boys with deep tans and big dicks." According to him, the video received positive reviews in several magazines and would be of interest to those "into Latins, outdoor sex scenes, or young hairless beach boys surfing in the nude." The video sold for $69.95 plus $3.00 shipping and could be ordered from the San Francisco–based mail order company International Wavelength.[74] Similarly, Moss shoot *5 Guys in a Hammock* in Zihuatanejo in the early 1990s; this was one of the last videos he made. This hour-long video sold for $49.95 plus $3 shipping.[75] Since the US Hispanic market had constructed strong ideas about what constituted Hispanic identity, Moss's "authentic" representations of Latin American men in Latin American settings were arguably important. As Arlene Dávila notes, "conceptualizations of the Hispanic market have tended to reproduce biases toward the foreign-born and Spanish-dominant Hispanics; consequently, the Latino or Hispanic identity of the English-dominant or US-born Latino is downplayed if not erased."[76]

Moss's work is just one example of the many shared histories between the production of gay printed magazines and films, in which many editors were also involved. For example, in the 1950s and 1960s many physique photographers across North America and Europe, including the publisher Bob Mizer, began producing physique films. Many of these films were advertised in physique magazines for mail-order purchase, and by the mid-1960s they were being shown in many urban theaters.[77] In the 1980s, Hidalgo de la Torre also began commercializing gay videos that had been produced in the United States. Juan Jacobo Hernández recalls that the editor had ten videorecorders that allowed him to produce ten copies of the same video simultaneously. At first, Hidalgo de la Torre sold these videos by mail. Then, he sold them at his gay sex-shop El Ángel Azul, which he operated with his partner Víctor Hugo Villalobos Leaño in the same house where *Macho Tips* was produced. None of these videos was advertised in Hidalgo de la Torre's magazines, though, perhaps to avoid calling attention to copyright. Not even the ads for El Ángel Azul mentioned the availability of any sort of videos.[78]

Throughout the 1980s and 1990s, the gay porn video industry was highly profitable, and the selling cost of Moss's Latin American videos was consistent with the market—though considerably higher than other Latino gay porn. By way of comparison, an average gay porn video in the late 1980s and early 1990s in the United States sold anywhere from $39 to $69 USD. In 1989, Latino Fan Club advertised "New XXX All-Latin Male Feature Videos" from only $39.95 USD, while Catalina Video sold material with a white cast by film director Scott Masters for $69.95 USD.[79] Other white and Black porn videos by Marksman Productions sold for $59 USD each, with the option of ordering two and deducting $8, ordering three and deducting $16, and ordering four and deducting $32.[80] Specialized material such as "muscle bondage videos" from Zeus Studio sold anywhere from $50 to $80 USD in 1994.[81] The cost of Moss's videos was within this range, and although the archival record of the commercialization of his work is scant, we do have some numbers. For instance, in August 1989 Rowberry sold the distribution rights of *Viva Macho 2* to Rollo, Inc., for the considerable sum of $15,000 USD.[82] Within that context and in a world where most gay porn depicted white men, it would have made sense to come up with something different and innovative, such as porn films shot in Mexico and Central America with local men.[83]

Moreover, Moss's video-making and Hidalgo de la Torre's business took place against the backdrop of the transition from adult film to video, an important change that, in Stephen Prince's words, "enabled the adult industry to expand its output, reach a bigger slice of audience, and enjoy skyrocketing revenues."[84] The work of Moss, Edwards, Rowberry, and even Hidalgo de la Torre must be situated within this larger context of porn-video production, as well as within the context that led to the emergence and growth of the Hispanic market in the United States. The growth of this market made clear that the production of gay pornography in videos and magazines that featured Mexican and Latino men could be highly profitable, considering the absence of these men in mainstream gay pornography. But their videos and magazines did not simply portray Mexican or Latin American men. Their work drew on what white, gay, middle-class consumers imagined Mexico or other Latin American countries to be. As such, the pornography and erotic imagery they produced was deeply influenced by power relations between races and by a colonial mindset. This influence persisted in the pornography that followed the tradition that Moss, Rowberry, and other pornographers like them had set into motion in the late 1980s and early 1990s, thereby complicating the potentially liberating aspects of gay pornography. This complex relationship between racialized pornography and gay liberation is the focus of the final section of this chapter.

Marketing Fantasy and Desire

This book has examined different ways in which the visual content of gay periodicals in North America contributed to the project of gay liberation, not only at local or national levels, but also at the international one. The work of Hidalgo de la Torre, Moss, and Rowberry was part of this larger, transnational history of gay print and visual cultures. The magazines and images they produced over the 1980s and early 1990s, as well as the contexts in which they operated, were dramatically different from those of the early gay liberation era, where politics were far more important than profits. Magazines like *Hermes*, for instance, had little resemblance to the Mexican publications *Política sexual* or *Nuestro cuerpo*, both examined in chapter 1. Even *Del otro lado*, which committed gay activists like Juan Jacobo Hernández produced, was dramatically different from those two titles, even though he had been one of their creators. Nonetheless, one thing that all these magazines shared was their commitment to liberating, celebrating, visualizing, and catering to homoerotic desires, either for profit or as part of political and editorial activism. This commitment, though, was not without pitfalls. The interest of Hidalgo de la Torre, Rowberry, and Moss in featuring Mexican or Latino men in their publications and pornography evokes the work of Winston Leyland in the 1970s and 1980s. As discussed in chapter 3, despite being committed to a liberationist project that fought against structures of oppression, the Latin American content that Leyland produced for *Gay Sunshine* and Gay Sunshine Press built on and profited from neocolonial imaginaries of non-Western sexualities. The work of Hidalgo de la Torre, and especially of Rowberry and Moss, followed a similar path. The depiction of Mexican and Latino men in their magazines and pornographic videos expanded the repertoire of gay imagery available to men with liberated desires and fantasies. But this repertoire largely perpetuated stereotypes of nonwhite bodies and sexualities, and in some cases, it was constituted through exploitative practices.

For example, the pornography that Moss created, and Rowberry sold, was not particularly concerned with offering accurate representations of Latin America or with diversifying the ways in which Latin Americans had been represented in US gay cultural production. Instead, this pornography simply aimed to comply with viewers' expectations of and desires about the region. While this could arguably be the case with any pornographic representation, because "porn foregrounds and exaggerates difference in order to exploit its erotic potential,"[85] it is important to scrutinize how some of these representations and practices reproduced stereotypes and structures of oppression. The marketing of Moss's work in the United States illustrates how the Latin American models who worked with him were often misrepresented to cater to international consumers' demands, particularly of those who were white. For instance, his porn video *Guys from Guatemala* was indeed shot in Central America, but as scholar Whitney Strub observes, the video has nothing to do with Guatemala or Guatemalans: "The 'truth' of race could be inscribed through the very act of white voyeurism."[86] In their pornography, Moss, Rowberry, and Ken Edwards also aimed to present an image of Latin America as backward to better cater to US consumers' ideas of the region. For example, in the letter addressed to Moss and Rowberry where Edwards expressed his intention to make a porn film with Mexican actors, he attached a nine-page "orientation course for visiting Gringos." In this guide, Edwards explained what he understood to be Mexican sexual beliefs and practices. Mexico, he claimed, "is an alien place to a western mind. Modern Mexico is superficially westernized, but 'Old Mexico' or 'The Real Mexico' is very different and alien."[87] The real Mexico that Edwards referred to was the "lower class and rural Mexico," which one could also find in some regions of the country or among the populations of cities "made up of recent immigrants from the country." Though Edwards was not explicitly framing his discussion in racial terms, it is clear that the immigrants he referred to were the poor indigenous and mestizo people moving to the cities from rural areas. Mexico, he went on, was "industrializing very rapidly. 'The Real Mexico' will soon disappear."[88] These sweeping statements signal what Edwards and other gay men like him aimed to capture in their pornography depicting Mexican men, that is, an essentialist version of "real" Mexicans and Mexico. This version was similar to that of the poor, backward, and tradition-bound Mexico that people like Nikos Diaman, Edward Lacey, Winston Leyland, and many others like them had been portraying for anglophone, North American gay consumers since the 1970s (see chapter 3). It was precisely this kind of image that Moss's video *Viva Macho* portrayed by evoking indigenous Mexico and by featuring rural landscapes and brown men dressed as peasants or rancheros. The film actually started with a solo scene titled "Aztec Stud" that featured the Mexican model Roger dressed in "indigenous" clothing.[89]

Indeed, the use of stereotypes was key to a successful marketing of Latin American or Hispanic erotica and pornography. This is a common practice in advertising that, as Arlene Dávila notes, has never been disconnected from larger social issues. Dávila writes: "What makes stereotypes so troublesome is not that they order and simplify information by reducing complexities to a few limited conventions, but that in doing so, they both reflect and, more important, engender social hierarchies."[90] This is clear in the imagery of *Hermes* and similar periodicals that depicted Mexican models building on cultural stereotypes—brown, macho men in tropical settings that situate them as closer to nature and/or more primitive. It is also clear in the way magazines like *Uncut* fetishized Latin models: While the magazine featured men from all racial backgrounds, including white men, Latino men were prominently featured. The magazine was launched in 1986, and although Rowberry sometimes referred to it as his "weakest" magazine, it printed the considerable number of eighty thousand copies.[91] It also sold much better than other magazines with racialized men such as *Black Inches*, which according to its publisher George Mavety "was a disaster sales wise"; but *Uncut*, he said, "did reasonably well."[92] Portraying Latin American or Latino models with foreskin in porn videos and magazines must have been crucial to the success of these materials, as it seems to have been one of their main features. Latino Fan Club's twenty-volume series *Horse Hung Hispanics* includes numerous close-ups of actors playing with their foreskin; similar scenes are also present in Jim Moss's *Viva Macho*, particularly in Roger's solo scene. A description in promotional material for *Horse Hung Hispanics 2* (1990) captures some of the racialized fantasies that these videos encourage as well as the central role of the foreskin in those fantasies: "This second in this popular Latino Fan Club release series offers more teasingly erotic self-love by super-hung, foreskinned, thug-alicious Latinos.... If you like Latin men with huge hooded dicks, look no further."

Pornography such as that presented in *Horse Hung Hispanics* and *Viva Macho* seems to have catered to a mostly white male consumer base and provides us with an opportunity to gauge the tensions between gay liberation and oppression. On one hand, one may consider the "pejorative nature" in the language of some titles or descriptions of pornography featuring nonwhite casts; as John Burger points out, this language "resonates with the injustice of the white erotic subordination of ethnic minorities." *Horse Hung Hispanics*, he maintains, "denote[s] racial and sexual subjugation for those who want it, and 'stay away' for those who need to maintain segregational practices in their sexual fantasies."[93] In his analysis of late 1980s and early 1990s Chicano and Latino pornography, Christopher Ortiz also argues that much of this material was constructed around a presumed white gaze. He warns that gay pornography "is often viewed in its best light as an almost utopic space of sexual liberation for the homoerotic representation of desire and as free of the aforementioned hierarchies"; however, it "consciously mobilizes dominant discourses on race and ethnicity to produce its sexual meaning."[94] Indeed, racialized pornography reveals a tension between the liberatory and oppressive potential of such representations, particularly when they build on colonial imaginaries of racial subjugation.

The analysis presented in this chapter, and indeed throughout this book, is aware of the different ways in which liberation and oppression may come together in erotic, sexualized, and pornographic visual representations. Nonetheless, the analysis is also informed by the interpretive frameworks that scholars like Mireille Miller-Young and Jennifer Nash have developed. Their work has sought to complicate readings of racialized pornography by considering the intricacies of desire and the difficulty of reading erotic and pornographic material with nonwhite actors. Referring specifically to Black-oriented pornography that draws on, celebrates, and exploits power relations among races, Miller-Young states that "to simply call all pornography that commodified images of black and interracial sexual relations 'racist' would be to miss the complexities of desire within these forms, to reduce racial fantasy to mere racist domination, and to ignore how performers also intervened in their own sexualities for their own purposes of desire and fantasy."[95] Nash has made a similar case when reading racialized pornography with Black female subjects. Responding to Black feminist readings of violence in racialized pornography, Nash focuses on the complex circuit of desires and pleasures in those representations to avoid "rendering black female pleasures invisible."[96] A closer reading of the pornographic work by Moss, Rowberry, and Hidalgo de la Torre in order to gauge the applicability of Miller-Young's and Nash's theories is beyond the scope of this book. One major complication in conducting this kind of analysis is the difficulty of interviewing the male performers with whom these editors and pornographers worked; despite numerous efforts to track them, none of these performers could be identified and interviewed for this book—most did not use their real names, and at least one of them, Roger, has passed away. Nonetheless, despite the difficulty of understanding to what extent they intervened in their own representation, it is possible that some of these men did exercise a high level of agency during their sessions. Models like Roger and Sergio Andrade—who was also named Valentín and Marc Anthony in gay magazines—seem to have had significant control over their representation. As figures 4.10, 4.13, and 5.8 demonstrate, these men looked directly at the camera in all sessions, appearing to enjoy the photographic moment, and at no point acting passive, submissive, or degraded.

But beyond a theoretical discussion of the intricacies between desire, pleasure, liberation, and oppression in gay print culture, there are some concrete examples that allow us to gauge the reception of racialized pornography in gay magazines and the way in which this content could be incompatible with the project of gay liberation. For instance, the controversy at an international conference on the topic of "Gay Shame," which took place at the University of Michigan in 2003, offers an opportunity to examine how the visualization of certain homoerotic desires has different implications for different viewers. In *A Taste for Brown Bodies*, Hiram Pérez recounts a disturbing experience at this conference, where he was the only participant of color. During this event, scholar Ellis Hanson delivered a talk on Plato's *Symposium* while displaying pictures from the premier issue of *Latin Inches*. These pictures featured Kiko, one of the actors in Enrique Cruz's porn film *Learning Latin*.[97] For Pérez, this presentation was devastating. During the talk, Hanson wore a uniform identical to Kiko's—a uniform that Pérez describes as "akin to a colonial schoolboy uniform." Pérez argued that Hanson's wearing of the uniform suggested "a colonial nostalgia" and criticized how the latter did not offer any "substantive reading of the images flashing behind him."[98] Pérez considers that his reaction to Hanson's presentation was the product of a "collective trauma" because "the images displayed have a context and a history that are meaningful to [him] in ways very different from the way they are meaningful . . . for Hanson."[99] Furthermore, Pérez considers that Hanson and some scholars from the audience reduced Kiko "not just to body, but to dick," and that they failed to offer a meaningful discussion about his representation, or about white fantasy, racialized desire, or about Hanson's reading of Plato.[100] The alleged reduction of Kiko to a penis at this academic event evokes the selling language used in the ad for *Horse Hung Hispanics*. However, the fact that this alleged reduction occurred not in a porn ad but at an academic conference, among a predominantly white audience, explains Pérez's reaction to the event.

It is also troubling that Jim Moss could indeed have exerted exploitative practices with the Mexican and Latin American models he worked with. His own guideline "How to Make Your Own Porno Videos" raises questions about his interactions with models, as he suggests, among other things, to pay them little and never in advance so they comply with what he wanted.[101] An incident that occurred in 1991, and which could have precipitated his death, seems to have been connected to such practices. Based on letter exchanges between John Rowberry, John Shown, and the Edwards couple, it seems that Moss had a severe incident with some "boys" he had photographed in Zihuatanejo. When Moss showed them the magazine where their pictures had been published, the boys reacted negatively and called the police. By that time, Moss's health was already declining due to AIDS, and after the incident he was arrested and deported to the United States. He was hospitalized at the Veterans Hospital in San Antonio, Texas, where he died shortly after, on September 20, 1991.[102]

Although the lack of archival documents does not allow us to fully reconstruct the work of Jim Moss and his interactions with Hidalgo de la Torre and the Mexican models he worked with, his role in the transnational history of gay print culture is clear. Over the 1980s and 1990s, he connected gay artists, editors, and entrepreneurs across borders, and he took an active role in the visualization of homoerotic desires, both in printed magazines and in pornographic videos. Like Hidalgo de la Torre and Rowberry, Moss wanted to expand his audience by exploring untapped markets. One of these markets was the production of erotica and pornography depicting racialized men for both Mexican and US gay consumers. The production of this content expanded the repertoire of erotic and pornographic representations available for gay men. And though liberatory for some, this content not only celebrated, but also fetishized brown Mexican and Latino sexualities and individuals.

EXAMINING THE PRODUCTION, RECEPTION, and circulation of the erotic and pornographic imagery of gay magazines like *Hermes, Del otro lado, Uncut*, and many other publications like these offers valuable insight into the role of print culture in the transnational history of gay liberation. First, the study of this content allows us to appreciate how the erotic and sexual imagery in gay consumer culture emerged from a transnational production of homoerotic desires that was directly connected to transnational networks of editors, activists, artists, and entrepreneurs. The network that Hidalgo de la Torre, Jim Moss, and John Rowberry formed in the late 1980s had a significant outcome. By being pioneers in a growing market that eroticized brown Mexican and Latino men, they played an active role in expanding the range of erotic and pornographic imagery available to gay consumers. And in doing so, they also advanced the project (intentionally or not) of celebrating, liberating, and visualizing homoerotic desires. In the case of Mexico, Hidalgo de la Torre created spaces to circulate these representations through *Macho Tips* and *Hermes*. He not only created a gay market for the brown Mexican-looking body, but also presented this body as a valid object of desire in both magazines. While other Mexican gay magazines such as *41 soñar fantasmas, Del otro lado, Apolo, Boys and Toys*, and *Adanes* recentered white desirability in the 1990s, *Macho Tips* and *Hermes* had challenged that dominant desire since the late 1980s. In the United States, Jim Moss and John Rowberry helped to strengthen a market that other entrepreneurs such as Brian Brennan were beginning to develop in the 1980s and that people like Enrique Cruz would finally consolidate in the 1990s. And even though their work could be objectionable in some regards, particularly because of the fetishization and/or exploitation of racialized men and nonwhite sexualities, they both contributed to the reconfiguration of gay eroticism by tapping into new gay markets.

After Moss's death, Rowberry and Hidalgo de la Torre continued their communication for a few years, but the 1990s would see the demise of their editorial work. As mentioned above, Rowberry helped the Mexican editor find material for *Hermes* in 1993, but he would die that same year. Also in 1993, Hidalgo de la Torre became sick and by 1994 he was facing financial hardships. As a result, he sold his magazine to another gay entrepreneur, Arturo Coste, who turned *Hermes* into *Boys and Toys*. While there were many similarities between *Hermes* and *Boys and Toys*, especially regarding content and formal features, they also differed in one important respect: *Boys and Toys* did not follow Hidalgo de la Torre's tradition of celebrating Mexican male beauty. At first sight, the magazine looked like most US gay periodicals, with an English title and erotic photographs of white men on its covers. Hidalgo de la Torre continued struggling with his health during the following years until his passing in 1999, leaving behind an invaluable legacy in the Mexican gay press.

Examining the work of all these editors and artists in relationship to the larger history of gay liberation does not mean that the latter simply became commodified and packaged as porn in the 1990s. However, this relationship does remind us that the production and visualization of homoerotic desire have always been constitutive of gay liberation, as they legitimize and celebrate gay sexuality even when they aim to make a profit. Ever since the late 1960s, pleasure, desire, and the body became intertwined within the politics of gay liberation. In the 1980s and 1990s, this imbrication became less political and more oriented toward profit. For this reason, printed magazines and the video industry became closer and mutually constitutive in their efforts to produce and cater to homoerotic desires, including racialized desires. The commercial nature of this enterprise does not undermine its role in the transnational history of gay liberation, but it does reveal a changing landscape whereby the production of homoerotic desires was shaped by a complicated relationship between gay liberation, race, and the market.

conclusion

Gay Print Culture has examined how gay periodicals provided gay communities across the Americas with a space to discuss, reflect on, and visualize the political goals of gay liberation, particularly those concerning gay sexuality and homoerotic desire. From the beginning of the modern gay liberation movement in the late 1960s and early 1970s, gay activists, editors, publishers, artists, and readers developed and circulated a rich visual culture that aimed to advance liberationist movements. Published in gay periodicals, this visual culture included numerous depictions of gay pride, resistance, and joy, such as photographs of gay protests and of public displays of same-sex love. It also included images that defied heterosexism, police violence, and homophobia, as well as images that celebrated the body, homoeroticism, and gay sex. From large magazine covers to small vignettes illustrating their pages, the visual content of these periodicals served an important purpose. As Charles P. Thorp claimed in the 1970 gay liberation manifesto quoted in chapter 3, gay magazines constituted powerful technologies to advance the gay liberation movement, build communities, and develop a gay identity. Thorp invited his readers to use this and other techniques such as gay art shows and theater "to assault the system with an alternative and with a show of the total beauty of our life-style."[1] Indeed, over the three decades covered in this book, numerous gay communities across the Americas (and elsewhere) put their energy and art into developing vibrant print and visual cultures and into circulating their work across borders. The histories behind the production, circulation, and reception of such cultural production constitute the focus of this book.

My study of the relationship between gay liberation politics, periodicals, and images has shown the transnational nature of these histories. As *Gay Print Culture* demonstrates, the gay magazines published in the Americas during the period of study had a shared history. The gay communities involved in the production of these periodicals were part of local, national, and international networks of communication and support. These networks aimed to exchange information, to circulate periodicals and images, and in some cases to make a profit. The book has discussed how such aims enabled the formation of local, national, and international communities. It has discussed how some of these periodicals developed a shared visual and political language that was legible across borders. And it has also discussed how some periodicals exchanged content or drew from each other because they catered to a similar consumer base, even if they published in very different cultural contexts. The people who participated in the production and circulation of all these periodicals—leftist activists, radical liberationists, entrepreneurs, photographers, visual artists, models, pornographers, and readers, among many others—had different goals in mind. Their aims included advancing revolutionary projects, connecting with like-minded people across borders, getting international attention and support, and expanding their markets. One thing that many of them shared was their conviction that gay periodicals were an effective tool for establishing connections across borders and for advancing a core project of gay liberation: the celebration and visualization of homoerotic desire.

Considering this core project of gay liberation, I concur with gay activist and writer Tom Warner's rejection of "the notion that lesbian and gay liberation died out as a phenomenon" in the 1980s. This notion, as the author wrote in the early 2000s, seems implicit in much of the literature about gay and lesbian advocacy.[2] Warner refers to gay and lesbian liberation "as an ideology or ethos situated within, and which continues to exert varying degrees of influence on, a broad and still manifest movement for social and sexual change having many dimensions even today," beyond the lesbian and gay rights movement.[3] Gay and lesbian activism, he contends, has not been "exclusively devoted to achieving equality rights and launching legal challenges. Liberationist issues such as sexuality, censorship, and police harassment" have remained part of their agenda.[4] Warner may or may not have thought about the visual representation of homoerotic desire as a liberationist goal when he wrote these lines, but this representation did of course intersect with the other issues he referred to. Magazines like *The Body Politic* in Toronto and *Macho Tips* in Mexico City, as discussed in chapters 2 and 4, faced censorship attempts because of their brave depictions and defense of homoerotic desires. Defending their right to publish was an undeniable liberationist struggle. And despite the obvious differences between both magazines—their content, focus, and overall purpose were dramatically different—this struggle makes them part of the same history of gay print culture.

Of course, the politics of gay liberation, as originally conceived, goes beyond the liberation and visualization of homoerotic desire. At the time the movement emerged, it was also about fighting structures of oppression. For example, in the early 1970s, members of Argentina's Homosexual Liberation Front published a manifesto declaring that "eroticism is a fundamental instrument of freedom" and that "the homosexual has the right to live out his or her eroticism as seems best to him or her." The anti-homosexual society, these activists argued, "is a society which is anti-sexual and anti-erotic, forcing its people in the name of morality to experience with guilt most of the pleasures which human beings pursue in order to realize their tendency to be happy." For the members of this group, it was important to challenge this repressive society, while also bearing in mind that the "abolition of anti-homosexual taboos would be an illusory victory" if other structures of oppression, such as those based on gender and class, remained unchallenged.[5] Many gay liberation activists across the Americas expressed similar concerns, particularly during the 1970s. However, for very few of them, these concerns continued to be central to their political projects throughout their lives. One of those exceptions is Tim McCaskell, a former member of *The Body Politic* collective who has been committed to anti-apartheid and other advocacy movements since the 1970s to the present. Another exception is Juan Jacobo Hernández, a founding member of the homosexual liberation movement in Mexico and of several gay magazines who also remains a strong advocate not only of LGBTQ+ rights, but of human rights more broadly.

The idea that gay liberation was also about fighting other structures of oppression was particularly present in the first gay liberation periodicals published in the Americas, but it became less prominent over the years. In contrast, the centrality of eroticism in gay liberation remained at the core of the gay periodicals that were published both at the beginnings of the movement and through the 1980s and 1990s. *Gay Print Culture* has examined the evolution of that project in the transnational history of gay print culture by focusing on a selection of gay periodicals from across North America. The analysis ends in the mid-1990s because this period coincides with the rise of the desktop computer and the internet. With this technological transformation, digital periodicals, online platforms, and social media began to occupy a more central role in LGBTQ+ activism and community-building. Emerging scholarship in LGBTQ+ studies has begun to elucidate this evolution. For example, media scholar Avery Dame-Griff has recently examined how computers, the internet, and digital technologies have provided trans individuals in the United States with a source of community and support since the late 1990s to the present. As the author explains, his work "spans the gap not just between two generations of the community, but two archive eras: physical material and born-digital multimedia documents."[6] The study of digital periodicals was beyond the scope of my study, since my focus was on print culture. But it is important to emphasize that gay periodicals and digital platforms after the mid-1990s carried on the project of gay liberation. And in many instances, eroticism continues to be at the center of that project.

The liberation of sexual desire in the name of human liberation is obviously not above criticism. In fact, this book has examined with critical distance the production and visualization of certain homoerotic desires in gay periodicals, particularly those that capitalized on racial and class differences and imbalances. The purpose of this book has been neither to simply condemn or celebrate the histories of these publications. Instead, the aim has been to analyze how activists, editors, entrepreneurs, artists, photographers, models, and readers of gay periodicals conceived of the relationship between desire and liberation, and how they navigated and negotiated the meanings of that relationship in their cultural production. The periodicals and images they produced and circulated were invariably shaped by these men's racial, class, and gender identities, as well as by their location. Therefore, analyzing their work and imaginaries with critical distance is as important as recognizing their contributions to LGBTQ+ history.

Even though this book has discussed how the editorial work of some gay activists provided inspiration for others, the goal has not been to simply identify who influenced whom. Indeed, gay liberation groups in anglophone North America were the first ones to use the press to advance their movements and build communities. When gay liberation activists in Latin America launched their own periodicals in the 1970s, they were often drawing from those North American publications that preceded them. In a similar way, when Mexican editors and entrepreneurs like Aurelio Hidalgo de la Torre launched lifestyle and erotic magazines like *Macho Tips* in the 1980s, they were also drawing from other North American publications, as discussed in chapters 4 and 5. However, those who published gay periodicals in anglophone North America were not oblivious of the editorial endeavors of gay activists in Latin America. On the contrary, many of those publishers and activists in the North sought to establish connections with Latin American gay communities, as well as exchanges with their publications, in order to advance their own editorial endeavors.

For various reasons, connecting with, conducting research on, and writing about gay communities in Latin America was important for those publishers in the North. One of the reasons was to support their claims for gay rights. As briefly noted in chapter 3, historian David Churchill coined the term "homophile anthropology" to refer to those accounts from the Global North that provided evidence of the naturalness and universality of homosexuality with the aim of legitimizing homophiles' claims to legal protection and consideration.[7] Though Churchill was specifically referring to homophile communities and periodicals, this kind of content was also present in gay liberation publications, in which genealogies of homoerotic desire across time can be traced. These publications aimed to both normalize and celebrate gay sexuality, even if from essentialist approaches that misrepresented non-Western constructions of homoerotic desire. Another reason for some gay activists in the North to connect with and publish content on Latin America was their commitment to transnational solidarity and to a fight against structures of oppression, such as sexism, capitalism, and imperialism. Since gay activists struggled with these structures everywhere across the Americas, many of them conceived of their movement as international in nature. Supporting each other and reporting on gay movements in different latitudes was one of the main roles of gay periodicals during the period studied in this book. As chapter 1 has argued, it was because of this shared struggle that gay periodicals across the Americas developed a shared political and visual language that was legible across borders. Yet the interest of some North American publishers in establishing connections with Latin America sometimes had a more commercial nature. This was particularly true for the network that John Rowberry, Jim Moss, and Hidalgo de la Torre created in the late 1980s. As explained in chapter 5, these editors created a network to circulate erotica and magazines across borders in order to expand their markets and diversify their representations of the erotic.

Thus, this book does not mean to reproduce the scholarly discourse of "global queering," which began to emerge in the late 1990s and early 2000s to grapple with the relationship between globalization and the emergence of LGBTQ+ identities and cultures around the world. Proponents of global queering, including Dennis Altman (who coined the term), Arnaldo Cruz-Malavé, and Martin Manalansan, among others, have suggested that "globalization has led to the 'Americanization' of homosexuality through the exportation of practices that originated in gay communities in the United States."[8] "Global queering," Omar Guillermo Encarnación explains, is one of the approaches that seek to "explain how the international arc of gay rights spread by the Stonewall Rebellion travelled from New York City to many other parts of the world."[9] But Encarnación is among a growing number of scholars who have decentered this rebellion in other histories of gay liberation, particularly of Latin America. For example, in their transnational and comparative analysis of gay liberation movements in Latin America, Felipe Caro Romero and Patricio Simonetto compellingly refer to the Stonewall riots as a "hinge in the global history of gay liberation." The authors argue that gay liberation movements in Latin America had a hybrid nature. On one hand, the Stonewall riots helped to consolidate already existing forms of gay resistance in the region. On the other, aside from drawing inspiration from

Global North movements, gay activists in Latin America also drew from each other and were significantly shaped by local events involving state violence, leftist organizing, and feminist movements, among others.[10] *Gay Print Culture* joins these calls for a more nuanced analysis of the local, national, and international dimensions of gay liberation and cultural production, an analysis attentive of turning points and landmarks at various levels, as well as of spaces of contestation, negotiation, adaptation, inspiration, and innovation, none of which necessarily exclude the other.

Focusing on cultural production has allowed me to conduct precisely this kind of analysis. Although periodicals and images were central to gay liberation movements in the Americas from the late 1960s to the 1990s, the body of scholarship analyzing these sources is still small compared with the scholarship that focuses on the social and political dimensions of these movements. *Gay Print Culture* contributes to our understanding of such dimensions by focusing on their relationship with cultural production. Moreover, it contributes to our understanding of the local, national, and international dimensions of gay liberation movements and their cultural production. Adopting a transnational lens, developing an interdisciplinary methodology, and engaging with a range of disciplines and sources has been crucial to conducting this work. Some readers might wish that I had addressed or engaged with other histories, periodicals, communities, or bodies of scholarship. This is one of the challenges of conducting transnational research; every periodical and connection I came across opened a new range of possibilities and demanded an engagement with a new body of scholarship. My selection of certain publications and cultural contexts was a natural response to make the project more manageable. It is my hope, however, that my work helps to illuminate other histories outside the scope of this book by providing a methodological framework to approach those histories.

The visual representation of homoerotic desires continues to be taboo in many places. In fact, homophobia and anti-LGBTQ+ discrimination and violence continue to be prominent not only across the Americas but around the globe. Gay periodicals in the period covered in this book were the most important resource for gay men to have a visual representation of their communities, desires, sexualities, experiences, and struggles. Digital platforms and even the mainstream media are now fulfilling that role, and in so doing they are building on the legacies of gay periodicals. The publications studied in this book, and their visual content, opened spaces and opportunities for other cultural expressions to visualize and advance LGBTQ+ liberation.

notes

INTRODUCTION

1. *Nuestro cuerpo*, no. 1, May 1979.

2. In Mexican gay culture, *ambiente* is a word that connotes the "gay scene" or "ghetto." To be "de ambiente," means to be gay. See Monsiváis, "De las variedades de la experiencia homoerótica," 166–68.

3. "Editorial," *Gay Sunshine*, no. 2, October 1970, 5.

4. Grupo Lambda de Liberación Homosexual, letter to *The Body Politic*, Mexico City, July 9, 1979, Box 22, F0002-02-364, The ArQuives, TBP Fonds, Toronto (hereafter TBP Fonds).

5. Tim McCaskell, letter to Carlos Max Mejía, Toronto, November 4, 1979, Box 22, F0002-02-364, TBP Fonds.

6. D'Emilio, "Foreword," 10.

7. Szulc, *Transnational Homosexuals in Communist Poland*, 129.

8. Dunn, *Contracultura*, 56.

9. Szulc, *Transnational Homosexuals in Communist Poland*, 129–30.

10. Stein, *City of Sisterly and Brotherly Loves*, 237. In *Imagined Communities: Reflections on the Origin and Spread of Nationalism* (1983), Benedict Anderson argued that print culture was instrumental in defining nations and national identities in the nineteenth and twentieth centuries. Through print culture, people were able to imagine national communities and to visualize their national belonging.

11. Johnson, *Buying Gay*, 19.

12. Johnson, *Buying Gay*, 150.

13. Meeker, *Contacts Desired*, 5.

14. Meeker, *Contacts Desired*, 11.

15. Meeker, *Contacts Desired*, 72.

16. Ross, *The House That Jill Built*; D'Emilio, *Sexual Politics, Sexual Communities*; Smith, *Lesbian and Gay Rights in Canada*; Kinsman, *Regulation of Desire*; Gentile, Kinsman, and Rankin, *We Still Demand!*; Boyd, *Wide-Open Town*; Churchill, "Personal Ad Politics"; Churchill, "Transnationalism and Homophile Political Culture in the Postwar

Decades"; Stein, *City of Sisterly and Brotherly Loves*; Stein, *Rethinking the Gay and Lesbian Movement*; Warner, *Never Going Back*; Mumford, *Not Straight, Not White*; Hobson, *Lavender and Red*; McCaskell, *Queer Progress*.

17. Green, *Beyond Carnival*; Mogrovejo, *Un amor que se atrevió a decir su nombre*; Laguarda, *Ser gay en la ciudad de México*; Díez, "El movimiento lésbico-gay"; Díez, "La trayectoria política del Movimiento Lésbico-Gay en México"; Grinnell, "Lesbianas Presente"; Fuentes Ponce, *Decidir sobre el propio cuerpo*; Encarnación, *Out in the Periphery*; Ben and Insausti, "Dictatorial Rule and Sexual Politics in Argentina"; Simonetto, *Entre la injuria y la revolución*; Caro Romero and Simonetto, "Sexualidades radicales"; Fernández Galeano, "Cartas desde Buenos Aires"; Caro Romero, "Más allá de Stonewall"; Simonetto, "La otra internacional"; González Romero, "La revolución sexual."

18. Streitmatter, *Unspeakable*; Meeker, *Contacts Desired*; Johnson, *Buying Gay*; Szulc, *Transnational Homosexuals in Communist Poland*.

19. Meyer, "Gay Power circa 1970"; Hilderbrand, "A Suitcase Full of Vaseline"; Dewhurst, "*Gay Sunshine*"; de Groot, "Out of the Closet and into Print"; Simonetto, *Entre la injuria y la revolución* (specifically chapters 3 and 4); Hrynyk, "Pin the Macho on the Man"; Korinek, "*VOICES* of Gay, Lesbian, and Feminist Activists in the Prairies"; Phipps, "Look over here, look over there, lesbians are everywhere"; Pitts, "Hung, Hot, and Shameless in Bed."

20. See Haritaworn, Moussa, and Ware, "Marvellous Grounds," 3.

21. Barthes, *Camera Lucida*, 115.

22. Domínguez-Ruvalcaba, "From Fags to Gays," 116.

1. PERIODICALS, COMING OUT, AND THE VISUALIZATION OF GAY LIBERATION

1. Numerous historians consider it important to acknowledge the significance of the Stonewall riots, their crucial role in the history of gay liberation, and their international impact. However, they also consider it important to acknowledge the various trajectories that gay and lesbian liberation movements followed around the globe. For instance, some scholars have argued that pre-Stonewall gay and lesbian subcultures in the United States were not only visible and thriving, but also contributed to the emergence of the gay liberation movement. See, for example, Lapovsky Kennedy and Davis, *Boots of Leather, Slippers of Gold*; D'Emilio, *Sexual Politics*; Stein, *City of Sisterly and Brotherly Loves*; Boyd, *Wide-Open Town*. Canadian scholars have also decentered the history of gay and lesbian liberation from the 1969 Stonewall riots. See, for example, Grube, "No More Shit"; Smith, *Lesbian and Gay Rights in Canada*; and Millward, *Making a Scene*. Likewise, various Latin American scholars have reconceptualized the emergence of homosexual liberation movements in this region by highlighting both local and transnational influences. See Encarnación, *Out in the Periphery*; and Caro Romero and Simonetto, "Sexualidades radicales."

2. Hobson, *Lavender and Red*, 8.

3. See foreword and contributions to Jay and Young's *Out of the Closets*; Kyper, "Coming Out and into the GLF," 33; Stein, *Rethinking the Gay and Lesbian Movement*, 109; McCaskell, *Queer Progress*, 54; Hobson, *Lavender and Red*, 2.

4. See Streitmatter, *Unspeakable*, 125–28; Mumford, *Not Straight, Not White*, 89–97.

5. See Jackson and Persky, *Flaunting It!*; Zorzi, "The Start-Up of *The Body Politic*"; Jackman, "*The Body Politic*"; Hrynyk, "Pin the Macho on the Man"; Phipps, "'Look over here, look over there, lesbians are everywhere.'"

6. Bébout, "On the Origins of *The Body Politic*." For more on the history of gay collectives and communes, see Vider, "The Ultimate Extension of Gay Community."

7. For a firsthand account of how the Student Homophile League came about, see Moldenhauer, "The Cornell Student Homophile League." The Student Homophile League was the second gay rights organization among US universities and followed the student league founded at Columbia University in 1966. See Stein, *Rethinking the Gay and Lesbian Movement*, 81.

8. See Brown, "Canada's First Gay Student Activist Group."

9. Zorzi, "The Start-Up of *The Body Politic*."

10. McLeod, "Moldenhauer, Jearld," 288–89.

11. Hooper, "Queering '69", 258. See also Maynard, "1969 and All That."

12. Gentile, Kinsman, and Rankin, "Introduction," 3–4; Chenier, "Liberating Marriage," 33.

13. See the chapter "After Stonewall: Transforming a 'Moment' into a 'Movement,'" in Streitmatter, *Unspeakable*, 116–53.

14. Meyer, "*Gay Power* circa 1970," 447.

15. *Come Out!*, no. 1, November 14, 1969, 1.

16. Smith, "Interview with Chris Bearchell," 256.

17. McCaskell, *Queer Progress*, 9.

18. McCaskell, *Queer Progress*, 21, 25.

19. Ed Jackson, interview by the author, Toronto, January 26, 2019.

20. See, for example, Churchill, "Personal Ad Politics"; and Haritaworn, Moussa, and Ware, "Marvellous Grounds."

21. Winsa, "Before Pride, There Was a Kiss."

22. "Beso de a $1,500.00 Dolares," *Macho Tips*, no. 15, 1987, 5.

23. Meyer, "*Gay Power* circa 1970," 450–52.

24. John Kyper, "Mexico: A Movement Under the Gun," June 1981, Box 1, Folder 9, p. 1, GLBT Historical Society, John Kyper Papers, San Francisco (hereafter John Kyper Papers).

25. Kyper, "Coming Out and into the GLF," 31–39.

26. See Johnson, *Buying Gay*.

27. Macías-González, "LGBTQ+ Archives and Public History Projects in Mexico," 194.

28. To learn more about the homosexual liberation movement in Mexico, see Díez, "El movimiento lésbico-gay"; Díez, "La trayectoria política"; Argüello Pazmiño, "Identidades en disputa"; and Lumsden, *Homosexuality, Society and the State in Mexico*.

29. Servín, "Another Turn of the Screw," 372–73; Allier-Montaño, "From *Conspiracy to Struggle for Democracy*," 132–33; Agustín, *La tragicomedia mexicana 2*, 154–55.

30. McCormick, "Torture and the Making of a Subversive During Mexico's Dirty War," 255–56.

31. Herrera Calderón and Cedillo, "Introduction," 5.

32. Herrera Calderón and Cedillo, "Introduction," 8.

33. Labastida Martín del Campo, "Legitimidad y cambio del régimen político en México," 197.

34. For a more detailed analysis of these publications, see Mezo González, "La prensa de liberación homosexual en la ciudad de México."

35. John Kyper and David Lamble, "Interview with Ignacio Alvarez of the Frente Homosexual de Acción Revolucionaria of Mexico City," July 11, 1981, Box 1, Folder 9, p. 1, John Kyper Papers.

36. Kyper and Lamble, "Interview with Ignacio Alvarez," July 11, 1981, Box 1, Folder 9, pp. 2–3, John Kyper Papers.

37. Juan Jacobo Hernández, interview by the author, Mexico City, June 19, 2019.

38. Hernández, interview by the author, Mexico City, June 19, 2019.

39. All the interviews with Mexican individuals cited in this book were conducted in Spanish. All quotations from these interviews are my translations from the original. Hernández, interview by the author, Mexico City, June 19, 2019.

40. Macías-González, "The Transnational Homophile Movement."

41. Danny Laird, interview by the author, Mexico City, December 19, 2019.

42. Hernández, interview by the author, Mexico City, June 19, 2019.

43. López Cámara, *La cultura del 68*, 11–18; 36–37.

44. McCaskell, *Queer Progress*, 54–56.

45. Peralta, *Los nombres del arcoíris*, 93–94.

46. Translation mine. Simonetto, "La otra internacional," 9.

47. Escoffier, *American Homo*, 125–26.

48. Teresa Incháustegui, interview by the author, October 17, 2022.

49. Marcuse, *Eros and Civilization*, 201.

50. Unless otherwise noted, all the quotations from the Latin American gay periodicals studied in this book are my translations of the Spanish-language original text. Frente de Liberación Homosexual, *Sexo y revolución*, 6.

51. Hernández, interview by the author, Mexico City, June 19, 2019.

52. Hernández, interview by the author, Mexico City, June 19, 2019.

53. See de Groot, "Out of the Closet and into Print," 30–31; and Lewis, "We Are Certain of Our Own Insanity," 110–11.

54. Hernández and Rafael Manrique, "10 años del movimiento gay en México: El brillo de la ausencia," Mexico City, August 29, 1988, fond 1, exp. K 152, Movimientos sociales, Serie identidades sexo-genéricas, 5–6, Centro Académico de la Memoria de Nuestra América, Mexico City.

55. Frascà, "Mario Mieli."

56. Frascà, "Mario Mieli."

57. Mieli, *Homosexuality and Liberation*, 167.

58. *Gay Sunshine*, no. 2, October 1970, 20.

59. Cited in Jackman, "Bawdy Politics," 250.

60. Vider, "The Ultimate Extension of Gay Community," 868–71.

61. Vider, "The Ultimate Extension of Gay Community," 871.

62. Hannon, "Celebrate the Body: Towards an Alternate Aesthetic," *TBP*, no. 5, July–August 1972, 12–13.

63. "Letter from Mexico," *Gay Sunshine*, no. 11, 1972, 2.

64. Hernández, interview by the author, Mexico City, June 19, 2019.

65. Translation mine. Peralta, "Del prejuicio a la libertad."
66. Whittier, "Identity Politics, Consciousness-Raising, and Visibility Politics."
67. Kissack, "Freaking Fag Revolutionaries," 121.
68. Hernández, interview by the author, Mexico City, June 19, 2019.
69. Kyper and Lamble, "Interview with Ignacio Alvarez," July 11, 1981, Box 1, Folder 9, p. 2, John Kyper Papers.
70. Reynolds, *From Camp to Queer*, 93.
71. Delap, "Feminism, Masculinities and Emotional Politics," 577–78.
72. Vider, "The Ultimate Extension of Gay Community," 873.
73. "Gay Yoga: On Body, Mind, and Politics," *Fag Rag*, no. 3, Summer 1972, 14–15, 21.
74. See McCaskell, "'We will conquer a space filled with light': Gay Life and the Liberation Struggle in Argentina," *TBP*, no. 26, October 1976, 8–9; "Gay in Colombia: Hiding, Hustling and Coming Together," *TBP*, no. 69, December 1980, 25–27; "Sex and Sandinismo: Gay Life in the New Nicaragua," *TBP*, no. 73, May 1981, 19–21.
75. For more on Tim McCaskell's biography, see McCaskell, "Before I Was White I Was Presbyterian," 31–39; and McCaskell, *Queer Progress*.
76. McCaskell, interview by the author, Toronto, April 25, 2016.
77. Hobson, *Lavender and Red*, 8, 98.
78. "Juan Jacobo Hernández Interview Edited and Introduced by John Kyper," August 15, 1979, Box 1, Folder 9, John Kyper Papers. See also Grinnell, "Lesbianas Presente," 118–19.
79. McCaskell, interview by the author, Toronto, April 25, 2016.
80. McCaskell, "We will conquer a space filled with light," 8–9.
81. McCaskell, "We will conquer a space filled with light," 9.
82. McCaskell, "We will conquer a space filled with light," 9.
83. Kyper, "Coming Out and into the GLF," 37.
84. Kyper, "Coming Out and into the GLF," 37.
85. Green, "Desire and Revolution," 244.
86. Green, "Desire and Revolution," 245. For an analysis on how leftist activists worldwide celebrated, idealized, or tried to emulate Che Guevara's revolutionary image, see Prestholdt, "Resurrecting Che."
87. Grinnell, "Lesbianas Presente," 58.
88. Perlongher, *Prosa plebeya*, 81–82.
89. McCaskell, "We will conquer a space filled with light," 9.
90. David Thorstad, email message to author, November 5, 2019. The gay activist Kurt Hill recalls having met Forgione in New York City in the late 1970s, when the former was based in this city. In the 1970s, Hill was an unpaid staff writer for the *USLA Reporter*, a periodical of the US Committee for Justice to Latin American Political Prisoners, and a former SWP member. Kurt Hill, email message to author, November 5, 2019. Impelled by their commitment to the left and gay movements, Thorstad, Forgione, and Hill edited two volumes on the relationship between gay liberation and socialism: Thorstad, *Gay Liberation and Socialism*; and Forgione and Hill, *No Apologies*.
91. Steve Forgione, letter to McCaskell, New York, August 16, 1981, Box 22, F0002-02-359, *TBP* Fonds.

92. McCaskell, letter to Forgione, Toronto, August 29, 1981, Box 22, F0002-02-359, TBP Fonds. For more on McCaskell's view on the Nicaraguan Revolution, see McCaskell, "Sex and Sandinismo."

93. Kyper wrote in *GCN* that Hernández visited San Francisco because members of FHAR wanted "to make American gays know we exist, to raise funds and make contacts." To that effect, they also got in touch with the Comité de Homosexuales Latinoamericanos (COHLA), in New York City, and with many groups in San Francisco, including the Third World Gay Caucus and the Gay and Latino Alliance (GALA). By that time, FHAR was also in communication with gay groups in Costa Rica, Guatemala, Colombia, and Brazil. See "Juan Jacobo Hernández Interview," August 15, 1979, Box 1, Folder 9, John Kyper Papers.

94. "Juan Jacobo Hernández Interview," August 15, 1979, Box 1, Folder 9, John Kyper Papers.

95. "Juan Jacobo Hernández Interview," August 15, 1979, Box 1, Folder 9, John Kyper Papers.

96. Hernández, letter to John Kyper, Mexico City, March 30, 1989, Box 1, Folder 10, John Kyper Papers; Álvarez, letter to Kyper, January 11, 1986, Box 1, Folder 10, John Kyper Papers; and Álvarez, letter to Kyper, May 15, 1986, Box 1, Folder 10, John Kyper Papers.

97. See letters to Kyper from Álvarez dated July 14, 1982; July 1, 1983; July 11, 1986; January 4, 1984; and October 23, 1984, in Box 1, Folder 10, John Kyper Papers.

98. Kyper and Álvarez, "In Mexico: May Day March Draws Gays," *GCN*, May 23, 1981; "Third Pride March Held in Mexico City Despite Renewed Government Repression," *GCN*, July 11, 1981.

99. Hernández, letter to Kyper, Mexico City, January 15, 1989, Box 1, Folder 10, John Kyper Papers.

2. SEXUAL IMAGERY, TRANSNATIONAL COMMUNITIES, AND THE POLITICS OF VISUALIZATION IN *THE BODY POLITIC*

A previous version of this chapter was published in *Left History* as "Contested Images: Debating Nudity, Sexism, and Porn in *The Body Politic*, 1971–1987."

1. Ken Popert, "State of Circulation," June 23, 1982, Box 3, F0002-01-054, TPB Fonds.
2. Phipps, "Look over here, look over there, lesbians are everywhere," 1–2.
3. McCaskell, *Queer Progress*, 183.
4. Nash, *The Black Body in Ecstasy*, 1.
5. Nash, *The Black Body in Ecstasy*, 6.
6. Jearld Moldenhauer, interview by the author, May 23, 2016.
7. "Gaylup Poll," *TBP*, no. 3, March–April 1972, 2.
8. Zorzi, "The Start-Up of *The Body Politic*"; Phipps, "Look over here, look over there, lesbians are everywhere," 56.
9. Moldenhauer, email to author, March 4, 2017.
10. Ed Jackson, "Nudity and Sexism," *TBP*, no. 21, November–December 1975, 12.
11. Jackson, "Nudity and Sexism," 12.
12. Because of the enormous diversity within the feminist movement, women envisioned different ways of fighting oppression and adhered to different fractions of feminism, such as lesbian feminism, radical, cultural, liberal, separatist, and socialist, among others. For more on second-wave feminist theory and history in the US and Canadian

contexts, see Friedan, *Feminine Mystique*; Millett, *Sexual Politics*; Firestone, *Dialectic of Sex*; Lorde, *Uses of the Erotic*; Evans, *Personal Politics*; Moraga and Anzaldúa, *This Bridge Called My Back*; Golding, "Knowledge Is Power"; Valverde, *Sex, Power and Pleasure*; Echols, *Daring to Be Bad*; Ross, *House That Jill Built*; Hesford, *Feeling Women's Liberation*.

13. Ken Popert, interview by the author, April 28, 2016.
14. Jackson, "Nudity and Sexism," 12.
15. Phipps, "Look over here, look over there, lesbians are everywhere," 79.
16. Phipps, "Look over here, look over there, lesbians are everywhere," 6.
17. Ken Popert, "The Future and Everything," December 31, 1984, Box 3, F0002-01-058, *TBP* Fonds.
18. Phipps, "Look over here, look over there, lesbians are everywhere," 204–5.
19. Smith, "Interview with Chris Bearchell," 253.
20. Smith, "Interview with Chris Bearchell," 257–58. For more on LOOT, see Ross, *The House That Jill Built*.
21. McCaskell, *Queer Progress*, 67.
22. Phipps, "Look over here, look over there, lesbians are everywhere," 33.
23. Phipps, "Look over here, look over there, lesbians are everywhere," 199.
24. Phipps, "Look over here, look over there, lesbians are everywhere," 144–45.
25. Teresa Incháustegui, interview by the author, October 17, 2022.
26. Doug, "Gaylup Poll Results," *TBP*, no. 4, May–June 1972, 8.
27. Doug, "Gaylup Poll Results," 8.
28. Doug, "Gaylup Poll Results," 8.
29. Duffy, *Remake, Remodel*, 33.
30. Johnson, *Buying Gay*, 5.
31. Johnson, *Buying Gay*, 226.
32. See note 62 in chapter 1.
33. *TBP* collective, "We're Gonna Close You Down," *TBP*, no. 19, July–August 1975, 1; "Editorial: Thought Police," *TBP*, no. 19, July–August, 1975, 2.
34. *TBP* collective, "We're Gonna Close You Down," 1.
35. Jackson, "Nudity and Sexism," 25.
36. Jackson, "Nudity and Sexism," 13.
37. "Editorial: Thought Police," *TBP*, 2.
38. Gerald Hannon, "Obscenity Laws & the Uses of Sexual Guilt," *TBP*, no. 20, September–October 1975, 1.
39. Anonymous, "Harold Hedd," *TBP*, no. 20, September–October 1975, 28.
40. Greg Snyder, "Letter," *TBP*, no. 21, November–December 1975, 24.
41. Ms. Ann Onymus, "Mother and Son Like Harold Hedd," *TBP*, no. 21, November–December 1975, 24.
42. Richard A. Maecker, "Harold Hedd Cartoon Sexist?," *TBP*, no. 21, November–December, 1975, 2, 24.
43. John Kyper, "More Hedd," *TBP*, no. 22, January–February 1976, 2.
44. Jackson, "Nudity and Sexism," 12.
45. Jackson, "Nudity and Sexism," 12.
46. Jackson, "Nudity and Sexism," 13.
47. Hoffman, *An Army of Ex-Lovers*, xiv.

48. Hoffman, *An Army of Ex-Lovers*, xiii.
49. Hoffman, *An Army of Ex-Lovers*, 111.
50. Hoffman, *An Army of Ex-Lovers*, 112.
51. Hoffman, *An Army of Ex-Lovers*, 112–13.
52. Hoffman, *An Army of Ex-Lovers*, 113–15.
53. Hoffman, *An Army of Ex-Lovers*, 115.
54. Hoffman, *An Army of Ex-Lovers*, 115–16.
55. Jackson, "Nudity and Sexism," 13.
56. "Gaylup Poll," 2.
57. Doug, "Gaylup Poll Results," 8.
58. "Editorial Page," *TBP*, no. 4, May–June, 1972, 2; The Collective, "Sex and Money, or What Can You Find Wrong with This Picture?," *TBP*, no. 41, March 1978, 2.
59. "True Confessions," *TBP*, no. 70, February 1981, 21–24.
60. "True Confessions: Report No. 2: Getting—And Getting into—*TBP*," *TBP*, no. 78, November 1981, 47.
61. Hoffman, *An Army of Ex-Lovers*, 3–4.
62. Hoffman, *An Army of Ex-Lovers*, 116.
63. Hoffman, *An Army of Ex-Lovers*, 116–18.
64. "Editorial," *Gay Sunshine*, no. 16, January–February 1973, 2.
65. Craig, "Madison Avenue Versus *The Feminine Mystique*," 15; Valverde, *Sex, Power and Pleasure*, 133; Bronstein, *Battling Pornography*, 143–45.
66. Ross, *House That Jill Built*, 264.
67. Ken Popert, interview by the author, April 28, 2016.
68. The Collective, "Sex and Money," 2.
69. The Collective, "Sex and Money," 2.
70. Young, "Out of the Closets," 25–26.
71. See Altman, *Homosexualization of America*; D'Emilio, "Capitalism and Gay Identity"; Johnson, *Buying Gay*; Sender, *Business, Not Politics*.
72. Through the 1970s and early 1980s, both *TBP* and gay businesses were targeted by Toronto police's systematic harassment and entrapment against the gay male community. *TBP* was raided in December 1977, and the next year, on December 9, the police raided the Barracks, a bathhouse where patrons could practice S&M sex. The raid preceded the February 1981 "Operation Soap," the name given to a series of bathhouse raids that resulted in close to 300 charges. See Kinsman, *The Regulation of Desire*, 339–40; Nash, "Consuming Sexual Liberation," 83; Smith, "Interview with Chris Bearchell," 260.
73. Nash, "Consuming Sexual Liberation," 83, 97–98. See also Ken Popert, "Gay Business: Its Interests and Ours," *TBP*, no. 52, May, 1979, 18; and Gerald Hannon, "Putting on the Pressure," *TBP*, no. 74, June, 1981, 8–10.
74. "True Confessions," *TBP*, no. 70, February 1981, 23.
75. Michael Lynch, "A Working Paper for *The Body Politic*," December 1979, Box 3, F0002-01-070, *TPB* Fonds.
76. Chris Bearchell, "Contribution to the 'Think Tank,'" December 13, 1979, Box 3, F0002-01-070, *TPB* Fonds.

77. Lynch, "A Working Paper for *The Body Politic*," December 1979, Box 3, F0002-01-070, TPB Fonds.

78. For an analysis of how TBP mediated understandings about gay male masculinity, see Hrynyk, "Pin the Macho on the Man."

79. The Collective, "Sex and Money," 2.

80. Greg Bourgeois, "Letter," TBP, no. 42, April 1978, 2.

81. Jackson, "Nudity and Sexism," 12.

82. John Duggan, "Club Bath Ad," TBP, no. 43, May 1978, 2.

83. Duggan, "Club Bath Ad," 2.

84. Paul Goldring, "Letter," TBP, no. 43, May 1978, 2.

85. Douglas A. Campbell, "Images and Responsibility," TBP, no. 42, April 1978, 2.

86. Jackson, "Nudity and Sexism," 12.

87. Mariana Valverde, "False Controversies in the Media Marketplace," TBP, no. 69, December 1980–January 1981, 32.

88. The Collective, "When Are Cocks Offensive?," TBP, no. 68, November 1980, 3.

89. Warren A. Putas, letter, TBP, no. 70, February 1981, 6.

90. See letters section in TBP, no. 70, February 1981, 6.

91. Hrynyk, "Pin the Macho on the Man," 50–51.

92. Mariana Valverde, "Resignation Letter," May 29, 1979, Box 3, F0002-01-070, TBP Fonds.

93. Tim McCaskell, interview by the author, April 25, 2016. See also Kinsman, "Queer Resistance and Regulation in the 1970s," 140.

94. Tim McCaskell, interview by the author, April 25, 2016.

95. According to Ross, by the early 1980s Ryan Hotchkiss, along with Sue Golding, Gillian Rodgerson, "and other sex radicals/militants and biker women[,] had begun to articulate a distinctive pro-sex feminism that positively foreshadowed the coalescence of lesbians, sex workers, transvestites, gay men, transsexuals, and transgendered people under the 'queer' banner in the 1990s." Ross, *House That Jill Built*, 129.

96. Bronstein, *Battling Pornography*, 2; Hunter, "Contextualizing the Sexuality Debates," 15–28; Strub, *Perversion for Profit*, 213–14.

97. Ross, *House That Jill Built*, 113; Warner, *Never Going Back*, 124–26.

98. Lacombe, *Blue Politics*, 30; Cossman et al., *Bad Attitude/s on Trial*, 21; Warner, *Never Going Back*, 124–26.

99. Dworkin and MacKinnon, *Pornography and Civil Rights*, 69; Cole, *Pornography and the Sex Crisis*, 22, 47, 68–69.

100. Lacombe, *Blue Politics*, 33.

101. The letter was signed by George Hislop from Community Homophile Association of Toronto (CHAT), Charles Hill from UTHA (University of Toronto Homophile Association), Jearld Moldenhauer from TBP, Tony Metie from Toronto Gay Action (TGA), and Roger Wilkes from York University Homophile Association (YUHA). TBP, no. 2, January 1972, 1.

102. Churchill, "Personal Ad Politics," 126.

103. Warner, *Never Going Back*, 127; Lacombe, *Blue Politics*, 57.

104. Bronstein, *Battling Pornography*, 141.

105. Vance, "Pleasure and Danger," 3–4.

106. Warner, *Never Going Back*, 127–28.

107. In 1992, the Toronto Police brought criminal charges against Glad Day for selling *Bad Attitude*, a magazine of erotic lesbian fiction. The magazine was deemed obscene, and the bookshop and its owner were charged with obscenity. See Cossman, *Bad Attitude/s on Trial*, 4; Cossman, "Censor, Resist, Repeat," 55.

108. *TBP*, no. 45, August 1978, 12–13.

109. "Pornography," *TBP*, no. 44, June–July 1978, 2.

110. Richard Mohr, *TBP*, no. 45, August 1978, 13; Richard Mehringer, "Re: Porn," *TBP*, no. 47, October 1978, 4.

111. "Memo to: The Collective," June 1985, Box 3, F0002-01-074, *TBP* Fonds.

112. Robert D. Butchart, "Celebrating Pain?," *TBP*, no. 126, May 1986, 10.

113. Gillian Rodgerson, *TBP*, no. 126, May 1986, 10.

114. Rodgerson, *TBP*, no. 126, May 1986, 10.

115. Nash, *Black Body in Ecstasy*, 3.

116. See, for instance, Craig Hanson, "S&M and Gay Lib," *Gay Sunshine*, no. 14, August 1972, 7; Michael Holm, letter, *Gay Sunshine*, no. 15, November 1972, 14; Ian Young, "S&M," *Gay Sunshine*, no. 16, January–February 1973, 10.

117. Lewis, "We Are Certain of Our Own Insanity," 110.

118. See Califia, *Sapphistry*, 118; Cole, *Pornography and the Sex Crisis*, 126; Butler, "Lesbian S/M," 172; Russell, "Sadomasochism," 176; Mariana Valverde, "Feminism Meets Fist-Fucking: Getting Lost in Lesbian S&M," *TBP*, no. 60, February 1980, 43–44.

119. Rechy, *Sexual Outlaw*, 262.

120. See Valverde, "Confessions of a Lesbian Ex-Masochist," *TBP*, no. 56, September 1979, 18; Valverde, "Feminism Meets Fist-Fucking," 43.

121. Phipps, "Look over here, look over there, lesbians are everywhere," 159–60. See also Peg McCuaig, "Power Trip or Fun and Games: Lesbian S&M, Part 2," *TBP*, no. 61, March 1980, 43; letters section of *TBP*, no. 62, April 1980, 4.

122. Popert, "The Future and Everything."

123. B. Benson, "Take Sex out of *TBP*," *TBP*, no. 125, April 1986, 11.

124. K. McCarthy, "Classified Porn," *TBP*, no. 126, May 1986, 10.

125. David G. Thomas, "Taking the Cake," *TBP*, no. 127, June 1986, 11–12.

126. Dewhurst, "*Gay Sunshine*," 215, 219.

127. The Sheaf Collective, "Glaring Pornography," *TBP*, no. 127, June 1986, 11.

128. The Sheaf Collective, "Glaring Pornography," 11.

129. Gerald Hannon, "The Collective Responds," *TBP*, no. 127, June 1986, 11.

130. See David Churchill's analysis of this episode in "Personal Ad Politics."

131. Churchill, "Personal Ad Politics," 127.

3. LIBERATIONIST POLITICS, COLONIAL OPTICS, AND THE DESIRE FOR LATIN AMERICA IN *GAY SUNSHINE*

1. See Balderston and Quiroga, "A Beautiful, Sinister Fairyland."

2. Balderston and Quiroga, "A Beautiful, Sinister Fairyland," 96.

3. Dewhurst, "*Gay Sunshine*," 214.

4. For a general history of queer culture in the San Francisco Bay Area, see Stryker and Van Buskirk, *Gay by the Bay*. For a history of homophile and pre-1969 gay cultures

and activism in the San Francisco Bay Area, see D'Emilio, *Sexual Politics, Sexual Communities*; Boyd, *Wide-Open Town*; Meeker, *Contacts Desired*. For a history of gay liberation and transnational solidarity in the San Francisco Bay Area, see Hobson, *Lavender and Red*.

5. Boyd, "San Francisco's Castro District," 240–41. See also Stryker and Van Buskirk, *Gay by the Bay*; Armstrong, *Forging Gay Identities*; Castells, *The City and the Grassroots* (specifically chapter 14).

6. Leyland, "Introduction," 17–18; Hobson, *Lavender and Red*, 26–29; Dewhurst, "*Gay Sunshine*," 222–23.

7. Meeker, *Contacts Desired*, 16.

8. Leyland, "Introduction," 17.

9. See "Biographical Notes on Editor and Author of Proposed Books," Box 38, Folder 2 "Now the Volcano: An Anthology of Latin American Gay Literature (2 of 2)," ONE National Gay & Lesbian Archives, *Gay Sunshine* Records, Los Angeles (hereafter *Gay Sunshine* Records); Leyland, "Introduction," 18; "Winston Leyland," LGBT Religious Archives Network.

10. Leyland, "Introduction," 17.

11. Leyland, "Introduction," 18.

12. Dewhurst, "*Gay Sunshine*," 223.

13. Leyland, "Introduction," 18.

14. Leyland, "Introduction," 19.

15. Dewhurst, "*Gay Sunshine*," 224.

16. "Note on Gay Sunshine Press," Box 38, Folder 2 "Now the Volcano: An Anthology of Latin American Gay Literature (2 of 2)," *Gay Sunshine* Records.

17. "Editorial," *Gay Sunshine*, no. 9, October–November 1971, 2.

18. Leyland, letter to Jearld Moldenhauer, Toronto, March 31, 1974, Box 15, F0002-02-004, TBP Fonds.

19. There are several letters from people such as Zapata, Nigro, and Regazzoni in the *Gay Sunshine* Records at the ONE National Archives (see Box 62, Folder 10). In these letters, many of them with dates of 1976 and 1977, these men thank Leyland for sending recent or past issues of *Gay Sunshine*.

20. Leyland, "Appeal to Gay Sunshine Readers," *Gay Sunshine*, no. 28, spring 1976, 9; Leyland, "Open Letter," *Gay Sunshine*, no. 28, spring 1976, 26.

21. Nick Benton, "Who Needs It," *Gay Sunshine*, no. 1, August–September 1970, 2.

22. Charles P. Thorp, "A Gay Liberation Manifesto," *Gay Sunshine*, no. 3, November 1970, 8–9.

23. Dewhurst, "*Gay Sunshine*," 226.

24. Cited in Dewhurst, "*Gay Sunshine*," 226.

25. *Gay Sunshine*, no. 3, November 1970, 2.

26. Benton, "Who Needs It," 2.

27. Benton, "Who Needs It," 2.

28. "Editorial by the *Gay Sunshine* Magic Editorial Machine," *Gay Sunshine*, no. 10, January 1972, 2.

29. "Editorial by the *Gay Sunshine* Magic Editorial Machine," *Gay Sunshine*, no. 10, January 1972, 2.

30. Royal Murdoch, Mexico City, 1980, Box 27, Folder 7 "Gay Sunshine Journal #46, 47," *Gay Sunshine* Records.

31. Churchill coins the term "homophile anthropology" to refer to those accounts from the Global North that "provided proof of a universal homosexuality that was nonetheless contingent on the temporally and spatially located, not to mention racialized, other. These others, caught in historical time, were evidence of the naturalness of homosexuality and thus legitimated claims of Westerners to legal protection and consideration." In these accounts, Churchill explains, Global North lesbians and gay men often distinguished and separated "themselves from their supposedly more primitive brethren." Churchill, "Transnationalism and Homophile Political Culture," 57.

32. See Gleibman, "The Madness of the Carnival."

33. Gleibman, "The Madness of the Carnival," 877.

34. Encarnación, "International Influence, Domestic Activism, and Gay Rights in Argentina," 693.

35. See Ben and Insausti, "Dictatorial Rule and Sexual Politics in Argentina," 299; Encarnación, "International Influence, Domestic Activism, and Gay Rights in Argentina," 693; Theumer, "Políticas homosexuales en la Argentina reciente (1970–1990s)," 110–13.

36. Taylor, Carrier, Figueroa, and Diaman wrote the articles "Mexican Gaylife in Historical Perspective," "Gay Encounters in Guadalajara," "Mexican Gay Oppression," and "Reflections on the Pyramid: A Mexico City Diary," respectively. See *Gay Sunshine*, no. 26–27, winter 1975–1976.

37. As Ben and Insausti observe, *El caudillo* was run by people connected to the government, and in December 1975 it "called for the 'eradication' of all homosexuals by either confinement or mass murder." Ben and Insausti, "Dictatorial Rule and Sexual Politics in Argentina," 319.

38. Nikos Diaman, interview by the author, October 8, 2019. Nikos Diaman—born Nikolaos Aristotle Diamantidis—was an early member of the New York Gay Liberation Front, the San Francisco Radical Faeries, and other gay organizations, including the gay community in Greece. See Laird, "GLF Pioneer Nikos Diaman Dies."

39. Diaman, interview by the author, October 8, 2019.

40. Diaman, interview by the author, October 8, 2019.

41. "'Brazil' No Gay Sunshine," *Lampião da esquina*, no. 9, February 1979, 12.

42. Diaman, "Reflections on the Pyramid," *Gay Sunshine*, nos. 26–27, winter 1975–1976, 5.

43. Diaman, "Reflections on the Pyramid," 5.

44. *International List of Gay Organizations and Publications*, September 19, 1973, Box 21, Folder 4, Microfilm Reel #15, New York Public Library, Gay Activists Alliance, 1970–1983, GALE, Archives of Sexuality and Gender, Document Number GALE|GMCLUX502424575.

45. Gerald Hannon, "Anatomia del homosexual: Oppression in Mexico," *TBP*, no. 13, May–June 1974, 16–17.

46. These travel arrangements can be traced through Leyland's correspondence with friends and acquaintances based in the United States and Latin America. See, for instance, Leyland, letter to Luis Zapata, San Francisco, April 27, 1983, Box 47, Folder 4 "Adonis García, Luis Zapata," *Gay Sunshine* Records.

47. Leyland, letter to Lacey, San Francisco, July 4, 1976, Box 3, Folder "June 1974–Dec. 1976," McMaster University Archives and Research Collections, Edward Lacey Fonds, Hamilton (hereafter Edward Lacey Fonds).

48. "Biographical Notes on Editor and Author of Proposed Books."

49. See Edward Lacey, "Autobiographical Statement," Box 3, "General Autobiography," Edward Lacey Fonds; Henry Beissel, "Introduction"; Sutherland, "Introduction"; Sutherland, *Lost Passport*.

50. Beissel, "Introduction," 5.

51. Lacey, "Autobiographical Statement," Edward Lacey Fonds.

52. Beissel, "Introduction," 9–14.

53. In 1991, Lacey suffered a serious car accident in Thailand that forced his return to Canada—according to Fraser Sutherland, "a speeding car ran over him as he lay in a drunken stupor in a Bangkok street." He died of a heart attack in Toronto in 1995. See Balderston and Quiroga, "A Beautiful, Sinister Fairyland," 91; Sutherland, "Introduction."

54. Fernández Galeano, "Cartas desde Buenos Aires," 620.

55. Balderston and Quiroga, "A Beautiful, Sinister Fairyland," 96.

56. Balderston and Quiroga, "A Beautiful, Sinister Fairyland," 89–90.

57. Leyland, letter to Lacey, San Francisco, May 10, 1978, Box 4, "*Gay Sunshine* Records," Edward Lacey Fonds.

58. Lane, letter to Lacey, Guatemala, May 22, 1978, Box 4, "*Gay Sunshine* Records," Edward Lacey Fonds.

59. Lane, letter to Leyland, Guatemala, September 21, 1978, Box 38, Folder 6 "Now the Volcano," *Gay Sunshine* Records.

60. Leyland, letter to Lane, San Francisco, February 16, 1979, Box 38, Folder 6 "Now the Volcano," *Gay Sunshine* Records. This disagreement worsened some already existing tensions between Leyland and Lane, and it led to the end of their friendship, "traumatized and broken" by Lane in the early 1980s, according to Leyland. See Leyland, letter to Lacey, San Francisco, March 5, 1991, Box 41, Folder 7 "Gay Roots, permissions," *Gay Sunshine* Records.

61. Leyland, letter to Joe Fuoco, San Francisco, October 16, 1980, Box 27, Folder 7 "Gay Sunshine Journal #46, 47," *Gay Sunshine* Records.

62. Balderston and Quiroga, "A Beautiful, Sinister Fairyland," 97.

63. For an analysis of how this stereotype is reproduced in US popular culture, see Bender, *Greasers and Gringos*. For a discussion of how the term "volcano" has been used as a metonym for Latin America, see Fonseca, *Literature of Catastrophe*, 11; Anderson, *Disaster Writing*, 109.

64. Ian Young wrote to Edward Lacey in 1975 to let him know that Winston Leyland wanted to get in touch with him. Leyland wanted to include some of Lacey's poems in an anthology and wanted him to contribute to the magazine. Young gave Leyland the Peru address of Lacey and Leyland established contact shortly after. See Ian Young, Letter to Lacey, Scarborough (Canada), March 7, 1975, Box 3, Folder "June 1974–Dec. 1976," Edward Lacey Fonds.

65. Leyland, letter to Lacey, San Francisco, April 30, 1976, Box 3, Folder "June 1974–Dec. 1976," Edward Lacey Fonds.

66. Leyland, letter to Lacey, April 30, 1976, Edward Lacey Fonds.

67. Young, letter to Lacey, Scarborough, July 25, 1976, Box 3, Folder "June 1974–Dec. 1976," Edward Lacey Fonds.

68. Leyland, letter to Lacey, San Francisco, June 24, 1976, Box 3, Folder "June 1974–Dec. 1976," Edward Lacey Fonds.

69. In several letters, Lacey expressed his lack of interest in politics, the left, and the gay movement. However, he did support gay periodicals such as *TBP* and *Gay Sunshine*. For instance, he contributed with "a very generous cheque" to *TBP* Free the Press Fund when the magazine was fighting a legal battle against censorship in 1978. By that time, *TBP* had already lost its first two appeals on the legality of the search warrant used to raid their office. Since the Ontario Supreme Court and the Ontario Court of Appeal had decided that the warrant was perfectly legal, *TBP* decided to take the matter to the Supreme Court of Canada. See Hannon, letter to Lacey, Toronto, May 17, 1978, Box 4, Folder "Ian Young," Edward Lacey Fonds. A couple of years prior, Lacey had also offered to support *Gay Sunshine* financially. See Leyland, letter to Lacey, San Francisco, June 24, 1976, Box 3, Folder "June 1974–Dec. 1976," Edward Lacey Fonds. By that time, several periodicals from the beginnings of the gay liberation movement were facing financial difficulties, including *Gay Sunshine*.

70. Initially, Molina wanted to move to Spain or Canada, and Stajnsznajder was considering Canada and Israel but ended up fleeing to Spain. See Pablo Stajnsznajder, letter to Edward Lacey, Buenos Aires, July 15, 1976, Box 3, Folder "June 1974–Dec. 1976," Edward Lacey Fonds; Molina, letter to Hannon, Montreal, December 9, 1976, Box 15, F0002-02-006, *TBP* Fonds.

71. Stajnsznajder, letter to Ed Jackson, Buenos Aires, June 17, 1976, Box 15, F0002-02-006, *TBP* Fonds.

72. Hannon, letter to Stajnsznajder, Toronto, July 8, 1976, Box 15, F0002-02-006, *TBP* Fonds.

73. Molina asked for these issues on three occasions. He was determined to get them because gay activists were leaving Argentina, and if he waited too long to send them, there could be no one to receive them. See exchanges between Molina and Hannon contained in boxes 15 (F0002-02-006) and 17 (F0002-02-040) of *TBP* Fonds.

74. Green "Desire and Revolution," 248–49. See also Domingos de Oliveira, *Desejo, preconceito e morte*, 92–93.

75. "'Brazil' No Gay Sunshine."

76. Leyland, editor's note, Box 26, Folder 10 "Gay Sunshine Journal #38/39," *Gay Sunshine* Records.

77. In a letter to Lacey, Leyland wrote that during a trip to Mexico and Guatemala in 1977 he received an invitation from the activist João Antônio Mascarenhas to visit Rio de Janeiro and stay at his extra apartment; had he not received this offer, Leyland "could never have afforded it." Leyland, letter to Lacey, San Francisco, November 29, 1977, Box 4, Folder "Gay Sunshine (Winston Leyland)," Edward Lacey Fonds.

78. Leyland, "Open Letter," *Gay Sunshine*, no. 28, spring 1976, 26.

79. Puar, "Circuits of Queer Mobility," 110–11; Rushbrook, "Cities, Queer Space, and the Cosmopolitan Tourist," 188, 198.

80. Starkey, "Human Rights, Cosmopolitanism and Utopias," 25.

81. Pérez, *Taste for Brown Bodies*, 5.

82. Pérez, "You Can Have My Brown Body and Eat It, Too," 176.
83. Nyers, "Abject Cosmopolitanism," 1072.
84. Nyers, "Abject Cosmopolitanism," 1072.
85. Nyers, "Abject Cosmopolitanism," 1073.
86. Pérez, *Taste for Brown Bodies*, 105–6.
87. Waitt and Markwell, *Gay Tourism*, 46.
88. To read more about the gay photographers who represented youthful male bodies during the Pictorialist era at the turn of the century, see Waugh, *Hard to Imagine*, 71–80.
89. Amin, *Disturbing Attachments*, 40.
90. Zapata, letter to Leyland, Mexico City, February 1981, Box 47, Folder 4, *Gay Sunshine* Records.
91. Leyland, letter to Zapata, San Francisco, April 11, 1982, Box 47, Folder 4 "Adonis García, Luis Zapata," *Gay Sunshine* Records.
92. Leyland, letter to Zapata, San Francisco, October 31, 1981, Box 47, Folder 4 "Adonis García, Luis Zapata," *Gay Sunshine* Records.
93. Leyland, letter to Zapata, April 11, 1982, *Gay Sunshine* Records.
94. Leyland, letter to Zapata, San Francisco, April 27, 1983, Box 47, Folder 4 "Adonis García, Luis Zapata," *Gay Sunshine* Records.
95. Pérez, *Taste for Brown Bodies*, 23.
96. Waitt and Markwell, *Gay Tourism*, 43–44.
97. Salvatore, "Enterprise of Knowledge," 82–83.
98. Waitt and Markwell, *Gay Tourism*, 88.
99. Brennan, *What's Love Got to Do with It?*, 195–96.
100. Rivers-Moore, *Gringo Gulch*, 7.
101. Rivers-Moore, *Gringo Gulch*, 8.
102. Rivers-Moore, *Gringo Gulch*, 63.
103. Diaman, "Reflections on the Pyramid," 6.
104. Gleibman, "Madness of Carnival," 877.
105. One example is the cover of *Grecian Guild Pictorial*'s third issue, which featured physique artist George Quaintance's *Aztec Sacrifice* (1952). At the center of this image, a muscular brown man wearing a thong and a headdress made of feathers is chained against a monolith that evokes the Aztec sun stone. See *Grecian Guild Pictorial*, no. 3, spring 1956.
106. Thomas E. Wright, letter to Leyland, Guatemala, May 8, 1978, Box 38, Folder 2, *Gay Sunshine* Records.
107. Diaman, "Reflections on the Pyramid," 5.
108. See Bustos-Aguilar, "Mister Don't Touch the Banana."
109. Bustos-Aguilar, "Mister Don't Touch the Banana," 153.
110. Bill, letter to Leyland, Santa Mónica, December 20, 1975, Box 25, Folder 1, *Gay Sunshine* Records.
111. Balderston and Quiroga, "A Beautiful, Sinister Fairyland," 92.
112. Balderston and Quiroga, "A Beautiful, Sinister Fairyland," 91.
113. See Lacey, letter to Ian Young, Guatemala City, October 22, 1974, p. 1, Box 3, Folder "June 1974–Dec. 1976," Edward Lacey Papers; Lane, letter to Leyland, Guatemala City, March 16, n/y Box 38, Folder 2 "Now the Volcano," *Gay Sunshine* Records.
114. Kirtley, "Let the Sunshine In."

4. GAY MASCULINITY AND THE COMMODIFICATION OF THE MEXICAN BODY IN *MACHO TIPS*

A previous version of this chapter was published in *Hispanic American Historical Review* as "Consuming the Mexican Body: Gender, Race, and the Nation in *Macho Tips*, 1985–1989."

1. For a discussion of how the PRI used this discourse of revolutionary nationalism in the 1980s to legitimize its rule and respond to the challenges it faced following the 1982 debt crisis, see Sheppard, "Nationalism, Economic Crisis and 'Realistic Revolution' in 1980s Mexico," and Sheppard, *A Persistent Revolution*.
2. See Johnson, *Buying Gay*.
3. See Domínguez-Ruvalcaba, *Modernity and the Nation in Mexican Representations of Masculinity*; and Macías-González and Rubenstein, *Masculinity and Sexuality in Modern Mexico*.
4. Appelbaum, Macpherson, and Rosemblatt, "Introduction," 2, 17–18. See also Radcliffe and Westwood, *Remaking the Nation*; Wade, *Music, Race, and Nation*; Wade, Urrea Giraldo, and Viveros Vigoya, *Raza, etnicidad y sexualidades*; Sue, *Land of the Cosmic Race*.
5. Macías-González and Rubenstein, "Introduction," 5–6.
6. Macías-González and Rubenstein, "Introduction," 6.
7. Radcliffe and Westwood, *Remaking the Nation*, 156–57.
8. Aurelio Refugio Hidalgo de la Torre, "Editorial," *Macho Tips*, no. 7, June 1986, 3.
9. The information regarding Hidalgo de la Torre's academic credentials is publicly available through Mexico's national registry of professionals (Registro de Cédulas Profesionales). For an announcement regarding his wedding see the "Sociales" section of *El Informador*, November 20, 1971, Guadalajara, Jalisco, 6-C, Hemeroteca Nacional, Mexico City.
10. Grinnell, "Intolerable Subjects," 93.
11. Grinnell, "Intolerable Subjects," 93.
12. González Romero, "Contra el agandalle de la tira," 93–94.
13. Meyer, *Liberalismo autoritario*, 31.
14. Díez, "La trayectoria política," 699; Lumsden, *Homosexuality*, 64.
15. Díez, "La trayectoria política," 701.
16. *Macho Tips*, no. 11, December 1986, 38.
17. José Luis Bueno, interview by the author, Mexico City, February 20, 2019.
18. Johnson, *Buying Gay*, 114.
19. J.R., letter to the editor, *Macho Tips*, no. 9, September 1986, 2.
20. Oscar Emilio Laguna Maqueda, interview by the author, Mexico City, February 18, 2019.
21. Rubén P. L., letter to the editor, *Macho Tips*, no. 14, 1987, 2.
22. Laguna Maqueda, interview by the author, February 18, 2019.
23. Federico Campbell, "El sida se hace tema central de órganos de cultura e información de homosexuales," *Proceso*, Mexico City, May 16, 1987.
24. Gonzalo Pozo Pietrasanta, interview by the author, March 11, 2019.
25. The Unión de Expendedores y Voceadores de los Periódicos de México (Union of Retailers and Paperboys of Mexico's Periodicals).

26. Pozo Pietrasanta, interview by the author, March 11, 2019.

27. For more on *Crisálida*, see Lázaro, "La conformación del movimiento LGBT en Guadalajara, Jalisco," 260.

28. Mosex, "Cronica de un viaje anunciado: *Gay Pied*, de París de visita en México," *Macho Tips*, no. 10, 1986, 37–39. *Macho Tips* also translated and published materials from the French magazine in the third and tenth issues.

29. Milton Robles, interview by the author, Mexico City, July 30, 2019.

30. Hidalgo de la Torre, "Editorial," *Macho Tips*, no. 6, May 1986, 1.

31. Lizarraga Cruchaga, *Una historia sociocultural de la homosexualidad*, 166.

32. Xabier Lizarraga Cruchaga, interview by the author, Mexico City, February 18, 2019.

33. Alejandro Brito, interview by the author, Mexico City, February 19, 2019.

34. Peralta, *Los nombres del arcoíris*, 94–95.

35. Following Argüello Pazmiño, assimilationism in this context could be understood as the accommodation of collective actors to normative orders of class and gender. See Argüello Pazmiño, "Identidades en disputa," 43.

36. Oster, *Mexicans*, 234.

37. Johnson, *Buying Gay*, 25–26.

38. The Comisión Calificadora is an administrative body of the Mexican Secretariat for Home Affairs (Secretaría de Gobernación) that evaluates the title and content of publications and illustrated magazines in the country to declare their licitness or illicitness should a publication infringe the law. For a thorough analysis of how the Comisión Calificadora operated through the twentieth century, see Rubenstein, *Bad Language, Naked Ladies, and Other Threats to the Nation*.

39. The opening pages of every *Macho Tips* issue stated that the magazine was in the process of obtaining this certificate. For the Comisión Calificadora's asessment of *Hermes*, see "Certificado de licitud de contenido," Mexico City, July 2, 1991, exp. 1/432"90"/6827, 46, Comisión Calificadora de Publicaciones y Revistas Ilustradas, *Hermes* Files (hereafter *Hermes* Files). From the *Hermes* Files in the Comisión Calificadora's archive, one infers that the magazine got a first certificate in June 1990, but it was later revoked and granted again in 1991. See "Certificado de licitud de contenido," Mexico City, June 29, 1991, exp. 1/432"90"/6827, 32, *Hermes* Files.

40. "Suspenden 47 publicaciones por ilicitudes," *El porvenir*, December 23, 1987, Monterrey, Nuevo León, 4, Hemeroteca Nacional, Mexico City.

41. Translation mine. Alianza Nacional para la Moral, letter to the Comisión Calificadora, Guadalajara City, November 19, 1990, exp. 1/432"90"/6827, 40, *Hermes* Files. See also 34 and 35 in the same files.

42. Campbell, "El sida se hace tema."

43. José Antonio Izazola Licea, interview by the author, March 12, 2019.

44. Hidalgo de la Torre wrote that "la motivación primordial de nuestra publicación, es la lucha contra el sida y todas aquellas cosas que van en contra de la salud humana; así como la información y la diversión sana para nuestros lectores." Hidalgo de la Torre, letter to the Comisión Calificadora, Mexico City, May 21, 1990, exp. 1/432"90"/6827, 36, *Hermes* Files.

45. Hidalgo de la Torre, letter to the Comisión Calificadora, Mexico City, May 21, 1990, exp. 1/432"90"/6827, 29, *Hermes* Files.

46. For instance, Hidalgo de la Torre forwarded to the Comisión Calificadora an article that the Culiacán-based newspaper *El debate* had reprinted from *Hermes* on June 15, 1990: "El SIDA, lo que debemos saber" (AIDS, everything we should know). Hidalgo de la Torre, letter to the Comisión Calificadora, Mexico City, August 10, 1990, exp. 1/432"90"/6827, 9, *Hermes* Files.

47. Hidalgo de la Torre wrote that "además de los aspectos informativos, se incluye el atractivo visual para de este modo conseguir, una más fácil aceptación y mejor entrada en el gusto de los lectores." Hidalgo de la Torre, letter to the Comisión Calificadora, Mexico City, November 6, 1990, exp. 1/432"90"/6827, 36–37, *Hermes* Files.

48. "Vivir en libertad es vivir en responsabilidad y en amor por uno mismo y por los demás. El egoísmo, la inconsciencia y la ceguera social son incompatibles con los ideales libertarios y con el México que todos deseamos." Hidalgo de la Torre, "Editorial," *Macho Tips*, no. 9, Sept. 1986, 3.

49. Lumsden, *Homosexuality*, 68.

50. Lumsden, *Homosexuality*, 68.

51. Juan Jacobo Hernández, interview by the author, Mexico City, July 19, 2019.

52. Hidalgo de la Torre, "Editorial," *Hermes*, no. 25, 1994, 5.

53. Informants who touched on this topic have asked to remain anonymous; therefore, the specific interviews that inform this observation are not cited.

54. Hidalgo de la Torre, letter to the Comisión Calificadora, Mexico City, November 6, 1990, 37, *Hermes* Files.

55. Translation mine. Hidalgo de la Torre, letter to the Comisión Calificadora, Mexico City, November 6, 1990, 38, *Hermes* Files.

56. Rubenstein, *Bad Language*, 134.

57. Levine, *Gay Macho*, 4–5.

58. Levine, *Gay Macho*, 5.

59. Davis, *Queer Beauty*, 247–48, 254.

60. Hrynyk, "Pin the Macho on the Man," 310.

61. "Tendencias: tres generaciones," *Macho Tips*, no. 8, July 1986, 46–47.

62. Irwin, McCaughan, and Nasser, "Introduction," 15. See also Monsiváis, "Los gay en México."

63. Macías-González and Rubenstein, "Introduction," 11.

64. Macías-González and Rubenstein, "Introduction," 11. See also Cano, "Unconcealable Realities of Desire," 45.

65. de la Mora, *Cinemachismo*, 7.

66. Macías-González and Rubenstein, "Introduction," 2.

67. Subero, *Queer Masculinities in Latin American Cinema*, 7.

68. See Macías-González and Rubenstein, "Introduction," 13–14.

69. Macías-González and Rubenstein, "Introduction," 14.

70. For a more detailed discussion of these tensions, see Argüello Pazmiño, "Identidades en disputa," 32–35.

71. Hidalgo de la Torre, "Editorial," *Macho Tips*, no. 20, 1988, 3.

72. Levine, *Gay Macho*, 29.

73. "[El Taller] Está concebido y pensado para brindar a TODOS LOS HOMBRES QUE GUSTAN DE LOS HOMBRES un espacio amplio y cómodo con un concepto totalmente revolucionario en nuestro país." "El Taller," *Macho Tips*, no. 8, July 1986, 26.

74. According to Lumsden, González de Alba tried to establish a dress code in his bars by offering discounted cover to men wearing jeans and white T-shirts. Lumsden, *Homosexuality*, 38.

75. Hrynyk, "'Pin the Macho,'" 33.

76. Since Brooks Higginbotham coined the term in 1993 to refer to the rejection among African Americans of "'negative' public behavior" in order to eradicate racism, "the politics of respectability" has been used to signal a particular strategy through which marginalized groups seek social acceptance. Higginbotham, *Righteous Discontent*, 14–15.

77. Víctor Villalobos Cuevas, "La separatidad en el ambiente gay," *Macho Tips*, no. 5, March 1986, 29–30.

78. According to Boivin, El Eco was frequented by the middle and upper classes and by the political and intellectual elite. Due to its location on Sullivan Street, it offered an alternative to the working-class bars in downtown Mexico City. Boivin, "*L'organisation sociale et spatiale*."

79. Villalobos Cuevas, "La separatidad," 30.

80. Julián Pizá, "Libertinaje vs. Gay," *Macho Tips*, no. 9, September 1986, 43–45.

81. O.G.B., letter to the editor, *Macho Tips*, no. 9, September 1986, 2.

82. S.M.D.F., letter to the editor, *Macho Tips*, no. 8, July 1986, 2.

83. Quoted in Argüello Pazmiño, "Identidades en disputa," 42.

84. See *Macho Tips*, no. 6, May 1986, 6–7; *Macho Tips*, no. 14, 1987, 26–29; *Macho Tips*, no. 21, 1989, 25–27.

85. Infinity was the only bar whose ads in the magazine featured imagery reflecting the drag queen show it promoted. See *Macho Tips*, no. 1, July 1985, 28.

86. Boivin, "*L'organisation sociale et spatiale*."

87. Grinnell, "'Intolerable Subjects,'" 93–94. See also González Romero, "Contra el agandalle de la tira," 71–88.

88. *Macho Tips*, no. 6, May 1986, 49; *Macho Tips*, no. 11, December 1986, 26; *Macho Tips*, no. 19, 1988, 56.

89. *Macho Tips*, no. 12, 1987, 3.

90. In our conversations, Lizarraga Cruchaga, Laguna Maqueda, and González de Cosío, among others, readily associated both magazines with the featuring of Mexican-looking men.

91. Moreno Figueroa, "Distributed Intensities," 387–88. See also Knight, "Racism, Revolution, and *Indigenismo*"; Stepan, *The Hour of Eugenics*; Sue, *Land of the Cosmic Race*.

92. Mallon, "Constructing Mestizaje in Latin America," 171.

93. Miller, *Rise and Fall of the Cosmic Race*, 6.

94. Gutmann, *Meanings of Macho*, 240–41.

95. José Luis Bueno, interview by the author, Mexico City, January 11, 2018.

96. Antonio González de Cosío, interview by the author, March 7, 2019; Pozo Pietrasanta, interview by author, March 11, 2019.

97. Wade, *Music, Race, and Nation*, 15.

98. *Macho Tips*, no. 19, 1988, 32.

99. *Macho Tips*, no. 9, September 1986, 32.
100. *Macho Tips*, no. 21, 1989, 50–53.
101. Hilderbrand, "A Suitcase Full of Vaseline," 390.
102. Hilderbrand, "A Suitcase Full of Vaseline," 380.
103. Pérez, *Taste for Brown Bodies*, 83.
104. Johnson, *Buying Gay*, 25.
105. Johnson, *Buying Gay*, 34.
106. Brown, *Work!*, 218.
107. *Macho Tips*, no. 16, 1987, 32.
108. *Macho Tips*, no. 20, 1988, 32.
109. *Hermes*, no. 3, 1991, 14–18.
110. Brown, *Work!*, 132.
111. Brown, *Work!*, 148.
112. Brown, *Work!*, 84.
113. Brown, *Work!*, 148–49.
114. Subero, "Gay Male Pornography and the Re/De/Construction of Postcolonial Queer Identity in Mexico," 121–22. See also Subero, "Gay Mexican Pornography at the Intersection of Ethnic and National Identity in Jorge Diestra's *La putiza*."

5. THE GAY EDITORIAL MARKET AND THE TRANSNATIONAL PRODUCTION OF RACIALIZED DESIRES

1. For a discussion of the emergence and growth of the US Hispanic market, see Rodriguez, "Commercial Ethnicity"; Halter, *Shopping for Identity*, chapter 6: "A Rainbow Coalition of Consumers"; Dávila, *Latinos, Inc.*; Nevaer, *Rise of the Hispanic Market in the United States*.

2. Scholars have long debated the positive or damaging outcomes of pornography. Feminist scholars have been particularly prolific in writing about pornography, especially in the context of the anti-porn debate, also known as the "sex wars" (see chapter 2). To a lesser extent, gay men have also participated in this debate, taking either a pro- or anti-pornography stance. For a succinct analysis of how gay men have participated in this debate, see Corneau and van der Meulen, "Some Like It Mellow." Some representative literature in the study of gay pornography includes Kimmel, *Men Confront Pornography*; Waugh, *Hard to Imagine*; Kendall, *Gay Male Pornography*; Escoffier, *Bigger than Life*; Dean, *Unlimited Intimacy*; Nguyen, *View from the Bottom*; Mercer, *Gay Pornography*; Johnson, *Buying Gay*; Escoffier, *Sex, Society, and the Making of Pornography*.

3. The amount of forty thousand issues is given in *Hermes*'s application for a license to publish. See "Application for a 'Certificado de licitud,'" Mexico City, March 20 (no year), exp. 1/432"90"/6827, 24, *Hermes* Files.

4. The conservative group Alianza Nacional para la Moral, which sent letters regularly to the Comisión Calificadora to complain about *Macho Tips* and *Hermes*, may have played a role in the censure of *Macho Tips*. In one of their letters, the Alianza implied that the Comisión Calificadora had revoked *Macho Tips*' license in 1990 because of their previous complaints, especially about "the classifieds section, where homosexuals and lesbians offered all class of abhorrent services" (translation mine). Alianza Nacional

para la Moral, Letter to the Comisión Calificadora, Mexico City, February 24, 1992, exp. 1/432"90"/6827, 6, *Hermes* Files.

5. See Pitts, "Hung, Hot, and Shameless in Bed."
6. Iqani, *Consumer Culture and the Media*, 9–10.
7. Iqani, *Consumer Culture and the Media*, 10.
8. Hrynyk, "Pin the Macho on the Man," 50.
9. Like *Macho Tips*, the size of *Hermes* was about 8.85 × 6.49 inches and its pages were mostly black and white. However, around the same time that *41 soñar fantasmas* and *Del otro lado* began publishing in 1992, *Hermes* increased its size and began to include more color pages in each issue.
10. Sánchez Crispín and López López, "Visión geográfica de los lugares gay de la ciudad de México," 4.
11. This article claimed to be based on field research with 50 *"chacales."* Rodolfo N. Morales S., "Chacales: príncipes de la fauna urbana," *Del otro lado*, no. 1, January–February 1992, 58–61.
12. Morales S., "Chacales: príncipes de la fauna urbana," 58–61.
13. Monsiváis, "Nightlife," 180. For the Spanish original of this article, see Monsiváis, "La noche popular."
14. "Los homosexuales mexicanos, ¿racistas?," *Del otro lado*, no. 5, March 1993, 2–3.
15. "Los homosexuales mexicanos, ¿racistas?," 2.
16. "Los homosexuales mexicanos, ¿racistas?," 3.
17. See Waugh, *Hard to Imagine*.
18. Pitts, "Hung, Hot, and Shameless in Bed," 68.
19. Pitts, "Hung, Hot, and Shameless in Bed," 67–68.
20. "Los homosexuales mexicanos, ¿racistas?," 3.
21. The editors stated, "Si en el ejercicio de la búsqueda y la práctica del debate perdemos algunos lectores a quienes disgusta la discusión y que, teniendo otras opciones deciden que no quieren pagar para ver nacos, morenos, obvios o vulgares, démoslos por bien perdidos." "Los homosexuales mexicanos, ¿racistas?," 3.
22. See Suggs, "Porn Kings of New York," 85–89; Escoffier, *Bigger than Life*, 311–18; Miller-Young, *Taste for Brown Sugar*, 67, 109–10. For a critical discussion of the representation of Latinos and Chicanos in the US porn market during the late 1980s and early 1990s, see Ortiz, "Hot and Spicy." For a consideration of how the emergence of these specialized markets related to gay Asian pornography in North America, see Fung, "Looking for My Penis"; and Nguyen, *View from the Bottom*.
23. Suggs, "Porn Kings of New York," 86.
24. Escoffier, *Bigger than Life*, 316–17.
25. Escoffier, *Bigger than Life*, 315.
26. Suggs, "Porn Kings of New York," 85.
27. Suggs, "Porn Kings of New York," 85.
28. See Dávila, *Latinos, Inc.*, 25–27; and Rodriguez, "Commercial Ethnicity," 289.
29. Dávila, *Latinos, Inc.*, 40–44.
30. Dávila, *Latinos, Inc.*, 68.
31. Quiroga, *Tropics of Desire*, 180.

32. For biographical notes on Jim Moss, see Marsault-R and Muller, "*L'enfant terrible de Hollywood*," 26–29; Pozo Pietrasanta, "Entrevista a Jim Moss," *Macho Tips* no. 17, 1987, 49–52; Moss, "How to Make Your Own Porno Videos: Tips from a Professional," 1990, Box 7, Folder 4, 24, University of California Los Angeles Library Special Collections, John Rowberry Papers (hereafter John Rowberry Papers).

33. Brown, *Work!*, 254–55.

34. Marsault-R and Muller, "*L'enfant terrible de Hollywood*," 28.

35. See Strub, *Perversion for Profit*, 180, 208, 210–11; Miller-Young, *Taste for Brown Sugar*, 115.

36. Marsault-R and Muller, "*L'enfant terrible de Hollywood*," 26.

37. Marsault-R and Muller, "*L'enfant terrible de Hollywood*," 29.

38. Marsault-R and Muller, "*L'enfant terrible de Hollywood*," 28–29.

39. Marsault-R and Muller, "*L'enfant terrible de Hollywood*," 29.

40. Moss, "How to Make Your Own Porno Videos."

41. Some of Jim Moss's photographs were featured in the *Inches* issues of February, March, and April 1989; April and July 1990; April, May, and November 1991; and September 1992. Many of these seem to be pictures of Mexican or Latino models. See *Gay Erotic Archives*, "Inches Magazine."

42. See *Gai pied hebdo*, no. 211, March 15–21, 1986, 26–29; *Gai pied hebdo*, no. 442, November 1, 1990, 87; *Gai pied hebdo*, no. 454, January 24, 1991, 85–87.

43. Pozo Pietrasanta, "Entrevista a Jim Moss," 51.

44. Pozo Pietrasanta, "Entrevista a Jim Moss," 52.

45. For more on Rowberry's involvement in *Drummer*, see Fritscher, *Gay San Francisco*, 398–99.

46. "Do You Want to Reach the Most Affluent Audience in the World?," Mavety Media Group Ltd., Box 3, f. 5, 1990–1991, John Rowberry Papers.

47. Eduardo A., letter to *Uncut*, Los Angeles, July 5, 1990, Box. 6, f. 2, John Rowberry Papers.

48. Rowberry, letter to John Shown, n.d. (most likely 1993), Box 1, f. 6, John Rowberry Papers.

49. Rowberry wrote in a letter that Hidalgo de la Torre had been phoning and faxing him lately through his secretary Rocío Sosa, who, unlike the former, spoke "pretty good English." Rowberry, letter to Ken and Jackie Edwards, Carlsbad, California, September 8, 1993, Box 3, f. 1, John Rowberry Papers.

50. Rowberry, letter to Sosa, Carlsbad, California, September 3, 1993, Box 3, f. 1, John Rowberry Papers.

51. Rowberry, letter to Alain Baillon, Oceanside, California, April 21, 1993, Box 5, f. 5, John Rowberry Papers.

52. Rowberry, letter to Ken and Jackie Edwards, Carlsbad, California, September 8, 1993, Box 3, f. 1, John Rowberry Papers.

53. Hidalgo de la Torre seems to have been particularly interested in connecting with Bjorn, then a famous porn actor and producer. In August 1993, Febo Editores sent issue 17 of *Hermes* to Rowberry so he could forward it to Bjorn's agent, which Rowberry did shortly after. See Rowberry, letter to Hidalgo de la Torre, Carlsbad, California, August 25,

1993, Box 3, f. 1, John Rowberry Papers; Rocío Sosa, letter to Rowberry, Mexico City, August 31, 1993, Box 7, f. 5, John Rowberry Papers.

54. Brown, *Work!*, 191.

55. John Shown's collage art was featured in book jackets and illustrations for various nationwide magazines, including the gay periodicals *The Advocate*, *Mandate*, *Torso*, and *In Touch*, as well as in museums and galleries. For instance, his collage exhibits *Texikon*, *Sexikon*, and *Mexikon* were featured at the University of Texas Health Science Center in San Antonio, at the Museo Universitario del Chopo in Mexico City, and in Hollywood. His films and other work were also shown at the Hibbs Gallery in New York City, at the Whitney Museum of Art, the San Antonio Museum of Modern Art, the Fleming Gallery in Houston, the Royal College of Art in London, the Witte Museum in San Antonio, and the San Antonio Art Institute, among others. See John Shown, Personal Journal, Box 2, University of Texas San Antonio Libraries Special Collections, John Shown Collection (hereafter John Shown Collection); Shown, "Mexikons Collage," Museo Universitario del Chopo, Mexico City, February 1990, Box 3, Exhibits 1979–1995, John Shown Collection; Jim Moss, "John Shown's Tarot," Box 7, f. 5, John Rowberry Papers; Pozo Pietrasanta, "Las mariposas de John Shown," *Macho Tips*, no. 20, 1989, 31; Charlene Rathurn, "John Shown at Robinson Gallery," *ArtScene*, spring 1984, p. 4.

56. John Shown, personal journal, Box OM3, John Shown Collection; Shown, letter to John Rowberry, December 3, 1990, Box 7, f. 5, John Rowberry Papers; Jim Moss, letter to John Rowberry, n.d., Box 7, f. 5, John Rowberry Papers.

57. Jim Moss, letter to John Shown, 1986, Mexico City, personal journal, Box OM3, John Shown Collection.

58. Ray (Murdock or Thomason), letter to Shown, California, personal journal, Box OM3, John Shown Collection.

59. Moss, letter to Shown, Edinburg, Texas, 1987, Box OM3, personal journal, John Shown Collection.

60. Moss, letter to Shown, Edinburg, Texas, 1987, Box OM3, personal journal, John Shown Collection.

61. Moss, letter to Shown, Edinburg, Texas, 1987, Box OM3, personal journal, John Shown Collection.

62. John Shown, "Sexikons," Box 3, Folder "Exhibits," John Shown Collection.

63. Shown, personal journal, Box OM3, John Shown Collection.

64. Shown, letter to *Forum* Board Members, San Antonio, September 1, 1987, Box 1, Folder "Forum, 'Correspondence, clippings, 1985–1987,'" John Shown Collection.

65. *Nuevo en todas las artes* was distributed free of charge. Its reportage focused mostly on Mexican socialites, famous photographers, celebrities, cultural events, art, and fashion. It also contained numerous ads for hairstylists, painters, art galleries, and designers.

66. Pozo Pietrasanta, "Las mariposas de John Shown," 31.

67. Jim Moss, letter to Tony DeBlase, Mexico City, November 23, 1989, Desmodus Correspondence, Jim Moss File (PERS-0016-04-02-0239), Box 14, Folder 43, Leather Archives, Chicago, Illinois [hereafter Leather Archives].

68. Shown, letter to Rowberry, December 3, 1990, Box 7, f. 5, John Rowberry Papers.

69. See "Contract," signed by John Rowberry, August 25, 1989, Box 3, f. 5, John Rowberry Papers; Moss, "How to Make Your Own Porno Videos."

70. Moss, letter to DeBlase, Box 14, Folder 43, Leather Archives.

71. Ken Edwards, letter to Gary and Rowberry, Guadalajara, Mexico, February 26, 1993, Box 1, f. 6, John Rowberry Papers.

72. Ken Edwards, "Notes to John Rowberry and Jim Moss," n.d., Box 1, f. 5, John Rowberry Papers.

73. Gonzalo Pozo Pietrasanta, interview by the author, Mexico City, July 25, 2019.

74. Moss, "How to Make Your Own Porno Videos."

75. Moss, "How to Make Your Own Porno Videos."

76. Dávila, *Latinos, Inc.*, 78.

77. Benshoff, *Queer Images*, 114–15.

78. Hernández, interview by the author, Mexico City, June 19, 2019.

79. See ads "Catalina Presents Two from Scott Masters" and "New XXX All-Latin Male Feature Videos!" in *Uncut Magazine*, no. 3, January 1989, 53–54.

80. See ad "A Special Selection of Marksman Bestsellers" in *Uncut Magazine*, no. 3, January 1989, 58.

81. See the ads in *Drummer*, no. 172, 1994, 10–14, and in other contemporary magazines.

82. All of these videos were available by mail from International Wavelength, but in 1989, John Rowberry sold the rights of *Viva Macho 2* to Rollo, Inc. The tape was a "90 minute feature mostly solo but with dual scenes in 3 episodes." See Moss, "How to Make Your Own Porno Videos." See also "Contract," signed by John Rowberry, August 25, 1989, Box 3, f. 5, John Rowberry Papers.

83. In relation to the selling costs of heterosexual pornography around the same years, Chuck Kleinhans comments that "retail cost drastically changes from $70 to $100 per feature-length tape, circa 1980, to $35 to $40 for new releases, $15 to $25 for basic features in 1990, with some discounters going lower . . . the cost of specialty videos (sadomasochist, transvestite, transsexual, etc.) remains high because the niche market will bear it." See Kleinhans, "The Change from Film to Video Pornography," 160.

84. Prince, *New Pot of Gold*, 359.

85. Mercer, *Gay Pornography*, 150.

86. Strub, "Indexing Desire," 138–39.

87. Ken Edwards, "Notes to John Rowberry and Jim Moss," n.d., Box 1, f. 5, John Rowberry Papers.

88. Edwards, "Notes to John Rowberry and Jim Moss."

89. Moss, *Viva Macho*, Pronger Collection, Sexual Representation Collection, University of Toronto, Toronto.

90. Dávila, *Latinos, Inc.*, 89.

91. Rowberry, letter to John Preston, Carlsbad, July 18, 1993, Box 1, f. 2, John Rowberry Papers.

92. Geroge Mavety, letter to Rowberry, Broadway, New York, June 26, 1990, Box 5, f. 3, John Rowberry Papers.

93. Burger, *One-Handed Histories*, 55.

94. Ortiz, "Hot and Spicy."

95. Miller-Young, *Taste for Brown Sugar*, 111.
96. Nash, *The Black Body in Ecstasy*, 149.
97. For Hanson's own recollection of this conference, see Hanson, "Teaching Shame," 156–57.
98. Pérez, *Taste for Brown Bodies*, 113.
99. Pérez, *Taste for Brown Bodies*, 113–14.
100. Pérez, *Taste for Brown Bodies*, 114.
101. Moss, "How to Make Your Own Porno Videos."
102. See letter exchanges between 1991 and 1993 among John Rowberry, Jackie and Ken Edwards, and John Shown in Box 1, fs. 5 and 6 of the John Rowberry Papers. See also "En memoria: Jim Moss," *Hermes* no. 10, 1992, 16–20.

CONCLUSION

1. Charles P. Thorp, "A Gay Liberation Manifesto," *Gay Sunshine*, no. 3, November 1970, 8.
2. Warner, *Never Going Back*, 4.
3. Warner, *Never Going Back*, 4.
4. Warner, *Never Going Back*, 4–5.
5. "Argentina: Gay Manifesto," *Gay Sunshine*, no. 15, November 1972, 7.
6. Dame-Griff, *Two Revolutions*, 21.
7. Churchill, "Transnationalism and Homophile Political Culture," 57.
8. Encarnación, "International Influence," 688.
9. Encarnación, *Out in the Periphery*, 21–22.
10. Caro and Simonetto, "Sexualidades radicales," 66.

bibliography

ARCHIVES

Archivo Histórico Gráfico de las Primeras Marchas, Colectivo Sol Online Archive
The Body Politic (TBP) Fonds, The Arquives—Canada's LGBTQ2+ Archives, Toronto, Canada
Centro de Documentación e Investigación de la Cultura de Izquierdas (CeDInCI) Online Archive
Desmodus Correspondence, Leather Archives, Chicago
Edward Lacey Fonds, McMaster University Archives and Research Collections, Hamilton, Canada
GALE, Archives of Sexuality and Gender
Gay Sunshine Records, ONE National Gay & Lesbian Archives, Los Angeles, California
Hermes Files, Comisión Calificadora de Publicaciones y Revistas Ilustradas, Mexico City
John Kyper Papers, GLBT Historical Society, San Francisco, California
John Rowberry Papers, University of California Los Angeles Library Special Collections
John Shown Collection, University of Texas San Antonio Libraries Special Collections
Magazines Collection, Colectivo Sol Online Archive
Pronger Collection, Sexual Representation Collection, Bonham Centre for Sexual Diversity Studies, University of Toronto
Robert Roth Papers, Cornell University Library, Division of Rare and Manuscript Collections.
Serie identidades sexo-genéricas, Centro Académico de la Memoria de Nuestra América (CAMeNA), Mexico City

PERIODICALS CONSULTED

41 soñar fantasmas, Mexico City, 1992–1993
The Body Politic, Toronto, 1971–1987
Come Out!, New York, 1970–1972
Del otro lado, Mexico City, 1992–1996
Fag Rag, Boston, 1971–1987
Gai pied, Paris, 1979-1992

Gay Community News, Boston, 1973–1999
Gay Sunshine, Berkeley and San Francisco, 1970–1982
Hermes, Mexico City, 1990–1994
Lampião da esquina, São Paulo, 1978–1981
Macho Tips, Mexico City, 1985–1989
Nuestro cuerpo, Mexico City, 1979–1980
Nuevo ambiente, Mexico City, 1979–1983
Política sexual, Mexico City, 1979
Somos, Buenos Aires, 1973–1976

LIST OF INTERVIEWS

Adriane Shown, Los Angeles, June 29, 2019
Alejandro Brito, Mexico City, February 19, 2019
Antonio González de Cosío, Skype, March 7, 2019
Armando Cristeto, Skype, May 25, 2020
Danny Liard, Mexico City, December 19, 2019
Ed Jackson, Toronto, January 26, 2019
Eréndira García Salazar, Mexico City, February 20, 2019
Gerald Hannon, Toronto, April 26, 2016
Gonzalo Pozo Pietrasanta, Mexico City, July 25, 2019
Gonzalo Pozo Pietrasanta, Skype, March 11, 2019
Jearld Moldenhauer, Skype, May 23, 2016
José Antonio Izazola Licea, Skype, March 12, 2019
José Luis Bueno, Mexico City, January 11, 2018
José Luis Bueno, Mexico City, February 20, 2019
Juan Carlos Yustis, Mexico City, February 15, 2019
Juan Jacobo Hernández, Mexico City, June 19, 2019
Ken Popert, Toronto, April 28, 2016
Mariana Valverde, Toronto, July 4, 2017
Milton Robles, Mexico City, July 30, 2019
Nikos Diaman, Skype, October 8, 2019
Oscar Emilio Laguna Maqueda, Mexico City, February 18, 2019
Pablo Stajnsznajder, phone conversation, November 26, 2020
Pedro Gellert, Mexico City, December 19, 2019
Ralf Marsault, Paris, August 12, 2019
Teresa Incháustegui, phone conversation, October 17, 2022
Tim McCaskell, Toronto, April 25, 2016
William Shown, San Antonio, February 18, 2020
Xabier Lizarraga Cruchaga, Mexico City, February 18, 2019

SECONDARY SOURCES

Agustín, José. *La tragicomedia mexicana 2: la vida en México de 1970 a 1982*. Mexico: Planeta, 1992.

Allier-Montaño, Eugenia. "From *Conspiracy to Struggle for Democracy*: A Historicization of the Political Memories of the Mexican '68." In *The Struggle for Memory in Latin*

America: Recent History and Political Violence, edited by Allier-Montaño and Emilio Crenzel, 130–46. New York: Palgrave Macmillan, 2015.
Altman, Denis. *The Homosexualization of America*. New York: St. Martin's Press, 1982.
Amin, Kadji. *Disturbing Attachments: Genet, Modern Pederasty, and Queer History*. Durham, NC: Duke University Press, 2017.
Anderson, Benedict. *Imagined Communities: Reflections on the Origin and Spread of Nationalism*. London: Verso, 1983.
Anderson, Mark D. *Disaster Writing: The Cultural Politics of Catastrophe in Latin America*. Charlottesville: University of Virginia Press, 2011.
Appelbaum, Nancy P., Anne S. Macpherson, and Karin Alejandra Rosemblatt. "Introduction." In Appelbaum, Macpherson, and Rosemblatt, eds., *Race and Nation in Modern Latin America*, 1–31.
Appelbaum, Nancy P., Anne S. Macpherson, and Karin Alejandra Rosemblatt, eds. *Race and Nation in Modern Latin America*. Chapel Hill: University of North Carolina Press, 2003.
Argüello Pazmiño, Sofía. "Identidades en disputa: discursos científicos, medios de comunicación y estrategias políticas del Movimiento de Liberación Homosexual mexicano, 1968–1984." In *La memoria y el deseo: estudios gay y queer en México*, edited by Rodrigo Parrini Roses and Alejandro Brito, 25–49. Mexico City: Universidad Nacional Autónoma de México, 2014.
Armstrong, Elizabeth. *Forging Gay Identities: Organizing Sexuality in San Francisco, 1950–1994*. Chicago: University of Chicago Press, 2002.
Avicolli Mecca, Tommi, ed. *Smash the Church, Smash the State: The Early Years of Gay Liberation*. San Francisco: City Lights Books, 2009.
Baim, Tracy, ed. *Gay Press, Gay Power: The Growth of LGBT Community Newspapers in America*. Chicago: Prairie Avenue Productions and Windy City Media Group, 2012.
Balderston, Daniel, and José Quiroga. "A Beautiful, Sinister Fairyland: Gay Sunshine Press Does Latin America." *Social Text* 21, no. 3 (Fall 2003): 85–108.
Barthes, Roland. *Camera Lucida*. New York: Hill and Wang, 1981.
Bébout, Rick. "On the Origins of *The Body Politic*: 'Conception and Birth.'" Accessed January 13, 2019. http://www.rbebout.com/oldbeep/concep.htm.
Beissel, Henry. "Introduction." In *A Magic Prison: Letters from Edward Lacey*, edited by David Helwig, 5–16. Ottawa: Oberon Press, 1995.
Ben, Pablo, and Santiago Joaquín Insausti. "Dictatorial Rule and Sexual Politics in Argentina: The Case of the Frente de Liberación Homosexual, 1967–1976." *Hispanic American Historical Review* 97, no. 2 (May 2017): 297–325.
Bender, Steven W. *Greasers and Gringos: Latinos, Law, and the American Imagination*. New York: New York University Press, 2003.
Benshoff, Griffin. *Queer Images: A History of Gay and Lesbian Film in America*. Lanham, MD: Rowman and Littlefield, 2006.
Boivin, Renaud René. "*L'organisation sociale et spatiale des minorités sexuelles à Mexico: Construction d'une économie culturelle au cours du XXème siècle*." *Métropoles* 14 (June 2014).
Boyd, Nan Alamilla. "San Francisco's Castro District: From Gay Liberation to Tourist Destination." *Journal of Tourism and Cultural Change* 9, no. 3 (December 2011): 237–48.

Boyd, Nan Alamilla. *Wide-Open Town: A Queer History of San Francisco, 1945–1965*. Berkeley: University of California Press, 2003.

Brennan, Denise. *What's Love Got to Do with It?: Transnational Desires and Sex Tourism in the Dominican Republic*. Durham, NC: Duke University Press, 2004.

Bronstein, Carolyn. *Battling Pornography: The American Feminist Anti-Pornography Movement, 1976–1986*. New York: Cambridge University Press, 2011.

Brown, Elspeth. "Canada's First Gay Student Activist Group." *Notches: Remarks on the History of Sexuality*, February 5, 2019. Accessed July 15, 2021. https://notchesblog.com/2019/02/05/canadas-first-gay-student-activist-group/.

Brown, Elspeth. *Work! A Queer History of Modeling*. Durham, NC: Duke University Press, 2019.

Burger, John. *One-Handed Histories: The Eroto-Politics of Gay Male Video Pornography*. New York: Haworth Press, 1995.

Bustos-Aguilar, Pedro. "Mister Don't Touch the Banana: Notes on the Popularity of the Ethnosexed Body South of the Border." *Critique of Anthropology* 15, no. 2 (June 1995): 149–70.

Butler, Judy. "Lesbian s/m: The Politics of Dis-Illusion." In *Against Sadomasochism: A Radical Feminist Analysis*, edited by Robin Ruth Linden, Darlene R. Pagano, Diana E. H. Russell, and Susan Leigh Star, 169–75. East Palo Alto, CA: Frog in the Well, 1982.

Califia, Pat. *Sapphistry: The Book of Lesbian Sexuality*. Tallahassee, FL: Naiad Press, 1988.

Campbell, Federico. "El sida se hace tema central de órganos de cultura e información de homosexuales." *Proceso*, Mexico City, May 16, 1987.

Cano, Gabriela. "Unconcealable Realities of Desire: Amelio Robles's (Transgender) Masculinity in the Mexican Revolution." In *Sex in Revolution: Gender, Politics, and Power in Modern Mexico*, edited by Jocelyn Olcott, Mary Kay Vaughan, and Gabriela Cano, 35–56. Durham, NC: Duke University Press, 2006.

Caro Romero, Felipe Cesar Camilo. "Más allá de Stonewall: El Movimiento de Liberación Homosexual de Colombia y las redes de activismo internacional, 1976–1989." *Historia Crítica*, no. 75 (January–March 2020): 93–114.

Caro Romero, Felipe Cesar Camilo, and Patricio Simonetto. "Sexualidades radicales: los movimientos de liberación homosexual en América Latina (1967–1989)." *Izquierdas* 46 (May 2019): 65–85.

Castells, Manuel. *The City and the Grassroots: A Cross-Cultural Theory of Urban Social Movements*. Berkeley: University of California Press, 1983.

Chenier, Elise. "Liberating Marriage: Gay Liberation and Same-Sex Marriage in Early 1970s Canada." In Gentile, Kinsman, and Rankin, eds., *We Still Demand!*, 29–50.

Churchill, David. "Personal Ad Politics: Race, Sexuality and Power at *The Body Politic*." *Left History* 8, no. 2 (March 2003): 114–34.

Churchill, David. "Transnationalism and Homophile Political Culture in the Postwar Decades." *GLQ: A Journal of Lesbian and Gay Studies* 15, no. 1 (January 2009): 31–66.

Cole, Susan. *Pornography and the Sex Crisis*. Toronto: Amanita Enterprises, 1989.

Corneau, Simon, and Emily van der Meulen. "Some Like It Mellow: On Gay Men Complicating Pornography Discourses." *Journal of Homosexuality* 61, no. 4 (February 2014): 491–510.

Cossman, Brenda. "Censor, Resist, Repeat: A History of Censorship of Gay and Lesbian Sexual Representation in Canada." *Duke Journal of Gender Law and Policy* 21, no. 1 (Fall 2014): 45–66.

Cossman, Brenda, Shannon Bell, Lise Gotell, and Becki L. Ross. *Bad Attitude/s on Trial: Pornography, Feminism, and the Butler Decision*. Toronto: University of Toronto Press, 1997.

Craig, Steve. "Madison Avenue Versus *The Feminine Mystique*: The Advertising Industry's Response to the Women's Movement." In *Disco Divas: Women and Popular Culture in the 1970s*, edited by Sherrie A. Inness, 13–23. Philadelphia: University of Pennsylvania Press, 2003.

Dame-Griff, Avery. *The Two Revolutions: A History of the Transgender Internet*. New York: New York University Press, 2023.

Dávila, Arlene. *Latinos, Inc.: The Marketing and Making of a People*. Berkeley: University of California Press, 2001.

Davis, Whitney. *Queer Beauty: Sexuality and Aesthetics from Winckelmann to Freud and Beyond*. New York: Columbia University Press, 2010.

Dean, Tim. *Unlimited Intimacy: Reflections on the Subculture of Barebacking*. Chicago: University of Chicago Press, 2009.

de Groot, Scott. "Out of the Closet and into Print: Gay Liberation Across the Anglo-American World." PhD diss., Queen's University, 2015.

de la Mora, Sergio. *Cinemachismo: Masculinities and Sexuality in Mexican Film*. Austin: University of Texas Press, 2006.

Delap, Lucy. "Feminism, Masculinities and Emotional Politics in Late Twentieth Century Britain." *Cultural and Social History* 15, no. 4 (October 2018): 571–93.

D'Emilio, John. "Capitalism and Gay Identity." In *The Lesbian and Gay Studies Reader*, edited by Henry Abelove, Michèle Aina Barale, and David Halperin, 467–76. New York: Routledge/Taylor and Francis Group, 1993.

D'Emilio, John. "Foreword: The Leading Edge of Change: The LGBT Press in the 1970s." In Baim, ed., *Gay Press, Gay Power*, 9–10.

D'Emilio, John. *Sexual Politics, Sexual Communities: The Making of a Homosexual Minority in the United States, 1940–1970*. Chicago: University of Chicago Press, 1998.

Dewhurst, Robert. "*Gay Sunshine*: Pornopoetic Collage, and Queer Archive." In *Porn Archives*, edited by Tim Dean, Steven Ruszczycky, and David Squires, 213–33. Durham, NC: Duke University Press, 2014.

Díez, Jordi. "El movimiento lésbico-gay, 1978–2010." In *Los grandes problemas de México*, vol. 8, edited by Ana María Tepichin, Karine Tinat, and Luzelena Gutiérrez, 135–54. Mexico City: El Colegio de México, 2010.

Díez, Jordi. "La trayectoria política del Movimiento Lésbico-Gay en México," *Estudios sociológicos* 29, no. 86 (May–August 2011): 687–712.

Domingos de Oliveira, José Marcelo. *Desejo, preconceito e morte: assassinations de LGBT em Sergipe—1980 a 2010*. Paripiranga: Faculdade AGES, 2014.

Domínguez-Ruvalcaba, Héctor. "From Fags to Gays: Political Adaptations and Cultural Translations in the Mexican Gay Liberation Movement." In *Mexico Reading the United States*, edited by Linda Egan and Mary K. Long, 116–34. Nashville, TN: Vanderbilt University Press, 2009.

Domínguez-Ruvalcaba, Héctor. *Modernity and the Nation in Mexican Representations of Masculinity: From Sensuality to Bloodshed*. New York: Palgrave Macmillan, 2007.

Duffy, Brooke Erin. *Remake, Remodel: Women's Magazines in the Digital Age*. Urbana: University of Illinois Press, 2013.

Dunn, Christopher. *Contracultura: Alternative Arts and Social Transformation in Authoritarian Brazil*. Chapel Hill: University of North Carolina Press, 2016.

Dworkin, Andrea, and Catharine MacKinnon. *Pornography and Civil Rights: A New Day for Women's Equality*. Minneapolis: Organizing Against Pornography, 1988.

Echols, Alice. *Daring to Be Bad: Radical Feminism in America 1967–1975*. Minneapolis: University of Minnesota Press, 1989.

Encarnación, Omar Guillermo. "International Influence, Domestic Activism, and Gay Rights in Argentina." *Political Science Quarterly* 128, no. 4 (2013–2014): 687–716.

Encarnación, Omar Guillermo. *Out in the Periphery: Latin America's Gay Rights Revolution*. New York: Oxford University Press, 2016.

Escoffier, Jeffrey. *American Homo: Community and Perversity*. Berkeley: University of California Press, 1998.

Escoffier, Jeffrey. *Bigger than Life: The History of Gay Porn Cinema from Beefcake to Hardcore*. Philadelphia: Running Press, 2009.

Escoffier, Jeffrey. *Sex, Society, and the Making of Pornography: The Pornographic Object of Knowledge*. New Brunswick, NJ: Rutgers University Press, 2021.

Evans, Sara. *Personal Politics: The Roots of Women's Liberation in the Civil Rights Movement and the New Left*. New York: Alfred A. Knopf, 1980.

Fernández Galeano, Javier. "Cartas desde Buenos Aires: el movimiento homosexual argentino desde una perspectiva transnacional." *Latin American Research Review* 54, no. 3 (September 2019): 608–22.

Firestone, Shulamith. *The Dialectic of Sex: The Case for Feminist Revolution*. New York: W. Morrow, 1970.

Fonseca, Carlos. *The Literature of Catastrophe: Nature, Disaster and Revolution in Latin America*. New York: Bloomsbury Academic and Professional, 2020.

Forgione, Steve, and Kurt Hill, eds. *No Apologies: The Unauthorized Publication of Internal Discussion Documents of the Socialist Workers Party (SWP) Concerning Lesbian/Gay Male Liberation. Part 2: 1975–1979*. New York: Lesbian/Gay Rights Monitoring Group, 1981.

Frascà, Paolo. "Mario Mieli." In *The Literary Encyclopedia*. https://www.litencyc.com/php/speople.php?rec=true&UID=14147.

Frente de Liberación Homosexual. *Sexo y revolución*. Second Edition. Buenos Aires, 1974.

Friedan, Betty. *The Feminine Mystique*. New York: Norton, 1963.

Fritscher, Jack. *Gay San Francisco: Eyewitness Drummer*, vol. 1. San Francisco: Palm Drive, 2008.

Fuentes Ponce, Adriana. *Decidir sobre el propio cuerpo: una historia reciente del movimiento lésbico en México*. Mexico: La cifra editorial, Universidad Autónoma Metropolitana-Xochimilco, 2015.

Fung, Richard. "Looking for My Penis: The Eroticized Asian in Gay Video Porn." In *How Do I Look?*, edited by Bad Object-Choices, 145–68. Seattle: Bay Press, 1991.

Gay Erotic Archives. "Inches Magazine." Last updated in February 2006. Accessed June 25, 2021. https://www.gayeroticarchives.com/22_listings/Monthlies/Inches.html.

Gentile, Patrizia, Gary Kinsman, and L. Pauline Rankin. "Introduction." In Gentile, Kinsman, and Rankin, eds., *We Still Demand!*, 3-25.

Gentile, Patrizia, Gary Kinsman, and L. Pauline Rankin, eds. *We Still Demand! Redefining Resistance in Sex and Gender Struggles*. Vancouver: University of British Columbia Press, 2017.

Gleibman, Shlomo. "'The Madness of the Carnival': Representations of Latin America and the Caribbean in the U.S. Homophile Press." *Journal of Homosexuality* 64, no. 7 (April 2017): 870–88.

Golding, Sue. "Knowledge Is Power: A Few Thoughts About Lesbian Sex, Politics and Community Standards." *Fireweed* 13 (1982): 80–100.

González Romero, Martín Humberto. "Contra el agandalle de la tira: el surgimiento del Movimiento de Liberación Homosexual y la resistencia a la razias policiacas en la ciudad de México, 1978–1984." *Sémata: ciencias sociais e humanidades* 31 (August 2019): 71–88.

González Romero, Martín Humberto. "La revolución sexual: debates públicos de sexualidad, política y cultura en la Ciudad de México, 1960–1984." PhD diss., El Colegio de México, 2021.

Green, James. *Beyond Carnival: Male Homosexuality in Twentieth-Century Brazil*. Chicago: University of Chicago Press, 1999.

Green, James. "Desire and Revolution: Socialists and the Brazilian Gay Liberation Movement in the 1970s." In *Human Rights and Transnational Solidarity in Cold War Latin America*, edited by Jessica Stites Mor, 239–67. Madison: University of Wisconsin Press, 2013.

Grinnell, Lucinda. "'Intolerable Subjects': Moralizing Politics, Economic Austerity, and Lesbian and Gay Activism in Mexico City, 1982–85." *Radical History Review* 2012, no. 112 (January 2012): 89–99.

Grinnell, Lucinda. "Lesbianas Presente: Lesbian Activism, Transnational Alliances, and the State in Mexico City 1968–1991." PhD diss., University of New Mexico, 2013.

Grube, John. "No More Shit: The Struggle for Democratic Gay Space in Toronto." In *Queers in Space: Communities/ Public Space/ Sites of Resistance*, edited by Gordon Brent Ingram, Anne-Marie Bouthillette, and Yolanda Retter, 127–45. Seattle: Bay Press, 1997.

Gutmann, Matthew. *The Meanings of Macho: Being a Man in Mexico City*. Berkeley: University of California Press, 2006.

Halter, Marilyn. *Shopping for Identity: The Marketing of Ethnicity*. New York: Schocken Books, 2000.

Hanson, Ellis. "Teaching Shame." In *Gay Shame*, edited by David M. Halperin and Valerie Traub, 132–64. Chicago: University of Chicago Press, 2009.

Haritaworn, Jin, Ghaida Moussa, and Syrus Marcus Ware. "Marvellous Grounds: An Introduction." In *Marvellous Grounds: Queer of Colour Histories of Toronto*, edited by Jin Haritaworn, Ghaida Moussa, and Syrus Marcus Ware, 1–20. Toronto: Between the Lines, 2018.

Herrera Calderón, Fernando, and Adela Cedillo. "Introduction: The Unknown Mexican Dirty War." In *Challenging Authoritarianism in Mexico: Revolutionary Struggles and the Dirty War, 1964–1982*, edited by Fernando Herrera Calderón and Adela Cedillo, 1–18. New York: Routledge, 2011.

Hesford, Victoria. *Feeling Women's Liberation*. Durham, NC: Duke University Press, 2013.

Higginbotham, Evelyn Brooks. *Righteous Discontent: The Women's Movement in the Black Baptist Church, 1880–1920*. Cambridge, MA: Harvard University Press, 1993.

Hilderbrand, Lucas. "A Suitcase Full of Vaseline, or Travels in the 1970s Gay World." *Journal of the History of Sexuality* 22, no. 3 (September 2013): 373–402.

Hobson, Emily. *Lavender and Red: Liberation and Solidarity in the Gay and Lesbian Left*. Oakland: University of California Press, 2016.

Hoffman, Amy. *An Army of Ex-Lovers: My Life at the Gay Community News*. Amherst: University of Massachusetts Press, 2007.

Hooper, Tom. "Queering '69: The Recriminalization of Homosexuality in Canada." *Canadian Historical Review* 100, no. 2 (2019): 257–73.

Hrynyk, Nicholas Andrew. "'Pin the Macho on the Man': Mediations of Gay Male Masculinity in *The Body Politic*, 1971–1987." PhD diss., Carleton University, 2018.

Hunter, Nan D. "Contextualizing the Sexuality Debates: A Chronology 1966–2005." In *Sex Wars: Sexual Dissent and Political Culture*, edited by Lisa Duggan and Nan D. Hunter, 15–28. New York: Routledge, 2006.

Iqani, Mehita. *Consumer Culture and the Media: Magazines in the Public Eye*. Basingstoke: Palgrave Macmillan, 2012.

Irwin, Robert McKee, Edward J. McCaughan, and Michelle Rocío Nasser. "Introduction." In *The Famous 41: Sexuality and Social Control in Mexico, 1901*, edited by Robert McKee Irwin, Edward J. McCaughan, and Michelle Rocío Nasser, 1–18. New York: Palgrave Macmillan, 2003.

Jackman, Michael Connors. "Bawdy Politics: Remembering Sexual Liberation." PhD diss., York University, 2013.

Jackman, Michael Connors. "*The Body Politic*: At the Genesis of Sexual Liberation in Canada," *Xtra!*, October 20, 2011.

Jackson, Ed, and Stan Persky, eds. *Flaunting It! A Decade of Gay Journalism from "The Body Politic": An Anthology*. Vancouver: New Star Books, 1982.

Jay, Karla, and Allen Young, eds. *Out of the Closets: Voices of Gay Liberation*. New York: Douglas Book Corp., 1972.

Johnson, David. *Buying Gay: How Physique Entrepreneurs Sparked a Movement*. New York: Columbia University Press, 2019.

Kendall, Christopher Nigel. *Gay Male Pornography: An Issue of Sex Discrimination*. Vancouver: University of British Columbia Press, 2004.

Kimmel, Michael S., ed., *Men Confront Pornography*. New York: Crown, 1990.

Kinsman, Gary. "Queer Resistance and Regulation in the 1970s: From Liberation to Rights." In Gentile, Kinsman, and Rankin, eds., *We Still Demand!*, 137–62.

Kinsman, Gary. *The Regulation of Desire: Sexuality in Canada*. Montreal: Black Rose Books, 1996.

Kirtley, Charles. "Let the Sunshine In: The Pioneering Role of Winston Leyland in Gay Publishing." Lesbian and Gay New York, Spring 1998. Accessed April 19, 2021. http://www.leylandpublications.com/article_leyland.html.

Kissack, Terence. "Freaking Fag Revolutionaries: New York's Gay Liberation Front, 1969–1971." *Radical History Review* 62 (Spring 1995): 104–35.

Kleinhans, Chuck. "The Change from Film to Video Pornography: Implications for Analysis." In *Pornography: Film and Culture*, edited by Peter Lehman, 154–67. New Brunswick, NJ: Rutgers University Press, 2006.

Knight, Alan. "Racism, Revolution, and *Indigenismo*: Mexico, 1910–1940." In *The Idea of Race in Latin America, 1870–1940*, edited by Richard Graham, 71–113. Austin: University of Texas Press, 1990.

Korinek, Valerie J. "*voices* of Gay, Lesbian, and Feminist Activists in the Prairies." *American Periodicals* 28, no. 2 (2018): 123–38.

Kyper, John. "Coming Out and into the GLF: Banned No More in Boston." In *Smash the Church, Smash the State: The Early Years of Gay Liberation*, edited by Tommi Avicolli Mecca, 31–39. San Francisco: City Lights Books, 2009.

Labastida Martín del Campo, Julio Alfonso. "Legitimidad y cambio del régimen político en México." In *Globalización, identidad y democracia: México y América Latina*, coordinated by Julio Alfonso Labastida Martín del Campo and Antonio Camou, 170–218. Mexico: Universidad Nacional Autónoma de México and Siglo XXI editores, 2001.

Lacombe, Dany. *Blue Politics: Pornography and the Law in the Age of Feminism*. Toronto: University of Toronto Press, 1994.

Laguarda, Rodrigo. *Ser gay en la ciudad de México: lucha de representaciones y apropiación de una identidad, 1968–1982*. Mexico City: CIESAS and Instituto Mora, 2009.

Laird, Cynthia. "GLF Pioneer Nikos Diaman Dies." *Bay Area Reporter*, November 11, 2020. Accessed October 21, 2021. https://www.ebar.com/news/news//299125.

Lapovsky Kennedy, Elizabeth, and Madeline D. Davis. *Boots of Leather, Slippers of Gold: The History of a Lesbian Community*. New York: Routledge, 1993.

Lázaro, Ch. A. "La conformación del movimiento LGBT en Guadalajara, Jalisco." *Argumentos* 27, no. 76 (September–December 2014): 241–73.

Levine, Martin P. *Gay Macho: The Life and Death of the Homosexual Clone*. New York: New York University Press, 1998.

Lewis, Abram J. "'We Are Certain of Our Own Insanity': Antipsychiatry and the Gay Liberation Movement, 1968–1980." *Journal of the History of Sexuality* 25, no. 1 (January 2016): 83–113.

Leyland, Winston. "Introduction." In *Gay Roots: Twenty Years of Gay Sunshine: An Anthology of Gay History, Sex, Politics, and Culture*, edited by Winston Leyland, 1–30. San Francisco: Gay Sunshine Press, 1991.

LGBT Religious Archives Network. "Winston Leyland." Accessed October 3, 2020. https://lgbtqreligiousarchives.org/profiles/winston-leyland.

Lizarraga Cruchaga, Xabier. *Una historia sociocultural de la homosexualidad: notas sobre un devenir silenciado*. Mexico City: Paidós, 2003.

López Cámara, Francisco. *La cultura del 68: Reich y Marcuse*. Mexico: Universidad Autónoma de México, Centro Regional de Investigaciones Multidisciplinarias, 1989.

Lorde, Audre. *Uses of the Erotic: The Erotic as Power*. Trumansburg: Out and Out Books, 1978.

Lumsden, Ian. *Homosexuality, Society and the State in Mexico*. Toronto: Canadian Gay Archives; Mexico City: Solediciones Colectivo Sol, 1991.

Macías-González, Víctor. "LGBTQ+ Archives and Public History Projects in Mexico, 1976 to Present." In *Sources and Methods in the History of Sexuality*, edited by Anna Clark and Elizabeth W. Williams, 191–202. Abingdon: Taylor and Francis Group, 2024.

Macías-González, Víctor. "The Transnational Homophile Movement and the Development of Domesticity in Mexico City's Homosexual Community, 1930–70." *Gender and History* 26, no. 3 (November 2014): 519–44.

Macías-González, Víctor, and Anne Rubenstein. "Introduction: Masculinity and History in Modern Mexico." In Macías-González and Rubenstein, eds., *Masculinity and Sexuality in Modern Mexico*, 1–21.

Macías-González, Víctor, and Anne Rubenstein, eds. *Masculinity and Sexuality in Modern Mexico*. Albuquerque: University of New Mexico Press, 2012.

Mallon, Florencia. "Constructing Mestizaje in Latin America: Authenticity, Marginality and Gender in the Claiming of Ethnic Identities." *Journal of Latin American Anthropology* 2, no. 1 (September 1996): 170–81.

Marcuse, Herbert. *Eros and Civilization: A Philosophical Inquiry into Freud*. Boston: Beacon Press, 1966.

Marsault-R, Ralf, and Heino Muller. "*L'enfant terrible de Hollywood*." *Gai pied hebdo*, no. 211 (March 15–21, 1986): 26–29.

Maynard, Steven. "1969 and All That: Age, Consent, and the Myth of Queer Decriminalization in Canada." *The Abusable Past*, September 6, 2019. Accessed July 20, 2024. https://abusablepast.org/1969-and-all-that-age-consent-and-the-myth-of-queer-decriminalization-in-canada/.

McCaskell, Tim. "Before I Was White I Was Presbyterian." In *Revisiting the Great White North? Reframing Whiteness, Privilege, and Identity in Education*, edited by Darren E. Lund, and Carr Paul R., 31–39. Rotterdam: Sense, 2015.

McCaskell, Tim. *Queer Progress: From Homophobia to Homonationalism*. Toronto: Between the Lines, 2016.

McCormick, Gladys I. "Torture and the Making of a Subversive During Mexico's Dirty War." In *Mexico Beyond 1968: Revolutionaries, Radicals, and Repression During the Global Sixties and Subversive Seventies*, edited by Jaime Pensado and Enrique C. Ochoa, 254–72. Tucson: University of Arizona Press, 2018.

McLeod, Donald W. "Moldenhauer, Jearld." In *Who's Who in Contemporary Gay and Lesbian History from World War II to the Present Day*, edited by Robert F. Aldrich and Garry Wotherspoon, 288–89. London: Routledge, 2000.

Meeker, Martin. *Contacts Desired: Gay and Lesbian Communications and Community, 1940s–1970s*. Chicago: University of Chicago Press, 2006.

Mercer, John. *Gay Pornography: Representations of Sexuality and Masculinity*. London: I. B. Tauris, 2017.

Meyer, Lorenzo. *Liberalismo autoritario: las contradicciones del sistema político mexicano*. Mexico City: Océano, 1995.

Meyer, Richard. "Gay Power Circa 1970: Visual Strategies for Sexual Revolution." *GLQ: A Journal of Lesbian and Gay Studies* 12, no. 3 (June 2006): 441–64.

Mezo González, Juan Carlos. "Consuming the Mexican Body: Gender, Race, and the Nation in *Macho Tips*, 1985–1989." *Hispanic American Historical Review* 100, no. 4 (November 2020): 655–87.

Mezo González, Juan Carlos. "Contested Images: Debating Nudity, Sexism, and Porn in *The Body Politic*, 1971–1987." *Left History* 23, no. 1 (November 2019): 28–61.

Mezo González, Juan Carlos. "La prensa de liberación homosexual en la ciudad de México: una lectura transnacional (1979–1983)." *Historia Mexicana* 74, no. 3 (January–March 2025): 1317–60.

Mieli, Mario. *Homosexuality and Liberation: Elements of a Gay Critique*. London: Gay Men's Press, 1980.

Miller, Marilyn Grace. *Rise and Fall of the Cosmic Race: The Cult of "Mestizaje" in Latin America*. Austin: University of Texas Press, 2004.

Miller-Young, Mireille. *A Taste for Brown Sugar: Black Women in Pornography*. Durham, NC: Duke University Press, 2014.

Millett, Kate. *Sexual Politics*. New York: Doubleday, 1970.

Millward, Liz. *Making a Scene: Lesbians and Community Across Canada, 1964–84*. Vancouver: University of British Columbia Press, 2015.

Mogrovejo, Norma. *Un amor que se atrevió a decir su nombre: la lucha de las lesbianas y su relación con los movimientos homosexual y feminista en América Latina*. Mexico: CDHAL, Plaza y Valdés, 2000.

Moldenhauer, Jearld. "The Cornell Student Homophile League." Accessed March 31, 2021. https://www.jearldmoldenhauer.com/wp-content/uploads/Cornell-Final5X.pdf.

Monsiváis, Carlos. "De las variedades de la experiencia homoerótica." *Debate Feminista* 35 (April 2007): 163–92.

Monsiváis, Carlos. "La noche popular: paseos, júbilos, necesidades orgánicas, tensiones, especies antiguas y recientes, descargas anímicas en formas de coreografías." *Debate Feminista* 18 (October 1998): 55–73.

Monsiváis, Carlos. "Los gay en México: la fundación, la ampliación, la consolidación del gueto." *Debate Feminista* 26 (October 2002): 89–115.

Monsiváis, Carlos. "Nightlife." In *The Mexico City Reader*, edited by Rubén Gallo and translated by Lorna Scott Fox and Gallo, 175–92. Madison: University of Wisconsin Press, 2004.

Moraga, Cherríe, and Gloria Anzaldúa, eds. *This Bridge Called My Back: Writings by Radical Women of Color*. Watertown, MA: Persephone Press, 1981.

Moreno Figueroa, Mónica G. "Distributed Intensities: Whiteness, Mestizaje and the Logics of Mexican Racism," *Ethnicities* 10, no. 3 (August 2010): 387–401.

Mumford, Kevin. *Not Straight, Not White: Black Gay Men from the March on Washington to the AIDS Crisis*. Chapel Hill: University of North Carolina Press, 2016.

Nash, Catherine. "Consuming Sexual Liberation: Gay Business, Politics, and Toronto's Barracks Bathhouse Raids." *Journal of Canadian Studies/Revue d'études canadiennes* 48, no. 1 (Winter 2014): 82–105.

Nash, Jennifer C. *The Black Body in Ecstasy: Reading Race, Reading Pornography*. Durham, NC: Duke University Press, 2014.

Nevaer, Louis E. V. *The Rise of the Hispanic Market in the United States: Challenges, Dilemmas, and Opportunities for Corporate Management*. London: Routledge, 2015.

Nguyen, Tan Hoang. *A View from the Bottom: Asian American Masculinity and Sexual Representation*. Durham, NC: Duke University Press, 2014.

Nyers, Peter. "Abject Cosmopolitanism: The Politics of Protection in the Anti-Deportation Movement." *Third World Quarterly* 24, no. 6 (December 2003): 1069–93.

Ortiz, Christopher. "Hot and Spicy: Representation of Chicano/Latino Men in Gay Pornography," *Jump Cut* 39 (June 1994): 83–90.

Oster, Patrick. *The Mexicans: A Personal Portrait of a People*. New York: W. Morrow, 1989.

Peralta, Braulio. "Del prejuicio a la libertad." *Milenio*, December 17, 2018. Accessed July 13, 2021. https://www.milenio.com/opinion/braulio-peralta/la-letra-desobediente/del-prejuicio-a-la-libertad.

Peralta, Braulio. *Los nombres del arcoíris: trazos para redescubrir el movimiento homosexual*. Mexico City: Nueva Imagen, CONACULTA, and INBA, 2009.

Pérez, Hiram. *A Taste for Brown Bodies: Gay Modernity and Cosmopolitan Desire*. New York: New York University Press, 2015.

Pérez, Hiram. "You Can Have My Brown Body and Eat It, Too." *Social Text* 23, nos. 3–4 (Fall–Winter 2005): 171–91.

Perlongher, Néstor. *Prosa plebeya: ensayos, 1980–1992*. Buenos Aires: Colihue, 2008.

Phipps, Kelly. "'Look over here, look over there, lesbians are everywhere': Locating Activist Lesbians in Queer Liberation History." PhD diss., Concordia University, 2019.

Pitts, Bryan. "'Hung, Hot, and Shameless in Bed': Blackness, Desire, and Politics in a Brazilian Gay Porn Magazine, 1997–2008." In *Ethnopornography: Sexuality, Colonialism, and Archival Knowledge*, edited by Neil L. Whitehead, Pete Sigal, Zeb Tortorici, 67–96. Durham, NC: Duke University Press, 2020.

Prestholdt, Jeremy. "Resurrecting Che: Radicalism, the Transnational Imagination, and the Politics of Heroes." *Journal of Global History* 7, no. 3 (November 2012): 506–26.

Prince, Stephen. *A New Pot of Gold: Hollywood Under the Electronic Rainbow, 1980–1989*. Berkeley: University of California Press, 2000.

Puar, Jasbir Puar. "Circuits of Queer Mobility: Tourism, Travel, and Globalization." *GLQ: A Journal of Lesbian and Gay Studies* 8, nos. 1–2 (April 2002): 101–37.

Quiroga, José. *Tropics of Desire: Interventions from Queer Latino America*. New York: New York University Press, 2000.

Radcliffe, Sara, and Sallie Westwood, *Remaking the Nation: Place, Identity and Politics in Latin America*. London: Routledge, 1996.

Rechy, John. *The Sexual Outlaw: A Documentary*. New York: Grove Press, 1977.

Reynolds, Robert. *From Camp to Queer: Remaking the Australian Homosexual*. Victoria: Melbourne University Press, 2002.

Rivers-Moore, Megan. *Gringo Gulch: Sex, Tourism, and Social Mobility in Costa Rica*. Chicago: University of Chicago Press, 2016.

Rodriguez, América. "Commercial Ethnicity: Language, Class and Race in the Marketing of the Hispanic Audience." *Communication Review* 2, no. 3 (November 1997): 283–309.

Ross, Becki. *The House That Jill Built: A Lesbian Nation in Formation*. Toronto: University of Toronto Press, 1995.

Rubenstein, Anne. *Bad Language, Naked Ladies, and Other Threats to the Nation: A Political History of Comic Books in Mexico*. Durham, NC: Duke University Press, 1998.

Rushbrook, Dereka. "Cities, Queer Space, and the Cosmopolitan Tourist." *GLQ: A Journal of Lesbian and Gay Studies* 8, nos. 1–2 (April 2002): 183–206.

Russell, Diana E. H. "Sadomasochism: A Contra-Feminist Activity." In *Against Sadomasochism: A Radical Feminist Analysis*, edited by Robin Ruth Linden, Darlene R. Pagano, Diana E. H. Russell, and Susan Leigh Star, 176–81. East Palo Alto, CA: Frog in the Well, 1982.

Salvatore, Ricardo. "The Enterprise of Knowledge: Representational Machines of Informal Empire." In *Close Encounters of Empire: Writing the Cultural History of US-Latin American Relations*, edited by Gilbert Joseph, Catherine LeGrand, and Ricardo Salvatore, 69–104. Durham, NC: Duke University Press, 1998.

Sánchez Crispín, Álvaro, and Álvaro López López. "Visión geográfica de los lugares gay de la ciudad de México." *Cuicuilco* 7, no. 18 (January–April 2000): 1–16.

Sender, Katherine. *Business, Not Politics: The Making of the Gay Market*. New York: Columbia University Press, 2004.

Servín, Elisa. "Another Turn of the Screw: Toward a New Political Order." In *Cycles of Conflict, Centuries of Change Crisis, Reform, and Revolution in Mexico*, edited by Elisa Servín, Leticia Reina, and John Tutino, 363–91. Durham, NC: Duke University Press, 2007.

Sheppard, Randal. "Nationalism, Economic Crisis and 'Realistic Revolution' in 1980s Mexico." *Nations and Nationalism* 17, no. 3 (January 2011): 500–519.

Sheppard, Randal. *A Persistent Revolution: History, Nationalism, and Politics in Mexico Since 1968*. Albuquerque: University of New Mexico Press, 2016.

Simonetto, Patricio. *Entre la injuria y la revolución: el Frente de Liberación Homosexual en la Argentina*. Buenos Aires: Universidad Nacional de Quilmes, 2017.

Simonetto, Patricio. "La otra internacional: prácticas globales y anclajes nacionales de la liberación homosexual en Argentina y México (1967–1984)." *Secuencia* no. 107 (May–August 2020): 1–37.

Smith, Miriam. "Interview with Chris Bearchell, Lasqueti Island, 1996." *Journal of Canadian Studies* 48, no. 1 (Winter 2014): 252–75.

Smith, Miriam. *Lesbian and Gay Rights in Canada: Social Movements and Equality-Seeking, 1971–1995*. Toronto: University of Toronto Press, 1999.

Starkey, Hugh. "Human Rights, Cosmopolitanism and Utopias: Implications for Citizenship Education." In *Human Rights and Citizenship Education*, edited by Dina Kiwan, 21–36. London: Routledge, 2015.

Stein, Marc. *City of Sisterly and Brotherly Loves: Lesbian and Gay Philadelphia, 1945–1972*. Philadelphia: Temple University Press, 2004.

Stein, Marc. *Rethinking the Gay and Lesbian Movement*. London: Routledge, 2023.

Stepan, Nancy Leys. *The Hour of Eugenics: Race, Gender, and Nation in Latin America*. Ithaca, NY: Cornell University Press, 1991.

Streitmatter, Rodger. *Unspeakable: The Rise of the Gay and Lesbian Press in America*. Boston: Faber and Faber, 1995.

Strub, Whitney. "Indexing Desire: The Gay Male Pornographic Video Collection as Affective Archive." In *Out of the Closet, into the Archives: Researching Sexual Histories*, edited by Amy L. Stone and Jaime Cantrell, 138–39. Albany: State University of New York Press, 2015.

Strub, Whitney. *Perversion for Profit: The Politics of Pornography and the Rise of the New Right*. New York: Columbia University Press, 2006.

Stryker, Susan, and Jim Van Buskirk. *Gay by the Bay: A History of Queer Culture in the San Francisco Bay Area*. San Francisco: Chronicle, 1996.

Subero, Gustavo. "Gay Mexican Pornography at the Intersection of Ethnic and National Identity in Jorge Diestra's *La putiza*." *Sexuality and Culture* 14, no. 3 (May 2010): 217–33.

Subero, Gustavo. "Gay Male Pornography and the Re/De/Construction of Postcolonial Queer Identity in Mexico." *New Cinemas: Journal of Contemporary Film* 8, no. 2 (November 2010): 119–36.

Subero, Gustavo. *Queer Masculinities in Latin American Cinema: Male Bodies and Narrative Representations*. London: I. B. Tauris, 2014.

Sue, Christina A. *Land of the Cosmic Race: Race Mixture, Racism, and Blackness in Mexico*. New York: Oxford University Press, 2013.

Suggs, Donald. "The Porn Kings of New York." *Out Magazine* 7, no. 12 (June 1999): 85–89.

Sutherland, Fraser. "Introduction." In *The Collected Poems and Translations of Edward A. Lacey*, edited by Fraser Sutherland. Toronto: Colombo, 2000.

Sutherland, Fraser. *Lost Passport: The Life and Words of Edward Lacey*. Toronto: Bookland Press, 2011.

Szulc, Łukasz. *Transnational Homosexuals in Communist Poland: Cross-Border Flows in Gay and Lesbian Magazines*. Cham: Palgrave Macmillan, 2018.

Theumer, Emmanuel. "Políticas homosexuales en la Argentina reciente (1970–1990s)." *Interdisciplina* 5, no. 11 (January–April 2017): 109–26.

Thorstad, David, ed. *Gay Liberation and Socialism: Documents from the Discussions on Gay Liberation Inside the Socialist Workers Party (1970–1973)*. New York: Thorstad, 1976.

Valverde, Mariana. *Sex, Power and Pleasure*. Toronto: Women's Press, 1985.

Vance, Carole S. "Pleasure and Danger: Toward a Politics of Sexuality." In *Pleasure and Danger: Exploring Female Sexuality*, edited by Carole S. Vance, 1–27. Boston: Routledge and Kegan Paul, 1984.

Vider, Stephen. "'The Ultimate Extension of Gay Community': Communal Living and Gay Liberation in the 1970s." *Gender & History* 27, no. 3 (November 2015): 865–81.

Wade, Peter. *Music, Race, and Nation: Música Tropical in Colombia*. Chicago: University of Chicago Press, 2000.

Wade, Peter, Fernando Urrea Giraldo, and Mara Viveros Vigoya, eds. *Raza, etnicidad y sexualidades: ciudadanía y multiculturalismo en América*. Bogotá: Universidad Nacional de Colombia, 2008.

Waitt, Gordon, and Kevin Markwell. *Gay Tourism: Culture and Context*. New York: Haworth Hospitality Press, 2006.

Warner, Tom. *Never Going Back: A History of Queer Activism in Canada*. Toronto: University of Toronto Press, 2002.

Waugh, Thomas. *Hard to Imagine: Gay Male Eroticism in Photography and Film from Their Beginnings to Stonewall*. New York: Columbia University Press, 1996.

Whittier, Nancy. "Identity Politics, Consciousness-Raising, and Visibility Politics." In *The Oxford Handbook of U.S. Women's Social Movement Activism*, edited by Holly J. McCammon, Verta Taylor, Jo Reger, and Rachel L. Einwohner, 376–97. New York: Oxford University Press, 2017.

Winsa, Patty. "Before Pride, There Was a Kiss: Toronto Gay Activists Look Back on 1976 Protest." *The Star*, Toronto, June 27, 2015. Accessed December 12, 2019. https://www.thestar.com/news/insight/2015/06/27/before-pride-there-was-a-kiss-toronto-gay-activists-look-back-on-1976-protest.html.

Young, Allen. "Out of the Closets, into the Streets." In *Out of the Closets: Voices of Gay Liberation*, edited by Karla Jay and Allen Young, 6–31. New York: Douglas Book Corp., 1972.

Zorzi, Peter. "The Start-Up of *The Body Politic*—Fall, 1971." Accessed July 24, 2021. http://onthebookshelves.com/bp01.htm.

index

Note: Page numbers followed by *f* refer to figures.

41 soñar fantasmas, 193–94, 196f, 197, 219, 247n9

Abbott, Steve, 112
activism, 17, 126; gay, 12, 25, 36, 38, 57, 65, 106–7, 117, 128, 142, 148, 222, 237n4; gay liberation, 28, 40, 68; gay periodicals and, 146, 214; gay political, 11, 35, 63–64; Hidalgo de la Torre and, 158; homophile, 108; lesbian, 25, 36, 38, 142, 148, 222; LGBTQ+, 223; "mail-order," 77; visualization of, 158
activists, 6–7, 13, 17, 21, 40, 47, 66, 113, 120, 124, 148, 150, 219; gay left, 62; homosexual, 58; Latin American, 21, 26, 70; leftist, 199, 222, 231n86; lesbian, 1, 25, 27, 35–38, 42–44, 56–57, 68, 75–76, 85, 147; lesbian liberation, 24, 155, 182; Mexican, 26–27, 38, 41–42, 48, 57, 63–64; queer, 25, 37; radical, 27–28. *See also* gay activists; gay liberation activists
Adanes, 219
Adonis, 191
advertising, 11, 85–88, 96, 101, 112, 151, 157, 164; agencies, 202; the body and, 71, 85; imagery in, 18, 76, 91; nudity and, 99; stereotypes in, 216
The Advocate, 35, 115, 248n55
AIDS, 145–46, 159–63, 219; articles about, 3; crisis, 142, 148, 182; epidemic, 155, 183, 188; programs for, 65, 160; raising consciousness about, 166
Alinder, Gary, 108

All Man, 163, 194, 204, 208
Altman, Dennis, 225
Álvarez, Ignacio, 38, 41, 52, 64–65, 159, 194
Álvarez Gayou, Juan Luis, 159
Amin, Kadji, 131
Anabitarte, Héctor, 126
Anderson, Benedict, 11, 227n10
Andrade, Sergio, 173, 175f, 176, 178, 204, 217
anti-apartheid movement, 55, 223
Apolo, 157, 219
Arenas, Reinaldo, 124
Arnal, Frank, 152
The ArQuives: Canada's LGBTQ2+ Archives, 14, 28, 179
art, 108, 136, 155, 168, 209, 249n65; cover, 46; homoerotic, 113, 120; Indigenous-related, 122; shows, 221. *See also* collages; photography
authoritarianism, 54–55, 118, 147

Balderston, Daniel, 106
bathhouses/baths, 88, 90–91, 136, 164; ads for, 166, 191; in Mexico City, 138
bathhouse raids, 87, 91–92, 234n72
Bárcenas, Tita, 150
Barthes, Roland, 17, 29
Beach Punk, 152
Bearchell, Chris, 28–29, 74–75, 88, 95

Bébout, Rick, 28
Beef Chunks, 152
Ben, Pablo, 13
Benton, Nicholas, 108, 112–13
Berlandt, Konstantin, 108
beauty, 221; female, 86; industry, 74, 86–87; male, 1, 47, 191, 193, 199–200; Mexican male, 3, 9, 144–45, 179, 182, 220; racialized male, 10; Western, 91; Western male, 183, 191, 193, 197, 199; whiteness and, 181
Bjorn, Kristen, 208, 248n53
Black Power: activists, 45; movement, 9
Blair, David (Terry David Silvercloud), 96, 97f
Blanton, Franklin D., 124
Blueboy, 152, 153f, 163, 201
body, the, 7, 44, 48, 53, 68, 85, 144, 170, 179; celebration of, 45, 47–48, 65, 72, 101, 221; community-building and, 24; contempt for, 94, 99; gay liberation and, 6, 19, 24, 27, 44, 52, 71, 75, 77, 132, 220; homosexual movement and, 1; liberation of, 4, 19, 42, 44–45, 47, 113; objectification of, 67, 72, 100; representation of, 66, 71; repression of, 51
The Body Politic (*TBP*), 1, 6–7, 15–17, 19, 26–34, 36, 40–41, 47, 54–56, 63, 65, 67–83, 85–92, 95–101, 112–13, 118, 127, 144–45; the body and, 44; censorship and, 222; Club Ottawa baths ad in, 191; community-building and, 23–24, 29, 31, 70, 81, 92, 115; erotic imagery in, 160; Figueroa and, 122; gay masculinity and, 164; on gay oppression in Argentina, 59f; *Gay Sunshine* and, 111; Hannon and, 135; on homosexual oppression in Mexico, 123f; "Hot Pics," 67, 69f, 92, 93f, 96, 97f, 99–100; nudity and, 46f, 155; sexually explicit content in, 152, 157; Toronto gay picnic and, 23, 24f; Young and, 126. *See also* McCaskell, Tim
Boivin, Renaud René, 169, 245n78
Bookpeople, 125, 132
Bourgeois, Greg, 88
Boyd, Nan Alamilla, 13, 108
Boys and Toys, 194, 219–20
Brainard, Joe, 113
Brand, Adolf, 131
Brennan, Brian, 201, 220
Brennan, Denise, 135
Brehton, Tony, 150, 171, 173, 174f, 176

Brito, Alejandro, 155
Brown, Elspeth, 177–79, 209
Brown, Pat, 35
Bueno, José Luis, 148, 150n71, 173, 178, 181, 198f
Burroughs, William, 111
Bush, Harry, 168
Bustos-Aguilar, Pedro, 138
Butchart, Robert D., 96
butterfly, 8f, 9, 58, 61, 62f, 160, 161f

Caballero, Luis, 130
Campbell, Douglas A., 90
Campbell, Federico, 159
Caminha, Adolfo, 124
La Cantina del Vaquero, 167–68, 170
capitalism, 4, 25, 54, 57, 87, 225; state, 163
Caro Romero, Felipe, 13, 225
Carrier, Joseph, 118, 138
Castro, Yan María, 57
Catalina Video, 208, 213
El caudillo, 118, 238n37
censorship, 27, 68, 92, 95–96, 98, 182, 222; laws, 155; *TBP* and, 101, 240n69; Hidalgo de la Torre and, 146, 155, 158–60, 162–63
Centro Académico de la Memoria de Nuestra América (CAMeNA), 14, 149f
chacales, 193–94, 197, 247n11
Churchill, David, 13, 94, 100, 117, 224, 236n130, 238n31
Ciao!, 136, 177
class, 10, 74, 127, 139, 165, 187; differences, 107, 224; hierarchies, 107, 135, 139; imbalances, 107, 128–30; *mestizaje* and, 173; mobility, 135; normative orders of, 243n35; oppression, 43, 223; otherness, 200
clone style, 91, 164–65
The Club (Ottawa), 88, 90–91, 191
Cocteau, Jean, 131
Cold War, 12, 37, 55, 57–58, 106, 117–18
Cole, Susan G., 94
Colectivo Sol, 169, 187, 194. *See also* *Del otro lado*
collages, 7–9, 17, 45–46, 61, 108, 113, 160, 161f, 209–10, 248n55. *See also* Mariah, Paul; Reed, James; Shown, John
colonial imaginaries, 9, 20, 105, 106, 214, 217
colonialism, 4, 25, 58, 117, 128
Colt Studios, 208

Come Out!, 26, 28–29, 61
Comisión Calificadora de Publicaciones y Revistas Ilustradas, 158–60, 163, 188, 243nn38–39, 244n46, 246n4
Comité de Homosexuales Latinoamericanos (COHLA), 232n93
community-building, 12, 16, 27, 42, 125, 223; the body and, 47; *The Body Politic* (*TBP*) and, 23–24, 29, 31, 70, 81, 92, 115; *Gay Community News* (*GCN*) and, 81, 83; gay liberation periodicals and, 77, 85; gay periodicals and, 11, 15, 19, 101, 134; *Gay Sunshine* and, 107, 112–13; Leyland and, 117; *Macho Tips* and, 20, 144, 164; queer consciousness-raising and, 52; sexual and erotic imagery and, 66, 183; transnational, 106
CONASIDA (National Council for the Prevention and Control of AIDS), 160
consumerism, 129, 144–45, 199; gay, 18, 20, 88
Cornell Student Homophile League, 28, 35, 229n7
cosmopolitanism, 128–29, 131
Crisálida, 61, 151, 243n67
Cruz, Enrique, 201, 218, 220; *Learning Latin*, 201, 218
Cruz-Malavé, Arnaldo, 225
Cuba, 120
Cuban Revolution, 36, 108
Cué, Antonio, 43, 52
Cumming Up, 163

Damata, Gasparino, 120; *Histórias do amor maldito*, 125
Dame-Griff, Avery, 223
Daughters of Bilitis, 108
Dávila, Arlene, 201, 212, 216
Davis, Whitney, 164
Day, Fred Holland, 131
De Groot, Scott, 14
De la Madrid, Miguel: moral renovation campaign of, 142, 147, 162, 170, 182–83
De la Mora, Sergio, 165
Del otro lado, 9, 15, 157, 186–87, 193–200, 214, 219, 247n9
D'Emilio, John, 10, 13, 237n4
Demi-Gods, 191
DeRosa, Tony, 110

desire, 4, 54, 100, 217–18; the body and, 19, 47, 220; brown body as object of, 207, 219; cosmopolitan, 132, 177; gay, 45; liberation of, 43, 224; male, 158, 177; Mexican men as, 183; production of, 179; racialized, 218; same-sex, 31, 107, 117, 134, 151, 200; sexual, 45, 70, 113, 187, 224; sexual liberation and, 47; white men as objects of, 9, 171. *See also* homoerotic desire
Dewhurst, Robert, 14, 99, 106, 111–12
Diaman, Nikos, 47, 118, 120, 122, 136, 138, 215, 238n38
Díez, Jordi, 13, 148, 229n28
digital periodicals, 223
discrimination, 4, 57, 86, 226
drawings, 17, 41, 48, 58, 62, 65, 108, 131, 168; gay sexuality and, 113; nude, 45, 47, 130
Drum (magazine), 11–12
Drummer, 164, 200, 204, 207, 209–10, 248n45; ads in, 250n81
Duffy, Brooke Erin, 77
Duggan, John, 90
Dworkin, Andrea, 94

Eakins, Thomas, 131
Echeverría, Luis, 37
El Eco, 169, 245n78
Edwards, Ken, 211–13, 215, 218
Der Eigene, 131
Embry, John, 204
Encarnación, Omar Guillermo, 13, 225
English, 15, 21, 27, 40–41, 117, 208, 210, 212, 249n49
entrepreneurs, 6–7, 13, 146, 157, 168, 202, 222, 224; gay, 201, 219–20
erotica, 7, 91, 142, 185, 187, 191, 193, 199, 211; circulation of, 225; locally produced, 10, 91; racialization and, 219; stereotypes and, 216
erotic imagery, 1, 4, 9–11, 15, 21, 38, 48, 66, 70–71, 86, 158, 186–87; in *The Body Politic* (*TBP*), 78, 91, 99, 101; in *Del otro lado*, 187, 199; disputes about, 19; in FHAR publications, 76; gay community-building and, 183; in *Gay Sunshine*, 112–13; in *Hermes*, 159–60, 163, 177, 187, 191, 193, 199–200; in *Macho Tips*, 141–42, 146, 157, 159, 170–71, 177–78, 182, 188, 199; in Mexico, 3, 5f, 146, 194, 207, 214; orientalist, 131

eroticism, 4, 6, 130, 223–24; gay, 220; genitality and, 45, 76; working-class, 197
erotic magazines, 3, 9, 12, 15, 19, 141, 145, 182, 186, 200, 224
Escoffier, Jeffrey, 201
Esquivel, Fernando, 38

Fag Rag, 26, 35, 54, 111, 118
Falcon Studios, 208
Febo Editores, 163, 258n43
feminism, 29, 38, 95, 232n12; pro-sex, 235n95; second-wave, 68, 71, 86
feminists, 75, 90, 95, 98; anti-porn, 68, 94; lesbian, 67, 71, 75–76, 87, 95, 100, 155; radical, 94; second-wave, 74; sex-positive, 68
Fernández Galeano, Javier, 13, 124
Figueroa, Bob, 118, 120, 122, 238n36
Folsom, 204, 205f, 207
Forgione, Steve, 62–64, 231n90
Forum, 209–10
Foucault, Michel, 45
Fowler, F. Ronald, 84f
French, 40, 122; gay periodicals in, 152, 207, 243n28 (see also *Gai pied*)
French theory, 45
Frente de Liberación Homosexual (FLH) (Argentina), 44, 57–58, 118, 126
Frente de Liberación Homosexual (FLH) (Mexico), 21, 36, 40, 48
Frente Homosexual de Acción Revolucionaria (FHAR), 21, 36–38, 51f, 56, 166; AIDS crisis and, 142; Black and Red Butterflies collectives of, 61; break between lesbian and gay activists in, 75; lesbians of, 75–76; need for literature, 64; nude bodies in periodicals of, 48, 76; periodicals of, 1, 3, 40–41, 44, 142, 147; in the United States, 232n93
Friction, 208
Fuentes Ponce, Adriana, 13

G Magazine, 199
Gai pied, 40, 152, 163, 203–4, 207, 209
Galdi, Vincenzo, 131
Gay Activist Alliance, 122
gay activists, 1, 14, 25–27, 30, 35–38, 41–45, 51, 53–54, 56, 61, 65, 68, 76, 85, 105, 108, 147, 240n73; assimilationism and, 169; bathhouse raids and, 87; the body and, 4; in Buenos Aires, 126–27; *Del otro lado* and, 214; editorial work of, 118, 224–25; Global South and, 117; "Kiss in" and, 31, 34f; Latin American, 62, 226; Mexican, 41, 48, 57, 63, 75, 157; networks of, 16, 20; personal papers of, 16; press and, 111; Toronto, 94; visual culture and, 221
Gay and Latino Alliance (GALA), 232n93
gay communes, 47, 229n6
gay communities, 4, 11–14, 25, 56; *The Body Politic* and, 6; gay periodicals and, 18, 35, 70–71, 106–7, 76, 134, 146, 158, 221; in Latin America, 117, 122, 128, 224; physique magazines and, 144; transnational, 54, 64, 117; in the United States, 225; violence against, 118
gay community, 29, 47, 70, 77, 112, 146, 179; *The Body Politic* and, 26, 87; *Del otro lado* and, 200; gay periodicals and, 15; in Greece, 238n38; *Hermes* and, 159, 162; *Macho Tips* and, 164, 183; masculinity and, 165, 182; normativity and, 96; sex and, 18, 92, 101, 125; Toronto, 91; transnational, 7, 56, 139
Gay Community News (*GCN*), 15, 19, 26, 36, 40, 64–65, 80–81, 83–86, 100, 101, 145; Forgione and, 63; Kyper and, 35, 64, 80, 232n93
gay history, 142; transnational, 20, 139,
gay identity, 11–12, 56, 129, 134, 146, 164, 169–70, 221
gay identities, 12, 18; modern, 107, 200
Gay lettres, 204
gay liberation activists, 4, 25, 42, 44, 54, 106, 117–18, 223; in Argentina, 126; *Del otro lado* and, 9; gay periodicals and, 10, 15, 19, 26, 54, 65, 224; *Gay Sunshine* and, 108; Gestalt therapy and, 53; in Latin America, 224; Mexican, 41; "Schizo-Culture" conference and, 45
Gay Liberation Front (GLF), 29, 35, 61, 108, 238n38; Berkeley, 108, 110; Boston, 35; Cornell, 28
gay liberation journals, 9, 45, 66, 68, 95, 111, 113, 150; advertising in, 86; the body in, 85; erotic imagery in, 160; nudity in, 71
gay liberation movement, 1, 4, 6, 19, 21, 24–29, 35, 47, 65, 68, 70, 92, 97, 111, 221, 226, 228n1, 240n69; in Argentina, 118, 126; the body and, 44; in Brazil, 127; commodification of gay culture and, 87; documentation of, 10; international solidarity work and, 56; in Latin America, 225; McCaskell and,

55; macho aesthetic and, 165; *Macho Tips* and, 157; in Mexico, 37–38, 40, 51–52, 64, 145–48, 155; photography and, 35, 115; in San Francisco Bay Area, 107–8, 112; *Sexual Politics* (Millett) and, 43; in Toronto, 75; transnational history of, 20, 144

gay liberation periodicals, 7, 10, 19, 26–28, 31, 35–37, 40–42, 48, 61, 65, 76–77, 85, 87, 100, 144–45, 200, 223; the body and, 24–25; commodification and, 112; homoerotic desire and, 105; in Latin America, 70; in Mexico, 3, 6, 131, 142; nudity in, 45, 47; sexualized and erotic imagery in, 71, 157, 204; visual language of, 53

gay liberation politics, 14, 65, 68, 70, 134; the body and, 48, 132; community-building and, 24, 106; consumerism and, 145; debates, 92; *Del otro lado* and, 199; *Hermes* and, 199; homoerotic desire and, 10, 105–7; homoeroticism and, 132; images and, 81, 101, 221; *Macho Tips* and, 157, 199; nudity in advertising and, 99; periodicals and, 3, 105, 221; pornography and, 94; print culture and, 101, 106; sex-positive lesbians and, 75; transnational, 3, 61, 158; visual culture and, 7, 80

gay magazines, 21, 55, 158, 168, 186, 191, 217, 221; commercialization and, 112; erotic imagery in, 187; Global North, 135; homoerotic desire and, 77; international, 163; in Mexico, 26, 91, 146, 163, 193–94, 200, 219, 223; Moss and, 203–4; non-white models in, 188; North American, 164, 199–200; obscenity laws and, 95; Polish, 12; pornography in, 218–19; sexual imagery in, 139, 155; Shown and, 209; white desirability and, 9

gay market, 7, 20–21, 35, 92, 131, 157, 219–20; Mexican, 10, 21, 183, 186, 193, 209

gay men, 1, 6, 12, 21, 28, 75–76, 81, 142, 165, 215; black, 201; of color, 70, 129; cosmopolitan, 138; *entendido* and, 125; erotic and sexualized imagery and, 72, 83, 100, 115; gay periodicals and, 11, 41, 112, 148, 158, 177, 226; Global North, 130, 135, 238n31; Hispanic, 186; homoerotic desire and, 107, 168; Latin American gay literature and, 118, 128, 130; Latino, 201; leftist homophobia and, 57; marginalization of, 170, 182; masculinity and, 166; massacre of (Chile), 58; in Mexico, 120, 144–46, 150–51, 157, 182; oppression of, 9; in Ottawa, 90; police harassment of, 52; pornography and, 95, 219; pro-sex feminism and, 235n95; S&M and, 98; sex and, 70, 88, 92, 99; sexually explicit content and, 152; sex wars and, 246n2; stereotypes and, 20, 164

gay periodicals, 3–4, 6–7, 11, 14, 17–19, 24, 55, 111, 127, 224–25; advertising and, 85; circulation of, 10, 12, 16, 27, 41, 48, 57, 62, 120, 164, 193; community-building and, 11, 18, 31, 64, 77; eroticism and, 223; foreign, 183; gay liberation and, 4, 26, 166, 182, 221–24; gay liberation imagery in, 155; homoerotic desire and, 170, 224; homoerotic imagery in, 71, 76; international, 40, 152, 158, 163, 171, 193; Lacey and, 240n69; Latin American, 66, 230n50; legacies of, 226; Mexican, 157; Mexican models in, 204; publishing, 146; radicalized desires in, 187; sexual and erotic imagery in, 101, 106, 131; transnational gay networks and, 10; US, 220; visual content of, 6–7, 13, 15, 17, 100, 136, 186, 214; white men as objects of desire in, 9, 181, 199

gay pride, 11, 17, 24, 35, 139, 221; march (Mexico City), 41, 42*f*, 53; picnic (Toronto), 24*f*

gay publishing, 1, 163; in Mexico, 3, 18, 20, 146, 187, 193; North American, 146; in the United States, 18, 139

gay rights, 4, 28–29, 30*f*, 224–25; movement, 112, 144, 194, 222; organizations, 229n7

gay sexuality, 7, 15, 65, 81, 113, 221; celebration of, 6, 17, 71–72, 76, 78, 101, 105, 125, 155, 197, 220, 225; Leyland and, 110; visualization of, 70–72, 76, 94

Gay Sunshine, 1, 4, 15–17, 26, 36, 65, 86, 105–22, 127, 129, 144; butterflies and, 61; erotic and sexual(ized) imagery in, 99, 101, 115, 157; gay liberation and, 20; gay liberation politics and, 101, 113; images in, 8*f*, 19, 45, 47–48, 50*f*–51*f*; Lacey and, 240n69; Lane and, 122, 124; Latin America and, 125, 135, 139, 214; Latin American special issues of, 118–21, 126, 131–32, 136–38; Leyland and, 105, 110–12, 117, 122, 128, 132, 139, 145, 157, 177, 214; Mexican activists and, 48; Moldenhauer and, 28; nudity in, 155; Records, 237n19; S&M sex and, 98; visual content of, 177; visual language of, 7; Young and, 126

Gay Sunshine Press, 19–20, 104f, 105–7, 111–12, 136, 157; Latin America/Latin American content and, 117, 122, 124–25, 129, 132, 139, 177, 214 (*see also* Zapata, Luis); Shown and, 210

gender, 18, 20, 48, 74, 77, 145, 223; assimilationism and, 243n35; divide, 75; expression, 197, 200; gay liberation and, 100–101, 144; hierarchy, 165; identity, 10, 224; *Macho Tips* and, 144, 170–71, 183; male homosexuality and, 164; *mestizaje* and, 173; national discourses of, 145, 182–83; stereotypes, 67; transgression, 136

Genet, Jean, 111

Gestalt therapy, 51–53

Ginsberg, Allen, 111

GLQ: A Journal of Lesbian and Gay Studies, 128

GLBT Historical Society, 14, 16

Global North, 20, 56, 66, 105, 139, 224; gay communities, 107, 117; gay consumers, 128, 134–35; gay men, 130, 135, 238n31; gay press, 118; lesbians, 238n31; movements, 226

Global South, 117, 129

Goldring, Paul, 90

Gómez-Tagle, Rubén, 143f, 150

González de Cosío, Antonio, 173, 245n90

González Romero, Martín H., 13

Grecian Guild Pictorial, 136, 191, 241n105

Green, James N., 13, 57, 127

Greene, David, 104f

Grinnell, Lucinda, 13, 147

Groves, Amy, 98

Grupo Lambda de Liberación Homosexual, 3, 36, 38, 48, 56, 63, 142, 147; *The Body Politic* and, 6; Laird and, 41; Sex-Pol and, 43. *See also Nuestro cuerpo*; *Nuevo ambiente*; *Política sexual*

Guatemala, 55, 63, 122, 232n93, 240n77; Guatemala City, 126. *See also* Lane, Erskine

Guerilla, 27

Guevara, Ernesto "Che," 57, 231n86

Gumier Maier, Jorge, 130

Gutiérrez, Trinidad, 57

Gutmann, Matthew, 173

Guzmán Delgado, Camilo César, 160

Hannon, Gerald, 28, 46, 77, 78, 95, 99–101, 135; "Celebrate the body," 47; Figueroa and, 122; "Kiss in" and, 31, 34; in Mexico City, 40; Stajnsznajder and, 127

Hanson, Ellis, 218, 236n116, 250n97

Heat, 152, 163, 207

Hefner, Hugh, 177

Heredia Filio, Mario Luis, 160

Hermes, 3, 9, 15, 20, 142, 148–52, 157, 159–64, 177–79, 181–83, 185–94, 199–200, 202, 204, 214, 220, 246n3, 247n9; Comisión Calificadora and, 159–60, 243n39, 244n46, 246n4; cultural stereotypes and, 216; erotica in, 10; erotic content in, 177, 188; international outreach of, 208; nudity in, 171, 188; pornographic imagery in, 219; Rowberry and, 248n53; sexual and erotic imagery in, 101, 159, 181, 187, 191, 193, 197. *See also chacales*

Hernández Chávez, Juan Jacobo, 9, 38, 40–41, 44–45, 51–52, 64–65, 213, 223, 232n93; *Del otro lado* and, 194, 197, 199, 214; *Macho Tips* and, 150, 152, 157, 194

heterosexism, 6, 221

Hidalgo de la Torre, Aurelio Refugio, 3, 7, 9, 20, 141–42, 144, 146–48, 150–52, 155, 157–58, 164, 166, 168, 181, 188, 193–94, 224, 248; academic credentials of, 242n9; brown models and, 179, 193, 199; censorship and, 160, 163; Comisión Calificadora de Publicaciones y Revistas Ilustradas and, 159–60, 163, 243n44, 244nn46–47; CONASIDA and, 160, 162, 183; editorial practices/work of, 177, 182–83, 191; *mestizaje* and, 173, 182; Moss and, 185–87, 202, 204, 207–8, 212–14, 217, 219, 225; PRI and, 162, 183; Rowberry and, 7, 152, 185–87, 202, 207–8, 213–14, 217, 219–20, 225, 248n49, 248n53; Shown and, 185–87, 202, 209–10. *See also Hermes*; *Macho Tips*

Hilderbrand, Lucas, 14, 176–77

Hobson, Emily, 13, 25, 56, 237n4

Hocquenghem, Guy, 27, 44–45, 98; *Le désir homosexual*, 42, 44; *Homosexualidad y sociedad represiva*, 45

Hoffman, Amy, 81, 83, 86

Holmes, Rand, 78, 79f; "Harold Hedd," 78–80

Hombres, 204

homoerotic desire, 101, 139, 144, 155, 168, 191, 220–21; celebration of, 3–4, 17, 19, 42, 65, 71–72, 76, 81, 107, 125, 182, 197, 214; genealogies of, 136, 225; images of, 7, 20, 71;

liberation of, 4, 17–19, 42, 71, 91, 100, 113, 186, 222; Mexican body and, 146; representations of, 1, 9–10, 15, 66, 186, 199, 222, 226; visual culture of, 131; visualization of, 11, 18, 20, 25, 35, 68, 70–72, 76–77, 81, 85, 91, 105–8, 113, 139, 144, 158, 166, 168, 170, 182–83, 186, 197, 214, 218–20, 222, 224
homophile anthropology, 224, 238n31
homophile periodicals, 12, 41, 117, 136
homophobia, 34, 54, 65, 200, 221, 226; internalized, 81; in leftist organizations, 57; resistance against, 31
homosexuality, 52, 58, 117, 139, 183, 204, 224, 238n31; Americanization of, 225; Bill C-150 (Canada) and, 28; clichés and, 169; domestication of, 98; Indian, 118; in Latin America, 125, 136; Latinx, 182; leftist homophobia and, 57; *Macho Tips* and, 145, 165–66; male, 164; stereotypes of, 146
homosexual liberation movement (Mexico), 36–37, 40–41, 56–57, 113, 147, 166, 169, 229n28; AIDS crisis and, 142. *See also* Hernández Chávez, Juan Jacobo; Laird, Danny
Honcho, 194, 200, 207
Honcho Overload, 208
Hooper, Tom, 28
Horse Hung Hispanics, 216, 218
Hot Chaps, 152
Hotchkiss, Ryan, 92, 93f, 96, 98–99, 235n95
Hrynyk, Nick, 14, 91, 164, 168
Hujar, Peter, 34

identity-formation, 12
illustrations, 17, 27, 77, 130, 191, 197, 201, 248n55
imperialism, 4, 25, 56, 117, 128, 225
Incháustegui, Teresa, 38, 44, 75–76
Inches, 150, 200, 204, 207, 248n41
Insausti, Joaquín, 13, 238n37
internet, 1, 4, 10
International Gay Association, 41, 61, 62f
International List of Gay Organizations and Publications, 122
Iqani, Mehita, 191
Isherwood, Christopher, 111
Izazola Licea, José Antonio, 160

Jackson, Ed, 28–29, 31, 34, 74, 78, 80–81, 85, 126–27

Jacobs, Don, 64
Jalisco, 61, 151, 212
Jamestown, New York, 80
Johnson, David, 11–13, 35, 77, 144, 146, 158, 177

Karlinsky, Simon, 124
Kenny, Maurice, 118
Kinsman, Gary, 13, 43
Kolb, Terry, 98
Kyper, John, 35, 57, 64–65, 80, 115, 232n93

Lacey, Edward A., 20, 58, 105–7, 117, 122, 124, 126–29, 215, 239n53, 240n69; Latin America and, 138–39; translation of *El vampiro de la colonia Roma*, 132; Young and, 239n64. *See also* Leyland, Winston
Lacombe, Dany, 94
Ladder, 108
Laguna Maqueda, Oscar, 151, 245n90
Laguarda, Rodrigo, 13
Laird, Danny, 41
Lampião da esquina, 26, 120, 127
Lane, Erskine, 20, 105–7, 117–18, 122, 124–29, 136, 138–39; *Game Texts: A Guatemala Journal*, 105, 124, 138; Leyland and, 239n60
Latin American men, 212, 214
Latin Inches, 200, 202, 218
Latin Men, 204
Latino men, 20, 219; in pornography, 186–87, 193, 201–2, 209, 213–14, 216 (*see also* thug porn)
leftist politics, 25, 38, 54, 64–65
Lesbian and Gay Rights Monitoring Group, 62
lesbian liberation, 25, 48, 70, 152, 222; activists, 24, 155, 182; movements, 13, 38, 43, 228n1
lesbians, 90; *The Body Politic* (*TBP*) and, 27–28, 68, 70, 74; *Come Out!* and, 29; *Gay Community News* (*GCN*) and, 83; gay periodicals and, 35; Global North, 238n31; Grupo Lambda and, 6; *Hermes* and, 159, 246n4; media representation of, 40; in Mexico, 36, 75–76, 147, 150, 162 (*see also* Frente Homosexual de Acción Revolucionaria [FHAR]; *Macho Tips*); Miss Canada Pageant and, 87; *Nuevo ambiente* and, 62; pornography and, 95; sex-positive, 75, 155, 235n95

Levine, Martin, 164, 166
Leyland, Winston, 20, 103, 105–7, 110–12, 128–29, 134, 136, 139, 145–46, 157, 168, 241; Brazil and, 127; community-building and, 117; gay cosmopolitanism and, 131; Lacey and, 239n64, 240n77; Lane and, 239n60; Latin America and, 115, 117–18, 122, 131, 138; Latin American gay writing and, 124–26, 132, 177, 214; Mexico and, 118, 120, 122, 215, 238n46, 240n77; Moldenhauer and, 111; Shown and, 210; Young and, 239n64; Zapata and, 132, 237n19. *See also Gay Sunshine*; Gay Sunshine Press
liberation, 10, 17, 35, 48, 68, 98, 115, 187, 217; body and, 1, 4, 6, 24, 44–45, 47–48, 113; community-building and, 24; contested meaning of, 70; in gay print culture, 9, 17, 218; of homoerotic desires, 4, 91, 100, 107, 113, 186, 222; LGBTQ+, 226; Marxism and, 19, 42, 44; national, 25; political, 1, 19, 26–27, 43; of sexual desire, 45, 224; women's, 25, 108, 145. *See also* gay liberation; homosexual liberation movement; lesbian liberation; sexual liberation
liberationists: gay, 25, 29, 68, 70, 81, 94–95, 98, 100, 128, 152; homosexual (Argentina), 57, 118; lesbian, 25, 68, 70, 94–95, 98, 152; radical, 222; sexual, 87
lifestyle magazines, 3, 9, 12, 15, 19, 145, 86, 224
Lizarraga Cruchaga, Xabier, 155, 245n90
López López, Álvaro, 194
López Portillo, José, 36–37
Lynch, Michael, 28, 88

machismo, 57, 165–66, 173, 182
macho aesthetic, 144, 164–66, 168
Macho Tips, 3, 5*f*, 7, 9, 15, 20, 101, 141–52, 154–83, 185–88, 191, 193, 197, 213, 219–20, 224, 247n9; censorship and, 222; Comisión Calificadora de Publicaciones y Revistas Ilustradas and, 243n39, 246n4; erotic imagery in, 141–42, 146, 157, 159, 170–71, 177–78, 182, 188, 199; gay liberation politics and, 199; Hernández and, 10, 150, 152, 157, 194; "Kiss in" photo and, 34; Moss and, 202, 204, 206*f*, 207; race and, 144, 146, 170, 183; Shown and, 209–11. *See also chacales*; Hermes

Macías-González, Víctor, 41, 145, 165–66
McCaskell, Tim, 6, 13, 28–29, 54–55, 65, 92, 231n75; anti-apartheid movement and, 223; Central American solidarity and, 63–64, 231n92; on gender divide between gays and lesbians, 75; "Kiss in" and, 31, 34*f*; Latin America and, 7, 54, 56–58, 59*f*, 118, 126; Marxist philosophers and, 43; on sexual desire, 70
McCormick, Gladys, 37
MacKinnon, Catharine, 94
Macpherson, Anne S., 145
McCuaig, Peg, 98
Maecker, Richard A., 80
malandros, 199
Male Insider, 207
Mallon, Florencia, 171
Manacle, 152
Manalansan, Martin, 225
Mandate, 200, 207, 248n55
Manpower!, 152
Marcuse, Herbert, 27, 43–44; *Eros and Civilization*, 42, 44
Mariah, Paul, 45, 110
marketing, 106, 177, 193, 201, 215–16
Markwell, Kevin, 134–35
Marxism, 19, 42, 45, 65
Marxist philosophers, 4, 43
masculinity, 141, 142, 158, 164–66, 168, 170, 177, 183; celebration of, 165, 168, 176; cult of, 144, 146, 182; gay, 20, 88, 91, 158, 164, 166, 168–70, 235n78; ideal of, 47; Mexican, 165, 178–79; performance of, 168; representations of, 146, 182–83; revolutionary, 57, 165; traditional, 37; working-class, 167
Mattachine Review, 108
Mattachine Society, 108
Mavety, George W., 207, 216
Mavety Media Group, 207–8
Mecos Films, 182
Meeker, Martin, 12–13, 108
mestizaje, 144–46, 171, 173, 183
Mexican men, 9, 183, 191, 210–11, 214–15
Mexican Revolution, 40, 165
Meyer, Lorenzo, 147
Meyer, Richard, 14, 29, 34–35
Mieli, Mario, 27, 44–45; *Elementi di critica omosessuale*, 42, 44–45

Miller, Marilyn, 171
Miller-Young, Mireille, 217
Mogrovejo, Norma, 13
Moldenhauer, Jearld Frederick, 23, 24f, 28, 30f, 46, 72–74, 76–77, 94, 235n101; Cornell Student Homophile League and, 229n7; *Gay Sunshine* and, 111
Molina, Carlos, 126–27, 240n70, 240n73
Monsiváis, Carlos, 36, 197
Montreal, 90, 126–27
Moreno Figueroa, Mónica, 171
Moss, Jim, 21, 150, 171, 179, 180f, 185–87, 202–20, 225; *5 Guys in a Hammock*, 211–12; Andrade and, 173, 175f; *Bronze Beach Boys*, 211–12; *Guys from Guatemala*, 215; *Inches* and, 248n41; *Viva Macho 1*, 211, 216; *Viva Macho 2*, 211–13, 250n82. See also Macho Tips
Mumford, Kevin, 13
Murdoch, Kenneth Royal, 115
musculature, 47, 181, 191; aesthetic, 91; male, 168
My Deep Dark Pain Is Love: A Collection of Latin American Gay Fiction, 124, 130

Nash, Catherine, 87
Nash, Jennifer, 72, 96, 217
neoliberalism, 92
newspapers, 14, 113; gay, 11, 64–65; gay liberation, 3; North American, 15; queer, 27
Nicaragua, 54–56, 63–64
Nicaraguan Revolution, 56, 231n92
Nigro, Alberto, 111, 237n19
Novo, Salvador, 124
Now the Volcano: An Anthology of Latin American Gay Literature, 124–25, 129–30
nudity, 1, 9, 47, 134, 155, 171; advertising and, 99; *The Body Politic* and, 71–74, 77, 80, 86, 88, 90–91; debates on, 19
Nuestro cuerpo, 1, 2f, 15, 26, 38–40, 42f, 44, 48, 52, 70, 111, 142, 145, 147, 199, 214; butterfly and, 61; Hernández and, 10, 38; nudity and, 155; Santamaría and, 47; women and, 76
Nuevo ambiente, 3, 15, 26, 38, 48, 49f, 61–63, 111, 142, 145, 147; *The Body Politic* and, 6–7; Laird and, 41
Nyers, Peter, 129

O.G., 204
objectification, 67, 70, 80, 83, 86, 91, 100–101, 155
Oikabeth, 36, 56, 76, 142
Oller, Carlos, 124–25
ONE Magazine, 41, 108
ONE National Gay and Lesbian Archives, 14, 16
Ortiz, Christopher, 217, 247n22
Ortiz, Enrique, 160
"The Other Mexico: Critique of the Pyramid" (Paz), 136
El otro, 26

Penteado, Darcy, 120, 124, 130
Peralta, Braulio, 38, 43, 52, 157
Perlongher, Néstor, 58, 124–25
Peru, 122, 239n64
Pérez, Hiram, 128–29, 132, 177, 218
Phipps, Kelly, 14, 74–75
photographers, 14, 96, 158, 171, 202, 222, 224, 249n65; gay, 208, 241n88; physique, 212; pictorialist, 131
photography, 17, 34–35, 77; fashion, 179; physique, 158; studios, 12
physique magazines, 12, 35, 144, 146, 158, 177, 191, 212; gay, 77
Physique Pictorial, 177
Pinney, Morgan, 110
Pitts, Bryan, 14, 199
Pizá, Julián, 169
Playboy, 177
Playgirl's Sexy Men, 152
Playguy, 200, 207
pleasure, 4, 6, 44–45, 72, 98–99, 139, 141, 217–18, 220, 223; masculine, 197; sexual, 94–95, 107; visual, 17, 85, 188
Plüschow, Wilhelm, 131
police, 7, 78, 219; brutality, 170; *Gay Sunshine* and, 8f; harassment, 222, 234n72; *Nuevo ambiente* and, 61–62, 63f; oppression of gay people and, 4, 52, 234n72; repression, 28, 48, 61, 64–65, 170; *Somos* and, 58; Toronto, 234n72; violence, 25, 36, 54, 57, 76, 221
Política sexual, 3, 10, 15, 26, 38, 40–41, 43–44, 111, 142, 145, 147; *The Body Politic (TBP)* and, 70; *Del otro lado* and, 199, 214
Ponce de León, Samuel, 160

Popert, Ken, 28, 74
popular culture, 20, 145; in Mexico, 165, 173; post-revolutionary, 144; US, 126
pornography/porn, 9, 18–19, 70, 80, 99, 115, 201–3, 207, 213–17, 219, 247n22; actors, 248n53; ads, 115, 218; anti-pornography movement, 68, 94–95, 98, 101, 246n2; Bearchell and, 75; *The Body Politic* (*TBP*) and, 27, 68, 86, 92; brown bodies and, 21, 187; censorship and, 95–96, 98; gay liberation and, 220; government repression of, 92; heterosexual, 250n83; industry, 201–2, 211; lesbian, 95; *Macho Tips* and, 152, 155; mainstream gay, 201; Mexican, 182, 186–87, 193, 211; producers, 208; racialized, 72, 217–18; racially diverse, 209; S&M and, 101; thug porn, 193, 201, 216; US market for, 247n22; women and, 74
Portuguese, 21, 117, 125
Posada, José Guadalupe, 39*f*
Pozo Pietrasanta, Gonzalo, 150–52, 173, 207, 211*f*, 212
PRI (Partido Revolucionario Institucional), 37, 142, 147, 162, 183, 242n1
Prince, Stephen, 213
Proust, Marcel, 131
Puar, Jasbir, 128
Puig, Manuel, 120, 124
Putas, Warren A., 90

queer theory, 18, 20
Quiroga, José, 106, 125, 138, 202

race, 18, 20, 74, 101, 127, 187, 215; gay liberation and, 128, 144; gay periodicals and, 10; gay pornography and, 217; homoerotic desire and, 220; Leyland and, 131; *Macho Tips* and, 144, 146, 170, 183; in Mexico, 9, 144, 171, 173 (*see also* mestizaje); national discourses of, 145, 182–83; nineteenth-century conceptions of, 134; sexuality and, 176–77; transnational gay community and, 139; *El vampiro de la colonia Roma* (Zapata) cover art and, 132
racism, 4, 25, 70, 87, 100, 200, 245n76; anti-Black, 31
Regazzoni, Ricardo, 111, 120, 122, 136, 137*f*, 237n19

Reich, Konnie, 96
Reich, Wilhelm, 27, 43; *The Sexual Revolution: Toward a Self-Governing Character Structure*, 42
Rechy, John, 98, 111
Reed, James, 7, 8*f*
repression, 31, 36–37, 56, 62, 147; allegories of, 9; of the body, 45, 51; police, 25, 28, 48, 61, 64–65, 170; of porn, 92; sexual, 44, 58; state, 37, 54, 91
Reuben, David, 78
Reyes, Rodrigo, 120
Rick, Bill, 110
Rivas, Mario, 57, 157
Rivers-Moore, Megan, 135
Robles, Milton, 152, 181*f*
Rodgerson, Gillian, 96, 98, 101, 235n95
Rosemblatt, Karin Alejandra, 145
Ross, Becki, 13, 233n20, 235n95
Roth, Robert, 122. *See also* International List of Gay Organizations and Publications
Rowberry, John, 21, 152, 185–87, 202, 207–10, 212–17, 219–20; *Drummer* and, 207, 248n45; Hidalgo de la Torre and, 7, 152, 185–87, 202, 207–8, 213–14, 217, 219–20, 225, 248n49, 248n53; *Viva Macho 2* and, 250n82. *See also* Moss, Jim; Shown, John; *Uncut*
Rubenstein, Anne, 145, 163, 165–66, 243n38
Rushbrook, Dereka, 128

sadomasochism (S&M), 9, 68, 75, 86, 94–96, 98–99, 101, 203–4, 207; sex, 234n72; subculture, 200. *See also Drummer*
Sabanosh, Michael, 155, 156*f*
Salazar Green, Juan, 159
Sánchez Crispín, Álvaro, 194
San Francisco Gay Rap, 64
Saylor, Jackie, 211–12
Santamaría, Guillermo, 1, 2*f*, 47
Secretaría de Salud (Ministry of Health), 160
Sentinel, 34
sex, 19, 70, 80, 86–88, 94, 128, 221; anal, 53, 113; *The Body Politic* (*TBP*) and, 90–92, 99; gay community and identity and, 18, 71, 92, 101, 125; industry, 96; intergenerational, 27, 68; interracial, 203; oral, 78, 113, 130; power dynamics in, 130; radicals/militants, 235n95;

roles, 54; safe, 155, 160, 161f, 210; scenes, 212; shops, 164, 213; tourism, 135–36, 138; toys, 86; workers, 75, 135, 147, 235n95
sexism, 4, 19, 25, 54, 56, 65, 70, 74–75, 80, 83, 100, 155, 225; ads and, 86; *TBP* and, 91, 101; gay men and, 6; lesbian feminists and, 67; pornography and, 94
Sex-Pol, 43, 52
sexual health, 3, 142, 146, 163, 194
sexual liberation, 43, 47, 53, 64, 217; erotic and sexualized imagery and, 115; Italian movement for, 45; the left and, 118; Marxism and, 42; pornography and, 152; racialized politics of, 100; sexual and erotic imagery and, 183
Sexual Politics (Millett), 43
sex wars, 68, 71, 75, 94–96, 155, 246n2
Shown, John, 21, 160, 161f, 185–87, 202, 209–11; collage art of, 248n55. *See also* Hidalgo de la Torre, Aurelio Refugio
Sicily, 131
Silva, Aguinaldo, 120
Simonetto, Patricio, 13–14, 43, 225
Skin Flicks, 163
Smith, Miriam, 13
Socialist Workers Party (SWP), 57, 62, 231n90
socialism, 29, 57, 231n90
social media, 223
solidarity, 6, 20, 56; Central American, 63; social, 29; transnational, 27, 54, 56, 106, 225, 237n4
Somos, 15, 26, 58, 60f, 61, 126
Sosa, Rocío, 150, 208, 248n49
South Africa, 55
Spanish, 15, 21, 40–41, 45, 117, 122, 125, 230n50; *Honcho* and, 194; *TBP* and, 126–27
Spartacu's (nightclub), 168–69, 179
Spartacus (travel guide), 135
Spiers, Herb, 28
Stajnsznajder, Pablo, 126–27, 240n70
Stallion, 207
Stein, Marc, 11–13
Sterling, Matt, 208
Stonewall riots, 25, 28, 108, 165, 225, 228n1
Streitmatter, Rodger, 13
Subero, Gustavo, 165, 182
Suggs, Donald, 201
Szulc, Łukasz, 11–13

El Taller, 167–68, 170, 244n73
Taller Documentación Visual, 150
Taylor, Clark, 118, 120, 122, 138
Third World, 115, 134, 138; sexualities, 129, 134
Third World Gay Caucus, 232n93
Thomas, David G., 99
Thompson, Michael, 83
Thorp, Charles P., 112, 221
Thorstad, David, 45, 231n90
Tlatelolco massacre, 36–37
Tom of Finland, 168
Toronto Gay Action, 27–28
Toronto Morality Squad, 78
Torso, 207, 248n55
trans people, 170, 223
transnational gay networks, 6, 10, 20, 106–7, 126
Trevisan, João Silvério, 120, 124
Trow, Robert, 31
Tuke, Henry Scott, 131

Uncut: The Magazine of the Natural Man, 200, 204, 206f, 207–8, 216, 219
Universidad Nacional Autónoma de México, 40, 53
University of Michigan, 218
University of Toronto, 124
University of Toronto Homophile Association, 128, 235n101
US Hispanic market, 21, 186–87, 193, 201, 212–13, 246n1

Valverde, Mariana, 90–91, 95, 98
Vaughan, Cherie J., 148, 150
Vector, 115
Vider, Stephen, 47, 229n6
Villa, Pancho, 165
Villalobos Cuevas, Víctor, 169
Villalobos Leaño, Víctor Hugo, 159, 181f, 189f–90f, 213
Villaurrutia, Xavier, 124
Villena, Enrique, 150
violence, 61–62; anti-LGBTQ+, 226; homophobic, 58; police, 25, 54, 57, 76, 221; in racialized pornography, 217; state, 55–56, 118, 226; against women, 74, 94, 98, 155
virility, 165, 168–69
visibility, 29, 35–36, 150, 204

visual culture, 34, 134; butterflies and, 61, 160; gay, 13, 27, 160, 191, 214; of gay consumerism, 18; of gay liberation, 35, 48, 58, 65, 80, 136, 221; gay liberation politics and, 7; gay liberation print culture and, 105; of gay periodicals, 15; of *Gay Sunshine*, 106, 113; homoerotic, 199; of homoerotic desire, 131; lesbian, 13; of *Macho Tips*, 142, 166; male beauty and, 193; Mexican Revolution and, 165; non-Western sexualities and, 9
Von Gloeden, Wilhelm, 131

Waitt, Gordon, 134–35
Warhol, Andy, 203
Warner, Tom, 13, 222
Where It's At, 204
white men, 9, 35, 83, 132; in *TBP*, 31; in *Boys and Toys*, 220; in *Del otro lado*, 186; gay porn and, 213; in *Hermes*, 181, 191; in *Macho Tips*, 9, 171, 181; Moss's photographs of, 204; in *Uncut*, 216; from the United States, 210
whiteness, 181, 191, 197; of the archive, 16; decentering, 199; gay male style and, 91; gay periodicals and, 186; macho style and, 168

Whitman, Walt, 131
Wilde, Oscar, 131
Women Against Pornography (WAP), 94
Women Against Violence Against Women (WAVAW), 86, 94
Women Against Violence in Pornography and Media (WAVPM), 86, 94–95
Wright, Thomas, 136
writers, 6, 14, 45, 117, 150; gay, 20, 111, 122, 124, 131

Xtra! magazine, 157

Yépez, Javier, 120, 122
yoga, 53–54
Young, Allen, 87
Young, Ian, 98, 126, 239n64
Young Adonis, 191
Yustis, Juan Carlos, 5f, 171

Zapata, Emiliano, 165
Zapata, Luis, 111, 124, 132, 237n19; *El vampiro de la colonia Roma* (*Adonis García: A Picaresque Novel*), 103–5, 131–32, 133f
Zorzi, Peter, 28, 72

www.ingramcontent.com/pod-product-compliance
Lightning Source LLC
Chambersburg PA
CBHW021851230426
43671CB00006B/349